W9-AFZ-776

THE
SONOMA VALLEY STORY

— Pages through the Ages —

THE
SONOMA VALLEY STORY

—— *Pages through the Ages* ——

Sonoma Valley through the eyes of
The Sonoma Index-Tribune family and staff

Robert M. Lynch

The Sonoma Index-Tribune, Inc. • Sonoma, California

To Celeste Granice Murphy, my "Aunt Celie," to whom I owe so much.

The Sonoma Valley Story
Pages through the Ages

Published by The Sonoma Index-Tribune, Inc.
Post Office Box C, Sonoma, California 95476 U. S. A.

Copyright ©1997 by The Sonoma Index-Tribune, Inc. All rights reserved.
No portion of this book may be reproduced or used in any form,
or by any means, without prior written permission of the publisher.

First edition printed 1997
10 9 8 7 6 5 4 3 2 1

Manufactured in the United States of America

Publisher's Cataloging-in-Publication Data
Lynch, Robert M., 1920–
The Sonoma Valley story: pages through the ages / by Robert M. Lynch—1st ed.

　　　329 p.   illus.　　cm.
　　　Includes bibliographical references and index.
　　　ISBN 0-9653857-0-1 : $29.95
　　　1. Sonoma (Calif.)—History.　　　　I. Title
　　　2. Sonoma Index-Tribune—History.
　　　3. Valley of the Moon (Calif.)—History.
　　　4. California—History, Local.

Library of Congress Catalog Card Number 97-91567
979.418

Printed on acid-free paper.

*About the cover: Design by Gina Bostian and Brandon Warner. Sonoma Valley vineyards
photo courtesy of Sonoma Valley Visitors Bureau; photo by Mike Banks. Photo of the
author by Jill Boeve.*

Contents

PART ONE: FROM SMOKE SIGNALS TO NEWSPAPERS
Excerpts from *The People of the Pueblo*

PART TWO: AS REPORTED IN THE I-T, 1879–1979
Significant Stories from *The Sonoma Index-Tribune*

PART THREE: SONOMA VALLEY NEWSMAKERS, 1980–1996

As We Come to the End of Our Story

Preface

For many years I have entertained the idea of leaving behind something lasting, in appreciation of the mostly happy life I have lived and of those responsible. This book, *The Sonoma Valley Story: Pages through the Ages,* is the culmination of that long-held idea. It was prodded into reality after a suggestion made by my eldest son, Bill, more than a year ago.

All of the ingredients, and the inspiration, for attempting a book seemed to be present. I was blessed with a great-grandmother who has been recognized as California's first woman novelist. Her eldest son, my maternal grandfather, purchased the weekly *Sonoma Index* and planted the family roots here in 1884. In 1915 my grandfather's eldest daughter, my aunt, succeeded him at the helm of the paper he had renamed *The Sonoma Index-Tribune.*

While editor of the *I-T,* my aunt wrote a book, *The People of the Pueblo.* The first edition was typeset and printed at our plant here 60 years ago and was the first published history devoted entirely to Sonoma and the Valley of the Moon. A large part of *The People of the Pueblo* has been excerpted and re-published in Part One of this book.

Along with the family legacy of putting words in type, I have also inherited a wealth of historic material. When I succeeded my aunt and her husband as editor and publisher almost a half-century ago, our newspaper archives included invaluable bound volumes of the *I-T* dating back to the 1880s. In addition, our files have been continually enriched with historic local photographs and other material through the kindness of history-minded individuals and organizations like the Sonoma Valley Historical Society and its Depot Park Museum. Our debt to these and many other sources is apparent from the long list on the Acknowledgments page.

Worthy of special mention is Jill Boeve, the devoted coordinator of *The Sonoma Valley Story.* Her skills, love of history, background in book publishing, energy and cheerful encouragement were invaluable contributions to this finished product.

To the reader, it should be emphasized that this book is not offered as a complete history of the Sonoma Valley; rather, it is a presentation of significant and interesting happenings that have contributed to the Valley's intriguing history.

Finally, I must say that my research of some 6,500 back issues of *The Sonoma Index-Tribune,* for this book, has given me increased pride in our community newspaper and its influence in reporting the Sonoma Valley story for 118 years, 113 of those years by the same family—mine.

Five Generations of a California Newspaper Family

INDEX-TRIBUNE ARCHIVES

Rowena Granice Steele: the family matriarch was an actress, novelist and newspaperwoman.

*L*ike the Sonoma vines and valley oaks, the roots of the *Index-Tribune* publishing family run deep—reaching back through five generations of the family that has published the *I-T* since 1884— a family whose members were involved in writing, printing and newspaper publishing in California from the days of the gold rush.

Family matriarch Rowena— actress, novelist, journalist

*T*he roots were planted on June 20, 1824, in Goshen, Orange County, New York, with the birth of Rowena Grannis. Rowena was to become the mother of Harry H. Granice, *Index-Tribune* publisher from 1884 to 1915; the grandmother of

Celeste Murphy, editor from 1915 to 1949; the great-grandmother of Robert M. Lynch, present-day publisher and this book's author; and the great-great-grandmother of Bill, Jim and John Lynch, fifth-generation newspapermen.

Rowena Grannis was six when her family moved to New York City. Her father died when she was 10, and she was educated by her mother, said to be refined and well read. At an early age, Rowena showed a talent for composition, but, being of an extremely sensitive nature, she often destroyed her efforts. Rowena was 20 when she married Thomas Claughley, an upholsterer, in 1844. Her mother died in 1849, and her first son, Harry Hale Claughley, was born that same year. A second son, George Law Claughley, was born in 1853.

In 1853 Thomas Claughley left New York for California to seek gold, telling Rowena he would send for her and the boys. From 1853 to 1856, Rowena was an actress at the New York Museum of Phineas T. Barnum. (Years later, Barnum would describe her as a highly respectable and accomplished actress in a letter published in the *San Joaquin Valley Argus*, the newspaper Rowena and her second husband were to publish. The letter was perhaps solicited, because any woman on the stage in the 1850s was considered by many to be less than a proper person—something rival editors could readily latch onto.)

When P. T. Barnum sold his New York American Museum in 1856, Rowena decided to go to California to find her husband. She left her two boys, Harry and George, with relatives, and boarded the ship *Golden Age*. A notice in the *New York Times* reported her departure. Her arrival in San Francisco was reported in the daily *Alta California*. She was using her stage name, Mrs. Rowena Granice, changing the spelling of her family name from Grannis to Granice. Said the *Alta California*, "This lady, who is not unknown to fame on the Atlantic side as an accomplished actress, will soon appear upon our theatrical boards."

The *Alta California* also reported Rowena's first performance in San Francisco on April 7, 1856, saying, "Mrs. Rowena Granice made her debut at The Union last evening in *The Yankee Housemaid*, in which she played the Yankee role of Jemima Sunflower very admirably." She drew large audiences for a short run in San Francisco, then went to Sacramento, where she likewise won applause for her performances.

The family records reveal that as an actress Rowena Granice had also operated "The Gaities, Temple of Mirth and Song," a melodeon theater at No. 77 Long Wharf, San Francisco, in the summer of 1856. It was called a "bit" theater, because you paid "one bit" to get in. She is credited with "discovering" a 12-year-old child actress named Lotta Crabtree in the fall of that year, when she gave her a chance to perform at The Gaities. Crabtree went on to become the toast of the West Coast as a performer. Rowena, however, not earning the income she sought, soon abandoned her theater and began that year, 1856, writing arti-

THE
FAMILY GEM;

MISCELLANEOUS STORIES.

BY ROWENA GRANICE.

SACRAMENTO:
PRINTED AT THE OLD STATE JOURNAL STEAM PRESSES, 40 K STREET
1858

INDEX-TRIBUNE ARCHIVES

Rowena Granice, as she was depicted on the cover of one of her books, *The Family Gem,* published in 1858. She began her literary career in 1856 and has been called California's first woman novelist.

cles for *The Golden Era* literary magazine and other publications.

She moved to Sacramento after her two sons joined her in 1857. The two little boys had arrived with name tags attached to their coat buttons, having made the sea voyage from New York virtually alone, except for kindly adult passengers who looked after them on the ship. Rowena supported herself and the boys by writing and giving parlor readings in Sacramento.

However, she evidently missed being an entertainer and returned to San Francisco two years later, reopening the former Gaities as "The Varieties" at the old place on Long Wharf. There, on Dec. 23, 1859, the now acclaimed Lotta Crabtree gave a performance of *Uncle Tom's Cabin* as a favor to Rowena, who shortly afterward closed down The Varieties and returned to Sacramento.

During the years when her boys were in school, Rowena devoted herself to writing. Her "neatly printed novelette," *Victims of Fate,* sold 5,000 copies, according to the *Alta California* in 1860. Another book, *The Family Gem,* published in 1858, included previously written articles for *The Golden Era* and other magazines. Her later works would include *Leonnie St. James; or, The Suicide's Curse*; a temperance novel, *Dell Dart; or, Within the Meshes*; and *Weak or Wicked.*

As R. Dean Galloway has written in an article for *The Pacific Historian,*

> The romantic stories of Rowena Granice Steele won for her only slight mention in the annals of early California literature, but they enabled her to triumph over a fate that would have crushed a less creative and determined woman. She survived desertion by her husband in California of the 1850s by writing, publishing and selling melodramatic Victorian stories and thus became known as the first California woman novelist. Her own turbulent life reads like one of her novels replete with misfortunes and trials over which the poor, but honest, heroine triumphs because of her strong character and indomitable courage. Unlike her stilted storybook characters, Rowena Granice was a genuinely heroic figure who brought culture to the crude frontier and for 40 years gave leadership to liberal causes in the San Joaquin Valley (p. 105).

Rowena had little or nothing to do with her husband after she arrived in San Francisco. Claughley had reportedly taken up with another woman and was drinking heavily. When he died in 1860, Rowena and her sons took the name Granice. In 1861 Rowena married Robert J. Steele, editor and publisher of Auburn's weekly *Democratic Signal.* A native of North Carolina and a veteran of the Mexican War, Steele had crossed the plains to California in 1849. After trying his luck, successfully, at gold mining in El Dorado County, he turned to newspaper work in 1852. In 1856 he bought a half-interest in the *Columbia Gazette.* In November 1858 he bought the *Placer*

INDEX-TRIBUNE ARCHIVES

Harry H. Granice, successful *Sonoma Index-Tribune* publisher from 1884 until his death in 1915. He was involved in a tragic Merced shooting 10 years before coming to Sonoma, after a rival newspaperman printed a slur on the character of his beloved mother, Rowena Granice Steele.

Courier at Yankee Jim's and later moved it to Forest Hill. He bought the *Democratic Signal* in Auburn on Dec. 10, 1860.

Rowena and Robert Steele lived in Auburn until the spring of 1862. When her new novel, *Leonnie St. James; or, The Suicide's Curse,* was printed there, Rowena, with Harry and George, ages 12 and 9, peddled her books from door to door through the mountain counties.

The family of four went to Snelling in Merced County in June 1862 to start the *Merced Banner.* Rowena's memoirs recalled that it was on the 5th of July that year when the first issue was published, with the whole family assisting. A number of years later, the family moved to Merced, where they published the *San Joaquin Valley Argus.* It was in 1874 that 25-year-old Harry H. Granice, serving as foreman of the *Argus,* was involved in a tragic shooting.

A tragic shooting

Tales of newspaper feuds were commonplace in the Old West, and some of them even led to shootings when editorial exchanges became

Kate Keough Granice, Harry's wife, was a charter member of the Sonoma Valley Woman's Club.

The old Granice home, Morning Glory Villa, still stands on East Napa Street, Sonoma, a half block east of First Street East.

extremely insulting.

The author of this book was 40 years old when he first learned "the family secret" while visiting with his "Aunt Celie" and her husband, Walter, one evening at their residence in the refurbished Sonoma Barracks building on Spain Street. Discussing family roots over a few potent martinis, Walter let it slip. "You know, Bob, your grandfather, Harry Granice, shot and killed a guy over an editorial," he announced. My dear old aunt nearly swooned. It was a happening that this prim and proud lady never chose to discuss. But the secret was out.

Some years later I learned the complete story following a chance contact with Kathleen Duarte Menghetti of Modesto, a cousin. Mrs. Menghetti acquainted me with Stanislaus State University professor R. Dean Galloway. While compiling data on early-day newspapers in Merced County, Galloway had received from Mrs. Menghetti a copy of a narrative written by Harry Granice during five days at large after escaping from a "drunken, infuriated mob" intent on lynching him.

Galloway detailed the shooting incident as a foreword in reprinting Granice's own story titled "Hunted Down; or Five Days in the Fog. A Thrilling Narrative of the Escape of Young Granice—Written by himself while in jail."

In 1874, at age 25, Harry Granice was foreman of his mother and stepfather's newspaper, the *San Joaquin Valley Argus*. The *Argus* and the rival *Merced Tribune* were constantly feuding over politics, but a slur on the character of Granice's beloved mother, Rowena Granice Steele, actually precipitated the shooting.

Edward Madden, 24, editor of the *Tribune*, had printed an editorial comment Dec. 5, 1874, about Mrs. Steele, who was traveling around the state peddling her latest novel, *Dell Dart; or, Within the Meshes*. Madden had stated: "If any family desires to be posted in the life of a female in a house of ill fame, they can ascertain all the knowledge in that line they desire by a perusal of the publication referred to. The authoress evidently knows whereof she speaks."

Harry Granice, incensed, though frail and quite sick at the time, tearfully begged for a retraction. Madden, strong and robust, not only denied the request but called Granice a damned bastard, drew a pistol and pointed it at Granice's

INDEX-TRIBUNE ARCHIVES

INDEX-TRIBUNE ARCHIVES

face. The effect of the confrontation caused him to go home, where he lay sick in bed under a doctor's care.

Two days later, on December 7, as Madden walked to his office at 7:30 A.M., Granice accosted him on Front Street and shot him dead before Madden could draw the weapon he had in his hip pocket. Immediately afterward, Granice gave himself up to the sheriff, who lodged him in the calaboose—the jail not yet completed.

When an unruly lynch mob formed, Granice's attorney requested that he be taken to Modesto on the train at 1 P.M. to escape the mob. The sheriff failed to act on the request but, fearing mob action, at 5 P.M. sent Granice with a deputy out on the road toward Snelling. When part of the mob seemed ready to close in on them at a roadhouse where they rested, about six miles from Merced, Granice was turned loose by the friendly deputy, who did not believe in mob justice. Granice wandered for two days in the fog before obtaining aid from a rancher near Cressey, who kept him until December 12, when Granice turned himself over to the authorities in Modesto.

Meanwhile in Merced, the angry mob broke into the Steele family's newspaper, the *Argus*, destroying everything. It also sent a note to the family to leave and never return. They did leave briefly but were back by December 16, when Harry was returned to Merced. The Steeles had many friends and raised a large defense fund. Rowena's fame as an entertainer-author-newspaperwoman enabled her to retain the best attorneys, including the famed Judge David S. Terry of Stockton. After several trials and mistrials, Granice was set free on bail raised by Merced citizens and on Jan. 9, 1877, was formally set free by court order.

He married Kate Keough, daughter of neighbors in Merced, and went to San Francisco, where he worked as a compositor on the old *Bulletin* for several years. Still in frail health, Granice was advised by doctors to go to the country for the few years he had left.

So in 1884 he came to Sonoma, purchased the *Sonoma Tribune,* and not only became a leading and respected citizen but published the paper until his death in 1915.

As for Rowena, the matriarch of the family, she continued to act as associate editor of the

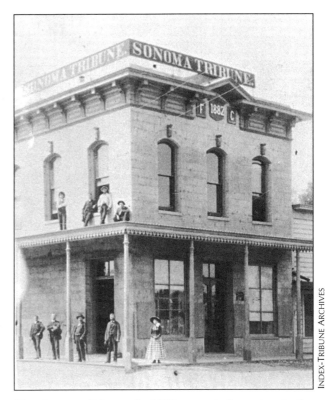

The *Sonoma Tribune* in 1883 occupied quarters in the second story of this building at the corner of Broadway and West Napa Street.

Merced Argus until 1877, when the failing health of her husband compelled her to take charge entirely. For seven years she was the editor and proprietor. According to Galloway, she "editorialized on the need for good wagon roads, schools, a pay increase for the county officials and a city cemetery. She scored the Mercedians for failing to grow enough fruits and vegetables for home consumption, and she urged the farm women to raise poultry" (Galloway, p. 121).

In 1884, assisted by her 21-year-old son Lee Richmond Steele, her only child by her marriage to Robert Johnson Steele, she started a daily paper in connection with the weekly. In 1889 her husband died. After successfully conducting the newspaper business in the same county for 28 years, she sold out.

In 1892 she was still an active writer and a leading worker in the temperance cause, and was listed as editor and proprietor of the *Budget* in Lodi. Before her death in February 1901 at age 76, she was a frequent visitor to Sonoma and wrote several columns for the *Index-Tribune* while visiting here.

Granice buys the *Tribune*

*I*n 1884, the year Granice became owner, editor and publisher of the *Sonoma Tribune* (formerly *The Sonoma Index*), the newspaper's offices were located in the two-story Clewe building at the southwest corner of Napa and Broadway, present site of Great Western Bank. The entrance to the newspaper quarters on the second floor, up a long flight of stairs, was on Broadway.

The editorial department had been elegantly furnished by the paper's previous owner, Edward J. Livernash, with Brussels carpet, Governor Winthrop desk and bookcase, swivel chair and shaded lamps. Livernash had just two employees at *The Sonoma Index*—a printer and a "printer's devil"—the three of them combining efforts to get out the four-page weekly each Thursday. Two of its pages were "ready-print" or "boiler plate," for-

warded from San Francisco each week. The local news was set in type by hand and printed in a room adjoining the editor's sanctum.

Other than the classy editor's office, Granice did not get much when he bought the *Sonoma Tribune* in 1884: an old Washington hand press, a few cases of type, some job printing equipment— and a lot of uncollected accounts. Granice turned the latter into an asset, spending his entire first week collecting from those who owed the paper money. He hauled in almost enough to cover the paper's purchase price!

With his excellent all-around newspaper background, the feisty, pint-sized Granice soon had the paper on its feet with lively editorials, solid news coverage and paid advertising. Granice changed the paper's name, combining the two old flags "Index" and "Tribune" to come up with *The Sonoma Index-Tribune*.

Granice was 5' 5" tall, had a fine handlebar

The *Sonoma Index-Tribune* had many competitors

What other newspapers, besides the 118-year-old *Index-Tribune,* have existed in Sonoma Valley in its history?

Alexander J. Cox started the *Sonoma Bulletin* in 1852—the first newspaper north of San Francisco.

For more than 20 years after the *Bulletin* passed out of existence in 1855, Sonoma apparently did without a newspaper until 1879, when Benjamin Frank started the four-page *Sonoma Index. The Sonoma Index* changed hands no fewer than 13 times before 1884 with a few name changes, including *The Sonoma Valley Weekly Index* (Frank K. Merritt, publisher) and *Sonoma Tribune* (Edward J. Livernash, publisher). Harry Granice combined the two names, creating *The Sonoma Index-Tribune* in 1884.

In 1889 an opposition paper called *The Sonoma Valley Expositor* was started. Its editors and owners through the early 1900s included W. O. Hocker, C. L. Newman, A. Chessmore, Watters and Hose, and J. K. Bigelow.

A tiny 4" x 6" newspaper called

the *Weekly Ray* was published at Schellville by the Ten Bosch brothers in the 1890s. One of the Ten Bosch brothers and Chessmore started *The Sonoma News* in 1896.

In 1889, the same year *The Sonoma Valley Expositor* was born, a breezy, well-edited newspaper called *The Sonoma Valley Whistle* was begun in El Verano, with Thomas Bewsy Holmes the editor.

A newspaper called *The Forum* was started here in 1915 by Harry and Adolph Lutgens. In that year Sonoma had no fewer than three newspapers—the *Expositor, The Forum* and the long-established *Index-Tribune.* Two years later *The Forum* was sold to Mr. Waters of the *Expositor* and merged to become *The Expositor-Forum.*

About 1926 a Rev. W. L. Gaston started *The Sonoma Valley Moon* with Martin Wittlinger, a printer, as his partner.

All of the aforementioned papers either went out of business or were eventually purchased by the *Index-Tribune* proprietors.

Celeste and Walter Murphy, who

took over the *Index-Tribune* in 1915 after the death of Celeste's publisher-father, Harry Granice, bought out *The Expositor-Forum* and *The Moon.* In 1935 Carl Anderson, a Vineburg printer, started a four-page weekly called *The Trading Post.* He suspended publication in 1941. Meanwhile, a Thomas McCabe had established the weekly *Sonoma Sentinel,* staying in business less than three years.

In 1946 E. A. Little, called The Colonel, started *The Valley of the Moon Review* in Boyes Springs. In 1948 Brent W. Payne bought the *Review* and in 1951 sold it to Newell Farrar. The *Review* was subsequently sold to Zan Stark, Sr. and Jr., postal card printers from Mill Valley. Operating as a weekly for several years, the *Review* went to daily publication as a free circulation newspaper but, after two years, went out of business in 1962.

Several weekly tabloid and even mimeographed publications have since been started in various Valley communities, but all were of short duration.

moustache, wrote potent editorials and would fight anyone at the drop of an insult. The *Index-Tribune* files contain a copy of a 1902 complaint against Granice on a battery charge filed by Louis Breitenbach, then City Clerk, in the Sonoma Township Justice Court of Joseph B. Small. Granice pleaded guilty and was fined five dollars.

A dedicated editor and unswerving champion for community betterment, during his more than 30 years at the helm of the *Index-Tribune*, Granice was recognized as the prime "mover and shaker" of Sonoma Valley. He had friends on all levels— and that is all he asked, that they be on the level. My mother, Ramona Lynch, recalled that her father parted company with but one man in the community, an office seeker who offered to buy the newspaper's editorial support—and was shown the door.

It would be satisfying for this writer to report that, upon his grandfather's death in 1915, the estate, including the *Index-Tribune*, was left to the three Granice daughters, all of whom had worked on the paper. But it didn't happen.

Some nine years after the death of his wife of many years, Kate Keough Granice, the aging Sonoma publisher had married an attractive, much younger woman from San Francisco, who swept him off his feet. Less than two months later, he was stricken ill and suddenly died. Despite a long, bitter court battle, Granice's entire estate, including the *Index-Tribune*, was handed over to his bride of two months. His three daughters received nothing.

However, the eldest daughter, Celeste, who had served as a reporter and editorial writer for the newspaper, was determined to acquire the business that had been in her family for more than 30 years. With her husband, Walter L. Murphy, who had learned the printing trade in Illinois, Celeste borrowed money from several old families in Sonoma and purchased the *Index-Tribune* from the estate.

The Murphy era— Celeste's return to the *I-T*

Cecilia Celeste Granice, the eldest child of Harry and Kate Granice, was born in Santa Clara July 27, 1881. Her sisters were Julie Hortense Granice,

born in Merced July 16, 1884, and Alice Ramona Granice, born in Sonoma Nov. 13, 1894.

It was Cecilia who, in later life, adopted the pen name Celeste (but was known to her close friends as Celie) and inherited the writing ability, drive and liberated ideas of her grandmother, Rowena, and the feisty spirit and editorial sense of her father, Harry.

The youngest Granice sister, called Ramona, was my mother. She worked at the *Index-Tribune* at various times and, in later years, handled reporting and advertising chores, in addition to operating the Linotype machine.

The third Granice daughter, Julie, had a beautiful singing voice and was "discovered" by a leading opera star of the 1890s—only to lose much of her hearing and a promising musical career

INDEX-TRIBUNE ARCHIVES

Cecilia Celeste Granice, shortly after her graduation from the University of California at Berkeley in 1901.

Celeste Murphy, author

Celeste Granice Murphy achieved recognition not only as a journalist, but also as an author and playwright. In 1937 she completed and published her book, *The People of the Pueblo: The Story of Sonoma*, recognized as the first complete history of the community and its residents.

The initial printing of Celeste Murphy's book was done at the *Index-Tribune* almost single-handedly by one man, Henry Steck, who for a quarter of a century ran the mechanical department of the newspaper and had charge of the job printing plant as well.

The second and third editions of *The People of the Pueblo* were printed by Binfords & Mort of Portland, Oregon.

In the preface to *The People of the Pueblo,* Mrs. Murphy wrote:

The Mexican pueblos of California have irresistible and enduring charm. The vanished past, which we glimpse in the gloomy adobe, the neglected garden, the friendly plaza, Mission church, modest marker or more imposing stone, urges the pilgrim to linger and find out more of the romantic background of historic localities.

The larger cities have chronicled their past. Their annals adorn many shelves, but the smaller pueblos, content with scattered mention, have been far too busy to reconstruct their beginnings, to people their streets with the characters of long ago. The old towns, chided with being "sleepy," dead" and "out of step," have spent time and money in modernizing, often at sorry cost as landmarks were scrapped and forgotten.

It is only when adobes are crumbling, old Missions being restored, plazas about to be sold or dignified by some pretentious pile or belated monument that the people of the pueblo begin to realize that history and landmarks are far more important than paved streets, concrete sidewalks, stucco store fronts, and all the pomp of Main Street. Time-scarred walls, hallowed soil and descendants of the old families should be the pride of every historic town, yet these often fail to impress those closest to them.

Years pass with little recognition until a generation growing anxious, lest a precious heritage slip away, awakes to the necessity of preserving the landmarks and traditions and recording the experiences of old settlers and descendants of the early families.

And so a chronicler makes haste to reconstruct the story of old Sonoma from scattered and fragmentary records interwoven with the history of state and counties, from old newspaper files, such as the *Sonoma Bulletin* of the early 1850s and San Francisco publications like *The Californian,* from writings of Gen. M. G. Vallejo and his contemporaries, official records, translated documents, pioneer correspondence, diaries, family letters and stories handed down from pioneer parents to their sons and daughters.

Literary treasures from the Bancroft Library at Berkeley and the shelves of the Society of California Pioneers have also been consulted in reconstructing Sonoma's past.

The writer of Sonoma's history is no wayfarer, but has known and loved the little pueblo—dignified as a city in its official classification—known and loved it and hoped for recognition of its historic soil and beautification of its friendly plaza for more than 40 years, recalls Commandante Mariano G. Vallejo in the waning hours of his glory as he sat on the porch of his hacienda, Lachryma Montis, where the red geraniums grew.

As an editor and journalist, the descendants of the pioneer families have been neighbors of the writer throughout the years. The Vallejo family have been close friends, particularly Mrs. Luisa Vallejo Emparan, most loved and amiable of the daughters and the very last of the family of the great Don.

Sonoma's beauty won the heart of the late Jack London, … and to its Indian name, "valley of the moon," he gave wide fame. On far-flung islands and continents, people read and ask: "What of this Valley of the Moon? Is there such a place?" Sonoma is the Valley of the Moon, and of it and of the people of the old pueblo and the Mission settlement I will tell.

Mrs. Murphy, one of the founders of the Vintage Festival renewal in 1947, also wrote and directed the Vintage Festival Pageant for several years. She was an active member of the Sonoma Valley Woman's Club (of which she and her mother were charter members), the Sonoma Valley Historical Society and the League of California Penwomen. She loved to travel, and her hobby was collecting bells.

At the time of her death, on May 10, 1962, shelves in her home at the historic Barracks here contained more than 300 bells.

Walter Murphy, Celeste's husband, was a community leader and served a number of years as Postmaster of Sonoma in the late 1930s and early '40s. He died Aug. 27, 1962.

The Murphys were genial hosts and, at their home in the Barracks, which they had refurbished, entertained several California governors, motion picture stars, national political figures, generals, admirals, noted literary personages, friends in the newspaper profession—and scores of their Sonoma Valley acquaintances.

while still a young woman.

Destined to carry on the journalistic tradition of her grandmother and father—and to impart to me, her admiring nephew, a love for journalism—Cecilia Celeste was raised amidst newsprint and printer's ink.

"I well remember my father pulling the lever on the old hand press, taking off the papers one by one; mother folding them; the apprentice inking the forms, while we little girls dozed on the bundles of newsprint," she once recalled.

As a keen student at Sonoma Valley Union High School in the 1890s, the eldest Granice child would, when needed, take over her often-ill father's editorial duties. Later, as a student at the University of California at Berkeley, she contributed to the campus newspaper and the major San Francisco dailies of the era.

Although she graduated from UC in 1901 and earned her teaching credential, her love of writing and her weaning on newsprint and ink combined to obliterate any thoughts of becoming a school teacher. Instead, the young college graduate suddenly found herself editing a weekly her father had started in Marin County, *The San Rafael Independent*.

The man who had been leasing the paper from her father worked hard but could not make it financially against two competing Marin papers. Not wanting *The Independent* to close up, Granice sent his talented daughter to save the paper's life.

"I first looked at the tiny office and cluttered print shop and wondered how it ever opened," my aunt told me many years later.

But she had instructions from her father: "You can write, so go to it. But remember, you must get new advertising, meet the payroll, rent and paper bills, and please the readers," Harry Granice admonished her.

W. E. Ortman, a Marin County old-timer whom she hired in 1902 as a young printer, recalled Celeste Granice in an article that appeared in the 100th anniversary issue of the *San Rafael Independent-Journal* in 1962:

> She was a small woman and, when not in an animated discussion, was quiet and unassuming. She generally wore a low-crowned straw hat with a feather alongside the ribbon band. Her street dress was a gray skirt and jacket and

Celeste Granice Murphy (left), editor and copublisher of *The Sonoma Index-Tribune* from 1915 to 1949. At right, Walter L. Murphy, copublisher of the *Index-Tribune*, served as Postmaster of Sonoma between 1936 and 1943.

white shirt waist. Her shirt waist had a high collar.

> Plain in appearance, she nevertheless, at times, changed her hair-do. She was not quick to changing hats.

"Those silly flower-pot affairs," she would scoff in disgust, "are made by male designers in Paris just to make women appear ridiculous. It's an organized move on the part of the inferiority complex of the masculine mind against women's superiority. And women aid and abet them by wearing these crazy creations!"

After fully giving vent to her pet peeve—"the acquiescence of American womanhood to male domination"—she would go to her desk and write an editorial, Ortman recalled.

Let it be said here that her editorials were not without force or punch. Miss Granice had a natural piquancy to her writings. Political personalities were of the stuff that nurtured her rasping pen.

Ortman, who remembers his salary as $1 per week for some 50 hours of work, still acknowledged that Miss "G," as she was called, worked harder than anyone—"soliciting all the advertisements, gathering all the news, writing the stories and then seeking job printing orders."

Celeste, in order to get a competitive edge,

INDEX-TRIBUNE ARCHIVES

This 1923 photo inside the *Index-Tribune* print shop shows copublisher Walter Murphy seated at the Linotype, mechanical foreman Roburt Stanleigh and Ramona Granice Lynch, a reporter and Linotype operator for the *I-T,* holding her three-year-old son, Robert, the author and current publisher.

turned *The Independent* from a weekly to a daily publication. Shortly thereafter her father sold what eventually became the 43,000-circulation daily newspaper known today as the *Marin Independent Journal*, owned by the Gannett chain.

Celeste returned to the *Index-Tribune* for a short period and then was hired by Fremont Older as the Marin County correspondent for the *San Francisco Bulletin*, her beat including San Quentin prison.

Later, during an interview for a reporter's job on the *San Francisco Examiner,* the editor there urged her to return to Sonoma, where he felt she had a great opportunity to run her father's paper.

She returned to Sonoma in 1904 and became associate editor of the *Index-Tribune*. In 1905 she married Walter Lewis Murphy, who had learned

the printing trade as a boy in Illinois. After serving with the California National Guard unit that volunteered during the Spanish-American War, Murphy had returned to Sonoma and entered the building construction business with his brother, Ralph.

After Walter and Celeste were wed at the Granice family home on East Napa Street, the couple moved to San Francisco, where builders were in demand to help restore the metropolis from the ravages of the earthquake and fire of 1906. They later moved to Alameda, and Mrs. Murphy continued to write, contributing to the San Francisco papers and *Life* and *Judge* magazines.

Following the death of Harry Granice in 1915, Celeste and Walter Murphy borrowed money from three old friends in Sonoma and purchased the

Index-Tribune from the Granice estate. My aunt became editor, and her husband was business manager and mechanical foreman.

They had a rough row to hoe. The paper had deteriorated in the months of Harry Granice's illness and death, and the subsequent settlement of his estate. Old equipment had not been replaced.

There was little type or printing material to work with, and, worst of all, there were two other newspapers already being published in Sonoma— *The Expositor* and a brand-new and modern publication, *The Forum*. The two later merged, and the Murphys had one less paper to compete with.

They plugged away, buying new equipment as they saved—working days and nights. My aunt told me she even walked from Sonoma to Boyes Springs and back to pick up advertising and news.

Old-timers encouraged the Murphys, telling them, "The roots of the *Index-Tribune* are deep— you'll succeed."

Succeed they did, buying out *The Expositor-Forum*, then a paper called *The Sonoma Valley Moon.*

Like her father before her, Celeste Granice Murphy led the fight for municipal ownership and improvement of Sonoma's water system, especially for fire protection and Plaza improvement. Other hard-hitting editorials favored the repeal of Prohibition, protection of our vineyardists and pure wines, and construction of the Black Point Cut-Off to provide improved accessibility to Sonoma and the Valley. She was an early booster for the Golden Gate Bridge bond issue, predicting the span could be built and would pay, despite many critics to the contrary.

Celeste Murphy's editorials and buttonholing

Taken in 1932, this photo of the *I-T* "back shop" shows the author's mother, Ramona Granice Lynch, at the Linotype. Looking on is printer Norbert Monson and (in foreground) Jasper, the Murphys' pet dog and *I-T* mascot.

INDEX-TRIBUNE ARCHIVES

of state officials are credited with saving many of our historic landmarks, including Mission San Francisco Solano de Sonoma. The Vallejo home, at the *Index-Tribune*'s urging, was acquired by the state as a monument.

The Murphys' love for the past, as well as the need for community improvement, was emphasized by their purchase of the old Barracks building in 1937. They restored the building and lived in it for the rest of their lives. Prior to their deaths in 1962, the Murphys sold the Barracks to the state for preservation as a historic landmark.

Celeste Murphy once said that her two proudest moments occurred in the same year, 1946. That was the year General of the Air Force H. H. (Hap) Arnold settled here and became a close friend and occasional columnist for the *Index-Tribune*. The same year, her nephew joined the paper as the family's third-generation representative.

Three years later the Murphys decided to retire and to give me the opportunity to purchase

INDEX-TRIBUNE ARCHIVES

Robert M. Lynch in 1949, when he became editor and publisher of *The Sonoma Index-Tribune* and began purchase of the family newspaper from Celeste and Walter Murphy.

The Sonoma Index-Tribune on the "installment plan." The payments began in mid-1949—and so did the Lynch family era of the then 70-year-old weekly newspaper.

An opportunity young Lynch couldn't refuse

The Sonoma Index-Tribune's present publisher and the author of this book, while having deep family roots in Sonoma, did not establish residence here until the late 1930s, following graduation from Alameda High School.

My father, Ernest (Brown) G. Lynch, a district supervisor for Standard Stations, Inc., and my mother, Ramona Granice Lynch, were working parents who, early on, acceded to a plea from an aging Alameda-based cousin—a widow—to "let Bobby come and live with me for a while."

The "for a while" turned out to be 12 years, my going all through school in Alameda, living with my cousin Agnes Turner, and spending the summers and long school holidays with my real parents, who lived alternately in Mendocino County, Berkeley and Richmond before returning to Sonoma in the 1930s.

My mother died here in 1937, while I was in my senior year at Alameda High School, and my Cousin Agnes passed away several months later in Alameda.

I lived in a boarding house until graduation, moving to Sonoma in 1938 and enrolling at Santa Rosa Junior College.

After graduation from SRJC, I fell in love with and subsequently married (on Nov. 9, 1941) Jean Helen Allen, a beautiful young legal secretary in the office of attorney A. R. Grinstead in Sonoma.

Interrupting my education, I took a civil service post at the Mare Island Navy Yard until the birth of our first son, Bill, Sept. 17, 1942.

After that I spent four years in the Navy during World War II, most of them as an enlisted man, and for a brief time as a line officer following graduation from Cornell University's midshipmen's school in 1945.

With my return from the service to Sonoma in 1946, Jean and I planned for her to live with her parents, Mr. and Mrs. A. E. (Jack) Allen, and for

INDEX-TRIBUNE ARCHIVES

California's Governor Goodwin J. Knight caught up with Jean and Bob Lynch at the Cloverdale Citrus Fair to present them with the *Index-Tribune*'s first-ever awards in statewide competition in 1953. The plaques for Best Editorial Page and Best Sports Page were to be the first of many state and national awards won by the Sonoma newspaper.

her to continue working while I completed journalism courses at the University of Oregon, where I hoped to finish my education.

I had taken writing courses in college, helped edit the campus newspaper at SRJC and edited my midshipmen's class magazine at Cornell—and was pretty sure I wanted to be a newspaperman.

But at the *Index-Tribune*, my aunt and uncle couldn't see waiting a year or more for me to finish school. They were tired, having hung on with little help at the paper during the war period. And they were both getting along in years.

They gave Jean and me a choice. Come in with them, or, if I chose to finish college, they would sell the newspaper to one of several eager prospective buyers.

We did a lot of soul-searching and accepted the opportunity provided by the Murphys.

It proved a wise choice. Three years after going to work for the paper—at $33 a week—the Murphys decided to retire and offered to sell us the *Index-Tribune*.

We gave them the few hundred dollars in War

Savings Bonds we had saved, as a down payment—and in just 11 years we had paid for the weekly *Index-Tribune*, which had grown during the prosperous post-war years from eight pages to 10 and 12, and sometimes 16 and 24, pages. In 1985 frequency of publication was increased from once to twice weekly—Tuesdays and Fridays. The number of pages per week now averages 60 pages.

During those first dozen fatiguing but happy growth years, I was editor, publisher, reporter, ad salesman, photographer, sports editor, society editor and job printing order-taker. A special job I had was posting printed notices of funerals on utility poles around the Plaza. This custom died out when people complained about the clutter.

On press nights I even ran the old Miehle No. 1 flatbed newspaper press. Afterward I helped our beloved shop foreman, Henry Steck, address and bundle the papers, after which I took them to the post office to be mailed. Early the next morning I would transport bundles of papers throughout the Valley, to be sold from news racks and store counters.

From our staff of six or seven people in 1946, we have grown to 65 today.

Meeting a demand for the printing of a variety of outside publications—newspapers, tabloids, inserts, booklets, etc.—the family-owned *Index-Tribune* corporation expanded its press, color, mailing and delivery capabilities several years ago. This arm of the *I-T* is called Sonoma Valley Publishing.

In 1992 The Sonoma Index-Tribune, Inc. stepped in to fill the void after the Scripps League newspaper chain, based in Charlottesville, Virginia, suddenly shut down its weekly paper, *The Clarion*, which had served Rohnert Park, Cotati and environs for many years. The *I-T* founded the weekly *Community Voice*, with offices in Rohnert Park—now in its sixth year. Key members of its staff include former *Clarion* employees.

The fifth generation— Bill, Jim and John

*T*he fifth generation of the *I-T* family became important cogs in the Sonoma newspaper operation beginning in 1969, when eldest son Bill, the paper's present editor and CEO, joined the staff.

INDEX-TRIBUNE ARCHIVES

Carrying on a family tradition—the author, *I-T* publisher Bob Lynch (third from left), with sons John, Jim and Bill. Bill, editor and CEO, has been with the Sonoma paper since 1969. Jim, who joined the staff about three years later, is the chief financial officer-business manager. John moved into the daily newspaper field in 1987 after 12 years with the family weekly.

Bill was followed about three years later by second son Jim. Today, as CFO, Jim keeps watch over the economic health of the business.

The "hat trick" came in 1975 with the arrival at the *I-T* of the youngest son, John, newly graduated from college. After several years, John departed the family business to enter the daily newspaper field. He has held editorial positions with the Lesher newspapers in the East Bay and the *Marin Independent-Journal*, owned by the giant Gannett chain.

All three sons are lifetime Sonoma Valley residents and graduates of Sonoma Valley High School. Bill and Jim graduated from UC Santa Barbara; John, from the University of the Pacific at Stockton.

Today, *The Sonoma Index-Tribune* is among the very few independent, family-owned newspapers still being published in California—or anywhere else in the United States.

A trend over the last 40 years, which reached its zenith in the early 1980s, is for large newspaper corporations to buy up smaller, successful or potentially successful community papers which become part of their chain or "group" operation. The ultimate control, and often the editorial policy, are dictated from a head office which can be thousands of miles distant.

The independence of the home-owned *Index-Tribune* is strengthened by the fact that in the 118 years since the newspaper's founding, the paper has remained under the same family's ownership and operation for 113 years.

Part One

FROM SMOKE SIGNALS
TO NEWSPAPERS

Excerpts from The People of the Pueblo

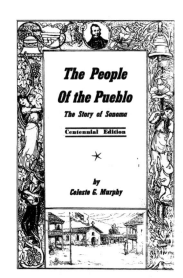

Introduction
to
Part One

FROM SMOKE SIGNALS
TO NEWSPAPERS

Part One of *The Sonoma Valley Story* was, for the most part, excerpted from *The People of the Pueblo,* a book written by Celeste G. Murphy when she was editor of *The Sonoma Index-Tribune.* The first edition of her book was printed on a small, sheet-fed press at the *I-T* in 1937. Two editions followed, in 1941 and 1948.

From my aunt I inherited the rights to *The People of the Pueblo* and herein rely largely on her account of Sonoma Valley's early history. Her book was too long to re-publish here in its entirety, so passages were selected, and connecting "bridges," identified as "Author's Notes," were written. After careful research, some of the material from *The People of the Pueblo* has been revised, added to and/or corrected. The use of brackets ([ ]) indicates where information has been updated.

Many photographs and drawings, contributed by local and outside sources, or selected from the *I-T* archives, enhance the material in Part One—from the time of Indian occupation of the Valley, through Mexican rule, the coming of the mission fathers, M. G. Vallejo's important role, the Bear Flag revolt and American occupation—taking the reader up to 1879, the founding year of *The Sonoma Index.*

1 The Indians Were Here First
... and called it Sonoma

The moon rises over the Sonoma Valley. Some say the name "Sonoma" is a Miyakmah Indian word for "town," while others translate it as "many moons." According to a local legend, early Indian inhabitants claimed to see the moon rise seven times over the ridges of a mountain range on the Valley's eastern rim, creating a supernatural effect.

INDEX-TRIBUNE ARCHIVES

*S*onoma, former pueblo of California, has so much natural charm, beauty and romance that all the world should know its history. Here beauty teems, and at the threshold of each year the madcap spring runs roughshod o'er a puzzled winter. Wild mustard fields of vivid yellow, feathery acacia heavily laden with its drowsy scent, golden poppies opening their chalices to the sky, orchards blossoming for the droning bee.

Days are glorious, and the silvery moon of Indian-summer nights stirs the soul and wakens old romance.

Prior to 1823 (the year Mission San Francisco Solano de Sonoma was founded) few, other than the Indian tribes, knew Sonoma Valley, whose roots they dug, game they killed, insects they relished, fish they caught, and seeds and acorns they pounded in their stone *metates* (mortars). Indian women made their way through tall wild oats or along Sonoma Creek and other meandering streams. They gathered seeds for food and tules to make boats. They gathered brush and wood.

The Valley of the Moon was the Indians' paradise. The summer sun was mild, the moonlight a heaven-sent wonder. Was there ever such moonlight as bathed this valley in the long ago? Sonoma—Indian vale of many moons! The Indians who named it have gone. Gone are the grizzly bears, monarchs of the seven ridged hills. The moon alone remains the same, to wander as of old on nights as glorious as before the white man came.

AUTHOR'S NOTE: Vinson Brown, an *Index-Tribune* columnist in the 1970s and '80s, widely recognized historian, author and environmentalist, wrote about Sonoma's Indians in a column titled "Early Indians around Sonoma," which follows.

He noted that their true identity is not known, because the area was a border country between the Wintun-speaking Patwin (or the Tulukai in Napa Valley) and the Miwok-speaking Tchokoyem to the west. Coast Miwok also resided in Sonoma Valley.

Just north of present-day Glen Ellen began the territory of the people who called themselves the Miyakmah.

Vinson Brown wrote that it was probably the Miyakmahs who named the area Sonoma, as "noma" in their language meant "town." Others, like Celeste Murphy, repeated the legend that Sonoma was an Indian word for "many moons."

In a letter to the editor of the *Index-Tribune* dated Nov. 4, 1891, a Charles Spindler claimed the name "Sonoma" is taken from a mineral called "sonomaite"—silky, colorless hydrous magnesium and aluminum sulphates—discovered by mission fathers years ago.

Still another translation is "big nose," which explains why more romantic-minded historians (and certainly the Sonoma Valley Chamber of Commerce) might prefer the "many moons" version.

COURTESY, THE BANCROFT LIBRARY

The two lower figures painted by artist Louis Choris in 1816 have been identified by modern archaeologists as Coast Miwoks of the Numpali tribelet, one of several groups who were Sonoma's first inhabitants.

When the Spanish Franciscan Padre José Altimira first came to the Sonoma Valley in 1823, what did he find? He found a delightful valley, well watered and lush, and decided to establish there what eventually became the Mission San Francisco Solano de Sonoma. He also found Indians already disturbed by early Spanish intrusions and ready to flee when they saw the armed men of the new nation of Mexico. For some years the earlier mission at San Rafael had been sending out what amounted to raiding parties to bring in Indians from the north and northeast to be Christianized, and the process was far from a gentle one!

Actually the Sonoma Valley before the white men came must have closely approached a paradise on earth. The spread of the Kuksu cult over what is now north central California had caused a religious inspiration and unity over wide areas, so that parties from various tribes often crossed borders to take part in dances, and chiefs were inspired to prevent wars and other trouble by mediation.

In this peaceful atmosphere, villages such as Huchi and Wugilwa, along Sonoma Creek, had probably existed for many centuries with little outside disturbance. Grass and tule-thatched huts were often as much as 30 or 40 feet long, housing in each several families, with a central place for cooking and for pounding acorns in stone mortars.

Healers and chiefs taught the idea of a creator god, gained probably from Kuksu, the hero god of the south, who may actually have existed at one time as a great Indian saint and also taught high standards of conduct. Lies and juvenile delinquency were nearly unknown among these people, because the minds of the children were strongly conditioned by religious ceremonies to be afraid to act otherwise. Ash devils (men covered with ashes) were used to handle, rather roughly, teenagers who had shown rebelliousness against group patterns of conduct. Usually, afterward they became quite meek!

The main rhythm of life centered around the gathering and preparation of food, and all these were woven into religious songs, prayers and legends that taught people the right attitude, and sometimes the right ways, to use in finding food. The great harvests were of acorns from the oak trees and pine nuts from the digger pines. Women and children gathered them into baskets, which were carried to the village for storage. Pine nuts were eaten raw, but the acorns had to be ground, dried, leached carefully with several washings of water and then baked into bread or boiled into mush.

When the end of the winter rains came and the earth took on new life in the spring, what a joy it was for the women and children to get out of the cramped village quarters and hunt for edible roots, herbs, bulbs and fruits of the spring growing! And the men were away on the first great hunts. It was a good time to be alive.

INDEX-TRIBUNE ARCHIVES

A basket of the type made and used by early Indian inhabitants of the Valley of the Moon, from the Sonoma Valley Historical Society's Depot Park Museum collection.

2 A Mission Is Founded

JACK BRADBURY/INDEX-TRIBUNE

The illustration above is an *I-T* artist's conception of the cross planted at the original site of the Sonoma Mission. According to Altimira's journal, the site chosen was south of the present city of Sonoma, at what was later called the Rancheria Pulpula. The mission was subsequently established at its present location. Of all the California mission founders, only Altimira had no assistant and hardly any military backup.

One night in the year 1823, the Indians of the peaceful vale received an alarm. Signal smoke contained the message that a cavalcade of men and horses were en route. Daylight revealed Spaniards, unknown Indian guides, soldiers, Don Francisco Castro representing Mexico's Gov. Luis Arguello, and priests led by Padre José Altimira, all from the village of Yerba Buena (later San Francisco), 50 miles away. Guides, speaking to the Indians in their native language, asked what they called this northern land, so fair, so fertile and fortunate in its sparkling streams and timber. "Sonoma," meaning "many moons," they were reportedly told.

"No one can doubt the benignity of this cli-mate after viewing the trees," wrote Father Altimira in his diary. He told of finding 607 springs of crystalline water in the area, and stone of which a second Rome might well be built. "We are all highly pleased with the site," wrote Altimira that July 4 morning so many years ago, envisioning no doubt the opportunity to acquaint the Indians with the Christian God, and praying for success of the new Mission San Francisco de Asis in the chosen valley of Sonoma.

An ardent Franciscan, Padre José Altimira was raised in the same part of Spain as Padre Junipero Serra, founder of the California mission chain. During three years at San Francisco de Asis (today often referred to as "Mission

Dolores"), Altimira saw the need for the ailing northern mother mission to be transferred to a new site in the great, wonderful wilderness beyond Tamalpais and San Pablo; and with it should be joined its *asistencia* (attending mission), San Rafael Arcangel.

The two missions were regarded as insufficient because of their climate at a time when alarming sickness had developed and more abundant crops were an increasing necessity. A new Mission San Francisco de Asis was needed in the north, Altimira concluded.

In a letter to the Padre Prefect, Father José Senan, Altimira wrote: "San Francisco is on its last legs, and San Rafael cannot subsist alone."

Thus it was that, after several days of exploration with his party of horsemen, a delighted Altimira, near bounteous springs and sheltering hills, planted the Christian cross in Sonoma on July 4, 1823.

A deterrent to Russian expansion at Fort Ross

*H*istory reveals that the purpose of establishing a mission at Sonoma was not only to solve a food shortage and to convert the Indians to Christianity, but also to remind the bold and enterprising Russians of Mexico's territorial rights in California. The Russian-American Fur Company had become a great monopoly and power, occupying all the Aleutian Islands and having one settlement, Sitka, on the American coast.

The Russians, seeking expansion of their rich harvest of otter pelts and land on which to grow foodstuffs—which their wet, cold, extreme northern clime did not afford—as early as 1809 established a colony in the Bodega Bay area, where they fished and hunted the rich ocean waters, grew food and cut timber from the equally rich forests of the rugged California coast.

Thirty miles north of Bodega Bay the Russians built Fort Ross, dedicated in 1812.

The Russians from Sitka who swooped down on California's abundant waters to plunder them of otter had found the Bodega area on the Sonoma County shore a good hideout. Farther south, the Spaniards kept a watchful eye on bays and harbors. Prior to 1823 most of the plunder had come from waters north of Bodega, but about that year the Russians ventured nearer San Francisco Bay. The mission at Sonoma was a deterrent gesture, but it did not stop the continued inroads of boats taking valuable furs up and down the California coast, even entering San Francisco Bay.

Despite Padre Altimira's recommendations, the San Francisco de Asis (Dolores) and San Rafael missions were not disbanded in favor of the mission at Sonoma, which for a year was known

Fort Ross in 1841 by V. V. Ushanoff, based on Bernard Duhaut-Cilly's early sketch of the Russian outpost on the northern California coast.

COURTESY, SONOMA VALLEY HISTORICAL SOCIETY

INDEX-TRIBUNE ARCHIVES

Saint Francis Solano, for whom Sonoma's mission was named, was born in the Andalusian area of Spain in 1549. His violin playing is said to have been the foundation of his friendship with Indians of the Andes in South America.

as New San Francisco.

As a result, a new patron saint named Francis had to be found for the new Sonoma mission. Chosen was Saint Francis Solano, apostle to the South American Indians some 200 years before. Thus, Saint Francis, founder of the Franciscan Order, holy man of Assisi, Italy, remained enshrined at his church on the Arroyo de los Dolores (Dolores River) in the city that was to be named for him. The mission at San Rafael was also spared.

On the 4th of April, Passion Sunday, 1824, the dedication ceremonies of the Mission San Francisco Solano de Sonoma took place. Last of all the missions to be built (and the first, and only one, built under Mexican rule), Sonoma became the support of other missions in the area.

Here 500 neophytes [new converts] from the three missions of San Rafael, San Jose and San Francisco were sent, pleasing the zealous heart of Padre Altimira. As at all the missions, neophytes had to conform to strictest rules. They were given religious instruction, fed and clothed. The sexes were given separate quarters, the women taught to sew by the soldiers' wives, the men trained to work at various crafts and trades.

The first mission buildings in Sonoma were of redwood, built by the Indians in the vicinity. The church was 25 by 105 feet, whitewashed on the outside. There was also a house for the padre, seven houses for the soldiers and their families, and a granary for which 100 redwood beams were cut. Fire twice swept the local mission, but by 1829 a substantial church of adobe brick with tiled roof would grace the land of many moons.

Six years after the founding of the church, Sonoma reported 760 neophytes on the rolls, and 650 Indians had received baptism. Grain fields had yielded 2,000 bushels. Two thousand head of cattle, 725 horses, 4,000 sheep and many swine were pastured.

Water had been piped from the crystalline springs. Rich, red soil was being tilled for fruit and vines. Herds were increased for hides and tallow. Adobe brick was drying in the sun. (Making adobe was often a punishment in early California.) Near tawny walls the purple grapes grew luscious for the autumn wine. Three thousand vines were coming into bearing.

The Indians learned to weave, to make their blankets and to tan hides for saddles and shoes.

AUTHOR'S NOTE: While the mission at Sonoma prospered in those early years, it was not without its problems. Despite his devotion and hard work in administering the mission he had founded, Father Altimira was deeply hurt by reports received by the mission authorities in Alta California that the Indians at Sonoma resented the conditions and their treatment by Altimira here.

In an article (excerpted on the next page) for an *Index-Tribune* special supplement on the occasion of the Sonoma Mission Sesquicentennial, author Robert S. Smilie described Altimira's departure from California and the succession of priests who followed him.

In the fall of 1826 after a bountiful harvest, Indians either from gentile tribes or some neophytes, or both, raided the storerooms and set fire to some of the lesser buildings. Altimira, discouraged, quickly left for Mission San Rafael, abandoned his mission at Sonoma and asked to be sent to Mission Santa Barbara.

However, he was sent to Mission San Buenaventura, southeast of Santa Barbara, where he remained until Jan. 23, 1828. Then, with another Spanish priest, he secretly left from Santa Barbara on the U. S. brig *Harbinger* for Spain. It caused quite the mission scandal of the period, as no permission had been requested or granted from the mission authorities. Altimira was later reported living in Spain.

Soon after Altimira abandoned Mission San Francisco Solano, Father Buenaventura Fortuny, in September 1828, was transferred from Mission San Jose to Sonoma. Under Fortuny's supervision, a large mission establishment was built, with an adobe church equal in

size to most of the other California mission churches. In January 1831, with the mission in excellent condition, Fortuny, now 57, asked that a younger padre take over the duties at San Francisco Solano.

Father José Maria Gutierrez, 32, arrived in Monterey in January 1833 and was sent to Sonoma that March. After Fortuny left in September, Gutierrez was the only padre at the mission. He carried on the building plans of Fortuny, and the crop and field operations through the winter. His lack of administrative experience and understanding of the neophytes and their problems led to complaints of too severe punishments and work tasks. The result was his transfer in February of the next year to Mission Dolores.

Father José Lorenzo de la Concepción Quijas was sent up from Mission Dolores early in 1834. Father Quijas was a large, robust, active padre, reported originally from Ecuador—an early muleteer and trader who joined the Franciscan College of Zacatecan in

A ceremonial gathering at the San Francisco Solano de Sonoma mission, circa 1832, from a painting by Oriana Day.

INDEX-TRIBUNE ARCHIVES

Mexico. At his new mission, he carried on the expansion started by Fortuny, building the large *monjerio* (priests' quarters) and storehouses, and completing the large adobe church.

The Mission became a favorite stopping place for the hide traders and traveling merchants and explorers of the period, where they were always welcome.

Then at the zenith of the Mission's prosperity came the order of secularization in August 1834. Inventories and accountings of all former church properties were demanded, from San Diego to Sonoma. The rancho lands, cattle and implements, etc., were supposedly to be divided among the freed neophytes—the churches to become parish churches, with a small supporting area in each mission pueblo settlement. An administrator was appointed for each mission, with major-domo and other assistants; the existing padre was to be the parish priest until replaced.

In Sonoma, Lt. Mariano G. Vallejo, then Commander of the Presidio of San Francisco, was appointed administrator of the Mission by the then governor of Alta California, José Figueroa. Vallejo soon installed Guadalupe Antonio Ortega as major-domo and his younger brother, Salvador Vallejo, as assistant. Father Quijas turned over all properties, ranchos, cattle, etc. to them and all authority to the neophytes. He retained only the use of the church and living quarters in the padres' house. Ortega and Salvador Vallejo gave little consideration to Father Quijas and his needs, or to those of the church. The proud padre complained to Lt. Mariano Vallejo but received no response or offer of help.

Finally, he could not stand the debauchery of Ortega or the insolence of Salvador Vallejo and, in June 1835, moved his residence to Mission San Rafael Arcangel, where he continued to carry out his duties for the Sonoma church. Father Quijas sent a letter of explanation of his actions and reasons to his superiors: thenceforth, he would care for the church duties at Sonoma but would not reside there unless Ortega was removed.

The ranchos of the Mission were being granted, one by one, to friends or relatives of Mariano Vallejo, with a small number to retired soldiers. Few neophytes remained—most having returned to their native rancherias. The buildings at the Mission were fast being dismantled—the materials being used to construct public and private houses around the new Plaza.

Anticipating total destruction of the Mission, Father Quijas requested in 1835 and received a plot of ground on the east edge of the proposed pueblo area for a public cemetery (the present Catholic Cemetery on East Spain Street near Fifth Street East). Finally, a small chapel was built in 1841–42 on the site of the original plank church, for use as the parish church for the local families. Part of the padres' house, still standing, was used for housing, when Father Quijas used rooms while attending the Mission from San Rafael and visitors came to the pueblo.

Mission San Rafael was undergoing the same deterioration as at Sonoma, as Mariano Vallejo was also its administrator. However, Don Timoteo Murphy was the major-domo at San Rafael and took better care of the neophytes. Father Quijas and Murphy became boon companions, the two elderly comrades reportedly relieving the monotony and frustrations of the deteriorations of their mission empires with their wine cellars. Records verify a story that the two were once locked up, on Gen. Mariano Vallejo's orders, at the calaboose in Sonoma for visiting the Russian colony at Fort Ross—which was definitely "off limits."

Father Quijas was also caring for Mission Dolores until 1843, when he was appointed vice-commissary by the

Franciscan College and made his head-quarters at Mission San Jose. He returned to Mexico in 1844 and never returned to California. Sonoma and the other missions in which he had served had all been reduced to poor parishes and were occasionally served by padres from as far south as Santa Clara and Monterey. Their wealth had been confiscated and dissipated by the destroyers under the guise of secularization in a few short years.

As the lives of the missions ended, so did those of the Indians in Sonoma Valley whom the padres hoped the church could educate and bring under the Christian banner. Wars and smallpox—which broke out first at Fort Ross and spread to all tribes—combined with an inability to adapt to the new way of life being foisted on them, left but a scattered remnant of Native Americans here by the 1880s. The Indians shifted for themselves or were taken in by settlers. The Vallejo family and early-day pioneers like Franklin Sears of Sears Point and the Carriger, Morris, Champlin, Fowler and other families had Indians in their employ.

The will of Nick Carriger, dated 1886, requested that "the Indian Vicente and tribe be allowed to remain on the home place in the western foothills of Sonoma ... and have the same privileges of wood, water, fishing and gardening as they enjoyed in my lifetime." Vicente lived to be over 100 years old. Some of his descendants may still be living in this vicinity.

INDEX-TRIBUNE ARCHIVES

Vicente Carillo, a Native American, survived a tragic smallpox epidemic in Sonoma Valley that decimated his people. Born in 1788, he witnessed a procession of historic events and people that boggles the imagination. Pictured here on the occasion of his 107th birthday, Vicente, as he was known to generations of Sonomans, died in 1902 at the age of 114.

3 M. G. Vallejo

Courtesy, Sonoma Valley Historical Society

This likeness of Mariano Guadalupe Vallejo is thought to have been painted about the time the young lieutenant was serving as the military commandant of the presidio at San Francisco, a few years before he was ordered to establish a garrison at Sonoma. In June 1835 Governor José Figueroa named the ambitious and vain—but competent—Vallejo military commandant and director of colonization of the northern frontier, titles that proved to be a solid foundation for garnering huge land grants, wealth and prestige in the years to follow.

AUTHOR'S NOTE: Mariano Guadalupe Vallejo was born in Monterey on July 4, 1807, the Spanish blood of his Castilian ancestors in his veins. Called Guadalupe by his family, he was described not only as a handsome young man, but also as highly intelligent and ambitious, cultivating friendships with those in high places in early Alta California from boyhood.

Vallejo's earliest mentor was no less a personage than Gov. Pablo Vicente de Sola, a former associate of his soldier-father, Ignacio Vicente Ferrer Vallejo. Governor Sola selected the quick-witted Mariano for special tutoring in English, French and Latin, and also provided schooling in business and accounting from European educators who were among early California settlers.

In 1822 Governor Sola returned to Mexico to serve in the legislature. Vallejo, although just 15 years of age, became personal secretary to Sola's successor, Gov. Luis Arguello. The teen-age wonder was in that post when word was received in California that Mexico had become independent of Spain, and he reportedly penned the news in a flowing script for circulation throughout Alta California.

At Governor Arguello's urging, young Vallejo followed family tradition and entered military service as a cadet in the Presidial Company of Monterey in 1824. He thrived on the discipline, pomp and ceremony, won promotions to corporal and sergeant, and in 1827 was promoted to the officer's rank of *alferez* (ensign or second lieutenant). The confident and ambitious Alferez Vallejo actually started his political career, too, in that same year he received his commission as a military officer—being named a provisional member of the Territorial Assembly at Monterey by then Governor of California José Maria Echeandia. Conveniently, Vallejo's nephew (his junior by just two years) Juan B. Alvarado was also elected to that body, along with his boyhood friend José Castro.

Before taking over his military duties at the San Francisco presidio, Ensign Vallejo participated in several skirmishes with Indians in the San Joaquin Valley, but is said not to have relished his victories. He expressed the feeling that the often-bloody forays against the Indians were inhumane. In this, he was unlike his brother, Salvador, who gained the reputation of being quite ruthless in his dealings with Indians. Don Mariano, at 22, was also unhappy with the way the powers in Mexico were ruling California, and he and his friends and relatives, when alone, often expressed a desire for a free and independent California. He was encouraged in his desire to improve California's disjointed administration with the arrival in 1833 of José Figueroa, successor to Gov. Manuel Victoria, who took an immediate liking to Vallejo.

Vallejo, by then, had been married (in 1832) to the 17-year-old Francisca Benicia Carrillo, whom he had met and fallen in love with Jan. 24, 1830, in San Diego.

In the spring of 1833, the young couple (he was 25) were living at the presidio of San Francisco, where Vallejo was serving as military commandant and where their first child, a baby boy christened Andronico, was born on March 4, 1833.

The tragic death of their first offspring six months later added to the depression of the young couple, who found it hard to adjust to the drab presidio of San Francisco and its shortages of finances, food, clothing and furnishings—and disgruntled soldiers—due to a disinterested Mexican government. It was his friend Governor Figueroa who rescued Lieutenant Vallejo from the doldrums of presidio life and its nearby ramshackle, sparsely populated village of Yerba Buena, which was destined to become, in a relatively few years, the sparkling metropolis of San

COURTESY, SONOMA VALLEY HISTORICAL SOCIETY

Francisca Benicia Vallejo was a member of the prominent Carrillo family of San Diego. In her 58 years of marriage to Mariano Guadalupe Vallejo, she bore 16 children, including the first Californio admitted to West Point and the first native-born physician in the state.

Francisco beside the Golden Gate.

In *General M. G. Vallejo and the Advent of the Americans,* Vallejo biographer Alan Rosenus writes that in mid-April 1833, Governor Figueroa sent the young officer a set of orders "which prepared the way for Vallejo's virtual autonomy in northern California and also helped to establish the foundation of his personal wealth" (p. 14).

Vallejo, with a military escort, was sent to check out the Russians who had established a flourishing colony and military outpost at Fort Ross, 85 miles north of the San Francisco Presidio. Not only was he to remind the Russian American Fur Company leaders—who had, without permission, established Fort Ross in 1812 and been plundering the coastal waters of its fur-bearing riches—that Bodega Bay and environs belonged to Mexico, but that incursions farther south would not be tolerated.

At the same time, Figueroa ordered his

young friend to inspect the area for a presidio site north of San Francisco Bay—subsequently authorizing Vallejo to establish the military post at Sonoma, the site of Mission San Francisco Solano de Sonoma. "It was probably no accident that the site choice was made on the eve of the secularization of the missions," Rosenus writes (p. 14).

The Indians greet Vallejo

*I*n 1835, with Russian affairs tense and with mission secularization insisted upon by the Mexican congress, Lieutenant Vallejo came to Sonoma, where he had been ordered to re-establish and extend his domain in the direction of Fort Ross. He came via San Rafael and from there made his way with eight soldiers and several Indian guides in two schooners, sailing up the sloughs to what is now called Novato.

ROD RULOFSON/COURTESY, VACAVILLE HERITAGE COUNCIL

Chief Solano, formerly Sem Yeto, as sculpted by Bill Huff in 1934. The statue was at first mounted on a rock above a weigh station at Cordelia and became a great target. It was later moved to the library in Fairfield.

In his *Historia de California* Vallejo painted a graphic picture of the country and its inhabitants. He found great numbers of Indians, who shot arrows at his boats and, failing to make an impression with these, tried to wade out in the slough and climb aboard.

Vallejo had landed at San Rafael and concluded a treaty with the Licatiut tribe, of which Marin and Quintin were the chiefs. He then proceeded to Novato and, from there, to another landing close to the rancheria of Captain Pulpula, later the J. A. Poppe ranch near Embarcadero (near present-day Schellville), afterward so important in the transportation of the area.

Here Chief Solano and 3,000 Indians were massed in curious if not friendly gesture to see the white men land. Tents were erected among the tules and messengers dispatched in many directions, urging the leaders of the region to come and make treaties with the head of the Mexican government.

Vallejo claimed that within 48 hours his small force faced a gathering of 11,000, of which only a third were of proven friendliness. Chief Solano of the Suisuns was interpreter and harangued those assembled, urging them to be friendly, take gifts and receive the help the white men could give them in punishing enemy tribes. Trinkets were lavished on the natives, after which Vallejo and his men were feted.

Vallejo befriends Solano, founds Sonoma pueblo

*A*UTHOR'S NOTE: Chief Solano, referred to above, was to become a very important person in Vallejo's life as an ally, intermediary with tribes, brave and unyielding fighter in battles, close friend and protector. A big, powerful man, over 6 feet 5 inches tall, chief of the Suisun tribes, his Indian name was Sem-Yeto (The Mighty Arm). He had been baptized into the Christian faith at the Sonoma Mission and christened Francisco Solano, by which name he was afterwards known.

The *Sonoma Index* of Dec. 4, 1880, carries a reprint of an address given by General Vallejo on the Fourth of July, 1876, in Santa Rosa. In the lengthy speech, Vallejo spoke reverently of the chief of the Suisuns who, after his conversion, came to Sonoma and "rendered most important services to the cause of civilization and Christianity and in the pacification of all the territory north of the bay of San Francisco. Solano, to whom we gave the title of 'Prince,' must occupy a prominent place in the history of California," said the General.

In his address, Vallejo retold the story of one of the few times he had to rebuke Solano—when the giant chieftain attempted to kidnap beautiful Helena, wife of Russian nobleman Baron Alexander Rotcheff, governor of the Russian colony at Fort Ross. The incident occurred in June 1841, when Rotcheff, Baroness Helena and a party of Russians were returning from a visit to Mount Mayacamas, where they placed a copper plate, christening the mountain Saint Helena in honor of the patron saint of their Imperial Mistress, Helena, Empress of Russia.

General Vallejo had learned of the expedition and sent his brother Salvador and Solano with a party of Indians to find out what the Russian party was about. Near Santa Rosa they closed in on the Rotcheff entourage, which they outnumbered, surrounding them. When the startled Russians saw muskets in the hands of Chief Solano and the Indian band, they drew their own weapons in defense. Don Salvador quickly appeared and warned the Russians, who had brandished their weapons, not to shoot, or face annihilation. Meanwhile, the legend, retold in history, tells of Solano becoming enraptured at the beauty of Baroness Helena and announcing that the Russian men would die, but "the woman, Solano keep!" (McKittrick, *Vallejo, Son of California,* p. 186).

Don Salvador, unable to dissuade the stubborn Indian chieftain from his intended capture of the Russian beauty, finally convinced him to stay his course until General Vallejo could be contacted. The general, it is said, personally appeared at the site of the pow-wow, convinced Solano of the flaws in his romantic abduction plan, and personally escorted the Lady Helena and party back to Fort Ross (McKittrick, p. 188).

Vallejo, as his Fourth of July, 1876, speech quoted many years later in *The Sonoma Index-Tribune* reveals, was very proud of his friendship

This simple depiction of Chief Solano was carved in sandstone by the General's son Platon, who knew Solano well.

with Chief Solano, and it is evident in the giant leader's loyalty to the youthful officer whom Governor José Figueroa sent here to found the pueblo and administer the secularization of the mission, that the friendship was mutual. In those busy early days of planning the village, fortifying it and building barracks, plus the many secularization duties, Solano proved to be a valuable friend and ally.

On June 24, 1835, Vallejo received a formal order from Governor José Figueroa. In addition to laying out a pueblo in the valley of Sonoma, Vallejo was to be administrator for the secularization of the mission here.

Vallejo's rule over the mission lands was accompanied by his first big gift of property, a 10-league grant from Governor Figueroa known as the Rancho Petaluma, later expanded to 66,000 acres. "This land was Vallejo's to dispose of as he wished—the beginning of his personal empire," notes Rosenus (p. 14).

*F*rom Monterey came these instructions, evidently after due inspection and recommendations for this particular locality:

In conformity with the orders and instructions issued by the Supreme

Government of the Confederation respecting the location of a village in the valley of Sonoma, this commandancy urges upon you that according to the topographical plan of the place it be divided into quarters or squares, seeing that the streets and plaza be regulated so as to make a beginning. The inhabitants are to be governed entirely by said plan. This government and commandancy approves entirely of the lines designated by you for outlets recognizing as the property of the village and public lands and privileges the boundaries of Petaluma, Agua Caliente, Rancho de Huichica, Lena de Suhr, Salvador, Vallejo and La Veronica on the north of the pueblo of Sonoma as the limits of the property, requesting that it be commenced immediately around the hill where the fortification is to be erected to protect the inhabitants from incursions of the savages and all others.

... You will divide each square (*manzana*) into four parts, as well for the location of each as to interest persons in planting kitchen gardens so that everyone shall have a hundred yards more or less ... which the government deems sufficient, and regulations on the subject, in such manner that at all times the town shall possess the legal title.

This government and commandancy general offers you thanks for your efforts in erecting this new city which will secure the frontier of the republic, and is confident that you will make new efforts for the national entirety, God and liberty.

José Figueroa

*T*hus Sonoma, well planned for beauty and symmetry, for the protection of its people and their welfare and to encourage thrift and industry, came into being, built and laid out in conformity with a definite plan. Before long it became the center of official life and social gaiety north of San Francisco Bay, its importance not then equaled by Yerba Buena, the straggling village of which Sonoma was the acknowledged rival. The mecca of distinguished visitors and emissaries to California, it was described in reports of travelers and scientists in the 1840s. Vallejo summoned many prominent men to confer with him here, and Sonoma was widely known long before the making of that crude emblem destined to be the state flag,

COURTESY, SUNSET MAGAZINE

In this painting by an unknown artist, General Vallejo reviews troops at the Sonoma garrison in the early 1840s.

and a decade before the cry of "Gold!" left bewildered families wondering at their deserted village.

The Pueblo of Sonoma was begun near the Mission church and was built around a plaza in true Mexican style. Vallejo knew the plan well, for Monterey, where he was born and raised, also had its plaza. He envisioned the Pueblo of Sonoma, with its parade ground for troops and an eight-acre square over which the green and white emblem of Mexico would fly, with promenade area for the populace. The army barracks, iron-barred and foe-resisting, were started. A cannon was mounted on Battery Hill, the eminence back of the town on the north. Guns frowned from the plaza walls, emphasizing the military import of Sonoma, though perhaps the town would not have long resisted a siege had real trouble come.

With pocket compass, the far-seeing founder staked out the plaza and plotted the streets adjacent thereto, providing for a 110-foot-wide avenue leading south from the plaza—main artery of the new pueblo—for in that direction four miles distant was the embarcadero and navigable water. (This thoroughfare is the Broadway we know today and is still the important avenue of traffic to and from San Francisco, where motor cars speed along on a smooth state highway—once the dust-clouded or muddy road over which plodding oxen and horses hauled freight and brought travelers to and from the schooners at the landing.)

After fortifying the hill back of Sonoma Mission, as ordered by Governor Figueroa, Indians were put to work on the building of the barracks west of the church. In these early days there were neither tool shops nor lumber yards, so redwood timbers, hand-hewn in the upper valley, were cut and hauled by ox team to the site. With sun-dried bricks, laborers built quarters for the troops and around the barracks erected an adobe wall with loopholes for guns. In later years Vallejo declared the barracks had been built with his private funds at a cost of $9,000, a sum which he had never been repaid, and that $4,000 was owed him for the troops.

In 1841 the military post of Sonoma had a payroll of $11,000. Sgt. José de Berryessa and Salvador Vallejo were in command, some of the soldiers at times doing garrison duty in San Francisco. Seven guns had been mounted, and Vallejo stated he was keeping up the Sonoma gar-

Juan B. Alvarado, General Vallejo's nephew, named himself governor of Alta California in 1836.

COURTESY, CALIFORNIA STATE LIBRARY

rison at a cost of approximately $1,000 monthly. On an average, however, there were fewer than 100 soldiers at Sonoma and San Francisco. Vallejo complained that this force was inadequate and invited attack because of its small number and inferior equipment. Despite later confirmation of his fears, the military commander was given little help by his government. Sonoma's cannon was eventually transferred to San Francisco and mounted on Telegraph Hill to protect the entrance to San Francisco harbor.

Town lots in Sonoma were allotted to many residents, and outlying areas comprising vast land grants were distributed to friends of the administration. The Spanish grants had been restricted to three square leagues, but under Mexican allotment as many as 11 square leagues were obtainable. Mexican citizens, and those who had become naturalized citizens of Mexico, shared Governor Figueroa's favor.

Figueroa, sixth Mexican governor of California (1833–35), died in the midst of efforts to secularize the missions, do justice to the Indians and colonize the country in the vicinity of Sonoma.

He believed in a gradual break-up of the missions and fair partition of their lands and vast herds, the Indians to share in the distribution. His plan seems to have been that half the mission properties should be granted the Indians dependent upon them; that a fund should be maintained for the support of the churches by secular authorities; and that the Indians were to give their labor to public work, part time. They were not to sell property distributed to them or to indiscriminately kill their cattle.

Named commandante-general, military governor

AUTHOR'S NOTE: Vallejo's political fortunes did not suffer from the passing of Figueroa, his special friend and benefactor. Vallejo's nephew, Juan Bautista Alvarado, had headed a brief rebellion in 1836 proclaiming Alta California independent of Mexico, naming himself as governor. Alvarado was confirmed as governor by Mexican authorities in 1838, followed by the announcement that his uncle Mariano was promoted (from second lieutenant) to colonel of cavalry. Vallejo's official title was even more impressive—commandante-general and military governor of the newly declared state of Alta California.

Family ties made for pretty impressive political results. Vallejo and Alvarado, both still in their 20s, were now virtually in control of California.

For the rest of his life, the commandante-general of Alta California was known to all as "General" Vallejo, despite his highest military ranking being that of colonel.

He was kept busy with his duties overseeing the Mission and the Indians, keeping his eye on the Russian colony at Fort Ross, and constantly trying to keep track of the political personnel moves in central and southern California and Mexico that might upset his role as commandante-general and the power, respect and wealth it generated for him and his growing family.

Despite gaining a reputation for sometimes being "a rigorous disciplinarian, haughty, aristocratic and strict" (Hunter, *Vallejo: A California Legend,* p. 38), Vallejo also was known to be considerate of others, generous (sometimes to a fault) and always hospitable to guests—particularly going out of his way to be friendly to visiting Americans and those from foreign lands who were arriving on the West Coast in larger numbers each year.

It would appear that General Vallejo became fed up with the disinterest of the Mexican government in its California colony. Unheeded were his warnings about the unauthorized influx of so many Americans and Europeans (despite his own hospitality) and the need for more military protection. So he pretty much decided to settle in and enjoy the "good life" he lived in Sonoma, strengthening his personal gains.

Dealing with unregistered foreigners

As far back as the late 1830s and very early in the 1840s, the foreigners in California were beginning to "feel their oats." In April 1840 Vallejo was advised of Governor Alvarado's intent to put down a conspiracy led by Isaac Graham, who had boasted of his intent to run the Mexicans out.

Vallejo got his orders to arrest foreigners who were unregistered in California and to deport all of those not married to natives of the country. He

Isaac Graham conspired against the Mexican government.

COURTESY, CALIFORNIA STATE LIBRARY

was given authority to secure a ship for their deportation and the power to seize those thought to be a menace to the territory. Vallejo obeyed instructions and secured the vessel *Joven Guipazcoasaat* at a cost of several thousand dollars.

While deportation was being arranged, Vallejo made a trip to San Francisco with his staff and 70 soldiers. Mounted on a spirited gray horse, he was a commanding figure as he paraded to Montgomery Street and up to the Jacob P. Leese house, where he conferred with the governor's representatives and arranged to place the presidio, mission and pueblo under martial law.

Vallejo left his actual deportation of undesirables (which history refers to as the Graham Affair) to then Capt. José Castro [later Commandante-General of California], who was subsequently court-martialed when those deported complained of great indignity and such harsh treatment that they won indemnity and were returned to California shores. (Among the 40 who complained were Peter Storm and Mark West, well known in the vicinity of Sonoma.) While the Graham Affair lasted, it bristled with excitement and prediction, and intensified bitterness between the foreigners and Mexicans up and down the coast.

AUTHOR'S NOTE: Isaac Graham, referred to above, was a rough and ready Tennessean, crackshot rifleman and revolutionist who entered California in the early 1830s and established a distillery near Monterey. Outspoken in his dislike for Mexican nationals, he surrounded himself with an equally rugged group of uncouth American riflemen.

In early 1840 Governor Alvarado, after receiving reports that Graham's followers were planning a takeover of the government at Monterey, gave the orders that caused the arrest

COURTESY, CALIFORNIA STATE LIBRARY

Gen. José Castro. After the Graham Affair, he became leery of American settlers.

of Graham and 38 other foreigners, mostly Americans. The prisoners were placed in Monterey's tiny jail and then sent to Mexico by ship. Later they were set free, but the repurcussions against Alvarado and his governing body were many, including a lengthy court-martial trial faced by Castro, who was eventually found not guilty of harsh treatment of the prisoners.

But history reveals that the bitterness sown by deportation of the Americans, many of them reputable settlers and not of Graham's ilk, would be a factor in what was to happen to General Vallejo, and Sonoma, six years later.

4 Sonoma in 1841

INDEX-TRIBUNE ARCHIVES

This 1840 drawing, which appeared in the June 14, 1896, issue of the *San Francisco Call*, is attributed to Col. Victor Prudon, General Vallejo's secretary. This is how the presidio of Sonoma opposite the north side of the Plaza would have appeared to Commodore Charles Wilkes, U. S. Navy, who visited Sonoma on an exploring tour in 1841.

AUTHOR'S NOTE: Had today's readers of this book been able to go back in time, and be invited guests of General Vallejo in early-day Sonoma, what would they have seen and experienced 156 years ago?

Commodore Charles Wilkes of the United States sloop-of-war *Vincennes,* on an exploring tour of California in 1841, made a visit to Sonoma, coming by water on a boat to Embarcadero, four miles south of Sonoma. In his narrative of the United States Exploring Expedition, 1838–42, he gives a graphic picture of the old pueblo of Sonoma.

General Vallejo knew Wilkes was coming and, to meet him at the landing, sent a sergeant, two soldiers and a drove of horses. From the drove were selected the best-looking animals, and they were lassoed for the Wilkes party. The travelers then mounted their steeds and, followed by a crowd of Indians and nondescript livestock, start-ed over flooded areas for the Vallejo home. As they neared Sonoma, a salute was fired in their honor and the Mexican colors were raised.

The palace (the Casa Grande) of Commandante Vallejo, adjoining the barracks, was not yet completed. In his narrative Wilkes said: "Through a gateway and courtyard we ascended a half-finished flight of stairs to the principal room of the General's house—50 feet in length, with many doors leading therefrom to other apartments." The place was indifferently furnished, recalled the visitor, some gaudy chairs from the Sandwich Islands making the greatest impression on him. He thought them in poor taste and said he could not imagine islanders designing such furniture.

Vallejo was ill, but Wilkes was received by his brother, Salvador Vallejo, and his brother-in-law, Jacob P. Leese. Finally, the commodore was taken to General Vallejo's quarters. The general proved courteous and hospitable, introducing the stranger to members of his household, including his wife and her sister, Mrs. Juan Wilson, whose husband, a Scot, was then commander of the schooner *California*. Mrs. Leese and a niece of the Vallejos were also presented. They invited Wilkes to be their dinner guest.

In writing afterward of the dinner, Wilkes complained that the meal was cold, having been brought in from an outside kitchen; but what it lacked of heat in one way was made up in another, for he said every mouthful eaten was "poisoned" with the everlasting compound of red pepper and garlic.

He thought himself a connoisseur of food and wine, and criticized the General's wine and complained that the tea was not to his liking. Leese was master of ceremonies at the dinner, which was served by an Indian boy who wore a loose shirt over bare legs and had cropped hair.

Salvador Vallejo and three soldiers took the Wilkes party for a trip around the surrounding country the next day. Sonoma seemed a paradise for sportsmen, with thousands of ducks and geese swarming the marshes or sunning themselves in the placid waters of the sloughs and creeks. Deer jumped up at every turn in the road. There were hundreds of deer, and the Mexicans killed them only for their firm white tallow, as they did not care for hunting.

The Indian village maintained near Sonoma after the Mission's decline was inspected by Wilkes, who described a group of 300 men, women and children existing in hovels made of tree branches. Their fare seemed to be the worst bullock joints and the acorns found in the vicinity. They wore few clothes and altogether presented a desperate picture.

The buildings in the town of Sonoma, described by Wilkes in his account of the pueblo, were the General's house, the barracks, Salvador Vallejo's residence, a billiard parlor, Leese's dwelling, the calaboose and a church which had replaced another church destroyed or fallen to decay. Wilkes probably saw the Mission buildings, or what was left of them, the church alone having been rebuilt by Vallejo. The style of the buildings, verandas, thick walls of adobe and partitions, and deep recessed windows greatly interested the traveler, who declared the large adobes had a roof built over each room. At the barracks he saw 13 troopers and said of them:

Salvador Vallejo, the General's brother.

If one may judge from the variety of the uniforms, each of the 13 constitute a regiment—the buffs, the blues, etc. They are mere boys with enormous swords and a pair of nascent moustaches, deerskin boots and that everlasting serape or blanket with a hole in the middle for the head.

Field pieces and cannon seemed more ornamental than useful, thought Wilkes.

He praised the orchard and vineyard at the rear of the General's home. In the evening there was another meal served with chili and tortillas, after which Salvador Vallejo and a trooper played guitars for dancing. The congenial company of the General's household were toeing and heeling until a late hour, singing in chorus and smoking, even the ladies puffing their cigarettes, quite evidently an old Spanish custom. Commandante Prado from the presidio of San Francisco was also a guest that evening. The festivities concluded with the singing of "Auld Lang Syne."

INDEX-TRIBUNE ARCHIVES

5 Seeds of Unrest

COURTESY, CALIFORNIA STATE LIBRARY

Manuel Micheltorena, named California's governor in 1842.

AUTHOR'S NOTE: When Brigadier-General Manuel Micheltorena was appointed the new governor of California in February 1842, both Alvarado and Vallejo relinquished their posts. Alvarado retired to private life, and Vallejo resigned his title as commandante-general, but received a promotion to lieutenant-colonel of the regular forces.

At the same time, Micheltorena appointed Vallejo commander of the northern frontier, from Sonoma to Mission Santa Ynez.

Vallejo apparently welcomed the new assignment, despite its lesser authority. Comfortable in Sonoma, the pueblo he had created, and rich in land and livestock, he was able to carry on his personal and family affairs. (Hunter, p. 42–43).

At the same time, he must have been concerned about the recurring turnovers in authority—either directed from Mexico or through minor revolutions involving would-be leaders in California. Too, he undoubtedly kept apprised of the inroads the United States was making in the West, and considered how it might affect his future.

American immigration, Mexican protectionism

A ticklish situation existed in California, now on the brink of American occupancy. Many so-called interlopers from across the Rocky

Mountains were married into Mexican families. Prominent dons had American sons-in-law. Sailors from Boston, ranchers from Missouri, and accountants from New York and Pennsylvania were equally popular with the ladies. Leaders from the states had proven indispensable in the conduct of affairs and were excellent businessmen, as Vallejo had acknowledged.

Yet Pío Pico, the Mexican governor (1845–46), was denouncing the impertinence of all the Yankees and openly advocated a French or English alliance to block American colonization. Pico indulged in such venomous descriptions of the new settlers as "lawless adventurers," "avaricious strangers," "a perfidious people." He publicly declared:

> We are threatened by hordes of Yankee emigrants; already the wagons of these perfidious people have scaled the almost inaccessible summits of the Sierra Nevadas, crossed the entire continent and penetrated the fruitful valley of the Sacramento. They are cultivating farms, establishing vineyards, erecting mills, sawing up lumber, building workshops and a thousand and one other things which seem natural to them but which Californians neglect or despise—we cannot stand alone against them.

He then declared for annexation with France or England, either one of which, he said, would buy California's beef and grain, substitute orderly government for "the miserable Republic of Mexico," and give Californians a chance to again lead "thoughtless and merry lives." It is quite apparent that Pío Pico wanted no responsibilities such as were likely under an energetic American regime.

Vallejo answered Governor Pico forcefully, and flatly disagreed with him as to his choice of a paternal government for California. He declared that the United States was the one nation to which his people should turn, not England or France.

He ignored the drastic order to drive the immigrants back across the mountains. He admired the new settlers in many ways, and his big heart, sound judgment and political sagacity

dictated the one wise course for him to pursue in the face of the gathering storm—watchful waiting.

A colonel's epaulets

Although California politicians sought to sidetrack Vallejo, he was plainly the man of the hour both in 1842 and in 1846. Mexico City had confidence in Vallejo's good judgment; and when Victor Prudon, his confidential secretary, argued on Vallejo's behalf for greater authority in California, he not only won Vallejo the higher rank of lieutenant-colonel but was given the rank of captain himself. Subsequently Vallejo received from the Mexican capital the gift of a pair of colonel's epaulets, which he proudly wore during his regime and finally handed down to his family as a cherished heirloom. Vallejo had the greatest ambition not only for personal advancement, but for California and particularly the town he had founded, the center of official life north of San Francisco Bay. Navy Lt. Charles Wilkes is quoted as saying: "Sonoma is to be the capital of this country, providing the General has power and lives long enough to build it up."

Vallejo recommended the organization of a civil government for Sonoma in an enthusiastic appeal to the citizens. On June 18, 1843, a meeting was held with Vallejo presiding and Prudon acting as secretary. Means for the support of the garrison were discussed and also financial assistance for the erection of a town hall, jail and

The silver epaulets awarded to Vallejo with his rank of colonel are today displayed at the Swiss chalet on the grounds of his second home in Sonoma, Lachryma Montis, now a state historic landmark.

COURTESY, ROBERT D. PARMELEE

John A. Sutter was sometimes called "General," having attained the rank of major general in the state militia.

cemetery. Thirty-one public-spirited residents subscribed the sum of $3,063 besides 155 *fanegoes* (bushels) of grain, 20 cattle, 1,100 feet of boards, 12,700 bricks and the help of 221 laborers. In August Vallejo turned over the plan of the pueblo and recommended that the same be followed under the civil government, as his commission as director of colonization was at an end. Sonoma then had 59 citizens, 12 foreigners and six Indians on its roll.

General Vallejo's frustrations increase

AUTHOR'S NOTE: Vallejo's respect for Americans, particularly those who were educated and skilled, was often expressed, and he made little attempt to hide the fact that, since his own countrymen showed little interest or talent in governing California, he would welcome its eventually becoming part of the United States. He admired the U. S. government. Two of his sisters were married to Americans, and the commandante-general had numerous friends from the States in high places. He was disturbed over the reports of increasing friction between newly arrived Americans and Californios. Many of the immigrants were being welcomed by Capt. John Sutter at his fort in the Sacramento Valley. The

wily Sutter was said to be handing out illegal land grants to them and encouraging a greater influx while stirring up the settlers from the U. S. against the badly divided Mexican government leaders.

General Vallejo's "comfort zone" in Sonoma, as potentate of the northern frontier, was disturbed some by his lack of confidence in the new governor, Micheltorena. Although personable and desirous of being popular, Micheltorena—in the view of Vallejo—lacked administrative skills. Vallejo also questioned the governor's sudden friendship with the opportunistic Sutter, self-proclaimed "king" of his busy fort at New Helvetia.

Too, Micheltorena was never forgiven for recruiting 300 criminals from Mexican prisons for military service in California. Still, when Vallejo's two old associates, Juan Bautista Alvarado and José Castro, led a revolt against Governor Micheltorena in November 1844 and sought Vallejo's aid, he declined.

Instead, Vallejo made a decision to become neutral. That same month, he discharged his Sonoma garrison of some 30 men, informing the governor that he could not continue to pay for them.

Vallejo's frustrations were multiplied as he took note of the events of 1845, the year James Polk became president of the United States. Polk, an expansionist, would declare war with Mexico in May 1846, after Mexico rejected his offers to purchase Texas and California. In California nobody would learn about the declaration of war until mid-July, a month after the Bear Flag revolt.

COURTESY, ROBERT D. PARMELEE

Sutter's Fort in the Sacramento Valley was a haven for American immigrants in the 1840s.

John C. Fremont

No individual in California during the early 1840s was the subject of greater speculation to natives and foreigners than John C. Fremont, lieutenant of engineers in the U. S. Army Topographical Service; Fremont, the Pathfinder, sent from Washington, D. C., to chart a course to the new West and find the most accessible approach to California. With him when he entered California in 1845, in addition to 50 other armed engineers, was the veteran mountain man and guide Kit Carson. Fremont gave concern to the Mexican population and was the hope of all American settlers who had preceded him here and realized the fast-growing hatred of Mexican officials toward them.

That Fremont was an officer of the Army Engineer Corps of the United States government with official instructions regarding the territory was known to all. Just how much authority he had and how far he would go in the event of a crisis were questions feverishly discussed, particularly around Sutter's Fort.

Californians disregarded Fremont's presence, until with him on later expeditions he brought immigrant trains he met along the way and helped settlers conquer the wilderness to reach California. These settlers attached themselves to him, and the growing numbers of strangers thus brought into California loomed as a danger signal to the jealous guardians of the country. Notices were sent by Mexicans to Eastern newspapers to try to halt immigration to California. A warning was published in the *Baltimore American* that colonists from the States would be unwelcome here. This notice appeared during 1843 and was inserted at the request of Mexican Minister of War Juan Almonte, the emissary to the United States, based in Washington, D. C.

Feverish preparations were undertaken to protect California from the newcomers who were flocking in. The Mexican authorities thought seriously of buying Sutter's Fort. Sutter was offered $100,000 but turned it down. Jacob P. Leese, representing California's Governor Pío Pico, and Victor Prudon, representing General Vallejo, talked it over at Sutter's establishment. Vallejo reported the conference and proposal to the war

Courtesy, Sonoma Valley Historical Society

John Charles Fremont, the Pathfinder, was a most ambitious and controversial figure in Alta California history.

department of Mexico City and said he considered the price high for what improvements Sutter had made, but that the strategic location of the Fort for the defense of California made its acquisition desirable.

Mexico promised to send troops to defend California. Californians were advised to organize for defense. It is evident that General Vallejo made no preparations for war. His American relatives, and the growing conviction of Sonoma's commander that California would come into its rightful destiny with the Stars and Stripes as protector, made Vallejo's neutral position a source of joy to United States Consul Thomas O. Larkin, whose ear had been to the ground for some time and who reported confidentially to Washington at intervals. It was evident that Vallejo's treatment of newcomers from over the Sierras was widely at variance with the Mexican orders to expel strangers as interlopers and enemies. Vallejo aided many a pioneer family up to the year 1846.

COURTESY, CALIFORNIA STATE LIBRARY

Thomas O. Larkin was named U. S. Consul in California in May 1843, with headquarters in Monterey.

AUTHOR'S NOTE: General Castro, a foe of Fremont and of American encroachment, met with Vallejo in Sonoma on June 5, 1846, seeking his help. Governor Pío Pico chided Vallejo for conferring with Castro, feeling that Castro's military preparations might actually be used in eventually ousting him (Pico). However, most believed that Castro was preparing to expel the American settlers and that his meeting with Vallejo was toward that goal. The truth was that Vallejo had decided to stay neutral.

Vallejo told Governor Pico that it was difficult to confer directly with him at Los Angeles (where Pico had chosen to make his headquarters, instead of at Monterey) on problems pressing for solution. He explained that he was duty-bound to aid Castro when he demanded horses or supplies to be used in the defense of California. Vallejo thus did his utmost to hold a steady course, although at times he was greatly misunderstood and his motives misinterpreted.

Many American settlers believed that Vallejo was aiding Castro against them, and that he might be declared governor of California. They feared that Vallejo, with his many connections, could unite the many factions which the weak regime of Pico had failed to conciliate. In their view Vallejo was the one man in Alta California who must be removed from the political picture if a move to take California away from the Mexicans was to succeed.

Meanwhile, the ambitious Captain Fremont was reportedly incensed by reports that Mexican authorities, led by General Castro, were not only attempting to halt immigration into California, but had vowed to evict settlers. Scores of concerned Americans, many of them living within the range of Sutter's Fort, looked to Fremont for guidance and protection.

Fremont was known to have little respect for the Californios. He showed that in March 1846 when he defied the orders of the previously cooperative Castro not to extend his explorations into the Salinas Valley, near Monterey, and was ordered by Castro to withdraw to where he had come from—apparently meaning Fremont's camps which he had established at Klamath Lake in southern Oregon or one near the Sutter Buttes in the Sacramento Valley.

It was from Fremont's Sacramento Valley camp that the rumors circulated about Castro's threats to drive all Americans from the territory. Word also spread that the land possessed by the hardy immigrants who had endured the hardships of wagon trains to settle here was to be confiscated.

Subsequently, Fremont was approached at his camp at Klamath Lake on May 9, 1846, by a messenger from Washington, Lt. Archibald Gillespie, with a packet of letters. It was said that Fremont used the receipt of these letters as though they contained orders from Washington to take aggression against the Mexican government, as represented by Mariano Guadalupe Vallejo, commandante-general at Sonoma. No such orders were ever given, other than by Fremont, who had absolutely no authority to act on behalf of the U. S. government, it is now known.

But Fremont returned to his camp in the Sacramento Valley, where Ezekiel Merritt and members of what was soon to be called the Bear Flag party gathered. There, Fremont reportedly named Merritt leader of the party which, acting on his (Fremont's) orders, set out to take the "stronghold of Sonoma," writes Hunter (p. 51). Fremont did not accompany them. Hunter is convinced that Captain Fremont acted on his own initiative and that "the Bear Flag incident was an embarrassment to the American authorities" (p. 52).

6 The Bear Flag Revolt

Kenwood artist Al Sondag's painting of the raising of the Bear Flag on the Sonoma Plaza. The mural was first displayed at the World's Fair on Treasure Island in San Francisco Bay in 1939. It is now a proud possession of the Sonoma Depot Museum.

The flag of Mexico was proudly waving over Sonoma's Plaza. The tower of General Vallejo's Casa Grande might have had sentries posted at the windows to scan the horizon for strangers who could approach from the marshland in the direction of Embarcadero where the boats landed, or from the hills to the east in the direction of Napa Valley and Sutter's Fort where the restless emigrants from over the Rockies made their rendezvous. This was mere precaution. The military government at Sonoma was by now military in name only, and Vallejo's title, military governor, sufficing for all purposes. The Mexican army had dwindled.

The garrison was but a remnant. There was no money to pay soldiers. Vallejo had pleaded in vain for funds for defense. Old Mexico was deaf to his appeals, believing that California should be self-supporting and that the mission wealth should provide surplus for defense. California's Governor Pico gave little financial assistance for protection of the northern frontier. His policy seemed to be one of free reign for political favorites who were permitted to feather their nests and were fat on every possible source of revenue.

Only six or seven rusty-looking soldiers patrolled the sun-drenched Sonoma Plaza. Mexicans aroused from their siesta hour by stories of trouble brewing around Sutter's Fort spoke together in whispered conference. Excited ones repeated the rumor that General Castro had

COURTESY, SONOMA VALLEY HISTORICAL SOCIETY

Vallejo around the time of the Bear Flag Revolt.

given the ultimatum to Fremont to get out of California and stay out. Fremont was something more than a "Brevet Captain of Topographical Engineers on a surveying expedition," confided the knowing ones. All agreed that the intruders from over the mountains were getting altogether too numerous. That they had designs on California, there was no question.

Vallejo was unalarmed by the reports. He felt that his people were in no danger from the new-comers in California, dubbed "lawless adventur-ers" by Castro. He felt no concern about Fremont's friendship, since admiration of the United States had been repeatedly voiced, and recently stressed by Vallejo at a junta in Monterey, where the destiny of California was the sole topic of the conference. However, the fact that a drove of Sonoma horses had been pur-chased by Lt. Francisco Arce made the Sonoma commander suspect that a clash between Castro

and the settlers might be imminent.

The news spread that the Mexicans were con-centrating an armed force for attack and that Castro meant business. The horses bought at Sonoma were ferried over the Sacramento River (at Knight's Landing), and the ferryman's wife told neighboring ranchers that they were to be used in a campaign against the Americanos. When the Yankee husband of one of the California women got wind of the plot, he rode to inform Fremont's men. Settlers took up the pursuit after the horses when informed by Fremont of the seri-ous turn of affairs. The horses were captured, and, when they were brought into camp, excitement was running high. Indignant and determined men of the Sacramento were ready to strike a concert-ed blow. Resentment over Mexican insolence flamed. Castro's vow to run the Yankees out was regarded as particularly audacious, as discredited officials had little or no support from old Mexico and were running the rich territory of California to suit themselves, exacting much and giving nothing in return. "Clean 'em up" was the cry of the settlers, tired of bravado and continuous insult.

It was an excited, rough-looking outfit which mobilized for action, action which was to make California history. Long-haired, wild-eyed men in greasy leather clothing, wearing coonskin caps and Indian moccasins, armed with long rifles, shotguns, bowie knives or pepper-box pistols— some with all of these weapons—comprised an army such as the world has seldom seen. They were dead-shots, callous to every danger and even to Mexican cruelty such as notorious fiends like the infamous "Three-Fingered Jack" Garcia of Sonoma could inflict. Whether Sonoma was regarded as the base of Castro's operations, or whether Fremont ordered the ride into the Valley of the Moon because of Vallejo's prominence in California affairs, will never be known, but the plans of the insurgents were definite. Sonoma was their objective.

The history-makers galloped away the night of June 13, 1846, on their ride of 120 miles to cap-ture General Vallejo and his stronghold in the valley of the seven moons. Sonoma, the destined cradle of a strange new flag, was to become the short-lived capital of a lusty young republic.

Vallejo family is roused, the General taken prisoner

Indian servants were stirring around the gardens and patio of Commandante Vallejo's two-story Casa Grande, adjoining the Sonoma barracks. June weather had brought out the loveliest of the fragrant pink Castile roses. The scent of orange blossoms filled the air. Birds chirped merrily to greet the sun. Grapes were beginning to form in tiny clusters on the vines. Fountains scattered spray in the welcome breeze. Indians worked indifferently at their morning tasks.

Upstairs the commandante and his family were not yet astir. Theirs was a house of mourning, and after long vigil at the little casket of a beloved child, sleep had come as an interlude to sorrow.

AUTHOR'S NOTE: The "mixed bag" of 30-odd horsemen who completed the ride between Sacramento and Sonoma in the early morning of June 14, 1846, crossed through the sleeping town and its dusty parade ground to General Vallejo's unprotected residence, the Casa Grande, on the north side of the plaza. The general and his wife were awakened by the commotion in the courtyard, and they hastily dressed. Mrs. Vallejo's pleas for her husband to flee before the rough-looking, loud and armed men were admitted met with the General's scorn as he sought to allay her fears.

Mrs. Vallejo's concerns were understandable, when considering the band of brigands at their door. Even Dr. Robert Semple, one of the party's leaders and less odious members, later wrote:

> Almost the whole party was dressed in leather hunting shirts, many of them were greasy; taking the whole party together, they were about as rough a looking set of men as one could well imagine. It is not to be wondered at that anyone would feel some dread in falling into their hands (McKittrick, p. 261).

General Vallejo, still an imposing figure at

John Grigsby — Robert Baylor Semple

COURTESY, ROBERT D. PARMELEE

COURTESY, CALIFORNIA STATE LIBRARY

age 38, greeted the motley group, poured wine and brandy for those who had entered the *sala* (parlor), and asked who was their leader—his American brother-in-law, Jacob P. Leese, serving as intepreter.

"Zeke" Merritt, the rawboned, stuttering frontiersman selected as spokesman by Fremont, attempted to blunt the General's expressed desire to put the discussion on a friendly basis.

Ignoring, briefly, the bottles and glasses proffered, Merritt said they hadn't come there to be entertained, but on serious business. "We mean to establish our own government in California, an independent republic, and are under arms to support it. You are under arrest, General, as the responsible head of the Mexicans hereabouts," said Merritt (Murphy, p. 103). Vallejo's brother, Salvador, and his secretary, Victor Prudon, were also announced as under arrest. Merritt and several of the other leaders who had entered Vallejo's Casa Grande proceeded to guzzle down the brandy and wine. Grog was also given to the impatient party members outside. Semple and Leese, meanwhile, drafted the articles of capitulation. They also prepared papers which guaranteed the safety of the residents of the pueblo of Sonoma and granted parole to all political prisoners who did not oppose the rebels. Outside, the party malcontents, having not heard from Merritt, elected John Grigsby as their new leader. Reportedly, Grigsby went inside and, himself, got caught up in the drinking, relaxing beside the prone Merritt.

According to some sources, a few of the

COURTESY, CALIFORNIA STATE LIBRARY

Jacob P. Leese, one of Vallejo's American brothers-in-law, served as the General's interpreter with the Bear Flaggers.

intruders forced their way into the house of mourning, where the little casket was located, as they searched the place. Some of the invaders are said to have ordered Vallejo's servants to make them some coffee. One of them indignantly grabbed a dirty sock from the yard and in it brewed the coffee which the uninvited guests gulped down.

Meanwhile, the impatient outsiders took another vote and selected teetotaler William B. Ide to represent them. The declaration drawn up by Leese and Semple protected all those not found in opposition to the cause and promised that property would not be destroyed. Best of all, the Vallejos and Prudon were to be allowed to remain in Sonoma. But the new leader, Ide, refused to accept the declaration. He insisted on taking the trio to Captain Fremont's camp in Sacramento. Ide told Leese that Fremont planned the entire undertaking. This, General Vallejo was happy to learn. He entertained no fears for his safety nor that of his family, convinced that a U. S. army officer would deal justly

with him. If only he knew.

At 11 A.M. on June 14 the three captives, General Vallejo, Capt. Salvador Vallejo and Prudon mounted their horses and began their trek to Sacramento escorted by an armed contingent of Merritt, Semple, Grigsby and a half-dozen others. Leese accompanied them at Vallejo's request, to serve as interpreter.

A garrison of 25 men was left at Sonoma with Ide as the elected leader. Vallejo's frightened wife, Francisca, was left at the Casa Grande with her five children. Her proud husband, one of California's most distinguished men, had ample opportunity to be rescued by friends, including his devoted Indian associate Chief Solano, while being escorted to Sacramento, but refused. He was looking forward to being part of the new United States government he had so hoped would be the successful occupant of his homeland. He felt certain he would be reunited with his wife and family soon after being greeted by Captain Fremont.

Alas! Fremont, fomentor of the rebellion, would not acknowledge his role in the raid and capture—even after Vallejo said that members of the Bear Flag party had told him the foray was conducted at the young officer's direction. Instead, Vallejo and his companions were made prisoners at Sutter's Fort on Fremont's orders. And the once-young commandante-general of Alta California was not to be united in Sonoma with his wife and children until the first week of August, when he would be released through the efforts of Commodores Robert Stockton and John Sloat of the U. S. Navy command.

Following Vallejo's "capture" back on June 14, Ide issued a glittering proclamation, and a symbolic flag of independence was made. Several of the raiders fashioned a flag that had a crude red star, cruder bear—which some say looked more like a pig—and a red flannel stripe below. Inscribed upon a field of white in black letters was "California Republic." While many in the party later took credit for sharing in the making of the historic emblem, the identity of those actually involved is still disputed today.

7 Who Made the Bear Flag?

This flag is believed to most closely resemble the original Bear Flag that flew over the short-lived republic based in Sonoma.

INDEX-TRIBUNE ARCHIVES

The Mexican emblem of green and white was flying from the flagstaff on Sonoma's plaza, and its challenging sweep nettled the Americans who demanded a flag of their own, an emblem of their "republic." They would show these Mexicans who was running California from this time on. One of the party agreed to make a flag if material could be found. William Lincoln Todd volunteered to do the work if they would decide what they wanted. Todd, a nephew of Mrs. Abraham Lincoln, was among the early immigrants to California.

The design of the new flag was hotly debated, but at last it was agreed that there should be a star like the one on the flag of Texas and a grizzly bear—the grizzly for strength and courage. The flag sewers were Ben Dewell and Thomas Cowie,

saddlers by trade and handy with their needles. William Mathews, express rider between Sonoma and Sutter's Fort, offered some red flannel from a clothesline of his home—some say the petticoat of his wife, others a man's shirt. A piece of unbleached muslin or manta cloth was donated by Mrs. John Sears, wife of the blacksmith, who had arrived with a party of emigrants from Missouri that very day. She had brought a bolt of home-spun cloth across the plains and tore off enough for the flag.

The red material was sewed on the bottom of the unbleached piece, and Todd painted the grizzly bear, which onlookers declared looked more like a pig. Some of the Mexicans discussed it in their own tongue. Little Platon Vallejo, son of the

INDEX-TRIBUNE ARCHIVES

Granville P. Swift

General, watched the flag making at the barracks, and in after years told how he had his new boots daubed with paint as he held the flag in place for Todd with his foot. The paint was hardly dry on the new emblem when the Bear Flag was raised on the Mexican staff amid cheers, which rose to yells of joy as the bear and the star flew over Sonoma.

The story of the making of the Bear Flag has often been told and there have been various tales of the incident. The one given here coincides with the letter written by W. M. Boggs, a son of Alcalde Lilburn Boggs, in after years to the Sears and Snyder families. Said Boggs in his letter:

The cloth that Mrs. John Sears furnished was the white cloth or unbleached domestic, commonly called by the Spaniards *manta,* of which Mrs. John Sears had a whole bolt at the time. Capt. John Sears was living with his family at the time we arrived in Sonoma, and we lived in the same row of adobe buildings near the northeast corner of the plaza, diagonally across from the old barracks, where the Bear Flag

was hoisted.

Mrs. Sears related to Mrs. Boggs, my wife, how that two or three of the Bear Flag men came to her door and roused her out of bed to get some cloth to make a flag, as they had been informed that she had a bolt of manta. She asked how much they wanted, and they said only a yard or two, and she tore off three yards and gave it to them, and that is what the real body of the flag was made of, and the man who made the flag, William Todd, who lived in our family a numbers of years, told us the same as related by Mrs. Sears, as to how the cloth for the Bear Flag was obtained, and Capt. [Granville] Swift and Capt. Henry L. Ford, who were present when the flag was made, told us how the red cloth for the stripe at the bottom of the flag was obtained.

I heard them relate the story often. There was an old sailor named Mathews, who had a Spanish wife. He was known as "Dirty Mathews," as he was untidy and not very clean in his wearing apparel. I have seen him many times in after years in Sonoma. Swift said that when a call was made for something red to put on the flag, that no one had anything to offer, and Dirty Mathews said that he could get something, and went and stole his wife's petticoat from the clothesline and brought it to Todd and old Peter Storm and old Nennigan Taylor who were assisting Todd in making the flag. When the flag was ready for inspection Todd asked what to paint on it for a motto. Capt. Henry L. Ford suggested a grizzly bear, and all agreed, as many of them were old-time grizzly hunters. I have been particular to give these facts in relation as to how the Bear Flag was made, for the reasons that many persons, through a faulty memory or desire to make themselves historical, have claimed they furnished the materials for the Bear Flag. They perhaps read different stories about it and became impressed with an idea how it was procured.

I have heard several pioneer ladies state that they furnished the material, but the foregoing facts as to the real and true way it was obtained were related by the men who made it and who took the most active part in supporting and upholding it after it was made, and those men became conspicuous in the service of Colonel Fremont's famous campaign in the conquest of California.

First of these was Capt. Granville P. Swift; next to Swift was Capt. Henry L. Ford, both of whom commanded companies in Colonel Fremont's regiment and did most of his scouting and fighting. Todd also served with Fremont. Capt. John Sears, a brother of the late Franklin Sears, also commanded a company. All of these men volunteered and joined Fremont. As soon as the Bear Flag was replaced at Sonoma by the American flag, it was the fortune of the writer to become personally and intimately acquainted with these men on my arrival in Sonoma in 1846 with my family, and lived a neighbor to them for a number of years after. William Todd was a nephew of Mrs. Abraham Lincoln. He lived three years in our family and clerked for my father in the store at the time in Sonoma. He and Swift and Ford often met there and talked and laughed over the way they made the Bear Flag.

Mr. Sears was one of the noble old Western pioneers, a class of men that are now nearly all gone. They were the forerunners of civilization and the founders of an empire state—conspicuous among whom was Maj. Jacob R. Snyder, one of the framers of the first constitution of the State of California, a man whom to know was an honor. He, as well as Franklin Sears, was my neighbor and friend for many years.

There are other versions of the making and appearance of the Bear Flag, such as the following account from *Pioneer Sonoma* by Robert D. Parmelee:

Bear Flag Party member Peter Storm in later years displayed the emblem he made and brought to Sonoma during the Bear Flag Party's raid on June 14, 1846.

The story goes that on the day before the capture of Sonoma, the Bear Flag men, as they were later to be called, had gathered at the ranch of John Grigsby near the present town of Yountville, Napa County, to make their plans. It was at this meeting that Peter Storm, a handyman from the Henry Fowler ranch, and a man with a flair for music and painting, designed an emblem for them to take on their Sonoma raid. Using material from two petticoats, one red and one white, he made a flag, red on the bottom and white on the top, without any lettering, with a blue star in the upper left corner and a grizzly bear rearing up on his hind legs, as if ready to spring forward at a foe. The finished product was made of four pieces of cloth with seams running through the center both vertically and horizontally, and the insurgents supposedly took this flag with them and used it the next day to replace Vallejo's Mexican emblem.

The account is retold in a 1949 treatise by Henry Fowler Mallett, grandson of Napa pioneer Henry Fowler, based on his mother's recollections, and is confirmed by other pioneers. Other stories conflict, and to speculate on the veracity of one version over another or on the fate of the flag itself is to stir up a hornet's nest of dissension and controversy more than a hundred years old. Either there never was any such thing as a Peter Storm flag ... or there was only one Bear Flag, the Revere flag, and that was destroyed in San Francisco in 1906 ... or it was buried with Peter Storm. Such confusion and quarreling about the flag is disheartening in the face of the significance of the movement itself. However, since no one of these various theories has been confirmed, there is always the exciting possibility that the first flag was not destroyed but has been concealed where one day it may still be uncovered.

Sonoma was in a tense state of excitement. William B. Ide, chosen head of the insurgents, and evidently relishing the job and hoping the republic would succeed, issued a proclamation guaranteeing protection to all citizens and residents of Sonoma and their properties so long as they remained peaceable and obeyed the rules of the new authorities. The proclamation was posted in both English and Spanish.

History has handed down the following names as those believed to have been with the Bear Flag party and identified with the short-lived and thrilling episode which precipitated the raising of the Stars and Stripes over California:

Henry Booker, Nathan Coombs, Thomas Cowie, Benjamin Dewell, William Bell Elliott, William Fallon, Josiah Ferguson, Henry L. Ford, Henry Fowler, John Gibbs, Sam Gibson, C. C. Griffith, John Grigsby, William Hargrave, David Hudson, William B. Ide, J. H. Kelly, Andrew Kelsey, Ben Kelsey, Sam Kelsey, Thomas Knight, William Knight, Lucien Maxwell, Pat McChristian, Ezekiel Merritt, Sam Neal, Harvey Porterfield, William Potter, Horace Sanders, John Scott, W. W. Scott, John B. Sears, Robert Semple, Ira Stebbins, Peter Storm, Granville P. Swift, William Levi Todd, Bartlett Vines and Marion Wise.

8 Vallejo's Imprisonment and Release

This drawing, depicting the raising of the American flag and lowering of the Bear Flag at Sonoma July 4, 1846, also shows the tower of Vallejo's first home in Sonoma, the Casa Grande, which burned to the ground April 13, 1867. At the time of the fire, of unknown origin, the historic building was utilized for residential and business rental units.

INDEX-TRIBUNE ARCHIVES

*W*hile General Vallejo was languishing as a prisoner at Sutter's Fort, his message asking United States naval officers to look into the plight of his family and conditions at Sonoma was followed by an investigation. At the order of the commander of the *U. S. S. Portsmouth* in San Francisco harbor, Lt. J. S. Missroon was dispatched with a number of sailors to Embarcadero, and from there they marched to Sonoma. As they approached the plaza, the town, now under martial law, wondered at their mission, but Missroon made it plain that he came merely as an ambassador of goodwill, stressing this both to Ide and to Alcalde Lilburn Boggs, as his commander had suggested. He explained that he came to look into the welfare of Señora Vallejo and children at the

request of Vallejo. He was urged by Bear Flaggers to call and see for himself that the family was not in any way being mistreated. Missroon called upon Señora Vallejo and assured her of his commander's interest in her safety and well being and that of her family.

Due to political maneuvers and the troubled times during which those charged with law and order were overly cautious, Missroon was not able to secure the release of the illustrious prisoners for almost two months, although it was his signature which finally went on the order for their release. The order signed Aug. 8, 1846, read as follows, quoting the document preserved in the Jacob P. Leese papers by the Society of California Pioneers:

I certify that I have this day released from imprisonment Mr. Jacob Leese, having received his pledge of strict neutrality during the continuance of the present war between the United States and Mexico, and also during the continuance of the authority of the United States in California, and I require all persons whatsoever to respect him accordingly so long as he shall act in good faith with his obligations.

J. S. Missroon, Lieutenant
U. S. Navy
Acting under the authority of the
Commander-in-Chief of the
United States Navy Land
Military Force in California
Fort New Helvetia
Aug. 8, 1846

A duplicate order for the release of General Vallejo was signed by Missroon, but during June and July, while the prisoners were locked within the walls of Sutter's Fort, the people of Sonoma were kept at high tension. Many stories were spread of Mexican reprisals and plots which might

COURTESY, DENVER PUBLIC LIBRARY

Kit Carson, explorer and trapper, who came to Sonoma with John C. Fremont.

be expected to develop any moment at the hands of Castro's followers or from bandits eager to take advantage of the situation.

July 4 to 9—a grand ball, the Stars and Stripes raised

Sonoma, under the Bear Flag for 25 days, was on the Fourth of July in 1846 at the zenith of its glorious though hectic career. William B. Ide probably foresaw the coming of more permanent government under the Stars and Stripes but was hopeful that independence under the star and bear might mean more power and success for him and those who had embarked with him in the little revolution to wrest California from Mexican authority. He was hardly prepared for the patriotic program which Fremont put on upon his return march to Sonoma on July 3rd.

Whether acting on orders from the United States or merely imbued with fervent patriotism, Fremont rode into the pueblo and announced that the Fourth of July, 1846, would be celebrated as never before in the land known as Alta California. Sonoma decided to fire off the Mexican cannon to herald the dawn of Independence Day and to hold exercises on the Plaza where the emblem of the Bears triumphantly waved.

July 4, 1846, was the greatest Sonoma had seen or was to see. In addition to the Bear Flag enthusiasts—the settlers, trappers, traders and riflemen collected by Fremont and Kit Carson—gathered for the big demonstration, from San Francisco came a number of officers and sailors from the U. S. Navy ships anchored in San Francisco harbor.

Officers and men attached to the warships in San Francisco Bay envied those who lived in the delightful climate of Sonoma, with its mineral springs, lovely scenery, señoritas and charming hospitality of its families.

Romance was in the air despite the conquerors and exigencies of a town in the hands of gruff captors. From many a window and balcony the dark-eyed daughters of California looked down upon the uniformed officers from the American ships as they gathered for the reading of the Declaration of Independence. The entire celebration was greatly enjoyed by the Mexican population, young and old.

Cheers and salvos echoed throughout the day, at a barbecue which concluded Sonoma's exercises, and into the convivial hours of the night. Many of the pioneer women and their families had taken refuge in Sonoma during the swift-moving hours of the revolution, including the Nathan Coombs family of Napa, and now felt a sense of security not experienced in days. When it was decided to have a grand ball on the night of the Fourth, quite a few of the fair daughters from the plains took courage and attended the dance, which was held at the adobe of Salvador Vallejo, now Fremont's official headquarters. By flickering lantern light, they joined in the thrills of the waltzes and the jollity of quadrilles, as fiddles squeaked and guitars twanged tunefully. Into the wee small hours of the morning the revelers made merry, despite the shaky political foundation of the country. Many of the menfolk could be heard in whispered conference and talk while the dance was in progress.

Ide was plainly disappointed when a vote was taken and it developed that he must give way to Fremont and affix his signature to a document in which the Bear Flag party pledged itself to annexation, the California Republic to be received ultimately into the Union of the United States. This pronouncement definitely ended any hope Ide might have cherished to head an independent state.

AUTHOR'S NOTE: On July 5, Fremont organized and assumed command of what historical accounts called the California Battalion, four companies of 224 men. One company, to protect the Sonoma garrison, was headed by John Grigsby. Fremont's other appointees as company commanders were Richard Owens, one of his own mountaineer scouts, and Bear Flag Party members Grigsby, Henry L. Ford and Granville P. Swift (Parmelee, p. 27).

General Fremont immediately left in pursuit of Castro, intent on avenging the insulting orders from the Mexican military leader ordering Fremont and his American followers to depart California, prior to the Bear Flag incident.

All eyes were on Sonoma because of the exciting incidents of the few weeks previous and the definite steps which had been taken to bring California under the Stars and Stripes. All

Lt. Joseph W. Revere, USN—who is said to have tucked the original Bear Flag into his pocket after its lowering in Sonoma on July 9, 1846—was a grandson of Paul Revere.

COURTESY, ROBERT D. PARMELEE

California buzzed with the developments. At the emigrant camps the situation created great speculation. At the haciendas it was hotly debated. At Monterey it was the topic at every gathering, both official and social. At Sutter's Fort, where the distinguished Mexican prisoners were held incommunicado, Sonoma's defying of Mexican authority and the taking of the reins by Fremont meant just one thing—the United States was going to step in.

The Stars and Stripes replaced the Bear Flag on the Sonoma Plaza flagstaff July 9. Lt. Joseph W. Revere put the crude little emblem in his pocket, remarking, "This is worth saving." The original Bear Flag was finally presented to the Society of California Pioneers in San Francisco and remained in its collection of California relics until 1906, when it was destroyed by the fire which followed the earthquake of that year. The flag design, however, was destined to live on and become the state emblem, officially adopted as California's state flag on Feb. 3, 1911.

COURTESY, SONOMA VALLEY HISTORICAL SOCIETY, O'NEIL COLLECTION

Vallejo's family mattered greatly to him. Shown here are one of his daughters, Luisa Vallejo Emparan (center), a daughter-in-law, Lily Vallejo (left), and their friend Emily Melvin (right).

Vallejo returns to Sonoma

When Vallejo came back to Sonoma in August 1846, he found his family growing up and his children evincing both talent and beauty. He was made agent of Indian affairs by the new regime and thus continued in an official capacity. As a private citizen he lavished money on pet projects and expended much time in the betterment of the town. He decided Sonoma should have the best schools and tutors and helped largely to maintain them, for in that day there were no public schools. He encouraged services at the Mission church,

repaired its crumbling adobe walls and built a belfry to replace the frame support of the bells which hung in front of the hallowed shrine.

While brought up in the Catholic faith, General Vallejo was not a narrow man in things spiritual. He believed people should worship as they saw fit, and he aided all denominations interested in the upbuilding of the country. Old Dr. Waugh, a traveling Methodist preacher, attested to this; also Dr. Ver Mehr, an Episcopalian who conducted an early-day school and was encouraged by Sonoma's founder to make his educational establishment the finest north of San Francisco Bay.

AUTHOR'S NOTE: When General Vallejo arrived in Sonoma after being released Aug. 1, 1846, from his "jail" at Sutter's Fort, his most rewarding welcome was being embraced by his devoted wife, Francisca, and their children, who fretted over his loss of weight and weakened condition from a malaria attack while imprisoned. An acknowledgement of Vallejo's long friendship with, and admiration for, the United States was the sending by Capt. John B. Montgomery, of the *U. S. S. Portsmouth,* the ship's assistant surgeon, Dr. Alexander Henderson, to render him medical services.

Some solace, too, for the proud former commandante-general of Alta California was seeing the Stars and Stripes flying over Sonoma, as he in earlier years had longed for, after the badly divided Mexican government showed its lack of interest or inability (or both) to strengthen and help develop its valuable coastal possession.

Vallejo's recovery to good health was swift, and he soon became involved in the activities of California and his own community, which included the greeting of, and cooperation with, the military units, their officers and personnel, who brought a lively and colorful atmosphere to the little pueblo.

9 Early Years under U. S. Rule

COURTESY, ROBERT D. PARMELEE

Col. Jonathan D. Stevenson, a New York native, commanded the U. S. Army volunteers who came to California in 1847.

AUTHOR'S NOTE: After the American flag replaced the Bear Flag in Sonoma Plaza on July 9, 1846, responsibility for law and order in the months that followed was in the hands of U. S. Navy officers, whose ships were anchored off Yerba Buena (now San Francisco Bay). Lt. Joseph W. Revere (a grandson of Paul Revere), who personally lowered the Bear Flag and raised the Stars and Stripes here, commanded the Army garrison at Sonoma until November 1846.

In a somewhat strange alliance, Lieutenant Revere received orders to enlist Bear Flagger John Grigsby and his local company of the California Battalion (formed by Captain Fremont) as a temporary U. S. occupational unit. Civil law was in the hands of John H. Nash, a former Alabama attorney who had been named area alcalde by the settlers.

Grigsby and Nash probably counted on Fremont's eventual return to garrison Sonoma. But it was not to be. Members of Fremont's battalion were discharged by Gen. Stephen W. Kearny in April 1847 and left to fend for themselves. Fremont, under Kearny's orders, "was to be returned to the United States under guard and eventually court-martialed for his irregular behavior" and unauthorized forays against the Mexicans (Parmelee, pp. 48–49).

*S*onoma under the Stars and Stripes: the moon just as wondrous as when the Indian tribes named

COURTESY, CALIFORNIA HISTORICAL SOCIETY

In a sketch possibly intended to represent himself, Lt. John McHenry Hollingsworth, a member of Stevenson's Regiment, illustrated the uniform of a New York Volunteer.

the vale; the climate as balmy as when the first padres breathed its wine-like air. The roses of old Castile had found in the soil the warmth of old Spain. Vines flourished and were bearing sugary grapes. An air of civilization and refinement surrounded the Sonoma ranchos in days when San Francisco streets were miserable ruts, the waterfront a haven of derelicts, the houses flimsy tents or gaudy dens to lure the lonely.

Stevenson's Regiment of New York Volunteers

AUTHOR'S NOTE: A lot of East Coast roots were planted on the West Coast—most specifically in Sonoma—after the U. S. takeover of Alta California following the Bear Flag incident. Some

of the deeper and most notable roots which played a major role in producing Sonoma's future leaders and shaping its destiny were established by the members of Company C, Stevenson's Regiment of New York Volunteers, who arrived here in April 1847 to garrison the pueblo, still attempting to adjust to the abrupt changes during, and after, the Bear Flag revolt.

Company C members were among three shiploads of young men recruited for frontier military duty by Col. Jonathan D. Stevenson, described by historian Parmelee as a "New York ward politician and state senator" (Parmelee, p. 51). The fact that President James K. Polk himself offered Stevenson command of the volunteers for the California duty would indicate that politics had a role in the appointment.

The recruits were carefully selected men, most of them not over 21 years of age. Their officers were graduates of West Point, and the companies were outfitted with everything a campaign such as the California solidification required. Most of Stevenson's recruits were skilled in trades or special lines of work. If they happened to be politically in tune with Polk and Stevenson, so much the better. The recruiting officers were told to accept men who had no reason to return East and who would colonize California at the conclusion of their army service. They were unmarried with but few exceptions.

Some of the young soldiers who had wives signed them up as laundresses aboard the ships, and they thus made the long voyage to California. (One of them was Hannah Cameron, bride of Corp. John Cameron, later to become the first mayor of Sonoma.) History records one baby born en route, a little girl christened Alta California. Her christening prompted a gala celebration.

The ship *Loo Choo,* in which the Company C men, commanded by Capt. John Brackett, sailed, arrived in San Franciso harbor in March 1847, the men ordered to proceed to Sonoma the following month. The two other companies recruited in New York by Stevenson were assigned to San Francisco and Monterey.

Imagine the excitement and flutter of hearts as the fine-looking young New Yorkers marched into Sonoma. Each soldier was nattily attired in a blue coat with scarlet trim. The trousers were of dark mixed gray material with scarlet strip up the seam of the leg. The uniform was topped with the latest-style French cap; "Very becoming," said newspapers of that day.

Company C garrisoned in Sonoma for a year or more, and the men became very popular with the residents. The Barracks, built by General Vallejo in 1836 for the Mexican troops, sheltered Stevenson's men, and an adobe belonging to John Ray was the mess hall for the officers. The Ray House, just east of the Blue Wing Inn, became the first Masonic Hall of Sonoma. Colonel Stevenson was a Grand Masonic Lodge Master of California.

Two of the biggest celebrations after the coming of American troops to Sonoma were their observance of Bear Flag Day in June and the Fourth of July, 1847. The holidays were heralded with the firing of salutes and there were feasting and dancing throughout the day.

A fandango, put on by a wily promoter, received bad publicity in a critical letter sent to the San Francisco papers by a disappointed soldier. When the dance was advertised, it was announced that there would be plenty of ladies to go around—that belles from Napa and señoritas from Benicia and Sonoma would join the merry whirl. When the fair ones failed to put in an appearance in sufficient numbers to interest the troopers, there was much grumbling. Ladies were scarce in California, and soldiers who had paid a big price for the dance, and were disappointed, complained about the "racket" in a letter to the press. Then, to take more joy out of life, the price of rum had "riz" in Sonoma "25 cents the horn," so the boys wrote home.

California's first theater born here

There were many pleasant diversions among the soldiers and officers in this pleasant presidio town. A number of the soldiers were talented, well-educated men, clever writers and ardent sportsmen. They organized theatricals, gave barbecues, rode spirited horses, lassoed wild mares and hunted waterfowl which swarmed the Sonoma marshes by the thousands.

General Vallejo turned over an adobe store-

The Ray House, just a block east of the Sonoma Plaza on Spain Street, was the site of the town's first Masonic hall. Today it is a private residence.

house to some enterprising soldier impresario, and a theater was opened by the soldiers, the first in California.

For those who like to read the reconstructed story of Sonoma's first theater, there is the article by Temple E. Allison, printed in the University of California *Chronicle*. Here is some of his description:

We enter and choose a place near the center of the house. Our eyes, accustomed to the dusk now, tell us that we are not the first to arrive. Near the door, at the farthest possible distance from the stage, sits an old Indian. The audience is increasing. Sparkling Mexican beauties in bright dresses and dark shawls, shepherded by calm and dignified señoras, take places far away. Across on the other side is a group of vociferous cowboys in clinking spurred boots and wide hats. Then the deposed Commandante himself and his complacent wife make their way to the box at the left of the stage. At the same time Alcalde Boggs and his wife enter the box at the right. The house is now filled to overflowing: Indians, Mexicans, Spaniards, cowboys, bandits, adventurers and soldiers, all sit side by side in this first English theater in California.

In that year, 1847, soldiers were the actors, and the play was Benjamin Webster's *The Golden*

COURTESY, ROBERT D. PARMELEE

Sonoma's first mayor, John C. Cameron, came here with Stevenson's Regiment of New York Volunteers.

Farmer. William Huefner was the farmer; Howard Scott was Jenny Twitcher, his daughter, and all the roles, male and female, were enacted by men. It was said there were only five English-speaking women within 100 miles of Sonoma, and their husbands would not allow them to act on the stage with soldiers.

Capt. John B. Frisbie, of Stevenson's Regiment, succeeded Captain Brackett at the Sonoma Barracks, and the exchange of posts by the officers was commented on in the columns of the *Californian* on Aug. 5, 1848:

> The military company under command of Capt. J. E. Brackett are today exchanging posts with Company H, under command of Captain Frisbie, both of the New York Volunteers. Company C has been stationed with us more than a year and much praise is due its members, not only for the military and soldierlike manner in which they have

acquitted themselves as a corps, but for their gentlemanly and orderly deportment, individually and collectively. We regret to part with them and cannot let them go without expressing a hope that, when peace shall have been declared, their regiment disbanded and their country no longer needs their services, they may have fallen sufficiently in love with our healthy climate and our beautiful valley to come back and settle.

The hope was not in vain, for many of the soldiers did return and made their homes in Sonoma, some engaging in business in the town and some buying land to farm and cultivate.

Members of Stevenson's Regiment who settled in the Valley included Capt. William Green, father of Louis Green, city treasurer of Sonoma during the 1930s. His ships the *Hamlet* and *Marguerite* hauled lumber and freight for several years between Sonoma and San Francisco. Other soldier-citizens were John Roane, of the regimental band, who started a shoemaker's shop on Napa Street; Peter Campbell, a notary; William C. Dotter; Alexander Cox, who founded *The Sonoma Bulletin,* Sonoma's short-lived first newspaper, in 1852; Harold Kamp, who became a business associate of C. T. Pauli, early-day merchant; John Cameron, first mayor of Sonoma; Henry Wohlgemuth, a wood carver; Robert Fleetwood, who started a store east of the Mission; E. B. Shirland and Matthew Purcell, who had a bakery on the east side of the Plaza; I. C. Blaneney, a barber; William M. Fuller, who became an alcalde of the pueblo of Sonoma, succeeding Gov. L. W. Boggs of Missouri; and Alexander C. McDonald, a sergeant-major in Stevenson's Regiment who later became the county treasurer. Dr. T. M. Leavenworth, chaplain of the regiment and San Francisco alcalde, came to Sonoma Valley and bought what is now the Boyes Springs area, his property embracing, in all, 800 acres. Capt. John Frisbie, who commanded the post and married Epifania Vallejo in 1851, often visited at the General Vallejo home in later years. He became very prominent in California, ran for lieutenant governor when General Sutter was candidate for governor, was defeated and finally went to Mexico, where he made and lost several fortunes.

INDEX-TRIBUNE ARCHIVES

An early photograph of the Blue Wing Inn (across from the Sonoma Mission), one of Sonoma Valley's least changed and most historic adobes.

The Blue Wing Inn

During barracks days much activity centered around the hotel or tavern known as the Blue Wing, which was one of the earliest public houses north of the bay and in later years the place where the stages stopped with travelers. The hotel was put up under the financial direction of General Vallejo, but was finally acquired by Capt. James Cooper, a seafaring man who left his ship and first tried his luck in San Francisco. He had a little money and bought a lot in the then "hopeless village of Yerba Buena." He soon traded his San Francisco holdings for the two-story, adobe Blue Wing Inn, across from the Sonoma Mission, and took a partner in the hotel business, Tom Spriggs, a ship carpenter.

The Cooper brothers often recalled how the miners coming to town after months at "the diggings" waxed sentimental at the sight of children and gave them nuggets. The hotel took gold dust in payment for meals and lodgings, and a pinch of gold would pay for a drink. The women folks in the Cooper hotel swept up enough of the precious waste each day to keep themselves in pin money.

The old inn on East Spain Street is in a fair state of preservation, and, for many years after its doors closed as a public house, the Blue Wing was used as a residence and winery.

The story of the people of the pueblo would be incomplete without the names of those listed in the account book of the Blue Wing Inn, starting in February 1848. Items purchased, listed opposite the names of native-born Californians, Mexicans, Spaniards and Americanos, including members of the New York Volunteers who garrisoned Sonoma, show that a convivial set frequented the old tavern. The accounts reveal that wines, liquors, rum, brandy (*aquadiente*), cigars, plugs of tobacco, and billiards contributed much to the joy of the patrons. Some dandies crossed the threshold of the thick walls to purchase expensive Panama hats, $60 serapes, $8 boots, cravats and neckerchiefs. Red calico indicates that there were womenfolk to be supplied with material to make dresses, or perchance the red (turkey red, they called it) was to please the Indians, said to be attracted to bright calico or glistening beads.

The Blue Wing Inn, on East Spain Street across from the Sonoma Mission, is just a half block from the Sonoma Plaza and Barracks, and close to the Ray House (mess hall of the officers), later the Masonic Hall. Tom Spriggs and Capt. James Cooper bought and sold various commodities, according to the records, and besides accepting gold dust for their goods, bought gold from men named Knight and Mason. Hides were purchased at $1.50 each, and a like sum was paid for tanned deerskin. Forty-five head of cattle were purchased for $90; a mule, for $75.

Landlord Cooper sold Captain Brackett 129 pounds of beef for his soldiers at two cents per pound. He also sold the troops 1,975 pounds of flour, in December 1848; 1,297 pounds in January, and 1,200 pounds in March of 1849. Eighteen-hundred pounds of flour were sold to Mark West.

The following are names just as they were signed on the Blue Wing books in 1848 and 1849:

Dr. Ames, Purvine Atwood, Oliver Bales, Frank Barrets, Don Sisto Berreyessa, N Berreyessa, Bill the Cook, Blain, Lilburn W. Boggs, Captain Brackett, Mr. Brooky, Mr. Brunner, Dr. Campbell, Julio Carillo, Evaline Carriger, Lissy Carriger, Nicholas Carriger, John Conway, Alexander Cox, Mr. Deadman, Mr. Eastin, Mr. Easton, Don Felipe, Holt Fine, Henry Fowler, William Fowler, Lenora Garcia, Elias Graham, Henry A. Green, John Griffith, William Hartgrove, Andrew Hoeppner, Hudspeth, J. P.

COURTESY, ROBERT D. PARMELEE

The rescue of the Donner Party in the Sierras, sketched by an unknown artist, showing almost-submerged chimneys at lower left. General Vallejo was among the first to provide personal funds for a search party. Of the Vallejos, Eliza Donner later wrote: "These people never asked unfeeling questions nor repeated harrowing tales and I did not learn until I was grown that they had been among the large contributors to the fund for the relief of our party" (Emparan, p. 260).

Huff, Aaron C. Inman, John Keisler, Andrew Kelsey, Benj Kelsey, Thomas M. Kelsey, Mr. Knight, Mr. Kreytisburg, Lieutenant Per Lee, J. P. Leese, J. P. Martin, William Mason, William McCutcheon, Edward McIntosh, Mr. Moore, D. Norris, Thomas Overy, Thomas M. Page, Don Picayune, T. Porter, Charles Prentiss, John G. Ray, Mr. Rhoda, Mr. Ritchie, Lieutenant Roach, George Rock, Mr. Rolette, W. W. Scott, John Sears, James Smith, Orren Smith, Don Soto, Auguste Stark, Mr. Strage, John L. Tanner, William E. Taylor, J. P. Thompson, David Tinkey, John C. Tivnen, William Todd, Don Marcus Vaka, M. G. Vallejo, Don Salvador Vallejo, Ramon Verrielsa, José Sanchez Verrielsa, Bartlett Vines, Sarah Walker, Lysander Washburn, Mark West, B. H. Whitmarsh, Isaac Wilson, Joseph Yatton, George Yount.

Many of the above names will be readily recognized by historians, although some of the spellings may be Yankee euphony, or nicknames. Quite evidently heads of the best families frequented the Blue Wing and rubbed elbows with some of the worst—that was early-day California custom.

The Donner girls

AUTHOR'S NOTE: Sonoma and its residents in 1846, only a few months after the Stars and Stripes were raised on the Plaza, were involved, indirectly, in circumstances surrounding the tragic Donner Party suffering and great loss of life in attempting to cross the snow-burdened Sierras.

Up to 1845 we are told that there were not more than 350 immigrants from the States in California, but by 1846 there were increasing numbers of Yankees who foresaw the coming of U. S. acquisition and were willing to face all dangers of the arduous trek across plains and mountains to seek land in the new frontier. But even the best-prepared and -equipped went through unbelievable suffering and hardships. Most tragic was the plight of the Donner family and party, whose story has become an epic of the West.

The Donner party was organized at Springfield, Illinois. It passed through Independence, Missouri, in May, and was joined by others until it contained between 200 and 300 wagons—when in motion extending two miles in length. Its timetable to escape snowfall in the Sierras was intact until after reaching Fort Bridger. There the Donner party chose a new route, called the Hastings Cut-off, south of the Great Salt Lake. Those who went by the old route reached California safely.

Winter set in early. On November 2 the main party, while resting overnight a few miles short of the Sierra summit, experienced a sudden snowstorm that blocked the pass. Most of the party was snowed in near Donner Lake until February, and many survived only by eating the flesh of the dead. Of 87 persons in the original group, 40 perished (Rawls and Bean, *California: An Interpretive History*, p. 66).

Gen. M. G. Vallejo heard of the plight of the Donner party and was among the first to contribute funds—$5,000, it is said—and organize relief units to be sent them. Brittan Greenwood was chosen as the guide, and with him into the winter fastness of mountains went James Reed and William McCutcheon. Reed had been previously banished from the Donner party after killing a fellow traveler in a fight, and thus forced to leave behind his wife and children. McCutcheon, a party member, had volunteered to go on ahead and seek help when the woebegone immigrants comprehended the gravity of their situation. Both had reached Sutter's Fort safely.

This was the second relief expedition to be outfitted, and it started from Sonoma, seeking to aid the trapped and starving pioneers. The terrible experiences of the survivors, including the Donner children, were soon the topic of discussion from Oregon to the Mexican border and were brought home in their stark realism when, a few months later, the Donner children arrived in Sonoma to live.

---

*I*t was in the fall of 1847 that the little girls, Eliza and Georgia, arrived. It was a hard trip from Sutter's Fort, and an Indian had to swim his horse across the streams and carry the children high and dry in order to bring them safely here. They made their home with Mr. and Mrs. Christian Brunner, a kind-hearted old couple who took the orphans to raise. Eliza Donner in after years wrote a graphic story of her early days in Sonoma.

COURTESY, ROBERT D. PARMELEE

Marie Brunner, who, with her husband, took Eliza (left) and Georgia Donner into her home in eastside Sonoma, operated a dairy. The girls' mother had been found in remarkably good condition by rescuers but refused to leave her dying husband in the mountains, a decision that rendered the little girls orphans.

She recalled the primitive methods of farming and transportation, the first school, services at the Mission church and the funeral of a soldier of Stevenson's Regiment. She described the military funeral cortege which passed her home on Second Street East, the riderless horse and the officer's boots hanging from the saddle.

The children had vivid recollections of customers from the Barracks who patronized their "Grandma" Marie Brunner's dairy and bought her good butter and cheese. Church services at the Mission and the wedding of General Vallejo's daughter Epifania to Captain Frisbie were recalled.

Until the 1930s a stone dairy house marked the place where the Donner children lived while they made Sonoma their home. In after years the place became the center of a lively industry—the raising and training of race horses, the J. B. Chase stock farm.

Locals bought their clothing and mining supplies in town at this store located at Napa and First Street East, now Pinelli's Corner Store. From an original tintype found in the Sonoma Barracks.

Gold!

*L*ife was leisurely and lovely in the vale of the moon until one day the cry of gold seemed to turn the land of the dons from dreams and siesta into a mad whirl. The cry of "Gold has been discovered on the American River!" reached Sonoma in January 1848, and engulfed it in a torrent of excitement.

The news swept staid citizens off their feet and started a stampede to the diggings in the vicinity of Coloma, a hundred miles distant.

Soldiers here on small pay were wild to try their luck and believed their presence in California at this moment a wondrous act of providence. Their officers and General Vallejo urged caution, and Alcalde Boggs was sent direct to Sutter's Fort and Coloma to verify the incredible stories of riches and to bring back gold dust, nuggets or specimens if possible. This the alcalde did and, with the official confirmation of the gold strike, most able-bodied men packed up and were off to the mines, regardless of family ties or business.

Official knowledge of the discovery which was to electrify the world was dispatched to General Vallejo by Gov. Richard B. Mason, who, with aide William Tecumseh Sherman and other officials, passed through Sonoma on an inspection tour of the mining area in the summer of 1848.

The trip started from Monterey. The governor's party made San Francisco without difficulty, but to cross the bay, the pilot of an old scow had to ferry the party and their horses across the Golden Gate. They stopped at San Rafael Mission with Don Timoteo Murphy, then went to Bodega, called on Capt. Stephen Smith, and also conferred with General Vallejo at Sonoma before proceeding to Napa and Putah Creek. From there they proceeded to the banks of the Sacramento River and were taken across by Indians in dugout canoes, their horses swimming the channel. They arrived at Sutter's Fort in time for a big Fourth of July celebration and were official guests at the ceremonies and feasting. Whether the round-about journey was entirely regarded as the best route, or whether a little prospecting may have been the objective, is not told, but it was a hard trip, later recounted by Sherman.

*A*UTHOR'S NOTE: Governor Mason's party had a first-hand look at the millrace, belonging to Sutter, where John Marshall first discovered gold. The governor's group also inspected Mormon Island, where already Sam Brannan and 300 Mormon emigrants were panning and washing gold—before returning via Dr. Robert Semple's ferry at Benicia. Semple, the 6-foot 6-inch respected member of the Bear Flag party, was both captain and crew. Six or eight horses were carried at a time across the Carquinez Straits, and it took two days in 1848 to cross the swift watercourse, where today crossing is accomplished in a few minutes by bridge.

*M*erchants of Sonoma and Embarcadero kept large stocks of goods which they exchanged for produce, hides and, later, for gold dust. Some of the early merchants were prompt to take advantage of a chance to advertise, although early-day papers such as the weekly *Californian* of San Francisco charged $100 per column for advertising space.

Sonoma merchants whose ads appeared in the *Californian* included Lilburn W. Boggs, whose ad was printed in both English and Spanish. Boggs stated that his goods would be sold "for cash or hides." Another enterprising firm was the Commerce House kept by Adler and Myers, "wholesale and retail dealers in general merchandise—produce taken in exchange for goods."

When miners began to bring in their gold dust, a rate of exchange was established, and in Sonoma some of the stores allowed from $4 to $5 per ounce. Change less than a dollar was so scarce that Guy Freeman Fling, a blacksmith, was employed to cut Mexican pesos into halves and quarters.

Sonoma lost little if any sleep over gold, which found its way into the homes and stores. Doors were seldom bolted. The unwritten law of the mining camps prevailed, and, before the riff-raff of the world began to pour into California, horse-stealing, quarrels and shootings over card games seemed to have been the principal crimes of the area.

The first rush to the mining country from Sonoma left the town practically devoid of men. The women carried on the business for the most part until mountain fever and bad luck began to send the miners homeward. A few came back with the precious gold dust, but the general opinion was that paydirt was hard to find. The men came back looking rough and disheveled after the rude life along the streams and in the hills, where common necessities of life were hard to get at any price.

The growing influx of gold seekers made fruit, vegetables, flour and all produce ridiculously high in price. Money and gold dust were plentiful, but everything else was scarce, for California was cattle country, selling principally hides and tallow and a limited quantity of grain. Farming and stock-raising loomed as the source of more certain revenue to many of the practical and those disillusioned of the easy wealth to be picked up at the mines. Jacob Leese sold 1,100 head of beef cattle from his Sonoma Huichica Rancho to James Marshall, of Coloma, as the latter began to supply the hungry hordes of gold seekers with meat.

10 Sonoma in the 1850s

An early engraving showing the northeast corner of the Sonoma Plaza and, in the background, Schocken Hill.

COURTESY, SONOMA VALLEY HISTORICAL SOCIETY

*F*or a time after the American occupancy of California there was a confused idea of authority and a clash among prominent leaders—Comm. Robert Field Stockton of the United States fleet, Gen. Steven Watts Kearney of the United States Army and Col. John Charles Fremont. Fremont's personally organized battalion of California volunteers was wanted in the regular army but withheld by Fremont's orders.

Some of his critics thought the officer should be tried for insubordination, and finally the situation became so acute that Kearney left to take up the quarrel with officials at Washington, and Fremont went with him. The latter was subsequently court-martialed but escaped penalty because of his political influence.

*A*UTHOR'S NOTE: Meanwhile, back in old Sonoma, politics were being played relative to the office of alcalde, probably the most important civil governing position in the sprawling post-U. S. occupation era. The alcalde designation has its roots in Spanish tradition and was used most extensively in Spain's overseas colonies. According to historian Dr. Theodore Givas, "Doubtless the most important single officer in the administration of local government in California, both before and after the American conquest, was the alcalde."

The alcalde acted not only as a mayor, but as chief law enforcement officer, judge, assessor, notary, tax collector and hide inspector. His symbol of authority was a silver-headed cane. The cane also served as a standard of measure. The alcalde, in his role as arbiter of land disputes and assessor, measured the land in question based on the length of his cane. His decision in the matter was final.

During Kearney's regime as military governor of California (1847), Sonoma had a lively experience with its alcalde, "Squire" John H. Nash. The position of alcalde was one of growing importance after the Mexican era because of the responsibility of land grants and titles, and the power of the judiciary vested in the alcaldes of the several districts. The alcalde by virtue of his office was treated with great respect by the people. His rank was indicated by the staff he carried, a cane with gold or silver knob interlaced with black cord or tassel. When this was raised, the populace bowed low, so the "big stick" was evidently an old Spanish custom.

After the Bear Flag incident, John Nash had succeeded to the office of alcalde. The honor seems to have gone to the old man's head, for when informed that General Kearney had appointed Lilburn Boggs alcalde, he defied the authorities, claiming that he had been the choice of the people. So obdurate was "Chief Justice" Nash that he flatly refused to turn over the records or books of his office to his successor, so Capt. J. E. Brackett was appealed to. Captain Brackett, not wishing to mix in the fight at such close range, appealed to Col. Richard B. Mason, Kearney's successor, asking him to straighten out the tangle and attempt to pry the alcalde of Sonoma loose from the honor he so dearly coveted. Mason's adjutant, William T. Sherman, was immediately dispatched from Monterey on horseback to Sonoma via San Francisco, then a settlement of just 400 people.

The stubborn Nash was found eating dinner at the home of friends named Green, with whom he lived in an adobe dwelling southeast of the Plaza. He was indignant when told that he was under arrest. There were threats and there might have been gun-play, but the alcalde was hustled to a waiting cart, driven to the cutter and put aboard. Nash had never been on a boat in his life, having come overland across the plains to California from Missouri. He was thoroughly frightened at the prospects of a rough trip on the water and the rougher treatment he was likely to receive at Monterey.

He finally arrived there and, after agreeing to turn over his office, all moneys and records, he was released and returned to Sonoma—subdued, penitent and obliging. Ex-Governor of Missouri Boggs, the new alcalde, proved able and fair in the administration of his district, which extended from Sonoma to Sutter's Fort.

State capital location became a question

With California's development a certainty, Gen. M. G. Vallejo, believing himself still a very wealthy citizen because of his vast ranchos, herds, grain fields, abundant water supply and many profitable deals, decided that the state capital or leading metropolis of the north should be in the vicinity of his holdings on Suisun Bay, its proximity to San Francisco Bay and to the great rivers of the Sacramento and San Joaquin making it outstanding. He wished to call the new city Francisca after his wife, Francisca Benicia Vallejo. When the village of Yerba Buena changed its name to San Francisco, he thought there would be too much similarity in the names of the rival towns, so he called the place Benicia.

Vallejo was encouraged in his views by army officers including Bvt. Maj. Gen. Persifor F. Smith, who arrived on the *California* in 1849 to assume military command of the whole Pacific Coast. In

INDEX-TRIBUNE ARCHIVES

The Sonoma adobe of "stubborn" alcalde John H. Nash on First Street East, today a private residence.

COURTESY, ROBERT D. PARMELEE

Gen. Persifor F. Smith moved his headquarters from San Francisco, which he deemed "in no way fitted for military or commercial purposes," to Sonoma in 1849.

early reports to the war department from San Francisco, General Smith said:

> Two companies of the second infantry will be stationed somewhere near, above the influence of the fogs; the company of artillery, at the Presidio; the cavalry, at Sonoma. They will require some additional inducements beyond their pay to prevent them from deserting. Such may be given by authorizing the quartermaster to employ them in public work.

The town of San Francisco is in no way fitted for military or commercial purposes; there is no harbor, a bad landing place, bad water, no supplies of provisions, and inclement climate, and it is cut off from the rest of the country except by a long circuit around the southern extremity of the bay. In time of war enemy could be landed for many miles south of the entrance of the bay on the sea beach and thus cut it off by a short line across the peninsula on which it stands.

Of military posts about the bay, Smith wrote in May 1849 to Brig. Gen. Roger Jones, Adjutant General, of

> … Benicia, a place on the straits of Carquinez, where is established the general depot for this division, and a military post garrisoned by two companies of infantry. A small company of dragoons is posted at Sonoma, a day's ride southwest from Benicia whence it can visit if necessary the country bounded by the Sacramento (latitude 42) and the ocean, said to be thickly inhabited by Indians. I am about to move my headquarters to Sonoma.

Andrew J. Smith (later to become a major general in the Civil War) and a company of dragoons occupied the Barracks here. Sherman, who became the adjutant general for the Commander of the Pacific, moved with him to Sonoma.

Persifor Smith could no longer endure the primitive conditions, the cold and hardships of the city by the Golden Gate. The servants Smith and his wife, a Southern woman, brought with them on their journey deserted the household, following the rest to the gold mines. The military commander and his wife were about desperate until they reached the hospitable settlement of Sonoma with its kindly population and more abundant supplies. Here they made their home in the adobe known as the Fitch House on the west side of the Plaza.

Maj. Joseph Hooker later succeeded Sherman as adjutant general of the division. Sherman became General Smith's aide-de-camp. Both Smith and Hooker thought so highly of Sonoma

Valley that they purchased land here. The Persifor Smith ranch of several hundred acres was sold to a Major Beck when Smith was finally ordered away from California—and then passed to the ownership of William Swift, brother of Granville Swift of Bear Flag fame. General Hooker bought a portion of the Agua Caliente grant and continued to make Sonoma Valley his home for some years, little dreaming that he was to win fame and the title "Fighting Joe" Hooker during the Civil War.

General Smith allowed Sherman, another destined hero of the war 'twixt North and South, to improve his opportunities financially while in the service. As a result of the big opportunities of the gold rush boom, Sherman, after a little time out at the mines, came back to Sonoma with a profit of $6,000. He did not pan out the gold or stake out a claim, but his business deals were profitable.

The district known as Sonoma comprised all the territory west of the Sacramento River and south of the Oregon line, but with the election of Mariano G. Vallejo, Robert Semple and Joel Walker as delegates to the Constitutional Convention at Monterey in 1849, one of the first matters taken up was the division of California into counties. Sonoma County was to include what was later Mendocino county and also a portion of Napa. The northern line of Sonoma was along the 40th parallel to the summit of the Mayacamas range, thence south to San Pablo Bay.

General Vallejo became a state senator in 1850. It was then that he made the amazing proposal to establish the state capital at the city of Eureka (later called for him Vallejo). He offered not only the land but thousands of dollars to carry out a public building program of magnificence. He believed the town of Vallejo was the true center of the state and said "that point which can be approached from all parts of the state in the fewest hours and at the cheapest cost is the true center."

He prophesied the coming of a railroad from the Mississippi River west to San Francisco, where the western terminus would connect with three-week steamers from China, and urged his colleagues to ornament California's shores with a capital worthy of their great state. As we know today, Sacramento won the honor.

COURTESY, SONOMA VALLEY HISTORICAL SOCIETY

General Vallejo was a delegate to the 1849 Constitutional Convention in Monterey and a state senator, but his plan to establish the state capital at present-day Vallejo was unsuccessful.

Sonoma loses county seat

Disappointed over the location chosen for the state capital and disturbed concerning his widely challenged land titles, General Vallejo began to realize that Sonoma, the city he had founded and regarded as the rival of San Francisco, was also likely to lose the county seat. While all business of the district was carried on at Sonoma, officially recognized as the seat of government after the formation of the county in 1850, a rival town had grown up at Santa Rosa, 22 miles north of the pueblo. New settlers there, with all the spirit of the new day, were conniving to win the county seat and erect a courthouse for Sonoma County.

The question of the courthouse and facilities to house the county offices and records split the county into rival camps, one advocating an imposing edifice at Santa Rosa, the other willing to continue on in the dilapidated adobe county seat headquarters at Sonoma.

A bill was engineered through the legislature, giving the voters of Sonoma County the right to

INDEX-TRIBUNE ARCHIVES

Founded in 1858, Sonoma's Cumberland Presbyterian Literary College was initially housed in the Salvador Vallejo adobe on the west side of the Plaza, until a new three-story structure (pictured above) was built for it on Broadway. Declared unsafe for classes after the 1906 earthquake, the building was torn down and rebuilt to serve as the Valley's first high school. It continued in that capacity until 1923, when the present high school was erected a block south.

vote on the question of changing the location of the county seat. J. W. Bennett, pledged to removal, had defeated Col. Joseph Hooker of Agua Caliente for the assembly. Bennett was author of the enabling act and followed up his advantage.

In July 1854 a grand barbecue was staged by Santa Rosa. People for miles around were invited to partake of the town's hospitality and, incidentally, primed for the courthouse battle. In the following September, a vote was taken on the removal of the county seat, and Santa Rosa won. Sonoma prepared to make an appeal and to declare the proceedings illegal. But while the people of the pueblo talked and *The Sonoma Bulletin* raved, the eager Santa Rosans sneaked up on them and, descending on Sonoma's adobe courthouse with a couple of go-getters and a mule team, loaded up the records and all the county paraphernalia, and disappeared in a cloud of dust.

Sonoma Valley's first schools

According to the census of 1851, the entire population of Sonoma County was only 561. D. O. Shattuck was chairman of the first board of supervisors. Roads and schools were the chief topics to

engage the attention of officials. Supervisors Randolph, Boggs and Shattuck were named on the road committee of the board, and Supervisors Shattuck, Boggs and John Lewis on the committee to consider the establishment of public schools. As there were only 250 children to be provided for, it was not a difficult problem. Sonoma, Santa Rosa and Analy were the first communities to have American schools.

The pueblo of Sonoma was always considered an educational center.

In a letter dated Nov. 5, 1855, the family of George Watriss wrote to friends in the East:

> Emma (Watriss) has gone to a boarding school located at Sonoma, called Saint Mary's Hall, kept by an Episcopalian clergyman, his wife and assistant teachers. You go on a steamer up the bay about 30 miles to a place called Lakeville and take a stage from there to Sonoma, a trip of three or four hours. The school is 265 by 60 feet long and has three acres of ground for recreation.

This school was patronized by General Vallejo, and his older daughters were educated there, including the late Natalia Vallejo Haraszthy. One of the teachers at Dr. Ver Mehr's academy was Mrs. Dorthea Duhring, a brilliant pianist, and wife of the Sonoma merchant. Prior to the opening of the Ver Mehr school, about 1852, General Vallejo had established a school in his own palatial home, where Frederick Reaer, a brilliant German scholar, was instructor and Andrew Hoeppner was music master.

Sonoma Cumberland College, founded in 1858, was a literary college referred to as the Cumberland Presbyterian Literary College. It was originally in the El Dorado Hotel building but in 1864 occupied a new building on Broadway that later became the first Sonoma high school. In fact, much of this high school building, with its three stories and mansard roof, was the original structure of the college founded by Professor W. N. Cunningham, Oxford graduate and Presbyterian clergyman. He became its principal, and his teaching staff were all college graduates.

One of the early schools mentioned in memoirs of pioneers of Sonoma and recalled by old-timers was the school that stood on the site of the old Methodist Church just over the bridge near the Sonoma grammar school. Here in the 1860s the old school bell rang from its ventilated tower, and many students, afterwards prominent in California, rode to Sonoma in carts, came on horseback, or walked to town after a long trudge from outlying ranches. Susie Formhals was an early teacher there, and also Henry Morris, a brother of J. B. Morris, the Agua Caliente pioneer. The Morris family then resided in an adobe on Spain Street. Here Henry Morris, described as "a refined young gentleman with the face of a Bret Harte," lived. George W. Jones was also an early-day instructor and was succeeded by a rough-and-ready educator whose principal accomplishment

seems to have been tobacco chewing. George Jones, Sonoma's first public school teacher, became the first county superintendent.

In 1868 the site was improved with a frame school house on a lot bought from John Lewis for $400. The building was designed by a San Francisco architect and thought to be the last word in school buildings. To this frame school house of several rooms, and the school yard with its rotund play houses and creaky pump, trooped many boys and girls at the sound of the 8:30 bell. A modern brick grammar school building [now utilized as the Sonoma Community Center] followed.

Sonoma young ladies of the 1860s were educated at the fashionable Napa Ladies Seminary,

INDEX-TRIBUNE ARCHIVES

Fifty-five boys and girls were enrolled at St. Joseph's Presentation Convent in Sonoma on its first day of classes, July 11, 1882. Today the site (shown here, looking north) at Napa and Third Street West is home to St. Francis Solano Church and School. The original buildings were destroyed by fire in 1896. The convent closed in 1918 after 35 years.

established in 1860, later conducted by Miss Maria McDonald and, at her death, by her sister, Miss Sarah F. McDonald.

Locust Grove school at Embarcadero, founded by Mr. and Mrs. C. W. Lubeck, was a private preparatory and boarding school of splendid reputation, and many prominent families sent their children there to prepare for college.

No account of old school days would be complete without mention of the Presentation Convent of Sonoma, where the good sisters of St. Francis Parish taught primary and advanced grades and otherwise directed the lives of Catholic boys and girls. Music was a specialty at the convent, whose entertainments and graduation exercises were most ambitious. With growing numbers of pupils entering the public schools each year, the parochial school was finally forced to close for lack of sufficient support. A new parochial school building was erected and opened to students in 1945. Known as the St. Francis Solano School, it was a gift from the late Samuele Sebastiani, wealthy Sonoma wineman.

11 Social Center of Alta California

INDEX-TRIBUNE ARCHIVES

Sonoma belles, like this unidentified beauty of the 1880s, and the social events they attended were once frequent topics in the *Index-Tribune*. An account from the March 10, 1888, issue stated: "The anniversary ball of Bear Flag Lodge #97, Knights of Pythias, which took place at Union Hall on March 5, was a pleasant and most enjoyable affair. The toilets of the ladies were very becoming, many of the costumes being quite rich."

AUTHOR'S NOTE: Sonoma was not only the principal place of business north of Yerba Buena (San Francisco) in the years following the American takeover, but was also looked upon as the social center of Alta California, even in the days following statehood, accorded in 1850.

In addition to early settlers, many of them members of prominent families in their home states, the coming of the aforementioned Stevenson's Regiment of New York Volunteers and the later choice of Sonoma as a place to live by top-ranking military personnel brought a social vitality to the pueblo. Following the arrival in California of Gen. and Mrs. Persifor Smith—and his choice of Sonoma for his head-quarters and residence—more and more people of good character and talent selected Sonoma as the ideal residential community, shunning the ever-growing but often lawless city by the Golden Gate, which the gold rush made even more of a problem for respectable people to accept.

Upon admission of California as a state, social affairs in which the native Californians and the new settlers joined were most cordial. The inter-marriage of Americans into leading California families, the coming of the wives and daughters of the immigrants from the States, the presence of the military officers and men of the army and navy foreshadowed brilliant social gatherings of the period.

On Oct. 29, 1850, nine days after the steamer *Oregon* had brought news of the admission of California into the Union on September 9, there was a glorious celebration in San Francisco in which prominent Sonomans joined. A parade and exercises on Portsmouth Plaza terminated with fireworks and a grand ball. Bonfires blazed on Telegraph Hill, and as rockets lit the sky and anvils heralded the glad news of statehood, 500 gentlemen and 300 ladies attended the most brilliant ball that had been witnessed in the city, declared "The Annals of San Francisco." Thus the admission of California as the 31st state of the Union passed into history. The Admission Day ball was long remembered by Sonoma's socially prominent, and invitations to the event bearing the names of many well-known social leaders of the day are treasured by pioneer families.

Following the example of Governor Boggs of Missouri, General Smith and other notables who chose Sonoma for their homes, Judge David O. Shattuck of Louisiana settled here in 1850. He arrived at San Francisco by steamer with his family and soon located in Sonoma Valley. A 10-room house had been shipped around Cape Horn in sections and was put together on a ranch three miles south of the town. Judge Shattuck saw great pos-

The name Glen Ellen was first used by Col. Charles V. Stuart as the name for his home, shown above, built in 1869 and named for his wife, Ellen. "Glen Ellen" later became the name of the town, and the ranch name was changed to Glen Oaks to avoid confusion. With its old stone buildings and virtually intact acreage, Glen Oaks appears to be the best-preserved historic agricultural property in the Valley.

sibilities in the rich new country of California and started the practice of law in San Francisco, though he had no desire to have his wife and family live in that wild and woolly seaport. Like Persifor Smith, he chose Sonoma as the ideal suburb. Shattuck had been president of one of the leading colleges of Louisiana and a presiding Judge of the Superior Court there. He became a Superior Court Judge in San Francisco also and presided in many important trials during the vigilante days, doing his utmost to curb the lawlessness of the times and hold in check the fiery spirits who would deal out summary justice.

Meanwhile, the Shattuck family kept the home fires burning in the valley of Sonoma, and no family was more typical of the hospitality of California and the old South. Frank Shattuck, a son of Judge David Shattuck, became the first Superior Court Judge of Sonoma County. His sister, Molly, and her daughters, Nonie and Nancy Spencer, were belles of the day.

Nonie married into the Cooper-Harris family, of Blue Wing Inn fame, and Nancy became the bride of a nephew of Col. George H. Hooper, San Francisco banker, who had bought a magnificent estate on the west side of Sonoma Valley, the famed Sobre Vista ranch, which he highly cultivated. Sobre Vista was winner of many gold

The 870-acre estate on the west side of the Valley known as Sobre Vista was deeded to M. I. Todd by General Vallejo. Todd sold it to Gen. Washington Sewall, U. S. Army, in 1860. Sewall, in turn, deeded it to Col. and Mrs. George F. Hooper in 1872 (photo taken during their residency). Sugar king Adolph Spreckels and his wife, Alma, acquired the property from the Hoopers in 1896.

medals for the excellence of its wines, brandies, grapes, olive oil and fruits.

Close to the Hooper property was the vast vineyard of the hospitable Eli T. Sheppard, wealthy Californian, who had been in the diplomatic service. He established his home in Sonoma Valley, calling his place Madrone Vineyard because of the red-hued native trees on the property. The Sheppards entertained in lavish fashion, a wedding reception for their daughter being recalled by old-timers because of the elaborate gowns worn by the ladies, and the elegance of a supper for which San Francisco caterers and an orchestra were engaged. The Madrone Vineyard was later acquired by Sen. George Hearst and, at his death, passed to Mrs. Phoebe Hearst, his widow, who eventually sold it to the California Wine Association.

A distinguished resident of Sonoma Valley in the early 1850s was William McPherson Hill, born in Philadelphia, a college graduate, lawyer and wealthy citizen. The Hill family acquired 1,400 acres in the Valley of the Moon, extending from

INDEX-TRIBUNE ARCHIVES

Beltane Ranch near Kenwood is today a guest ranch that invites visitors to reflect on the Valley's early-day history.

the summit of Sonoma Mountain to the fertile area along Sonoma Creek. The home of William McPherson Hill, with sons and daughter taking prominent part in the social life of the period, was one of the most hospitable north of the bay. A son, Robert Potter Hill, succeeded his father in the management of the estate.

Los Guilicos Rancho, in the upper valley,

COURTESY, WILLIAM RAMSAY AND JANET RAMSAY LOMBARDO

Ten Oaks Vineyard on Dunbar Road in Glen Ellen, where J.B. and Kate Warfield planted their first grapes in 1859.

COURTESY, WILLIAM RAMSAY AND JANET RAMSAY LOMBARDO

Dr. J. B. Warfield and Katherine Overton Warfield. After J. B.'s death in 1878, Kate, "a woman of rare pluck and energy" (Teiser and Harroun, p. 80), expanded their wine-making business significantly. Six years later Kate took first prize at the Louisville Exposition in 1884 with her Riesling wines. The previous year, when her brandy won first place at the state fair, her competitiors demanded a second judging; she won that, too.

where Hood Mountain towers, was the scene of many fine affairs in the early days. The William Hood and James Shaw ranches were showplaces of that scenic section. Hood was a Scotchman who arrived in California eight days after the American flag was raised at Monterey. He settled in Sonoma in 1849, on what is now the Pythian Home property. The Shaw ranch, Wildwood, adjoined it, and was highly improved with vineyard, some of the best cabernet wines in the world coming from this hillside. Louis Kunde succeeded Shaw.

The Stuarts of Glen Ellen, Dr. J. B. and Mrs. Kate Warfield and Col. J. H. Drummond were also prominent in the upper valley and noted for the elegance of their entertainment. Colonel Drummond was an Irishman, credited with perfecting his wines from European cuttings. His "Dunfillan Brand" wines were famous. Drummond and a brother in the old country, Hamilton Drummond, were partners in the Sonoma Valley enterprise, and the brother searched Europe for choice varieties of grapes, which were then planted in Sonoma soil. The wines took prizes wherever exhibited, and Colonel Drummond won many honors for Sonoma through

his consistent displays at all the big expositions in this and other countries. In addition to grape vines, 7,000 fruit trees were set out. Tropical fruits in many varieties, nuts and ornamental trees made his Sonoma estate one worthy of the princely hospitality dispensed there. After the dread phylloxera blight swept the vineyard, and after Drummond died, the place was sold to the wealthy Bell family of San Francisco. A Southern Pacific station, Beltane, named for the family, existed for a time at the site.

In this section of Sonoma Valley also settled the well-known Ashe family, the brothers Will, Porter, Gaston and Sidney Ashe coming to the country frequently. Here they kept their race horses. Will Ashe, who married the daughter of J. D. Peters, the Stockton capitalist, made his home near Glen Ellen.

Further down the valley, in the Agua Caliente region, was the Morris family—the late Tom Morris and Harry Madison, who went in for balls and parties and were social leaders of their day.

Of a fine old American family were also the Appletons, whose family tree gave them entree into the best society.

Then there was the Watriss family, and Joseph J. King, brother of James King of William, and his family.

Others equally prominent socially had homes and farms on the east side of the valley in the vicinity of Buena Vista and Rhine Farm, centers of early-day sociability. Buena Vista, originally the home of Col. Agoston Haraszthy, boasted a mansion in the Pompeian style, with stately columns, fountains and statuary. Colonel and Mrs. Haraszthy gave a party there of gaiety and splendor on Oct. 28, 1864. The affair was a vintage masquerade to which they issued elaborate invitations.

Invitations on white satin were issued by General and Mrs. Vallejo to a tea given in honor of Mayor and Mrs. John Cameron of Sonoma in 1850. Mrs. John Ross Martin of San Francisco, the Camerons' daughter, treasured this souvenir for many a day.

The double wedding of Natalia and Jovita Vallejo to the Haraszthy brothers, Attila and Arpad, was solemnized June 1, 1863, at the Vallejo home, and was followed by a reception of great brilliance. Five of the General's daughters were given away by him in the beautiful parlor of Lachryma Montis. For all these weddings and many others, orange blossoms grown in the Vallejo garden were used.

In later years Temelec Hall, home of the Col. W. K. Rogers family, was the scene of many brilliant affairs, as was the home of Sen. and Mrs. John Enos of Grand View; Orange Lawn, the residence of the Youngs; the homes of the Picketts, Dunns, Hayeses, Rufuses, Dresels, Ewells and other families of the pueblo.

The Buena Vista property passed from the ownership of Major Snyder and the Haraszthys to Robert and Kate Johnson of San Francisco, who built a three-story mansion, long known as The Castle, on the property. While the Johnsons lived a secluded life, they kept their country estate up to a high state of cultivation and were widely known for their charities. Kate Johnson's hobby was Persian and Angora cats. They became such an obsession with her that she turned over an entire floor of the Castle to her pets and, at her death, left a handsome sum for their care. The Castle was eventually sold to the State of California for a home for delinquent women and female narcotic addicts, who were credited with burning down the big frame mansion in March 1923. The house was never rebuilt. [A two-story building was later built by the state on the Buena Vista property for the rehabilitation of female delinquents. After the Buena Vista rancho was acquired at auction by Mr. and Mrs. Frank H. Bartholomew in the early 1940s, the building was used alternately as a hospital, rest home and winery.]

The organization of lodges in Sonoma during the pioneer days widened the social field and added interest to early life in the beautiful vale. On April 9, 1851, Temple Lodge, No. 14, Free and Accepted Masons, was organized with Col. Jonathan D. Stevenson, Grand Master, officiating at the ceremonies. The first lodge room was in the adobe on Spain Street known as the Ray House, which still bears the insignia of the Masonic order on its walls and upstairs floor. Charter members of Temple Lodge were H. Hendley, George H. Derby, James Long, M. Pelty, Jesse Davisson, William Burris, P. Hicklin, Stephen Akers, Jason Smith, E. Peabody and George Stevenson.

In July 1854 Sonoma Lodge No. 28,

Temelec Hall

Independent Order of Odd Fellows, was organized. It sponsored many early social affairs. A program of a Washington's Birthday ball given by the lodge in 1860 adorned the walls of the Odd Fellows hall for many years. The faded souvenir reveals that the floor managers were J. D. Long and N. Kavanaugh. Music was by Fuller's band, and on the committee for arrangements were F. Rohrer, N. Kavanaugh, John Adrian and B. H. Miller.

The 1860s were carefree, happy days despite the battles over land titles and feuds over squatters. Sonoma had a hall over the El Dorado Hotel

The Johnsons' "Castle." Count Haraszthy's land passed to the San Francisco couple in 1880 when, as the Jan. 8 *Sonoma Index* reported, "The Buena Vista Viticultural property was sold at auction on Wednesday at the courthouse in Santa Rosa to R[obert] C. Johnson ... the mortgagee, for $46,501."

COURTESY, ROBERT D. PARMELEE

Lt. George Derby, also known by his pen names Squibob and John Phoenix, was stationed in Sonoma with Stevenson's Regiment. A notorious practical joker, Derby once dressed several babies in each other's clothing while their mothers attended a party in the next room, leaving the ladies to discover the prank—in some cases, only after they arrived home with the wrong baby.

and also the Oakes or Union Hall on West Napa Street, the latter being the scene of many important events. Poppe's Hall, above the store of that name, was used as a lodge room and also for social affairs. Weyl Hall [today the Sonoma Hotel] was the scene of many social gatherings in the eighties, including the long-remembered reception and banquet given there to veterans of the Mexican War. Here the old Sonoma Valley Band always gave its concerts, and school entertainments, both public and parochial, offered their best talent before the flickering footlights and their tin reflectors.

Long before the Gay Nineties, parties were nonetheless popular in old Sonoma. In 1884 the Novelty Social Club gave a New Year's Eve ball with the following well-known citizens on the committee of arrangements: Capt. P. N. Stofen, Robert P. Hill, F. R. Corbaley, F. L. Clark, Carl Dresel; reception, T. S. Cooper, A. C. Haubert, Sam Lewis;

COURTESY, SONOMA VALLEY HISTORICAL SOCIETY

"Henry Weyl is about to put up a fine store building on the corner of Vallejo [Spain] and First Street West opposite the Plaza. ... We are glad ... as that corner needs filling up with a fine building. This, together with the railroad improvements going on, will make that side of the Plaza an attractive business site and lend much to the symmetry and attractiveness of the town." Dec. 25, 1879, *Sonoma Index*

floor manager, E. J. Mullen; floor committee, George Bachelder, R. J. Dunn, R. A. Douglas; reception, F. Ehrlich, G. S. Harris, M. F. Turley, Jesse Burris, Otto Rufus, R. J. Pauli.

A Leap Year party of the same period, given by Valley of the Moon Chapter, Order of Eastern Star, is of interest. On the committee were Mrs. P. N. Stofen, Mrs. P. H. Thompson, Miss Mattie Goodman; reception, Mrs. W. C. Goodman, Mrs. A. McHarvey, Mrs. William Brown; floor manager, Miss Mattie Goodman; floor committee, Miss J. Johnson, Miss E. Thompson, Miss Willie Akers; introduction, Mrs. P. N. Stofen, Mrs. E. Tobin, Mrs. George Clark; committee on fines, E. Cassebohm.

One of the flourishing organizations of the early days was the Clay Literary Society, which sponsored a dance to raise funds for a town library Dec. 30, 1887. Cirardi's string band, afterwards famed for its music on San Francisco ferry boats, where the old harp player was known to every traveler, was engaged for the occasion. Dances complimentary to the first families and their homes in the valley were indicated on the elaborate programs by their names: Orange Lawn, Bella Vista, Ivy Farm, Cherry Lawn, Willow Ranch, Three Oaks, Rose Vale, Temelec Hall, Shady Nook, Rhine Farm, Green Oaks, Locust Grove, Lone Pine Cottage, Saint Louis, Lachryma Montis and Buena Vista won favor.

At Weyl Hall Sept. 26, 1884, "The Four Hundred Social Club" gave a ball with the following committees: President, G. P. Dey; Secretary, J. J. Whstryk; committee on arrangements, G. P. Dey, G. W. Spencer, A. Dulon, J. J. Whstryk, O. Ehrlich, A. Haubert, George Bachelder, R. J. Dunn, R. N. Douglas, F. Ehrlich, G. S. Harris and M. F. Turley.

The Fourth of July and New Year's Eve were invariably celebrated with private and public parties, the celebration of Independence Day at the Eden Dale colonial mansion of the Honorable Robert Howe being an annual event typical of California hospitality. New Year's Eve was the date always conceded to the Volunteer Fire Department for its big annual benefit, and these dances were patronized by almost every family of Sonoma Valley.

Now and then it was a masquerade, and when the unmasking hour came, the banker's daughter was dancing with the butcher boy, the teacher found herself on the arm of the village blacksmith, the temperance advocate was bowing to the saloon keeper—social lines all forgotten in the giddy mazes of the quadrille. Sonoma people were deeply grateful to the firemen and showed it by their presence.

Elaborate suppers and banquets were the rule at all grand balls, the culinary art and bounty of Tony Oakes' establishment typical. In later years other bonifaces followed his example. The hand-outs of this day and age would have amused the former generations, and the cocktail parties which now clutter the social pages would have offended. While wine found its way onto the tables of the early-day parties, strong drink was taboo. Ladies who drank cocktails were few, and cigarette-smokers were never ladies in the eyes of the Yankees.

At a typical California ball in 1862, with 100 tickets sold, preparations for the supper included six good-sized pigs, 10 turkeys, 40 chickens and all the fixings.

The costumes of the ladies were no less extravagant: "White tarlatan, six flounces trimmed with broad black ribbon, head-dress black ostrich feather, jet jewelry." "White tarlatan trimmed with group of narrow ruffles ornamented with small bows of white satin ribbon, hair arranged in broad braids and looped with white

japonica." "Pink and white satin brocade overdress of pink illusion, three flounces elegantly embroidered." "Pink tarlatan, double skirt looped up at the side with wreaths of variegated flowers." Thus went the sweethearts of the '60s to the dance.

Lachryma Montis

General Vallejo's pride in his family's talent and education was supplemented with interest in his children's social happiness and success, and soon

An engraving of Lachryma Montis from the 1877 *Historical Atlas of Sonoma County*, showing the cottonwood trees that still line the drive. In General Vallejo's lifetime, the homestead included some 250 acres.

A state historic monument since July 1933, the house and 20 acres of Lachryma Montis are supported by the State Historic Park Association and its many donors and volunteers. Thousands of tourists visit the tree-shaded grounds, the old home and adjoining Swiss chalet annually.

COURTESY, BRIAN MCGINTY

Natalia Vallejo wed Attila Haraszthy June 1, 1863, in the same wedding ceremony that united her sister to her groom's brother.

COURTESY, FRANK H. BARTHOLOMEW FOUNDATION

In Attila Haraszthy's obituary, the *Index-Tribune* described him as "one of the best-known and enterprising citizens of Sonoma."

COURTESY, SONOMA VALLEY HISTORICAL SOCIETY

Jovita Vallejo married Arpad Haraszthy in the double ceremony at Lachryma Montis.

COURTESY, FRANK H. BARTHOLOMEW FOUNDATION

Arpad Haraszthy achieved fame as a maker of sparkling wines.

COURTESY, VALLEJO NAVAL & HISTORICAL MUSEUM

Epifania Vallejo Frisbie, reputedly the favorite daughter of M. G. Vallejo.

COURTESY, ROBERT D. PARMELEE

John B. Frisbie, one of M. G. Vallejo's sons-in-law.

the kindly don began to plan a magnificent residence, modern and elegant in the American and European fashion, with here and there a touch of the East. Oriental splendor ever captivated the imagination of Californians accustomed to viewing rich cargoes from China and the Philippines. Vallejo chose a homesite in the foothills of the matchless valley near the living spring, and named it Lachryma Montis (Tear of the Mountain) after reading poetry of old Granada. This remarkable spring, bubbling from the Sonoma hills in limitless quantity of clear, cold water, enriched the verdure of all the land bordering the town and was a major source of Sonoma's water supply over a period of years.

Orchards and vineyards flourished in the hill-protected area of Vallejo's new residence. Trees produced oranges, lemons, figs and olives; and tropical plants bore fruit and flowers. A terraced hill rose from a crystal lake, and fountains played before the doors—doors which opened on broad verandas where tales of love and sweetest music beguiled, and moonlit nights made this the paradise of romance. The Casa Grande adobe on the Plaza, which had been the home of the family, was going to decay. Bitter memories of the intruders of 1846, the lonely hours which followed that episode and the necessity for an appropriate residence for his charming family of young sons and daughters prompted the General and his wife to make Lachryma Montis the most comfortable and beautiful hacienda in the territory despite the fact that building costs were tremendously expensive, and the Vallejo fortune far less secure than in days gone by.

The home was finished in the early 1850s, when labor was in demand at the mines, and carpenters and other artisans received as high as $17 a day in wages. When Vallejo had paid his builders, when brick and marble had been shipped from Honolulu, redwood timber brought by ox team from the Sonoma County coast, summer houses of rare design imported from Germany, an avenue of stately trees set out, a Swiss chalet sent round the Horn and here assembled, he had spent more than $150,000 on his estate.

AUTHOR'S NOTE: Memorable at the lavish new home, Lachryma Montis, were the weddings there which united the Vallejos' eldest daughter,

Epifania (Fannie) and Capt. J. B. Frisbie, U. S. Army, commander of the Barracks at Sonoma under the new regime, in 1851; and the double ceremony when the Vallejos' daughters, Natalia and Jovita, married Attila and Arpad Haraszthy, respectively. The latter were the sons of Count Agoston Haraszthy, founder of the Buena Vista Viticultural Society, later to become known as the "Father of California Viticulture."

It should be noted here that the marriage of Epifania and Captain Frisbie was apparently a happy union, and that General Vallejo was greatly impressed by the New York-educated and ambitious young army officer. Frisbie and Vallejo had been closely associated in business prior to the captain's marriage to Epifania, the General's favorite daughter. But it was after the marriage

The General's Daughter restaurant on West Spain Street was once the home of Natalia and Attila Haraszthy. When constructed, the home was well within view of Lachryma Montis, the Vallejo property.

The home of Jovita and Arpad Haraszthy was purchased for them by Count Agoston Haraszthy from Col. R. B. Butler, who built the Greek Revival and Italianate home on a knoll on Sonoma's west side in the 1850s. Throughout its history the home has been a private residence and in 1990 won a historic preservation award.

that Frisbie became one of the many who took advantage of his father-in-law's trust and generosity, leading to Vallejo's financial distress.

The General, in July 1850, mistakenly gave full power of attorney, with control over his properties, to Captain Frisbie, whose self-centered schemes and misuse of his father-in-law's property and wealth led to Vallejo's near ruin.

Prior to his death Vallejo's only holding was his beloved Lachryma Montis property, its homestead a place of charm for four generations. Thanks to the generosity of history lovers and the largesse of the state of California, it has been saved for future generations to enjoy.

12 Setting Sonoma's City Limits

It's hard to believe, but the eight-acre Sonoma Plaza was once treeless and bordered by a picket fence. This photograph shows the business buildings that faced the Plaza's east side in 1871, just as cafes, a theater and shops do today.

General Vallejo was far-seeing regarding the value of California land and realized the importance of making those in possession of grants secure in their holdings, especially if they improved their acreage and lived up to the terms imposed upon them. As far back as 1837 the commandante urged the employment of a competent surveyor to put settlers in possession of the grants made to them.

After the American occupancy, the people could not agree upon the mode of extending General Vallejo's original survey. In 1835 the General, in conformity with the orders of Governor Figueroa, had laid out the Sonoma Plaza and one block of lots around it. He did the original work himself with a pocket compass and

Indian laborers to assist him. In consequence, the boundaries of the Plaza were not at right angles. To expedite the solving of land problems, military governor Richard B. Mason appointed a commission to investigate the situation in Sonoma and report to him. He instructed Alcalde Boggs to correct the old map, extend the survey of General Vallejo by leaving the Plaza as it then was, and run new lines of streets north and south at right angles, with lines of streets east and west parallel to the Plaza.

Boggs engaged Jasper O'Farrell, after whom O'Farrell Street in San Francisco is named, and J. M. Hudspeth, as surveyors, to resurvey the pueblo according to these instructions, and to make a map thereof. Hudspeth did the field work, and the O'Farrell map which he platted became the official map of Sonoma in 1848.

On April 4, 1850, Sonoma was incorporated as a city, its boundaries including all the outlots. Sonoma was the county seat of Sonoma and Mendocino counties inclusive until 1854 (when a questionable "vote" moved the county seat to Santa Rosa). A mayor, five councilmen, marshal, assessor, city clerk, attorney and treasurer were the city officers. Early-day mayors were John Cameron, M. G. Vallejo, Robert Hopkins, G. M. Miller, Sam R. Bright, Israel Brockman, Tony Oakes, H. L. Lindstrom and D. Cook.

By the Treaty of Guadalupe Hidalgo, the United States agreed to recognize and approve all valid grants of land in California made prior to the said treaty, not only to the pueblos, but also to private individuals. In order to carry out this provision, three land commissioners were appointed to examine grants and reject or approve same, the party aggrieved having the right to appeal to the United States District Court and Supreme Court. In 1852 Sonoma, through its city attorney, Robert Hopkins, brought the pueblo claim before the land commissioners, claiming the land lying between and bordered by the hills north of town, Agua Caliente Creek, Sonoma Creek to Arroyo Seco—one and three-quarters leagues. It was confirmed on June 22, 1856.

Claiming that the city authorities had mismanaged the people's affairs, had nothing to show for lots sold or taxes collected, that surplus funds had been loaned out of the city treasury at two percent interest per month and never returned, and pointing to an indebtedness of $1,200, the opponents of incorporation won out, and on April 26, 1862, disincorporation was approved. It was understood that three trustees should be elected to carry out the contracts of the former council; pay off, and liquidate the town indebtedness and declare which of the city streets should be public thoroughfares; and to sell streets not needed. The citizens chosen for this important work were D. O. Shattuck, John Walton and Dennis Beahan. The appeal from the decision of the United States District Court to the Supreme Court in regard to the pueblo land was dismissed. The trustees closed certain roads held unnecessary, and the owners of adjoining lots were given the preference of purchase. The sale of this land helped pay off

A respected American citizen in the 1850s and '60s, M. G. Vallejo nevertheless found his vast land holdings challenged on every front. In a letter to his wife in 1864, he wrote, "To remain poor because the most powerful government in the world has squatted on my most valuable pieces of property is not my fault" (Emparan, p. 215).

the town debt.

The United States District Court confirmed the decision of the land commissioners as to Sonoma's boundaries:

> In the west to Sonoma and Agua Caliente creeks, in the east to Arroyo Seco, in the south a line from the Trancas in Sonoma creek, high water mark in Schell creek, and in the north a line extending from the apex of a "prominent hill" lying north from the southwest corner of Lot 544 to the house on the Buena Vista ranch in an easterly direction and by shortest way therefrom to the Agua Caliente creek in a westerly direction.

Sonoma was caused a lot of annoyance in subsequent descriptions and litigation growing out of the fact that there are three "prominent hills" north of Sonoma—the wooded hill back of the General Vallejo home place; Battery Hill, so called because two cannon were originally placed there for the protection of the town when Vallejo first founded the pueblo; and the Jones Hill northeast of the others.

President Rutherford B. Hayes eventually signed the patent quieting title to the land sought by the town.

Sonoma, neglected by the board of supervisors, and with the cities of Santa Rosa, Petaluma and Healdsburg flourishing, decided in 1883 to forget factional squabbles and again incorporate as a municipality. Judge G. A. Johnson sent a copy of the enabling act to Henry Weyl of Sonoma. After conferring with A. F. Haraszthy and Judge F. Breitenbach, these leading citizens decided upon reincorporation, recognizing as in the city limits only the small lots as far south as Germany Street (now MacArthur Street) and also including Mountain Cemetery to the north. All outlots, comprising 32 acres of farming land adjacent to the town, were left out. Having decided on the boundaries, Judge Breitenbach petitioned the supervisors to call an election. The vote was a three-fourths victory for a new municipality which came into being Sept. 3, 1883. A municipality of the sixth class was created under the name City of Sonoma. The people of the pueblo rejoiced.

But as late as 1885 there were bitter and hard-fought land battles. Even the Catholic Cemetery title, originally a part of the Mission San Francisco Solano de Sonoma and agreed upon as part of the church holdings after secularization, was contested. William Pickett, who owned adjoining land, attacked the title. Many who might have testified concerning this land grant

COURTESY, SOCIETY OF CALIFORNIA PIONEERS

M. G. Vallejo is shown here (center) in 1874 dictating his history of California being compiled by Hubert Howe Bancroft. Next to Vallejo is Rosalia Vallejo Leese, his research assistant. Others are, from left, Henry Cerruti, an agent for Bancroft; Don José Abrego, in 1838 Treasurer General of the then independent state of California, and Don Vicente Gomez, another Bancroft associate.

were sleeping in the silent city; but fortunately General Vallejo, who knew the terms under which the church had been put in possession of the land, was a living witness and his testimony in the Sonoma County court won a decision for the church.

Archbishop Joseph Sadoc Alemany secured title for the Catholic church to all the California missions and had sought to have the Mexican government live up to its agreement of 1833 to compensate the Catholic church fund for moneys received after the missions were secularized and their properties sold.

The International Board of Arbitration at the Hague won a final victory for the Catholic churches of California in 1902.

AUTHOR'S NOTE: At age 42, the politically astute and widely respected General Vallejo entered state, and later local, politics. In 1849 he was named a member of California's first constitutional congress. He afterward represented the Sonoma district as a state senator and wrote the history and derivation of names of the various counties of California as set forth in the records today. He even offered lands and money to place the state capital at Benicia, the city named for his beloved wife and a site he believed ideally located for the purpose.

But in the zenith of his glory and munificence, his fortune faded. He had to curtail his prodigal philanthropies. Stripped of land, forced to sue for title to his thousands of acres, unable to recover large sums of money loaned to those he trusted, the old don found himself impoverished. In reduced circumstances he continued to show a fine public spirit and interest in his community. He served for two terms as mayor of Sonoma. Natural living springs on Lachryma Montis were developed as the town water supply, a public utility which in later years further impoverished his family, who could not afford the upkeep and improvements demanded. Mortgages were foreclosed on Vallejo's property; notes he held against men who had become millionaires were repudiated by them. His herds, which had numbered thousands, dwindled to the family cow and one old buckskin horse. "I had my day, a proud one," he would comment to those who came to pay him deference in his declining years.

13 Vallejo Loses Title to Thousands of Acres

A rare photograph of Gen. Mariano G. Vallejo without sideburns. An illness may account for his being clean-shaven here.

AUTHOR'S NOTE: The boundary and land grant questions which led to the disincorporation of the Sonoma pueblo in 1853 and the local land battles were prefaces to the costly court conflicts that were, in a few years, to dispossess General Vallejo of thousands of the acres granted him during his reign as commandante-general of Alta California.

The Treaty of Guadalupe Hidalgo, signed by the U. S. in 1848, supposedly guaranteed the property rights of the native Californians—and there was no bigger property owner than the then wealthy Vallejo. The property rights treaty provision was wantonly violated. Not only were many of his own property titles disallowed by government edict, but squatters were taking over land Vallejo had generously granted to many friends.

As previously noted, the trusting ex-commandante lost much of his fortune due to the greed and bad investments of his own son-in-law, Captain Frisbie, to whom he had inexplicably given full power of attorney in 1850.

General Vallejo was the friend and neighbor of most all the early settlers and seemed never to regret giving away the vast acreage he once owned—a veritable principality. The rich land had proven its fertility, and those who had settled on it years before were prospering. Charles Justi, Joseph Williams, Charles V. Stuart, William McPherson Hill and others received as high as

INDEX-TRIBUNE ARCHIVES

As a result of his many years on horseback, Salvador Vallejo suffered injuries that in later years required him to walk with a cane.

$1.50 each for their first peaches. By 1876 grape growers like Dr. J. B. Warfield had demonstrated what could be done with vines, for the census of 1876 reveals that he made 280,000 gallons of wine on his ranch and 10,000 gallons of brandy. Other lands of the Sonoma Valley were equally productive, and ranchos on which General Vallejo had formerly pastured droves of cattle began to teem with industry and the wealth of a new era.

Land grants and Vallejo's losses

AUTHOR'S NOTE: Charles the Fifth was king of Spain when the daring explorer Hernando Cortez conquered Mexico, land of the Aztec people, and brought to the Spanish sovereigns' rule their first great dominion in the New World. Cortez and

Juan Rodriguez de Cabrillo were believed to be the first explorers to send expeditions north, into what was to become known as California—and claimed for Spain as part of Mexico.

Original title to all land in California was in the name of the king of Spain, and while later held by the mission fathers for the Indians, a few grants were made by the Spanish crown. The ranchos granted while the flag of Spain flew over California were much smaller in area than when Mexico came into power in 1823. After secularization was ordered by Mexico, the spoliation of the mission holdings started, and over 700 vast land grants were recorded.

The Vallejo family members were made many grants—in Sonoma Valley; in the Pajaro Valley, where José Jesus Vallejo, a brother of the General, received the Bolsa de San Cayetano; and in San Francisco, where in 1839, Salvador Vallejo and his brother-in-law, Jacob P. Leese, were given Telegraph Hill. Governor Alvarado had granted them all the land in Yerba Buena along Vallejo, Front, Pacific and Davis Streets. Salvador Vallejo finally transferred his part of the Yerba Buena grant, which had been approved by the Departmental Assembly, to Leese, who experienced much squatter trouble and finally abandoned his waterfront property. Mr. Leese, however, seems to have been exceedingly alert in acquiring rich land in the vicinity of Sonoma, and successfully held on to his Rancho Huichica. By 1839 he was occupying this grant and had 200 acres of his five leagues of land under cultivation. His grant in all comprised 18,704 acres, and with its title confirmed, he was enabled to sell tracts to settlers after the American occupancy.

General Vallejo was less fortunate. Although a native son of California and at one time in control of 7,000,000 acres of land, he would die a poor man. His Sonoma home-place of a few hundred acres was all that remained of his holdings, and over that a mortgage hung for many a moon. Prodigal gifts to those he wished to befriend, and adverse decisions of the land commissioners and United States courts, stripped the proud don, as claimants squatted upon his possessions or brought action in the courts which, time after time, held his titles defective or ruled against him on some technicality.

INDEX-TRIBUNE ARCHIVES

Platon Vallejo with his father, the General.

INDEX-TRIBUNE ARCHIVES

An original letter written July 26, 1880, by M. G. Vallejo to his son Platon describes his birthday gift from Natalia and Attila Haraszthy of ink, pens, a penknife, paper, envelopes, postcards and stamps—an excellent gift for the prolific letter-writer.

For instance, Vallejo's Agua Caliente title was jeopardized because, prior to claiming this grant in Sonoma Valley, he already had in excess of the 11 leagues of land allowed any one claimant. Lazaro Pina, an artillery officer, was originally granted the Agua Caliente acreage. When he abandoned it and went back to Mexico, Vallejo acquired it.

The Agua Caliente grant

The Agua Caliente grant was a piece of land about 10 miles long, and extended up the valley from Sonoma Creek on the west to the hills on the east. Covered with large oaks, red-hued madrones and manzanita, with living springs and streams throughout its length and breadth, and possessed of hot sulphur springs long known as health-giving by the Indians, who bathed in the hot water of the Agua Caliente region, this grant was a beautiful and valuable one.

In 1846 General Vallejo exchanged 1,000 acres of it for piano lessons which Andrew Hoeppner, a music master, agreed to give the Vallejo family. Land was plentiful and money scarce, so the culture-loving Don and Professor Hoeppner signed an agreement giving Hoeppner land in exchange for five years or more of music lessons for the Vallejo children. The children seem to have made the most of their opportunity under the agreement with the music master, for they became good musicians, both boys and girls, and in after years enriched their communities with their talent and culture. (The writer of this story recalls Professor Andronico Vallejo, who gave lessons on the piano in Sonoma in the 1880s. Mrs. Natalia Vallejo Haraszthy, his sister, was also an accomplished pianist.)

The Agua Caliente grant had many prominent and colorful owners. In actions to clear the Agua Caliente title when the Vallejo claim to it was questioned, the names of Jacob Dopkin; Ernest Rufus, soldier under General Sutter and one-time owner of the German grant near Fort Ross; Beasley and Cooper, of the Blue Wing Inn; and Joseph Hooker, the army officer, appear as

INDEX-TRIBUNE ARCHIVES

Joseph Hooker, who was to achieve notoriety as a Civil War general, resided in the Sonoma Valley in the 1850s.

INDEX-TRIBUNE ARCHIVES

The June 15, 1880, *Sonoma Index* reported that "a patent has been granted to Gen. M. G. Vallejo of lands containing about 1,864 acres, and embracing that portion of the Rancho Agua Caliente confirmed to him." Vallejo later sold part of his Agua Caliente ranch to Joseph Hooker, who resided in this cabin, still standing today on the Serres property.

claimants. Hooker, who came to California as a soldier during the Mexican War, bought part of the tract. He laid claim to 550.86 acres.

Professor Hoeppner sold off several portions of the Agua Caliente grant but made good use of the hot springs on the place, for as early as 1847 he advertised the curative waters in the *Californian*. "No more rheumatism," read the advertisement, followed by the line "Warm Spring Annenthal," and the announcement that Andrew Hoeppner had recently fitted up the above medicinal spring for public use.

Alcalde Thaddeus Leavenworth of San Francisco, after whom Leavenworth Street was named, was another owner. He filed claim to 320.33 acres of the ranch in 1853. Titles to all this land were held valid. After Leavenworth came Capt. Henry E. Boyes, an Englishman who had been stationed in India. Boyes developed the hot springs on the property now called Boyes Hot Springs. In the upper valley, on the maps of the Agua Caliente grant, appears the name of William McPherson Hill, who acquired 2,000 acres in 1851.

After Hooker's leave-taking, the Watriss family settled on the Agua Caliente ranch and for years occupied the house which the army officer had fitted up for his use.

AUTHOR'S NOTE: Joseph Hooker, who sold his Agua Caliente rancho acreage to George Watriss and family in 1853, was to become the colorful "Fighting Joe" Hooker of Civil War fame. A West Point graduate, he had served as an adjutant to Gen. Persifor Smith during the Mexican War, 1846–48, rising to the rank of lieutenant colonel, and had joined Smith in Sonoma, where his commanding officer resided.

Bored with the inaction of army life here, Hooker secured a two-year's leave of absence from the army and purchased 550 acres of the original Agua Caliente grant (now the site of the Serres ranch on the west side of Highway 12 near the sheriff's substation). He built a small house and settled in to become a pioneer vineyardist. He liked it so well that on Feb. 1, 1853, he resigned his commission, according to an article by the late J. P. (Toots) Serres in the Sonoma Valley Historical Society publication *Saga of Sonoma*.

However, when the winegrape market became glutted before the year was out and prices fell sharply, Hooker sold to George Watriss. By some arrangement, Hooker continued to occupy the cottage he had built, living on the ranch until 1858. When the Civil War began, he returned to the army and became one of that conflict's most colorful generals.

The Agua Caliente grant, as noted previously, contained an abundance of natural hot springs, which Andrew Hoeppner was the first to advertise for their curative powers as early as 1847. Many years later, through the efforts of Captain Boyes, Theodor Richards and George Fetters, the summer resorts of Boyes, Agua Caliente and Fetters Hot Springs—with their hot tubs, swimming pools, dance pavilions and other vacation facilities—were to become major factors in establishing Sonoma Valley as a popular tourist destination.

*I*n addition to the famous Agua Caliente grant, Vallejo saw other grants slip away from him. His Rancho Yulupa, from which Sonoma mountain rises (Yulupa peak, where the sun goes down in Polynesian splendor), was but a claim of three leagues of land, but it was held invalid because it was not segregated from the public domain when originally granted to one Miguel Alvarado, so a technical land commissioner held.

Another grant, Soscol, in Solano County, given to Vallejo by the governor of California to compensate him for moneys paid from his own pocket for support of the military forces on the northern frontier (including the cost of the Sonoma Barracks, $9,000), was denied because the courts held that the governor had no authority to make land grants in payment of any claims or for money advanced by officials. The towns of Benicia and Vallejo were involved in this decision, for they were founded on land Vallejo had believed was his own and had planned to magnificently endow, should either town become the capital of California.

Then there was the Suisun grant of four leagues, which Vallejo gave to his Indian friend, Chief Solano, in 1842. This rancho was also the subject of long, drawn-out litigation, but the Vallejo title, as it appeared in old abstracts, was at last upheld, and Chief Solano came into his own.

The Petaluma Rancho

*O*ne of the finest grants made to Vallejo was the Petaluma Rancho. While ultimately confirmed to him, this grant led the proud don into many costly court battles, during which time it was neces-

M. G. Vallejo's Petaluma adobe, 10 miles southwest of Sonoma, was a thriving ranch and center of hospitality from the 1830s until sold by Vallejo in 1857. It has been preserved as a state landmark.

sary to mortgage or sacrifice much of his property. The land, extending from Suisun Bay, comprised all the area this side of Petaluma Creek into the hills of Sonoma Valley—a 12-mile strip—75,000 acres of land, assessed in later years for $3,000,000. On this rancho in the early 1840s, Vallejo's great adobe ranch house and the factories and shops of his establishment teemed with life and industry. The spacious house, dominating the landscape, was occupied at intervals by Vallejo and members of his family, and was always at the disposal of guests and travelers, as were most California homes of that day.

At the Petaluma Rancho were Vallejo's overseers, who trained the Indians in many crafts—the weaving of blankets and carpets, the making of saddles and bridles and shoes. Besides these artisans, there were hundreds of Indians employed in the planting and harvesting of crops, such as wheat, and in the curing of hides, the making of lard and tallow, the drying of beef to sell to the Yankees. In a letter written in after years (May 1889) Vallejo recalled the rich harvests of former seasons and said of the great rancho:

My harvest productions were so large that my storehouses were literally overfilled every year. In one wing of my house upstairs I lived with my family when we were in the Petaluma Valley. The south front was 250 feet and formed a large square, the house having an immense inner courtyard where every morning the laborers met and called the roll before dispersing for their various occupations.

The General at home in 1886.

The house was two stories high, and very solid, made of adobe and timbers brought by oxen from the redwoods and planed for use by the old-fashioned saw by four Kanakas (my servants) brought from the Sandwich Islands by my brother-in-law, Captain Cooper. It had wide corridors, inside and outside, some of which were carpeted by our own make of carpets. I sold the house to Mr. White about 20 years ago for $25,000.

Vallejo might have also recalled the fact that his ranch, during one *matanza* (butchering) season, yielded him revenue from as many as 8,000 three-year-old steers, approximately $80,000; the hides brought $16,000, and sales of wheat added more to his magnificent income.

The lordly adobe building between Sonoma and Petaluma [now a state landmark] dominates the countryside, with its imposing veranda and time-scarred walls. Within its hospitable portals the family of ex-Governor Lilburn Boggs of Missouri (later, a Sonoma alcalde), who arrived from across the plains in 1846, found shelter. William M. Boggs, his son, wrote:

On arrival in the night at this ranch, General Vallejo, who had gone ahead of our worn-out teams, had aroused the Indian servants to prepare supper for us. The tables were spread with linen tablecloths, sperm candles were in the chandeliers, and we had a regular Spanish-cooked meal, wholesome and plenty of it. With Spanish hos-

pitality, the General presided at the table, helping all the large family. After supper he handed Mrs. Boggs a large bunch of keys to the various rooms and assigned one large, well-furnished apartment to my wife and me. In this old adobe, Jan. 4, 1847, our eldest son was born. A few weeks after the young immigrant's birth, and while I was at Yerba Buena—an enlisted soldier in the war against Mexico—General Vallejo paid the baby gringo a visit. He was much interested in the youngster and inquired his name. He was named Guadalupe Vallejo Boggs.

The boy is said to have been the first white child born under the American flag in California. One or two female children were born in Sutter's Fort, probably before or about this time, said William Boggs.

Attacked right and left by avaricious land grabbers, forced into costly litigation and contests, Vallejo continued to befriend settlers and newcomers to the California he loved, despite the times and all its harsh exactions. Even when heavy losses were apparent and he had been the victim of a number of cruel decisions, he said, "Land is plentiful. God made it for us and I have plenty of it yet."

Vallejo's passing

AUTHOR'S NOTE: After a long illness, General Vallejo breathed his last breath at 1:30 in the morning darkness of Jan. 18, 1890, with his wife, Francisca, and eight of his children at his bedside. According to historian Hunter, it was 12-year-old Celeste Granice—who would grow up to be the editor of the *Index-Tribune*—who carried the news of Vallejo's death to her father at the newspaper.

The story of Vallejo's death appeared in the January 18 issue of the *I-T*. Heavy, black column rules, an editorial custom reserved for very prominent citizens, dominated the page.

The funeral services for Sonoma's founder and most prominent don in California history took place on January 21, an overcast and

INDEX-TRIBUNE ARCHIVES

gloomy day—as gloomy as the mood of the Sonoma citizenry over the loss of their distinguished resident. The flags were at half-staff, schools and businesses closed.

His body lay in state in the parlor of the family home. To the strains of Chopin's "Funeral March" played by a military band sent from the San Francisco Presidio, the General's body was borne from the house, down the tree-lined lane, to St. Francis Solano Church for the funeral Mass. En route to Mountain Cemetery, the funeral entourage made a memorial stop in front of the Barracks.

That brief stop was a trip back in time some 50 years, when a young Mariano Guadalupe Vallejo was reaping the benefits of influence and land acquisitions that led to great personal wealth.

But, alas! The casket contained the remains not of a rich prince, but of a pauper. Vallejo may have been a most effective military officer, astute politician and respected representative of the Mexican government. His ability to acquire property can not be denied. His respect for Americans and the United States, even after the Bear Flag incident, and his influence in fostering communication between the Yankee conquerors and the vanquished were widely acknowledged.

But it was his flaws that were responsible for Vallejo's being rendered penniless. Chief among these flaws appear to have been a lack of business sense and putting too much trust in his fellow man, particularly one man, his son-in-law John B. Frisbie. Also, Vallejo seemed to be unaware that there was a limit to the amount of land that he could give away, mortgage or sell. And when ruthless decisions by the U. S. Land Grant Commission invalidated claims to leagues of land long in his possession, his losses multiplied.

From 1850, when Frisbie acquired his father-in-law's power of attorney, Vallejo's holdings and wealth steadily dwindled as Frisbie sold off or mortgaged the General's properties. Even the family home was mortgaged. The mortgage

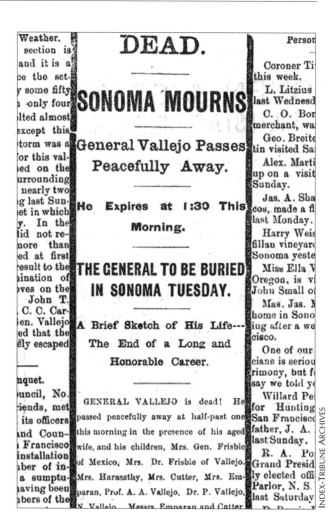

At the time of Mariano G. Vallejo's death in 1890, few Sonoma Valley residents knew what a pivotal role he had played in California's history. When his wife, Francisca, died the following year, her obituary in the *Index-Tribune* stated that "when [Vallejo] passed away ... his only inheritance to his aged wife and children was an honored name."

was eventually paid, but the Lachryma Montis property was Vallejo's only holding at the time of his death.

Perhaps a Mr. John R. McCauley of Alameda, in a letter published in the *Sonoma Index*, said it best in paying a tribute to General Vallejo:

"No unsavory record will ever taint the memory of this great man. ... At one time the richest Californian ... but he gave and gave, till he had nothing to give. ..."

14 Our Wine Industry's Roots

COURTESY, BARTHOLOMEW PARK WINERY MUSEUM

Photographer Edweard Muybridge visited the Sonoma Valley in the 1870s and photographed workers in the Buena Vista Viticultural Society vineyards. Agoston Haraszthy's villa is visible in the background.

As early as 1836, when Richard Henry Dana sailed before the mast and visited California, he observed that easy-going Californians bought many puncheons of inferior wine made in New England or Europe. They paid a fancy price for the shipment, although California had thousands of acres of fertile land and climate so favorable to grape growing that it might fill the cellars of the world. Thus a far-seeing Yankee was quick to observe and envision the viticultural possibilities of the hills and valleys of California; yet it was years before Sonoma, natural home of the vine and destined area of famous vineyards, realized the possibilities of the great wine industry, the fame and wealth it would bring.

Little dreamed the pioneer planters of the magnitude which this industry finally achieved following the unexpected blight of phylloxera, a parasite which attacked the grapevine roots; the triumph and recovery after vast losses and the devastation of thousands of acres; replanting and almost fabulous fortunes made from grapes and wine, only to be subjected later to the colossal blunder of Prohibition at terrific cost.

The mission fathers originally set out grapes in California, the limited plantings in the vicinity of the missions being made from cuttings brought from Spain. Sonoma's Mission had vineyards throughout its 14 acres, and the reddish soil, so like that of the wine-producing hills of Europe, was quick in bearing. The Indians labored in the vineyard, and the tilling of the soil, irrigating of the vines, picking of the grapes and crushing of the juice kept them busy from early spring until the bounteous fall.

Wine making was at first crude as in the peasant districts of Europe. The Indians tramped out juice in cowhide bags, and after fermentation the wines revealed unusual character and, with age, became magnificent. Worldwide travelers even then acclaimed them. The tang of the soil, in which had grown madrone and manzanita, bay and laurel, gave the red wines of Sonoma hills bouquet and color hard to equal. Demand for California wine was evident from the start.

Salvador Vallejo planted a vineyard in the foothills east of the Sonoma Mission close to a creek, water then held so necessary for irrigation. The site later became the nucleus of the Buena Vista Viticultural Society, embracing hundreds of acres of the most productive grape land in the state of California. Vallejo sold this vineyard to a prospector named Benjamin Kelsey, who had returned from the mines with plenty of gold dust. The place was promptly christened Kelsey's Vineyard and was the scene of California's first Methodist camp meeting in 1835. A lawyer named Julius K. Rose also owned the property, and all made money from the crops, although the custom of irrigating the vines precluded more extensive planting.

From rocky hillsides to the Mission's portals, luscious grapes developed, their foliage green in summer and riotous with the red and yellow tints of fall. The yield was uniformly good, and planting extended to other sections of this favored valley. General Vallejo planted a few acres at Lachryma Montis, and by 1850 a three-acre vineyard yielded several thousand dollars. In time his wines were winning honors, and among proud relics of the old grandee are numerous premiums and medals, also a solid silver pitcher, a State Fair trophy for his finest claret.

Colonel Haraszthy's great influence

Then came Col. Agoston Haraszthy to Sonoma Valley, a Hungarian of noble birth whose family had been through the throes of political upheaval in the Old World. He came to America to win new

Count Agoston Haraszthy was known as the "Father of California Viticulture." After 57 years of remarkable and lasting achievements, he died in Nicaragua, reportedly killed by a crocodile.

INDEX-TRIBUNE ARCHIVES

fame and fortune. In the late 1850s he arrived in California and, hearing of the vineyards Vallejo and others had developed in the Sonoma Valley, was much interested, for his native land had also grown grapes, particularly tokays.

Haraszthy was delighted and surprised to find the soil of Sonoma Valley so like that of the Old World's most famed grape sections. He was satisfied that the land would not only grow good grapes but would grow them without irrigation. He promptly invested in a vineyard at Buena

INDEX-TRIBUNE ARCHIVES

Agoston Haraszthy's villa at Buena Vista.

INDEX-TRIBUNE ARCHIVES

A replica of the Haraszthy Villa, completed in 1989 by the late Antonia Bartholomew as a memorial to her husband, Frank H. Bartholomew, and Colonel Haraszthy, is a centerpiece of Bartholomew Memorial Park at Buena Vista.

Vista, one mile east of Sonoma, and demonstrated the truth of his theory. He envisioned the golden future which would dawn on the mission settlement if choice cuttings could be brought from famed European localities to take root in the soil of California and become the foundation of vast wine-making enterprises.

With keen initiative and enthusiasm, Haraszthy went before the California legislature and agriculture department at Sacramento and convinced the state that potential wealth lay in the vineyard lands of California. He commended grapes as the one crop which could be grown with profit in red and rocky soil where little else would thrive. He outlined the vast business that could be developed.

So impressive was his presentation at the state capital that the legislature and Gov. J. G. Downey empowered the Sonoma grapegrower and prophet to make an official trip abroad for the purpose of investigating every wine-producing country, their methods of vine culture and wine making, and varieties of juice grapes, to the end that California might make extensive plantings and also become a wine-producing center. Haraszthy followed up his commission with zeal and enthusiasm and, after bidding his family and friends adieu, left San Francisco on the steamer *Golden Age* for New York, a journey of 24 days.

On July 6, 1861, he reached Washington, D.C. Senators Latham and McDougal presented Colonel Haraszthy, of Sonoma, to the Hon.

William H. Seward, secretary of state, who gave the ambassador of goodwill a letter to diplomatic agents abroad and to consuls in the foreign countries. The letter read:

> Department of State
> Washington, D.C.
> 6th of July, 1861
>
> Mr. A. Haraszthy, the bearer of this communication, has been appointed by the government of the State of California to proceed abroad for the purpose of collecting information in regard to wine-producing countries, and reporting the results of his observations and inquiries to that government.
> I will consequently thank you to extend to him any facilities which may be necessary for so important an object.
> I am your obedient servant,
>
> William H. Seward

After Haraszthy reached Europe, he made first-hand inspection of all the leading wine regions. The California emissary visited botanical gardens and nurseries, where he selected the most famous varieties of grape cuttings. In the Côte d'Or district of France, he tasted what he regarded as the most elegant of all wines sampled, and said of that locality:

> The soil here is red and gravelly, containing a good deal of limestone, sim-

ilar to our Sonoma soil which exists in almost every county of the state, and millions of acres of it. The redder the soil, the better the wine.

Weather varied in the wine countries of Europe during the vintage season, and dampness often caused great loss or inferior crops. Haraszthy, recalling Sonoma Valley's fine vintage weather, the Indian summers with warm dry days, the hills aglow at sunset with the ruby tint of the wine, was more anxious than ever to see the state launch this highly profitable and interesting grape-growing industry.

In Germany he visited a leading champagne manufacturer and found that the proprietor, Herman Dresel, was a brother of one of his neighbors in Sonoma, Emil Dresel, whose vineyard adjoined his own in the moonlit valley of California. Through Herman Dresel all the varieties of vines entering into champagne making were arranged for and also many implements necessary in the manufacture of the sparkling wine.

In Spain he bargained for several thousand trees and cuttings of vines and plants which would assure California the best olives, pomegranates, oranges, figs, lemons and other fruits. All these were to be shipped to California from Le Havre in France.

Italy's primitive farming methods astounded the traveler. He found the famed Asti and its hills similar to Telegraph Hill in size. After inspecting the grapes grown there, Haraszthy remarked, "The Asti vines will improve in our red soil." The success in later years of the great Asti Colony in Sonoma County, where Tipo Chianti and other wines were produced, proved the prediction. Italy's wine-making methods did not impress the traveler.

Haraszthy was also much annoyed by repeated allusions to the banditry and lawlessness of California, which seemed to be about all the Old World had heard of the land where gold was discovered. "If the press would bestow the same labor in statistical reports as they do in reporting and writing up crimes, I warrant that in a short time California and its great and varied wealth would be truly known all over Europe," commented the commissioner.

California's legislature met the following

Map showing Haraszthy's travels in Europe.

INDEX-TRIBUNE ARCHIVES

January, welcomed Haraszthy home and received his comprehensive report, but no compensation was granted through state appropriation. Mr. Haraszthy scoffed at the suggestion of a skeptical state senator that wine production might be overdone in California, pointing out that a worldwide market existed for a product which could not be excelled. Native California wines had the rare quality of keeping well during shipment. They could be exported and kept sound without a drop of brandy for fortifying—an unusual and valuable attribute, explained the expert.

Colonel Haraszthy had a number of enthusiastic Sonoma neighbors, for prior to his trip abroad he had subdivided and planted vineyards which he sold on contract, agreeing to care for the vines for several years. Newcomers seemed well pleased with the outlook.

Among men who helped finance the vast Buena Vista vineyards was Maj. Jacob R. Snyder. His extensive holdings in other localities were sold and the money diverted to the grape and wine enterprise in the Valley of the Moon. The Society of California Pioneers has the original records of many of these transactions, and in a "Memorial of Major Snyder" was printed an allusion to the prominent part this early-day capitalist played in the development of Sonoma as a wine-producing

INDEX-TRIBUNE ARCHIVES

Nicholas Carriger

INDEX-TRIBUNE ARCHIVES

Jacob Snyder

center. Said the Pioneer Society's *Bulletin*:

> He was one of the first to make wine in the valley and his wines (never sold until they were five years old) were among the finest in California, taking medals at the Mechanics Fair and at the State Fairs. The eastern distribution of his wines was in the hands of his several partners, located in Saint Louis. He remained in Sonoma, at work early and late, understanding, superintending every detail of the care of his vineyards and winery. His great stone cellar had a capacity of 300,000 gallons and was three stories high. That his investments in Sonoma Valley were very large is shown by his records in connection with the sale of his extensive real estate holdings in Sacramento, San Francisco and Santa Cruz, and the notation which followed each sale: "The money derived from the sale of these properties was reinvested in my vineyard at Sonoma."

It was not long before Haraszthy, prophet and pioneer in the viticultural industry, beheld the Sonoma foothills even to their topmost ridges cultivated with the choicest vines, and on the sloping hillsides great buildings to house the ruby caber-

net, the golden Johannisberg, the sparkling champagne. Massive cellars from the stone of Sonoma hills were built. Three tunnels, 100 feet long, ran into the Buena Vista hills for the storing and the aging of various wines. The champagne house was modeled after the most famous of Europe, and a vintner was imported to superintend the manufacture of champagne. The Buena Vista Viticultural Association gave work to many people, some being employed in the making of willow baskets for the wine, the willow being obtained from the creek on the Sonoma property. By 1874 there were 30,000 bottles of sparkling champagne aging in the tunnels of the Sonoma hills, and Haraszthy champagne was on the market, acclaimed by connoisseurs.

In later years the wine tunnels caved in, burying countless pints and quarts, so it is said.

Major Snyder and Colonel Haraszthy were not the only ones who brought fame to Sonoma Valley through grape growing. Prominent on the honor roll were men like Jacob Gundlach, Charles Bundschu, Emil and Gustav Dresel, and later Carl Dresel. The hardy pioneer Nicholas Carriger was among the first settlers to return from the mines after the discovery of gold and to announce that he was through with the uncertain fortune of mining and would go to farming. On his ranch in the western foothills he planted a vineyard, hav-

Champagne bottling at Haraszthy's vineyard in the early 1870s. The bottles were packed in wicker baskets made from local willow trees.

ing been quick to observe what Salvador Vallejo had accomplished on the other side of the valley. Thousands of gallons of wine and brandy were finally made by Carriger and stored in a massive cellar of stone and redwood that is believed to be standing today.

The costly ravages of phylloxera

In 1876 Sonoma Valley alone produced 2,335,000 gallons of wine. That figure dropped significantly in succeeding years. By 1901 only 5,000,000 gallons were produced in all of Sonoma County, and wine production in the entire state dropped to just 30,000,000 gallons. The ravages of phylloxera caused the drop in production. The growers faced a battle for existence when vineyards began to die from an unknown parasite, and grower after grower felt impoverishment.

While the disease of the vines was not confined to California, having been noted also in eastern grape centers, it was most pronounced in Sonoma Valley. As early as 1860 Colonel Haraszthy reported that he had been puzzled by

the dying of vines. When the prevalence of the blight became general and the whole state was alarmed, the legislature appointed a committee to investigate and report on the vine pest, its cause and origin.

In 1873 samples of vine roots from the O. W. Craig vineyard near El Verano in the Sonoma Valley revealed an insect held responsible for the great losses which the growers reported, as hundreds of acres of vineyard died off in this and other valleys. The Committee of Phylloxera Vine Pests and Diseases of the Vine of the State Viticultural Commission took up the matter and employed Horace Appleton of Sonoma and F. W. Morse of the University of California to make a detailed investigation. They finally made positive identification of the phylloxera pest and discovered that the disease had affected eastern grapes even prior to California plantings, and had caused millions of dollars worth of damage in France and other European countries.

Before the discovery of the cause and the knowledge of a resistant stock impervious to the pest, every vineyard in Sonoma and Napa was laid waste and a great industry was practically destroyed. A conservative estimate, declared a

Professor Bussman of the agricultural department, indicated that the phylloxera pest caused a loss of $1,000 per day to the growers as it swept the vineyards of this state.

Experiments, many of which were failures, were made to indicate just what resistant vines could be planted to withstand the scourge. Finally Dresel and Gundlach demonstrated the fitness and adaptability of some resistant stock for the Sonoma locality.

With advice from the state, the University of California and also the United States Department of Agriculture, which maintained experimental vineyards, replanting went forward and grape growing revived.

Pioneers beat pest, wines gain fame

*I*n reviewing the rise and fall of the vineyard industry and the tenacity of purpose which the

Grape phylloxera

pioneer grapegrowers and settlers of Sonoma Valley evinced in the face of ruin, the late Charles Bundschu recalled the following names of some of his associates in the battle: Aguillon, Appleton, Boyes, Cady, Chauvet, Clark, Craig, Davisson, Dowdall, Dresel, Drummond, Duhring, Enos, Erlich, Gundlach, Hall, Haraszthy, Haubert, Heller, Hood, Hooper, Hyde, Justi, Kohler,

The Gundlach family: (left to right) Freda, Carl, Rosa Gundlach Dresel, Heinie, patriarch Jacob, Bertha, Eva, Charles Bundschu and Francisca Gundlach Bundschu.

Leiding, Lounibos, Luttrell, McElroy, McEwen, Monahan, Nunn, Pickett, Poppe, Sears, Shaw, Sheppard, Snyder, Spencer, Steiger, Stier, Stuart, Thompson, Watriss, Watson, Wegener, Weil, Weise, Williams and Winkle. He could have mentioned many more who shared in the varying fortunes of the valley of the many moons.

> Then winter comes upon us,
>   with dreary days and cold,
> But we have the blood of Bacchus,
>   and the thoughts of days of old;
> And our hearts are filled with gladness,
>   though for summer we may pine,
> As we pass around the beaker,
>   singing praise of ruby wine.
>   — from a Bacchus Club song

Perhaps a less hardy generation would have abandoned hope after the vineyards were laid to waste in the late 1870s, but not so with the pioneer growers who settled the Sonoma region. They fought their way out and triumphed. The names

identified with the early history of the vine will ever be associated with industry, thrift, good cheer, genial friendships, hospitality and busy harvest seasons as old Bacchus finally looked down from the hillsides where flamed the tokays, and smiled with satisfaction as wine presses yielded bountifully and stalwart men grew rich.

All California shared in the industry's eventual triumph. By 1893, at the World's Fair in Chicago, 53 exhibitors from California displayed 301 varieties of wine and 33 distinct types. There were shown 143 varieties of white wine; 12 of red; 117 of sweet wine such as Malaga, muscatel and tokay; five kinds of sparkling wine and 44 kinds of grape brandies.

The Gundlach, Bundschu and Dresel families had many joyous vintage festivals on Rhine Farm to celebrate their success in conquering phylloxera and bringing back a bounteous yield to the hillsides of their homes. The Bacchus Club of Rhine Farm was organized in 1897, and, for several years, plays written by members of the family, and

Rhine Farm's Pansy Valley in 1898, a natural amphitheater for early vintage festivals.

COURTESY, GUNDLACH-BUNDSCHU WINERY

An early Gundlach-Bundschu poster

for which talented ones contributed verse in praise of wine, were produced at the farm.

The vintage festivals of the hills, with pageantry and song, goatherds, nymphs and the altar of Bacchus; and the hot spiced wine proffered to those who joined in the moonlit celebrations of the harvest season will ever remain a cherished memory of participants. The "Rhine Farm Song" for Sonoma's Bacchus Club, written by Ben Weed, who married Eva Gundlach, daughter of the pioneer vintner, is recalled:

> Fill the bowl with ruby wine,
> Round its rim the ivy twine,
> Pledge the god of Joy and Pleasure,
> Giver of the fruitful vine.
> On the old Rhine Farm so fair,
> Where we're freed from every care
> And we drink the richest vintage
> Of her vineyards old and rare.

At many expositions Sonoma Valley wines took honors and won premiums. The vintage of the Dresel vineyards won first prize at the Saint Louis fair.

At the Paris Exposition in 1900, medals, including the gold medal of highest award, were conferred upon the California Chambertin of the Gundlach-Bundschu firm, but these elegant wines and others are but memories. Their death knell was Prohibition.

The art of wine making, the part played in their excellence by old Father Time, the appreciation of the precious bits of earth, described by Robert Louis Stevenson in his *Silverado Squatters* as virtual bonanzas "where the soil has sublimated under sun and stars" to something finer than poetry itself, in the juice of the grape, again points to Sonoma Valley as the chosen spot of the vine.

An industry which has weathered two cataclysms of the proportion experienced by the grape and wine business, one of nature and one of fanatical man, an industry whose quantity production of new wines can bring the success achieved by Sonoma's late wine magnate and capitalist, Samuele Sebastiani, has a future already maturing. Sebastiani's enterprise and the golden era it has brought to the pueblo is but a forerunner of other successes. If Robert Louis Stevenson was right, Sonoma Valley holds the key not only to a prosperous ever-expanding industry, but to a golden age and renascence of grape culture.

The Buena Vista viticultural property and its great cellars and tunnels in the hills were initially restored by Frank Bartholomew, president of the United Press, who purchased the Buena Vista ranch in 1943 and replanted the vast vineyard. Wine was again being produced there after a lapse of 50 years.

Sonoma Valley held its first annual vintage festival since Prohibition in 1947, accentuating the historical background of the pueblo and recalling the Bacchus festivals of long ago at Rhine Farm.

AUTHOR'S NOTE: It should be noted that the foregoing chapter on the development of Sonoma's wine industry was written by author Celeste Murphy in the 1948 (last) edition of *The People of the Pueblo*. Since then, a remarkable growth in local wines and vines has taken place. Sebastiani Vineyards has become one of the largest wine producers in the U. S. Buena Vista Winery and Rhine Farm (now Gundlach-

Bundschu) have greatly expanded. And they are just three of some 36 wineries now located in the Valley.

The Gundlach-Bundschu and Dresel cellars on old Rhine Farm, dismantled after the enactment of the 18th Amendment, were reborn in 1971 when Jim Bundschu returned the historic winery to production again. The Rhine Farm vineyards had continued to bear premium grapes after Prohibition under the guiding hands of Jim's grandfather and father, Walter and Towle Bundschu.

The Bartholomews had purchased the 641-acre property (Buena Vista ranch) in December 1943 from the State of California at an auction. The property had previously been used as a state industrial farm for delinquent women. The Bartholomews' high bid of $17,600 was accepted, and it was several months later before they learned they had purchased one of the great legends of the wine industry—Col. Agoston Haraszthy's Buena Vista Viticultural Society vineyards and winery site.

After her husband left to cover the war in the Pacific for United Press International, Antonia (Toni) Bartholomew read up on everything she could find about Haraszthy, the history of the old vineyards and restoration of the vines. She was committed to seeing an old acre of zinfandel vines bearing grapes by the next fall, but she was frustrated by wartime conditions and her inability to hire workers for her ambitious vineyards project. She concluded one letter describing her problems to her war-correspondent husband overseas thusly: "Come home, you coward."

INDEX-TRIBUNE ARCHIVES

Frank and Antonia Bartholomew bought 435 acres of the former Buena Vista estate of Agoston Haraszthy, hardly knowing the property's history.

15 Early-Day Transportation

INDEX-TRIBUNE ARCHIVES

In the 1870s Sonoma travelers went by stage to Lakeville to board the *Antelope* for San Francisco, then three hours away.

AUTHOR'S NOTE: Early-day transportation to and from Sonoma Valley was by foot, canoe, horseback, stagecoach, a variety of sailing and steam-powered vessels and, eventually, limited rail service starting in the 1870s. The Valley's somewhat isolated location north of the San Francisco Bay affected the quality and mode of transportation. Even today the Valley of the Moon could be considered somewhat off the beaten track—not close to major highways, ports or air terminals—which many say accounts for Sonoma's "unspoiled" appeal and charm.

Schooners and captains

It was in November 1847 that a major trans-portation breakthrough occurred, with the inauguration of service proved by the 37-foot-long paddle-wheel steamer *Sitka,* originally built in Alaska as a pleasure craft for the Russian officers there. The regular passenger service between San Francisco and Sonoma was a cause for a local celebration reported in the San Francisco-based *Californian,* the item noting that toasts were given to the "rival towns of Sonoma and San Francisco."

The boat landing here was then known as Embarcadero, or Saint Louis, now known as the Wingo and Schellville areas.

In December 1847 the name of another craft sailing on schedules for Sonoma appeared in the shipping advertisements of the *Californian.* The

COURTESY, MILLERICK FAMILY

"The steamer *Sonoma* was compelled to cast anchor five miles off San Francisco during the severe storm last Friday evening. ... The passengers report the trip as rather risky." Jan. 15, 1880, *Sonoma Index.*

sloop *Stockton,* a "fast-sailing" vessel of which Captain Briggs was master, made the trips to Sonoma. "Fast-sailing" implied an all-day voyage from San Francisco, provided the tides were favorable; otherwise, passengers would find themselves high and dry on the mud banks of the sloughs. But accommodations such as the little boats provided were revelations to an age in ignorance of big liners, motorboats, streamlined trains, high-powered cars and great bay bridges. When at last the steamer *James M. Donahue* was put on the run to Sonoma via the Sonoma landing, that was believed to be the last word in transportation. Coupled with a good stagecoach, it satisfied the town for years.

AUTHOR'S NOTE: Other early-day names connected with ship transportation here included that of a Capt. Charles Justi, a pioneer resident of the Glen Ellen area. His vessels, operating during the period from 1850 to 1865, were the *Georgina* and the *Princess,* according to records of the N. W. P. Railway Company. In 1863 two brothers, John J. and Peter Stofen, actively engaged in freight and passenger hauling between Sonoma Valley and San Francisco. In 1874 they built, in company with William Green and others, the stern-wheel steamer *Sonoma,* extending freight and passenger service. Later, the Stofens put into service two sloops, the *Alice Stofen* and the *Gazelle.*

Of later vintage was the small combined power and sail schooner *Four Sisters,* which specialized in the shipping of fruit from the Valley and continued service until about 1898, owned and skippered by Capt. Peter Hauto. According to Louis Green, in *Saga of Sonoma* (pp. 7–8), Captain Hauto and the *Four Sisters* marked the last of regularly scheduled water transportation between the Valley and San Francisco.

COURTESY, ROBERT D. PARMELEE

The "mud wagon," drawn by a team of four horses, connected Sonoma to Santa Rosa in the 1870s. In the background of this 1879 photograph, the outline of the Mission is barely visible, and cattle can be seen grazing on the Plaza.

After stagecoach days

The year 1869 was one of prophetic import in the development of the West. That communities must have railroads to succeed was the general verdict.

Proud stage drivers, including those in the vicinity of Sonoma like Pat McAndrews and wise-cracking Jim Albertson, who handled the ribbons on six or eight horses, were the last ones to see that the day was fast coming when they would be deposed. They were far too busy looking after their teams and schedules as hoop skirts, linen dusters and carpet bags arrived and departed.

Tony Oakes' Union Hotel was the stopping place of the stages in Sonoma in the 1860s. Although Napa was but 12 miles distant, the stage carrying the mails there departed just once a week and took five hours to make the trip. Sonoma Valley clamored for better service and criticized the slow-going boats which met the stages on the trips to and from San Francisco. The "old tubs" were bitterly attacked in the papers of

the day, for it seemed that all the old derelicts of the waterfront were pressed into service for the Sonoma run.

Freight was handled from Embarcadero (near Schellville) by horses and ox teams, and Broadway, the main thoroughfare to Sonoma, was rough and dusty in summer and full of chuckholes and mudholes in the winter, sometimes under water as creeks overflowed. With the volume of business developed by grapegrowers and the growth of the basalt block industry as San Francisco paving contractors began the purchase of thousands of basalt blocks from Sonoma quarries, the Valley of the Moon finally saw the start of its first railroad.

Advent of the railroad

In 1875 the Sonoma Valley Prismoidal Railway Company was organized to build a single-track railroad from Norfolk, on Steamboat Slough off Sonoma Creek, to Sonoma, six miles distant. The road was built as far as Schellville but found

COURTESY, ROBERT D. PARMELEE

A single-track prismoidal railroad—so named for its prism-shaped wooden track—provided Sonoma Valley with its first rail service in 1876. Here, a drawing from a stock prospectus depicts the railway's terminal at Norfolk. The 3½-mile railway ran from a slough on Sonoma Creek through the marshes to a site near present-day Schellville. A narrow-gauge railroad followed only a few years later.

impractical, for its odd construction made it impossible to cross a wagon road, and so work was halted and a narrow-gauge railroad determined upon instead. Theodore Schell, after whom the station Schellville was named, was prominent in the promotion of this road, which ran through his thousand-acre ranch bordering the marshes southeast of Sonoma. Schell had been a supercargo on the old bark *Anahauc* and in that capacity had visited Sonoma as early as 1849, buying produce and trading with the merchants and farmers. He later became a purser of the Pacific Mail Steamship Company. In 1860 he purchased 1,400 acres of land in Sonoma Valley, convinced that all this section needed was better communication.

In 1878 the Prismoidal railway experiment was succeeded by the Sonoma Valley Railroad Company, which extended its line from Norfolk to Vineyard Station near the John Batto ranch. The new company built a wharf on Steamboat Slough and there maintained a freight terminal. It was hoped to extend the line from the mouth of Petaluma Creek into Sonoma city. While considering these improvements, the railroad sold its stock to Peter M. Donahue, San Francisco capitalist, in 1879, and he completed the narrow-gauge from Norfolk to Sonoma. A year later the line was extended to San Pablo Bay, and a landing, known as Sonoma Landing, where the steamer *James M. Donahue* carried freight and passengers to and from San Francisco, became the railroad terminal.

When the first narrow-gauge engine pulled

into Sonoma, General Vallejo and his family greeted it with warm enthusiasm, decorated the engine smokestack with evergreen garlands and flowers, and felicitated the company and crew. The little engine was called *The General Vallejo,* and Sam Lewis was the engineer. In those days the train came along Spain Street past the crumbling Mission church, where services were regularly held; but due to the dilapidated condition of the Mission and the noise of a railroad puffing and rattling by the place of worship, the resident priest and Archbishop Alemany of the diocese agreed that it would be best to sell the Mission property and consecrate new ground for the Sonoma church, to be dedicated to Saint Francis of Solano. In May 1881 the church sold its mission property to businessman Solomon Schocken of Sonoma.

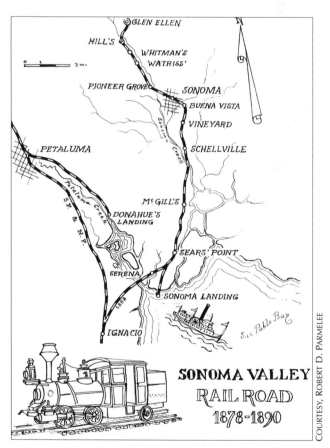

COURTESY, ROBERT D. PARMELEE

Sonoma Valley railroad service in 1878–90. "When [the narrow-gauge railroad] is finished, passengers from San Francisco will be able to reach Sonoma in two hours and a quarter, thus opening to travel one of the pleasantest routes from the city, and bringing within easy access one of the most picturesque and salubrious valleys in this state." April 10, 1880, *Sonoma Index,* quoting the *San Francisco Bulletin.*

INDEX-TRIBUNE ARCHIVES

In the 1880s, this eyesore on the north side of the Plaza turned the incoming train around at the track's terminus.

ARRIVAL OF TRAIN AT
EL VERANO, CAL. 7.

COURTESY, SONOMA VALLEY HISTORICAL SOCIETY

The arrival of the train at El Verano, circa 1889.

The advent of the railroad into Sonoma was not a bed of roses, even though the Vallejo family paid its floral tribute. A number of prominent old residents of the town fought the coming of the trains and defended the stagecoach days. They predicted that the railroad would take business out of town and declared that the tracks and the "iron hoss" ruined the appearance of Spain Street, where old adobes were strangely at variance with the changing scene. One vehement objector went so far as to tear up the ties in front of his property and threatened both railroad superintendent and employees with guns and injunctions.

To circumvent open hostilities and get Sonoma's first train over the road as scheduled, the section men worked all one night, with the result that the train pulled into town as promised before the astonished opposition could prevent it. A depot, workshops, round house, water tank and other buildings were erected on the historic plaza. The railroad continued to operate on Spain Street until Henry Weyl, property owner and city trustee, won a suit in 1886 against the Donahue railroad and forced the company to get new rights-of-way on the outskirts of town. Paved streets today obliterate every trace of the railroad ties which ired the old-timers.

In 1890 the railroad was broad-gauged from Sears Point to Glen Ellen, the Sonoma depot being erected on the northerly side of town "far from the madding crowd," but past the gateway of General Vallejo's always friendly homestead.

The Northern Pacific Railroad Company, afterward the California Northwestern and Northwestern Pacific, effected many improvements, connecting the Sonoma branch, at Ignacio, to the main line whose terminus was Healdsburg, Ukiah and finally Eureka. A drawbridge was built across the wide waterway, Petaluma Creek, at Black Point to accommodate freight and passenger trains to and from Sonoma Valley points.

Sonoma city had further opportunity from the Southern Pacific Company about 1888, when it was proposed to build a connection of that road from the main Sacramento line via Napa to Sonoma Valley and Santa Rosa. Sonoma citizens called a mass meeting to urge the establishment of a depot in Sonoma, but when it developed that fully $10,000 would be required to assure the Southern Pacific station and rights-of-way, enthu-

Constructed for picnickers when the railroad came to Sonoma, the Sonoma Plaza pavilion (later used as a city hall) was completed in November 1880. "The building is octagonal in shape, with a diameter of 70 feet and circumference of 220 feet. Height of ceiling, 16 feet. ... The building cost over $1,600, all of which is paid for," reported the Nov. 13, 1880, *Sonoma Index*.

siasm waned. The railroad therefore went ahead with prior plans, secured rights-of-way on the outskirts south and west of town, and built a pretentious depot called El Verano, two miles west of Sonoma.

In the late 1880s, El Verano became a boom town and for a time had the proud old pueblo of Sonoma much flustered over its seeming success. Promoters transformed the Craig ranch into a real-estate tract, sold town lots like hotcakes, built two-story residences and offered them for sale, put up a brick hotel block and started *The Sonoma Valley Whistle*, a weekly newspaper, "very shortly to become a semi-weekly." It was not long, however, before the boom went the way of other "blow-outs," and the *Whistle*, after a blast or two, was stilled forever. The rural charm of El Verano, however, continued to abide, and it won continued popularity as a summer recreation spot, with many family resorts popularized by the advertising of the Northwestern Pacific railroad, which established a depot called Verano a mile east of the Southern Pacific station.

Meanwhile, Sonoma maintained connections with the rival Southern Pacific town via a two-horse bus that carried the mail and railroad passengers which smiling Joe Ryan, diminutive Willie Peterson or the keen-eyed Ranny McDonell chanced to pick up in the salubrious suburb.

An open-air pavilion, built in the Plaza to accommodate picnics when the railroad came into

INDEX-TRIBUNE ARCHIVES

Jos. H. (Jim) Albertson, stage coach driver, later constable, stood firm against bicycle riding on the sidewalks.

Sonoma, became the city hall. The city pavilion, as it was long known, was finally enclosed and the fire bell mounted in a tower built on its rotund top. This little old frame city hall, with its red-hot stove in winter and its haze of tobacco smoke, was the scene of many heated battles over city affairs. Jim Albertson, the old stage driver, who became city marshal at the big salary of $15 per month, with his good-natured smile and familiar drawl, was the saving grace of many lively battles as city dads clashed and the president of the board pounded his gavel. Jim may have said the city "audiences" (ordinances) had to be printed to make them legal, and that it was a shame so many able-bodied families were on the "indignant" list, but his jocular smile and merry eye quelled many a battle.

16 Sonoma's First Newspaper

INDEX-TRIBUNE ARCHIVES

Alexander Cox founded Sonoma's first newspaper, the *Bulletin*.

AUTHOR'S NOTE: While Celeste Murphy mentions the *Sonoma Bulletin* and its founder, Alexander Cox, in *The People of the Pueblo*, it was the late Ed Mannion of Petaluma who first alerted me to the witty writings of Cox.

A Linotype operator with *The Petaluma Argus-Courier* for many years, and my friend, Mannion was a keen student and chronicler of Sonoma County history.

During the 1960s and '70s he contributed articles to *The Sonoma Index-Tribune*. One of them included Cox's breezy account from an 1852 issue of the *Sonoma Bulletin* of the removal of the county courthouse from Sonoma to Santa Rosa, quoted on the next page.

Much of the information that follows, about Cox and the *Bulletin*, was given to me by Mannion some years ago.

Sonoma can lay claim to having the first newspaper ever published north of San Francisco. It was called the *Sonoma Bulletin*, the first issue making its appearance on June 12, 1852. Its founder, editor, publisher and printer was Alexander J. Cox. A native of Charleston, South Carolina, Cox had come to Sonoma in 1847 with the soldier-colonists of Col. Jonathan D. Stevenson's Regiment of New York Volunteers.

Historian C. A. Menefee, in his 1873 *Sketchbook of Napa, Sonoma, Lake & Mendocino,* wrote that the *Bulletin* had "a sickly existence till in 1855 it ceased to be published. It was a diminu-

INDEX-TRIBUNE ARCHIVES

The *Sonoma Bulletin* first appeared in June 1852, just six years after the Bear Flag Revolt, and was the first California newspaper north of San Francisco.

tive affair and was issued as circumstances permitted, sometimes regularly, at other times with intermission, rarely ever prompt on the day announced for publication" (p. 314).

A caustic and colorful writer, Cox expressed himself on the events of his time in a witty and humorous manner, ranking him as an able forerunner of Mark Twain, Bret Harte and Ambrose Bierce. Here is his sharp-tongued description of the removal of the county courthouse from Sonoma (then the county seat) to Santa Rosa in 1852:

Departed—Last Friday the county officers with the archives left town for the new capitol amidst the exultant grin of some and silent disapproval (frowning visages) of others. We are only sorry they did not take the courthouse along—not because it would be an ornament to Santa Rosa, but because its removal would have embellished our plaza.

Alas old "casa de adobe!" No more do we see county lawyers and loafers in general, lazily engaged in the laudable effort of whittling asunder the veranda posts—which, by the way, required but little more to bring the whole fabric to the ground. The courthouse is deserted like some feudal castle, only tenanted perhaps by gnats, rats and fleas. In the classic language of no one in particular, "Let 'er rip."

Reconstructing Cox's life is like going to work on a jigsaw puzzle. From Sonoma he went to Vallejo and published a newspaper in the fall of 1855. The next year he is found in Napa as editor of Volume 1, Number 1 of *The Napa Reporter*. Cox left the *Reporter* in 1858 to begin *The Napa Semi-Weekly Sun*. Soon after, he returned to Sonoma County, lugging a hand press which had been with him from the beginning, and launched *The Healdsburg Review*.

The historical record shows that Cox founded no newspapers after that. In 1866 he and his little press were finally separated, the latter going to Lakeport and, eventually, to a museum. He continued working as a typesetter for various newspapers, including *The Mendocino Beacon* in 1882. A report of Cox's death appeared in the *Beacon* in September 1886. A Napa newspaper item of the time said he was buried in Los Angeles.

It should be noted here that with the departure of Alexander Cox and his little press in 1855, Sonoma was without a newspaper for some 24 years—until Volume 1, Number 1 of *The Sonoma Index* appeared on April 17, 1879.

Part Two

AS REPORTED IN THE I-T
1879–1979

Significant Stories from The Sonoma Index-Tribune

Introduction
to
Part Two

As Reported in the *I-T*, 1879–1979

Part Two of *The Sonoma Valley Story* covers events which played a role in shaping the community over a 100-year period, from 1879 (the year *The Sonoma Index* was founded) to 1979.

It was on July 19, 1979, that the *Index-Tribune* published a 114-page, centennial-issue supplement which was subsequently awarded second place in the National Newspaper Association's Better Newspaper Contest. The supplement, which was about the thickness of a Sunday *San Francisco Examiner,* had excellent support from advertisers and was free with every copy of the *Index-Tribune..*

Local artist Jack Bradbury created striking graphics for the supplement's cover and eight "front" pages. My three sons (Bill, Jim and John) and I (the editor then), and many other *Index-Tribune* staff members, researched our back issues and wrote stories. So did a number of community residents, who eagerly volunteered their services to dig through old editions of the *I-T* and write stories for their hometown newspaper. Among them were Robert D. Parmelee, the late Myron DeLong, Sam J. Sebastiani, Dr. Clinton Lane and Rose Murphy.

In Part Two of *The Sonoma Valley Story,* many of the photographs and stories we used in that 100th birthday edition have been included, along with names of the writers. Some new stories, a few of them real gems, have also been added—along with many heretofore-unpublished illustrations and photos from our archives at the *Index-Tribune.* As in Part One, "Author's Notes" and brackets indicate that information in a story has been updated.

17 Signs of Growth: 1879–1899

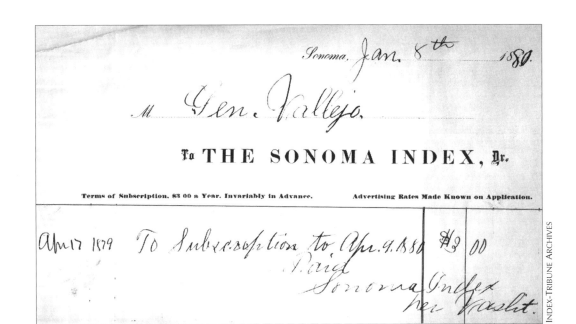

INDEX-TRIBUNE ARCHIVES

The original receipt, dated Jan. 8, 1880, showing General Vallejo's payment of $3 for a one-year subscription to *The Sonoma Index*.

Prodded by editorials, a sleepy pueblo awakens

*T*hose early years of the pueblo of Sonoma—from the time that Benjamin Frank started *The Sonoma Index* on April 17, 1879, until 1899—can perhaps be described as an era during which the long-sleeping vale got at least one eye open.

Between yawns and stretches, the few hundred inhabitants of city and valley granted that Mother Nature and history had combined to provide them with a very special place in which to live.

And it was during this 20-year span that Sonoma and Sonomans awakened at least partially, acknowledging—with some continual

prodding by *The Sonoma Index, The Sonoma Tribune* and its successor, *The Sonoma Index-Tribune*—the need to give Mother Nature, history, the economy and themselves a helping hand.

When changes came, they were painfully slow. Iron rails for first a narrow- and later a broad-gauge railroad were accepted reluctantly, horse-drawn coaches and wagons—and boats—still favored over smoke-belching engines.

Because the town had disincorporated in 1862, the move to once again make Sonoma a municipality in the 1880s was met with much opposition, but that "one open eye" of the drowsy pueblo focused on the need for reincorporation and approved it by the majority of votes on Aug. 28, 1883.

Sonoma had first been incorporated on April

INDEX-TRIBUNE ARCHIVES

The Leese-Fitch adobe near the corner of First Street West and Napa Street, opposite the Plaza, was originally the home and store of Jacob Primer Leese, brother-in-law of M. G. Vallejo. Leese sold the property to Vallejo and one of his sons-in-law, John B. Frisbie, who later leased it to Gen. Persifor Smith for his U. S. Army headquarters. The adobe was sold again in 1849 to a member of Mrs. Vallejo's family, was later leased to Rev. John Ver Mehr in 1853 for use as an academy for young women and today houses several businesses.

4, 1850, and was the county seat of both Sonoma and Mendocino inclusive until 1854.

It was an era during which at one time it appeared that even Sonoma Valley's famous grapevines would go into a sleep from which they might never awaken—after the dreaded phylloxera wiped out many vineyards here. While thousands of vines were plowed under, enough hardy stock survived, and a sufficient number of grape-growers, with faith and hard work, prevailed to carry on the vale's proud reputation for fine grapes and wines.

The instability of the community is indicated by the fact that after Benjamin Frank founded *The Sonoma Index* in 1879, it changed hands (and sometimes names) no less than 13 times before Harry H. Granice purchased it in November 1884.

The streets of the city were of compacted dirt, and the dust was a constant irritant and the watering by horse-drawn carts at city expense mostly insufficient in the summer and fall months. Mud was the standard winter hazard.

The historic Plaza laid out by Gen. M. G. Vallejo was a weed-filled eyesore, sometimes rented for pasture, and the butt of jokes and bitter editorials.

There was no adequate water distribution system, particularly as needed to fight the fires that seemed to break out with regularity to destroy homes and businesses.

Most lighting was by oil lamps, which resulted in further fire damage and strained eyesight.

Education in the community was limited to elementary and grammar school, at least until 1891, when a high school district was formed, somewhat reluctantly ... or so it seemed.

A group of civic leaders eventually formed a private company and supplied the city with its first electric light plant in 1898, after the city trustees failed to respond to the need—and to countless editorials by the *Index-Tribune* editor, Mr. Granice.

Homes, businesses and even major streets and the Plaza were eventually lighted, but because of an unwillingness by the users, including the city, to allow the private light company to charge necessary fees, the company dissolved and the plant shut down. Fortunately, a lessee was found and the electric light plant was put back in operation. That "one open eye" of the community at least appreciated the bright new light.

The weekly copies of the old *Index-Tribune* between 1879 and the 1890s reveal a shameful, demeaning racial movement directed against the Chinese who worked as laborers or domestics and operated laundries, the town's several gambling dens and, purportedly, even an opium den.

Open sewers and ditches around the town were constant sources of irritation, and if the "one eye" that opened during the era saw the menace, heard the squawking or paid any attention to the *Index-Tribune*'s constant reminders, it did little but blink at the problem. An old wooden dance pavilion placed in the Plaza was for many years the City Hall, reboarded and repainted whenever the city council could get a majority vote to do so—which was seldom. The town's jail was a disgrace—10 x 10 feet, musty and unsanitary.

Editor Granice perhaps captured the mood of Sonoma in an editorial on April 14, 1888, after voters had elected a city trustee opposed to bonding the town for improvements—water works, fire department, etc.—something the *Index-Tribune* and a few citizens "with a least one eye open" felt was needed. Said the editorial:

> Thirty years ago Sonoma was a city, while Napa, Petaluma, Santa Rosa and scores of other towns in this state were only small hamlets. Today the order of things is reversed, and what were small towns 30 years ago are now prosperous cities, if we except Sonoma. She has degenerated into a rural village ... caused by a hesitating policy and non-progressive spirit on the part of its leading citizens. It was this that lost us the county seat years ago. ... While other towns ... have kept up with the times, Sonoma, Micawberlike, has been and is still "waiting for something to turn up," with anything but satisfactory results.

Editor Granice contended that bonding the town would mean not only lessened taxation and reduced insurance rates (due to a water system and fire department), but "a prosperous, contented, happy and healthy community keeping pace with the march of improvement and progress."

Granice concluded his April 1888 comment, "Ah! Sonoma, you are backward and too slow for your own interest, but with your hospitable people, picturesque scenery and healthy climate, 'with all thy faults we love thee still.'"

But the "awakening years"—each one between 1879 and 1899—brought with them a slow but increasing awareness of what must be done for the community and the common good.

Before the turn of the century, the half-awake pueblo had indeed responded to self-criticism, and many of the tarnished facets of this historic, scenic jewel were polished by a growing community zeal.

Its vineyards and wines added to our fame. Agriculture products increased. Basalt blocks quarried in the northern foothills were produced in greater quantities than ever before and were used to pave the streets of San Francisco, San Jose and other growing cities.

Sonoma's streets and even sidewalks became

INDEX-TRIBUNE ARCHIVES

Sonoma had a large Chinese population in the 1870s and '80s. Several hundred Chinese laborers were employed on ranches and in vineyards, or worked as servants, launderers, fishermen, sailors and vegetable peddlers. Buena Vista Winery is said to have had the greatest number of Chinese vineyard workers. The young man here, identified only as Dan, worked in the home of Maj. and Mrs. Jacob R. Snyder on the eastern outskirts of town. A typical wage was a dollar for an 11-hour day.

the focus of improvement efforts. Boardwalks were being replaced by concrete sidewalks. The city trustees even denied the use of the Plaza for a sheep pasture and planted several hundred trees therein.

A separate old building was purchased for use as a high school, and the education program improved with each year, with as many as five people graduating from the high school by 1899.

A volunteer fire department came into being, with the members proudly wearing the uniforms they helped to purchase. Although bond issues to provide a city water system failed on two occasions, as the era ended another vote was being prepared.

A new jail was built, and there was more and more demand for a decent city hall.

Much of Sonoma's newfound enthusiasm can probably be attributed to the apparent "blossoming" of other nearby communities—like El Verano and Kenwood, both boom towns of the era in which promoters sold considerable stock.

Sonoma, although slow and reluctant in spending for improvements, nonetheless profited even more when the two boom-town schemes blew up in the faces of the promoters and the fleeced investors.

The narrow-gauge railroads here were extended to broad gauge, and travel extended from Napa Junction to Santa Rosa through the Valley.

Bridges were built, most important of which at the time was the span crossing Sonoma Creek at the west end of Napa Street. Others were built at Glen Ellen and Agua Caliente.

The California Home for the Feeble Minded, which was destined to become Sonoma County's largest employer as today's Sonoma Developmental Center, came into being at Eldridge.

Sonoma Valley joined with the rest of the state's population in curbing its racial prejudices, particularly as related to the Chinese, and by the turn of the century little or no prejudicial items or views were being publicized—at least in the *Index-Tribune.*

It was a time when the telephone first came into more general use in the area and Clewe's store boasted the first phone booth in town.

Capt. H. E. Boyes, a popular Englishman of the Valley, struck a flowing well of hot water with a temperature of 112 degrees at his Agua Rica Farm, two miles northwest of Sonoma in the community which later became Boyes Hot Springs. A like happening occurred at a nearby Agua Caliente rancho the same year, 1895.

The era seemed to bring a new interest in the community's history, evidenced by the respect shown the town patriarch and founder, General Vallejo, who died in this period, on Jan. 18, 1890, followed by his wife a year later. The 50th anniversary of the raising of the Bear Flag was a major celebration here in 1896, with some 5,000 participants, an unheard-of crowd for those days.

The very first "Vintage Festival" was held in the form of a Grecian production featuring Bacchus, God of Wine, in October 1896 at Rhine Farm.

Music and entertainment began to flourish, with Professor Maxwell and his Sonoma Brass Band, an orchestral society, minstrel shows, recitations and vocalists at Union Hall and Weyl

In the 1880s Glen Ellen had a thriving brickyard. Clay came from the London Ranch. The Pinelli family later moved the brickyard to Sonoma.

INDEX-TRIBUNE ARCHIVES

Hall (today, site of the Sonoma Hotel).

The social and club scene was further enlivened by the founding of the Native Sons and Native Daughters parlors during those years, to go along with a Masonic lodge, a chapter of Eastern Star, a United Workmans lodge, a Grove of the Druids, Rebekah Degree lodge of Odd Fellows, a Council of the Young Men's Institute, the Clay Literary Society and an athletic club known as the Sonoma Turners, specializing in gymnastics.

Four churches—Catholic, Methodist, Congregational and Episcopal—were also active in the period.

Our young men came home from faraway places with new perspectives based on their experiences—for this was the era of the Klondike gold rush and the Spanish-American War, and accounts of Sonomans who were participants in the ore search in the frozen north and the fighting in steaming Philippine jungles or on a foreign ocean were column items to be noted in pages of the *Index-Tribune*. It was truly the Era of Awakening. At least one of the old slumbering pueblo's eyes had fully opened. The other eye was fluttering as if to receive the light in the new century ahead.

– RML

Wines and vines were making comeback in '79

When *The Sonoma Index* was born in April 1879, the wines—particularly the vines—of the Sonoma Valley were actually making an unbelievable comeback.

Just five years before, in 1874, vineyards here were at their zenith. From the entrance over the dividing ridge on the old county road from Napa, our Valley appeared suddenly to be one vast vineyard—beginning with the foothills above San Pablo Bay and continuing some eight miles beyond Glen Ellen.

The thousands of acres of vines were in the hands of many small owners and several large ones. Buena Vista, for instance, had 500 acres of bearing vines, one of the largest vineyards in the state.

The vines flourished until the summer of 1874, when phylloxera infected several vine-

Taken in the late 1890s, this photo shows the prominent Rhine Farm proprietor, Carl Dresel, and his wife with their children. "Bunk" is on his mother's lap. Gustav is on his father's. Standing are (from left) Eva, Jupe and Otto.

COURTESY, GUNDLACH-BUNDSCHU WINERY

yards. In the course of but six years, nearly all the vines of the Valley were wiped out by this pest, reducing the vintage of two million gallons annually to less than three hundred thousand for the entire Valley. Although many vineyardists became discouraged and refused to replant, a few courageous winemen did so and, with the assistance of phylloxera-proof roots, conquered the pest, saving the Valley's nationally earned reputation as a premier winegrowing region.

Volume 1, Number 1 of *The Sonoma Index* on April 21, 1879, mentioned that "Wines are being shipped to the city by Messrs. Kohler & Frohling. They are quite active in the market now, and will be the means of making good times for Sonoma."

In August 1885, *The Sonoma Index-Tribune* reported that William Hill's new stone wine cellar was nearing completion at Hill's station (today known as Eldridge).

Mentioned, too, was that, of the $100 contributed toward the expenses of a special agent to take charge of the California wine and grape exhibit at the Louisville Exposition, all but $15 came from Sonoma Valley donors. Mrs. K. F. Warfield, Christian Weise, Capt. J. Drummond, Hill, Eli T. Sheppard, Capt. H. E. Boyes and I. DeTurk were among contributors.

Both Mrs. Warfield and Drummond won top awards for their wines at the Louisville Exposition.

Mrs. Warfield, Drummond, Hill and Sheppard were well-known vineyardists of the era. Kate Warfield was one of two women who operated vineyards and wineries in Sonoma Valley. The other was Eliza Hood. Sheppard owned the Madrone Vineyards and winery from 1880 to 1889.

The names of other vineyardists and winemakers of the 1879–99 era, as reflected in the pages of the *Index-Tribune*, included those of Gundlach and Bundschu, Julius and Carl Dresel, Jas. A. Shaw, J. Chauvet, Kohler & Frohling, G. P. Sears, Henry Winkle, T. S. Glaister, C. Aguillon, J. E. Poppe, George Hearst, Ed. Steiger, Burgess & Dominiconi, George Engler, Charles Stuart and Emanuel Goldstein. Samuele Sebastiani arrived in Sonoma in 1890, and while he made a small quantity of wine for himself and his friends, it was not until 1904 that he opened a small commercial winery—the beginning of the nationally famous and ever-growing Sebastiani Vineyards operation of today.

Other wine notes from pages of the *I-T* between 1885 and 1899:

• Sept. 19, 1885—Zinfandel grapes were sold for $22 per ton by Wm. McP.

Hill to J. Chauvet of Glen Ellen.

• Jan. 9, 1886—E. T. Sheppard of Glen Ellen has sold his entire cellar of red and white wines to J. Gundlach & Co. of San Francisco.

• Feb. 6, 1886—Eli T. Sheppard will set out 25,000 American resistant vines this coming season of the Lenoir, Riparia and Rupestria varieties. These vines are resistant to the dreaded phylloxera.

• July 3, 1886—$30 per ton offered for zinfandel grapes termed a "good" price.

• Sept. 25, 1886—A gold medal has been won at the Mechanics' Fair, San Francisco, by Gundlach & Co. for their display of table wines from Rhine Farm here. A large number of Chinese grape pickers are arriving daily in the Valley.

• Oct. 2, 1886—The Thos. S. Glaister vineyard (Green Oaks), four miles east of Sonoma, has 150 acres of

INDEX-TRIBUNE ARCHIVES

The Cutters, an early wine-industry family in the Sonoma Valley. Pictured in this 1884 photo are, left to right: Capt. E. P. Cutter, superintendent of the vineyards of the Buena Vista Vinicultural Society through the 1870s; his elder son, Ephraim Cutter, who worked at Buena Vista for some years; Gustave Chevassus (born 1880 and manager in 1947 of the Russ Building in San Francisco); B. Eugene Auger, for years trustee and a leading officer in the Buena Vista Vinicultural Society; Mrs. Edouard Chevassus, mother of Gustave; Miss Lina Auger, eldest daughter of Mr. Auger; and Mrs. Cutter.

COURTESY, SONOMA DEVELOPMENTAL CENTER

Founded in 1891 as a self-sufficient farming community (note vineyards), the Sonoma Developmental Center at Eldridge is today the oldest and largest center in California for persons with developmental disabilities.

choice bearing vines, including chasselas, malvoisies, Rose of Peru, tokay and other varieties.

• Dec. 3, 1886—Fifty tons and 40 pounds of grapes were picked from a block of just 3½ acres of Zinfandel vines in the Madrone Vineyards owned by Eli T. Sheppard this season—the largest yield of grapes reported in the history of grape production in this state.

• Oct. 8, 1887—As high as $2 per day and board is being paid to grape pickers in this Valley. With wine at 15¢ per gallon, we can hardly see where the winemaker's profit comes in.

• May 5, 1888—Sonoma Valley produced 1,500,000 gallons of wine in 1887, more wine than was made in the entire country 30 years ago.

• Aug. 17, 1889—The vintage for the coming season statewide is predicted to be 13,000,000 gallons, as compared to 18,000,000 gallons in 1888.

• Jan. 2, 1892—Julius Dresel, who came to Sonoma in 1869 with his three children—Carl, Helene and Gustav—and entered wine-growing, died in Wiesbaden, Germany, last Monday at 76. He is acknowledged as a California leader in perfecting dry wines and phylloxera-proof vineyards.

• Dec. 2, 1893—J. Gundlach & Co.,

with vineyards, wine cellar and distillery one mile east of Sonoma, have been awarded World's Fair premiums for their sauterne, semillon, chateau, chambertin, cabernet, sherry and tokay wines. Chas. Kohler of Kohler & Frohling said his Glen Ellen winery will pay $9 per ton for grapes.

• Dec. 8, 1894—Jacob Gundlach of Rhine Farm, pioneer winegrower of this Valley, died Tuesday at 76. He had been a vineyardist-winemaker here for 40 years. His children are Mrs. Chas. Bundschu, Mrs. Carl Dresel, Mrs. E. Schild, Mrs. A. Perutz, Miss Eva Gundlach, Chas. Gundlach and Henry Gundlach.

• Jan. 12, 1895—Carl Dresel has added an extensive bottling plant to his vineyards and winery here.

• May 11, 1895—J. Chauvet has purchased the Kohler & Frohling farm, with the exception of the cellars, which belong to the Calif. Wine Assoc.

• Oct. 3, 1898—Wine making has commenced in the Valley, with the price of grapes quoted between $18 and $22.50 per ton.

• Oct. 16, 1897—The Vintage Festival production at Rhine Farm was hailed as an outstanding "artistic success."   – RML

Bear Flag Party
survivors were guests

To Sonomans the raising of the Bear Flag in the Plaza June 14, 1846, was important not just for its place in state history, but because it marked the beginning of the modern history of their town.

Not only did some of the members of the Bear Flag Party stay in Sonoma, but other American settlers came soon after, some for farming and others on their way to or from the gold fields.

One of the first big celebrations to commemorate the Bear Flag Party took place on the 41st anniversary of the event, in 1887. Members of the Bear Flag Party and veterans of the Mexican War were invited as special guests.

Local storekeeper Robert Poppe had suggested the celebration in a letter to the *Index-Tribune* in March. He presented the idea as a way of attracting summer visitors and of catching the

attention of potential immigrants to the Valley.

The celebration took place on July 5, early enough so that it could be combined with Fourth of July festivities. Eager citizens kicked things off at 5 A.M. by ringing bells and firing a military salute.

Bear Flag Party survivors Calvin Griffith, John York and Harvey Porterfield raised the Bear Flag on the old pole.

Later in the morning a train carrying uniformed veterans of the Mexican War arrived on the old tracks which led into the Plaza.

The Sonoma Brass Band led a procession of veterans and citizens around the Plaza and to the flagpole, where the Bear Flag was taken down and the American flag run up.

A banquet for 150 guests was held for the veterans at Weyl Hall. In the afternoon the celebrants adjourned once again to the Plaza, where they had decorated the pavilion with banners and evergreens and had erected a large awning for shade.

There they continued with the typical

COURTESY, SONOMA VALLEY HISTORICAL SOCIETY

A parade on East Napa Street marked the 50th anniversary of the raising of the Bear Flag. Note the flags on buildings—plus parade participants marching east rather than west, as they do today.

Independence Day events: speeches, prayers, music and poetry recitations. Robert Poppe gave a well-received soliloquy on the history and meaning of the Bear Flag revolt. A grand ball at the end of the day culminated the celebration.

Fifty years after the revolt, early settler William M. Boggs gave the *Index-Tribune* a summary of Bear Flag survivors who remained in the area.

There were five in Napa County: William Baldridge, Harvey Porterfield, "Uncle" Jack York, C. C. Griffith and Henry Fowler. A sixth man, Benjamin Dewell, lived in Lake County.

Although Boggs did not mention him, James McChristian of Sebastopol was an eyewitness to events in 1846; his account was published in the *Sebastopol Times* in 1896.

Another survivor not mentioned by Boggs was Henry Beeson of Mendocino County, who would outlive all other members of the party.

For the 50th anniversary of the revolt, Sonomans staged a celebration grander than any before. Almost 5,000 people were in town, and most of these turned out for the parade.

Participants in the parade included "the Native Sons from Santa Rosa and San Francisco, the Pioneers (of the society founded by Nick Carriger), Mexican War veterans, delegates from the Grand Parlor of Native Daughters, members of the Grand Army (from the Civil War) and citizens in carriages," according to the *I-T* account. This time there were three bands instead of one.

Ben F. Dewell and Henry Beeson raised the Bear Flag; and then there was a great barbecue in the Plaza and another patriotic program of speakers and music.

Several townspeople opened their homes to visitors through the day, including editor Harry Granice, who made a point of hosting writers from other newspapers which could promote Sonoma.

Townspeople had also arranged tours of historical buildings. Later there was dancing at Union and Weyl Halls.

Such a grand celebration highlighted not only the past but the future as well, for it helped to carry Sonomans into a period of faster growth, more tourism and increased civic activity.

— SANDY SANDERS

Jim Martin's blacksmith shop at Hudson House, circa 1880, opposite the Sonoma Mission. Hudson House was named for Bear Flagger David Hudson.

1880 businesses: *Index* ads tell a colorful tale

What business firms advertised what in *The Sonoma Index* of 1879 and the 1880s?

Going through just a few of the weathered issues in our possession, we gleaned the following information:

General merchandise stores were operated by Solomon Schocken, Julius A. Poppe and G. T. Pauli. Schocken conducted his business in the old Barracks building, while Poppe and Pauli had their stores on the south side of the Plaza. Schocken's advertisement in 1879–80 copies of *The Sonoma Index* read:

> Schocken's New Store, Northeast Corner of the Plaza. Keeps a Fine Assortment of Groceries and Provisions, Furnishing Goods, Dry Goods, Clothing, Boots and Shoes, Hats and Caps, Notions and Cutlery, Tobacco, Tinware, Hardware, Teas of All Kinds, Flour, Feed, Etc., Etc., Etc. Agent for the Cal. Spool and Silk Co. The only Agency in town. Also Agent for the Cal. Home Mutual Ins. Co.

The advertisements of Poppe and Pauli, while not containing such a wide variety of offerings, had a number of things Schocken did not list. Poppe, for instance, advertised that he was a "Manufacturer of Wines" and an "Importer and

Breeder of Carp." Pauli, in addition to his "General Merchandise" listing, advertised "Crockery, Patent Medicines, Oils, Varnishes and Glass."

Meats were bought by Sonomans in 1879–80 from the Meat Market on First Street East which listed Cornelius, Lewis & Levy as proprietors.

Two bakeries advertised in those early-day *Sonoma Index* papers: City Bakery, operated by John Gardini, next door to the *Index* office; and Golden & Hunter's Union Bakery at the corner of Broadway and United States (now Napa) Street. The druggist in town was Ed. Wegner, whose ad read "Ed. Wegner, Dealer in Fresh Drugs, Perfumery, Stationery, Patent Medicines, Paints and Oils, Candies, Nuts, Cigars, Tobacco and General Merchandise," with "Prescriptions Carefully Compounded." Wegner was located on United States Street on the west side of the Plaza.

If you needed books and stationery, you went to J. Ruffner, one door north of Poppe's. He operated a general news depot and also advertised notions, candies, nuts and the "best cigars in town."

In need of boots or shoes? You had a choice between Martin Hester on United States Street,

near the Travelers' Home hotel ("Kip Boots to order, $6; French Calf Boots to order, $9"), or George W. Clark, whose shop was on the southwest corner of the Plaza.

He wore two hats, and advertised in an adjoining column as "G. W. Clark, Undertaker. Coffins, Burial Caskets, etc., Always on hand. Prompt attention to all calls."

With horses (buggies and wagons) the chief mode of conveyance in the 1879–80 period, folks relied on the Union Livery, Feed & Sale Stable operated by Corbaley & Carriger. "Gentle Saddle Horses, Fine Carriages & Buggies Always on Hand, Horses boarded by the Day or Week," read their advertisement. They were located next to the Union Hotel on United States Street.

Blacksmiths included R. B. Lyon, Broadway; Buchan & Deering, east side of the Plaza, and James Martin, northeast corner of the Plaza. Lyon, Buchan & Deering also were listed as wagon makers.

Louis Heydt operated a "Harness, Saddlery and Carriage Trimming Shop" on Vallejo (now Spain) Street, while opposite the Union Bakery on Broadway was the Sonoma Saddlery and Harness Shop.

Among the variety of other advertisers in

INDEX-TRIBUNE ARCHIVES

McHarvey and Hope's blacksmith shop. They were also wagon makers in the 1880s.

INDEX-TRIBUNE ARCHIVES

The Charles A. Poppe store in Glen Ellen, shown here in the 1880s, at the intersection of what are today Arnold Drive and London Ranch Road.

those first copies of *The Sonoma Index* were:

- A. Converse and J. W. Henderson, Carpenter and Builder
- W. B. Reed, Well Boring & Cleaning
- J. H. Sackett, Drayage and Hauling
- V. Bischoff, Barber & Hairdresser
- W. P. Wilson, House and Sign Painter, Paper-Hanger, Glazier, Whitener
- John Tivnen, Notary Public and Insurance Agent
- James U. Waters, Dealer in and Manufacturer of Tinware of Every Description

Wm. Green advertised his lumber yard located at Sonoma landing in the *Index* of 1880—"Lumber, Doors, Windows and Blinds. Bricks, Lime, Cement and all kinds of Building Materials. Also Hay, Barley, Oats, Corn and all kinds of Ground Feed." He also had a separate ad for grape stakes.

There was no need to go thirsty in old Sonoma. There were close to a dozen saloons in the pueblo. Among those whose ads appeared in *The Sonoma Index* were Pioneer Saloon, corner United States and First Streets East, Lewis Adler, Prop.; A. J. Hubsch's Saloon, United States Street; M. Powell's New Saloon, south side of the Plaza; Monahan's Wine Rooms, Odd Fellows' Building, Broadway, M. Muldry, Proprietor. You could also hoist a few at the local hotels—Union Hotel on United States Street, Sonoma House, Garibaldi House or Travelers' Home, on the southwest corner of the Plaza.

Professional services were advertised in one-column-by-one-inch ads appearing on the front page of *The Sonoma Index*. Reading the 1880 weekly paper you would find the advertisements of Attorneys and Counselors at Law Murray Whallon and C. A. Webb. Listed as "Physician, Surgeon & Obstetrician" were Doctors Chas. Van Geldern and C. M. Wells; and there was a card for D. J. P. Fuller, Homeopathist.

Property listings also appeared on page one.

In the March 6, 1880, *Sonoma Index,* 50 x 151.56 lots owned by General Vallejo on Vallejo Street were being offered for $250 each.

Also listed were "A splendid home and vineyard property only ½ mile from Plaza, 36 acres in grapes, house, large barn, good well, fruit trees, etc. for $8,500"; and "100 acres, 1 mile west of Sonoma, house of eight rooms, fine barn, beautiful grounds, two acres of orchard. Bounded by Sonoma Creek. $8,000."

In addition to the local ads were numerous advertisements from San Francisco, Petaluma and Santa Rosa for a variety of goods, supplies and services.

Most numerous were the old patent medicine or cure-all advertisements like these:

Hall's Pulmonary Balsam, 50 Cents. An immediate and Permanent Cure for Coughs, Colds, Asthma, Bronchitis, Croup, Influenza, Catarrh, Loss of Voice, Incipient Consumption and all Diseases of the Throat and Lungs. Sold by the Druggists.

Cure for Cancer. Red Clover cures Cancer, Salt Rheum, and all other blood diseases. Write W. C. Needham, sole agent, P. O. Box 422; San Jose, Cal.

The Deaf Hear Through the Teeth. Perfectly, all Ordinary Conversation, Lectures, etc. by New Channels to the Nerves of Hearing by means of a recent wonderful scientific invention—the Dentaphone. ... Send for descriptive pamphlet to the American Dentaphone Co., Cincinnati, Ohio.

Can you imagine what the governmental agencies, to say nothing of the medical fraternity, would have to say about advertisements like that appearing today?

The Sonoma Index, like all newspapers of the era, depended on advertising to stay in business. And that fact hasn't changed in more than 100 years.   – RML

The George Breitenbach harness and bicycle shop in 1896, with, left to right, Reynald McDonnel, G. H. Hotz, Lloyd Hotz, Col. Bob Atwood of Kentucky and George Breitenbach.

INDEX-TRIBUNE ARCHIVES

Early-day schools

While private schools existed in Sonoma and environs since about 1850, it was not until 1857 that Sonoma Township petitioned for the establishment of school districts under the public school system provided by the California legislature in 1851–52 legislation.

Initially there were four districts designated in the boundaries of Sonoma Township: Ash Springs, District No. 1; Dunbar, District No. 2; Watmaugh, District No. 3; and Sonoma, District No. 4.

The Sonoma District in that year had an average daily attendance of 13, according to county records.

Ash Springs School became the Oak Grove School and was discontinued in 1859.

The second year of the public school in Sonoma, 1858, the average daily attendance had risen to 69 with classes conducted in the Methodist church building.

A grammar school was built by the taxpayers in 1869 on East Napa Street, the four-room frame building costing $6,500. The site is where the Sonoma Community Center now stands. That brick building was built for the grammar school in 1915 for $30,000.

Other elementary schools of the early days included Watmaugh School in the southwest part of the Valley, founded in the 1860s; San Luis School at Schellville, established in the early 1880s; Locust Grove School on lower Broadway, just north of Schellville, in the 1870s; Harvey, Enterprise and Flowery; and the Summit Joint School near Los Guilicos.

When *The Sonoma Index* was founded in 1879, the Sonoma Public School taught groups designated First Primary, Second Primary, Grammar Room and High School. Students had to pass a stringent examination to participate in the high school classroom. In July 1887 the *Index-Tribune* reported 129 students in the primary and grammar grades, but only 18 in the high school room—14 girls and four boys.

In May 1888 the graduating class from the high school numbered just six—all girls.

There was no separate high school as such at that time. In 1880 the new state constitution pro-

Dunbar district school, 1895, from left: (at top) Zena Brand, Miss May White (Mrs. Lewis), teacher, and Milton Babkirk; (middle row) Phillip Brand, Martha Gordenker, Mary Finocchia, Will Youngman, Robert Babkirk, Robert Johnson, Percy Quien; (bottom row) Annie Quien, Stella Brand, Mike Gordenker.

vided that no money should be appropriated from the state school fund to be used to maintain high schools.

In order to avoid this clause in the constitution, Assemblyman Caminetti of Amador County put through a bill for what he very ingeniously called a "grammar school course." It was really a high school course in everything except name and was intended to prepare students for the state university in Berkeley.

Sonoma was among the first to avail itself of the provisions of the act and, by 1891, had already graduated five classes of "grammar school" (really high school) students.

In 1890 the legislature abolished the subterfuge and called for the establishment and maintenance of high schools as separate entities.

At a special meeting of the boards of trustees of the Sonoma School District on May 13, 1891, it was decided to take the necessary steps to establish a high school for the Valley, according to a lead story in the May 16, 1891, issue of *The Sonoma Index-Tribune*.

On July 11, 1891, voters in the Sonoma, Glen Ellen, Enterprise, Flowery, San Luis, Huichica, Harvey and Watmaugh school districts voted to form the Sonoma Valley Union High School District. Seventy-seven people cast ballots in the eight districts, 40 favoring the action. Of the 37 negative votes, 22 came from the tiny Enterprise district in the Trinity Road area north of Glen Ellen. In both the Watmaugh and San Luis districts there were three votes "for" the high school and four opposed.

Later, another vote took place, with Enterprise and San Luis again voting against participation in the high school district, while Watmaugh reversed its earlier vote and approved.

Eventually a tax rate of 6¢ on $100 of assessed valuation was set for the school district, the first board of which was composed of B. F. Campbell, Sonoma; P. H. Thompson, Huichica; H. Appleton, Flowery; J. B. Morris, Harvey; J. M. Zane, Glen Ellen.

Prof. Herbert Miller was hired as the teacher for $100 per month, and classes began Sept. 21, 1891, in the Sonoma district schoolhouse.

After a lot of bickering over the cost of leasing and fixing up the old Cumberland College building on Broadway for a high school facility, on Feb. 24, 1894, that move was made.

Sixteen students formed the student body. The principal was a Mr. Abshire. In July of that year he was succeeded by Mr. Benjamin Weed,

with Miss Georgia D. Reed as vice principal.

When the high school district trustees urged the purchase of the old college building, *I-T* editor Granice, in an Aug. 24, 1895, editorial, urged construction of a new building instead. But at an election held in January 1896, voters approved purchase of the old college building by a 168 to 104 margin.

When Sonoma Valley Union High School reopened after summer vacation on Aug. 3, 1896, with Benjamin Weed as principal and R. M. Sims, vice principal, the following students were enrolled:

- Sonoma—Doris Clewe, Lydia Wegner, Lydia Culberson, Marcella Glazier, Cecilia Granice, Helena Shaw, Mabel Thomas, Stewart Elliott, Frido Clewe, Malcolm Elliott, Wm. Chase and Bert Jones
- San Luis—Zarifa Howe and Berton Lawrence
- Harvey—Katie Morris, Grace M. Carmer, Bessie Carpenter, Wm. Sherman
- Glen Ellen—Katie Lang, Gussie Wright and Harry Hendley

COURTESY, SONOMA VALLEY HISTORICAL SOCIETY

Sonoma Grammar School students in 1899 were, left to right: (front row) Richard R. Emparan, Roy A. Pauli, Jack B. Knight; (second row) Maggie Fonts, Vira Fields, Julia Landgrebe, Emma Estes, Nellie Sullivan, Nellie Gordenker, Emma Griffith, Rena Small; (back row) Carlos V. Emparan, James B. Morris, James Modini, Bert Stockwell, principal W. O. Hocker, Roy Stockwell, Tom Mullen, William Castagnetto and Julius A. Poppe.

- Dunbar—Deme Gordenker
- Enterprise—Pauline Clawson, Lucy Clawson, Lucy Thompson, Laura Thompson, C. D. Clawson
- Flowery—Elsie Appleton, Sara Cady
- Watmaugh—Sadie Agnew, Eva Prunty, Rue Tate   – RML

The weather a century ago

A typical example of how the ravages of Mother Nature were reported appeared in the Nov. 19, 1887, edition of the *Index-Tribune* in an article headlined "A fearful gale!":

Thursday night at an early hour a slight breeze sprang up and by 12 o'clock it had increased to such an extent that it blew a perfect hurricane. Trees swayed to and fro, houses creaked and rocked, and the wind roared like a mighty bellows.

Fences were blown down and trees

uprooted in many parts of the Valley. But by far the most serious damage reported is that of the complete demolition of the new $12,000 hotel in the new town of Los Guilicos.

This fine structure was nearly completed and would have been turned over to the owners in a few days by the contractor, T. J. Ludwig. It is now a complete wreck, it having been leveled to the ground and reduced to kindling wood by the force of the wind. Old residents of the Valley say that never before have they experienced in this section such a terrific wind storm.

Accounts of heavy rains and subsequent flooding of lower Sonoma Creek, while common, were also newsmakers: "3.50 inches fell on Friday, January 24, alone. … Sonoma Creek overflowed," reported the Feb. 8, 1890, *I-T*. That season the Valley received an incredible 54.70 inches of precipitation, as compared to today's

INDEX-TRIBUNE ARCHIVES

These boys were students at the convent school built in 1882 under Father Esser and operated by nuns of the Order of the Sisters of Presentation. They are, left to right: (front row) A. Kiser, unidentified, Geo. Cornelius, Eddie Thomas, E. Mulphuft, Gus Marcy, Francis Mulphuft, Joe Infeld, Geo. Perazzo; (second row) Percy Wilson, Emmett Mullen, Jas. Modini, Jno. Laux, Wm. Mullen, George Laux, Charley Marcy; (back row) Jno. McDonald, Frank Perazzo, M. DeMartini, Jack Watt, Archie Stevenot, Paul Perazzo, Tom Mullen and A. Bertholome.

COURTESY, ROBERT D. PARMELEE

The A. D. Lowell family on their ranch east of Sonoma, circa 1880. Looks like the family found a great day for an outing.

seasonal normal of about 28 inches.

Property damage from heavy rains was noted in an Oct. 20, 1894, item:

> The rain which fell last Wednesday night and Thursday morning flooded the high school building to such an extent that the teachers dismissed the scholars for the balance of the week. The roof of the old building had been removed to make room for the new one, and when the rains came it flooded the classrooms to a depth of three inches. Furniture and books were damaged.

And talk about "raining on your parade," this item appeared in the July 6, 1895, issue: "Rain fell on the 4th of July here for the first time in 20 years. The rain in 1875 was very slight, while that of last Thursday amounted to a continuous downpour from 11 A.M. to 4 P.M., with an inch of rain falling. The bicycle races had to be postponed, along with many other amusements."

Rare snowfalls which occasionally dust our Valley were not unfamiliar to local residents during this period. As reported in the March 7, 1896, *I-T:*

> Early Monday morning a heavy snow storm set in and white flakes fell without interruption for several hours. By 7 o'clock the Valley and surrounding mountains were covered to a depth of several inches, giving Sonoma Valley a most wintry aspect.

A somewhat sensational account of a freak storm appeared Aug. 1, 1896:

> A tremendous hailstorm, the like of which has never before been known in California, hit Sonoma Valley Wednesday morning at about 3 o'clock. On the Goethe place, five miles from Sonoma, hailstones fell as large as hen's eggs and the family expected every minute to see the roof of their residence pelted in. Fortunately, the storm subsided as quickly as it came. While it lasted, however, it would have cost a man his life to venture outside.

Exaggerated reporting? Perhaps ... but it nevertheless illustrates once again the timeless value of the weather, in all its variations, as a news item.

– JIM LYNCH

Growing pains of Valley hamlets in late 1880s

While Sonoma was still the only incorporated town in the Valley after 1883, the pages of the old *Index-Tribune* reflect occasional reference to the growth and "booms" in the nearby hamlets of El Verano, Glen Ellen, Agua Caliente, Kenwood, Los Guilicos and Embarcadero in the 1880s through 1890s. The entire Sonoma Valley, in 1888, the so-called big boom year, had a population of approximately 3,000 people.

The story of El Verano's ill-fated boom and the promoters' dreams of it becoming a major Sonoma County metropolis in the 1880s and 1890s is covered in a related story.

Readers of the *Index-Tribune* of March 26, 1887, were told Glen Ellen was "booming ... in a lively, progressive state":

> It is the terminus of the Sonoma Valley Railroad and contains two blacksmith shops, two groceries, one candy and variety store, and two hotels—the Mervyn, managed by J. T. Peters, and the Glen Ellen, conducted by Chas. Crofoot. ... J. W. Gibson is constructing a slaughterhouse and a new butcher shop and post office are to be built within a few weeks.

C. J. Poppe and C. O. Borman ran the grocery (general merchandise) store. Jim's Retreat (Jimmy Crosby, prop.) was a favorite bar.

The Feb. 11, 1888, *Index-Tribune*, under the headline "New towns springing up," says the laying out of new town sites in the Valley during the past few months seems to be in anticipation of a demand for suburban residences by business and professional men of San Francisco upon the completion of the Donahue railroad extension from Pacheco to the Sonoma Valley Railroad:

> Agua Caliente, one of these new towns, already boasts of a post office, hotel, two saloons, livery stable, a general merchandising store, fish and meat

Glen Ellen in the 1890s: old Poppe store in foreground, Borman's general merchandise store at right. Buildings in the background include, from left, Chinese laundry, livery stable, Native Sons hall and, upper right, old station house.

INDEX-TRIBUNE ARCHIVES

market, blacksmith shop, a winery and swimming baths. North Glen Ellen is the name of another. The site of this town is laid off on Ten Oaks Vineyard, the property of Mrs. Kate F. Warfield.

The July 28, 1888, issue of the *I-T* reports receipt by editor Granice of the first issue of the *Los Guilicos Herald,* devoted to the interests of the new town of Los Guilicos, situated about 14 miles north of Sonoma. Charles Tarrant of San Francisco was the editor, and it was printed in San Francisco.

Embarcadero, which the *I-T* stated was "situated at the head of navigation on Sonoma Creek four miles southeast of Sonoma," was described as having "commenced to pick up" in an Aug. 25, 1888, news item.

The increased shipping of fruit from that place was credited with the spurt.

Located there were Vollmar's Hotel, Captain Green's lumber yard, and a number of neat sta-

tion buildings erected by the Santa Rosa and Carquinez Railroad.

The town of Schellville, laid out the latter part of 1888, bears a strong resemblance to Embarcadero, as described in the item in the Feb. 22, 1889, *Index-Tribune*:

It is located near the head of navigation on Sonoma Creek and at the junction of the Santa Rosa and Carquinez and Sonoma Valley Railroads, four miles from Sonoma. Laid out by Messrs. S. and M. P. Akers, it is surrounded on all sides by rich farming lands.

Schellville has a public school, a private boarding school, art school, a post office, express office, a general merchandising store, hotel and lumber yard.

– RML

INDEX-TRIBUNE ARCHIVES

Hood Mountain was the backdrop for this pastoral Kenwood scene of 1879.

COURTESY, ROBERT D. PARMELEE

El Verano upstaged Sonoma in the late 1880s with a new railroad depot (above), new hotel and new homes. Promoters of the boom town advertised building lots on signs like the one shown at left.

El Verano land booms— lots from $85 to $550

The community of El Verano, initially called just Verano (Spanish for "summer"), was born early in the year 1888, a child of the decision made by the Santa Rosa and Carquinez Railroad to place its new passenger and freight station on land two miles west of the city of Sonoma, across Sonoma Creek.

Divisive factions in Sonoma were responsible for the out-of-city placement of the new depot.

The May 5, 1888, issue of the *Index-Tribune* reported that "several hundred people from San Francisco visited Verano last Saturday to view the location of the new town and select lots, and as on several previous like occasions, a number were sold. ... The Verano Land Company is putting in magnificent drives, broad avenues, parks and water works as if by magic."

An earlier issue had noted that among the promoters of the new town was a Mr. F. P. Bacon, one of the founders of Pasadena.

On June 2, 1888, the *Index-Tribune* reported that the new depot building of the Santa Rosa and Carquinez Railroad at El Verano was nearing completion. "The handsome two-story structure" was built on the extreme northwestern corner of the 777-acre Clark ranch, which had been purchased by the railroad people who were promoting the new town of El Verano.

On June 9 of the same year it was revealed that the Clark place was the property of an organization called The Sonoma Valley Improvement Company, of which Chas. F. Crocker of the Southern Pacific Co. was president, and Messrs. Geo. H. Maxwell, F. S. Douty, F. A. Frank and Wm. Hood were directors.

F. P. Bacon of the Verano Land Co. was at that time bringing suit against the S. P. group over the land acquisition. (A judge ruled against him a month later.)

On June 23, a brief item in the *I-T* said that "all work on the new town of Verano has been suspended and the hotel closed, owing to a misunderstanding among the directors and a pending lawsuit."

Another item said, "A map of the new town of El Verano, located two miles northwest of this

COURTESY, ROBERT D. PARMELEE

Glen Ellen railroad depot in 1885.

city, on the line of the Santa Rosa and Carquinez Railroad, has just been issued by the Sonoma Valley Improvement Company."

An auction of town lots and acre tracts was held on June 30, 1888. More than 500 people attended the auction, the promoters stating that $30,000 in sales were made. Said the *Index-Tribune* of July 7, 1888:

> The lots brought fair prices, busi-
> ness corners on the streets facing the
> depot bringing from $400 to $550.
> Inside lots, 50 x 140, were sold for from
> $80 to $350. The people of this city
> were among the most spirited buyers,
> and they invested some $7,000 in lots
> and acre property.

Editor Granice reported the receipt of the first issue of *The Sonoma Valley Whistle*, published at El Verano on Feb. 22, 1889, a publication backed by the Sonoma Valley Improvement Company, promoters of the new town of El Verano.

The first mention of the boom town's apparent failure, after the item about the *Whistle* being started in El Verano, appeared in the April 13, 1889, *I-T* under "Glen Ellen gossip."

The columnist, after noting that west Glen Ellen will be lit up with gas in a few days, goes on to say, "The former enterprising town of Verano, which we are sorry to say is no more, has left well-graded streets and a half-finished con-

crete foundation, which we presume was intended for a Court House."

Said the Sept. 20, 1890, *Index-Tribune*: "It is rumored that Geo. Maxwell is to move his El Verano newspaper to Sonoma. ... Verily, Boomtown must be on its last legs."

And this piece: "It is stated that Maxwell cannot appeal the Bacon case which was decided against him last month. If this is so, investors in Boomtown lots and villa sites will have to look to Mr. Bacon for their titles. As Messrs. Bacon, father and son, have been taken in by the boom in this Valley, we have no doubt that they deeply empathize with their fellow victims," said the *Index-Tribune*.

It was about this time that the *Whistle* and Verano–El Verano promoters blew their last, or at least the *Index-Tribune* files through 1899 reflect little or no mention of the El Verano promotion being revived.

Perhaps "the last word" on the subject was this brief item in the Dec. 31, 1898, issue of the *Index-Tribune*: "George H. Maxwell, the founder of El Verano, will remove with his family to San Jose the coming month, where he will engage in the practice of law."

Kenwood, like El Verano, also experienced a "boom" that fizzled. In 1889 the Kenwood Land Company sold town lots, villa sites and acre tracts to eager buyers. The company had purchased 2,680 acres in Los Guilucos Valley from Mrs. Giconda Gianella but, when it could not satisfy the mortgage on the property, was foreclosed upon.

In September 1896 the property was sold, at sheriff's sale, back to Mrs. Gianella, for $58,903.89. There were 38 defendants in the case, many of whom had invested their all in the up-Valley boom town.   – RML

Social life, churches, clubs and Union Hall

Much of social life in Sonoma Valley—as reflected in the pages of *The Sonoma Index-Tribune* between 1879 and 1899—centered around the few existing churches, lodges and clubs, Union Hall and sometimes Weyl Hall, where most of the entertainment programs and large gatherings of any kind took place. The churches were St. Francis Solano (Catholic) and the Congregational and Methodist (Protestant) churches. Each had its own edifice. Episcopal services were also conducted in Weyl Hall and at the Flowery District School in Agua Caliente every other Sunday by a visiting minister.

The oldest fraternal organization in Sonoma was Temple Lodge, No. 14, F&AM, founded here May 6, 1851. Others included Sonoma Lodge No. 28, IOOF; Order of Eastern Star, Knights of Pythias, Pueblo Lodge, AOUW; Woodmen of the World, Crescent Council, No. 703; AL of H, and Verdant Rebekah Lodge, IOOF.

The Native Sons of the Golden West, Sonoma Parlor No. 111, was founded July 20, 1887; and a Glen Ellen NSGW parlor was founded Feb. 19, 1887. The Sonoma Native Daughters of the Golden West Parlor was started Oct. 22, 1887.

Other popular organizations of the era included the Clay Literary Society, founded in 1883, and the Sonoma Turn Verein (an athletic club).

The Sonoma Brass Band, under Prof. Hugh Maxwell, provided well-attended indoor and outdoor concerts during the 1880s, the *I-T* of Sept. 25, 1886, calling it "as fine a brass band as any interior town in the State."

In 1895 the same H. G. Maxwell was named as the director who put on the Sonoma Valley Band Concert June 28 at Union Hall. The 20-piece band, along with 12-year-old Julie Granice, daughter of *Index-Tribune* editor H. H. Granice and possessor of a beautiful, deep contralto voice, received fine reviews in *Town Talk* and *The Entertainer,* leading musical journals of San Francisco.

In 1899 two minstrel shows were given with great success at the Union Hall, one with an all-male cast, the other by a female aggregation called the Sonoma Lady Minstrels.

The stage curtain from Union Hall, with its advertisements and paintings, is today displayed in the Sonoma Valley Historical Society's Depot Museum.   – RML

Railroads and the *Index* were both born in 1879

Both *The Sonoma Index* and the railroads of Sonoma Valley were born in 1879. Up to that time (except for experiments), transportation had been by steamboat and stagecoach, colorful but slow and impractical for heavy loads.

In the year mentioned, the Sonoma Valley Railroad, a three-foot, narrow-gauge line, began daily service from Lions Station (Vineburg) to

Sonoma Valley Band, circa 1890, photographed on First Street West. Members were, left to right: Frank Riser, William Stone, Fred Clark, Leland Shaw, Claude Johnson, George Tate, Jim Albertson, Jake Wystrick, J. G. Marcy, Lucien Johnson, Alf. McLaughlin, Eph Cutter, Al Sutter, George Martin, Fred Ehrlich, George Porter, Frank Carmer, Charles Ward, Robert Wilson and Hugh Maxwell, leader.

INDEX-TRIBUNE ARCHIVES

COURTESY, ROBERT D. PARMELEE

The Kenwood railroad depot was built in 1887 by the Southern Pacific Railroad and has been preserved by residents for use as a community center.

Wingo (three miles below Schellville), where the train made direct connections with a paddle-wheeled steamboat destined for San Francisco.

In 1880 the railway track was extended to the Sonoma Plaza, and by 1882 it had reached Glen Ellen. From Schellville the railway track went straight north up Eighth Street East to Spain Street, turned west and proceeded to the Plaza, where a depot was built in February 1880. The track then continued west on Spain Street to near the present Highway 12, where it turned right and went north to Glen Ellen.

South from Schellville the railway went to Wingo, then to Sears Point and out into San Pablo Bay, where a pier was built to permit steamboats to stop on their way to and from Petaluma.

The railway had three locomotives—the *Sonoma*, built in 1878; the *Newton Booth*, built in 1879; and the *General Vallejo*, built in 1881.

The 1880 railway service was as follows: Passengers left Sonoma at 6:10 A.M., arriving in San Francisco at 9 A.M. The return left San Francisco at 4:30 P.M. and arrived at the Plaza at 7:20 P.M.

The Sonoma Valley Railroad had gotten its franchise from the Sonoma County Board of Supervisors. It needed no other authority, as the city of Sonoma remained unincorporated until 1883.

Traffic soon became difficult on Spain Street because of the railway track, and it wasn't long before the railway facility spread out over half the Plaza. Occupying the town square were the depot, a car barn, engine house, turntable, water pump, coal yard, brick pile and spur tracks, giving the Plaza the appearance of a railway junk-yard, full of weeds in the summer and just one big mud puddle in the winter.

Citizens became very critical of the condition of the Plaza, complaining about the mud and visual pollution. In part, the movement to rein-corporate the city in 1882 was an effort to get some control over the railroad's wanton disre-gard of the way things looked. Henry Weyl filed suit against the railway to try to get the line moved off Spain Street. He won the case in the Santa Rosa court, but the railway kept appealing the decision.

The railway's use of the Plaza might have lasted for a long time but for competition from the Southern Pacific Company, which forced changes for economic reasons.

In 1887 the Southern Pacific, acting under the title of the Santa Rosa and Carquinez Railroad, bought a right-of-way through the

Valley to run trains from Napa to Santa Rosa. It was Southern Pacific's intention to draw profits away from the Donahue railway system, of which the Sonoma Valley Railroad was a part.

Southern Pacific's tracks did not go into the town of Sonoma because S. P. sought to escape costs involved, since by this time Sonoma had reincorporated as a city. With much fanfare the S. P. opened its railway line in the spring of 1888.

It was obvious that the Sonoma Valley Railroad had to do something; the narrow-gauge railroad was too slow and the boat trip to San Francisco too long. The *Index-Tribune,* in editorials, urged that the Sonoma Valley Railroad be made standard-gauge and, of course, relocated off the Plaza. For a time it appeared as if the Sonoma Valley Railroad would be abandoned, but a management decision was made to fight the Southern Pacific.

This was to be accomplished, first, by extending the narrow-gauge track to Ignacio, where the trains would meet the standard-gauge Donahue line, thus doing away with the need for the boat to San Francisco (over which there had been considerable complaint because of the filthy conditions of the steamboats); and second, by making the railway standard gauge and moving the equipment off the Plaza.

By June 1888 the narrow-gauge track had been extended to Ignacio. By 1890 the Plaza railway equipment had been either demolished or moved two blocks north. There followed a period of approximately 30 years of exciting competition between the two railroads, working to the advantage of Sonoma both for price and convenience. Both railways increased the number of stations as the traffic warranted and served both Boyes Springs and Fetters Springs.

On the Southern Pacific Railway (Santa Rosa and Carquinez) one could leave from the San Francisco Ferry Building at 8 A.M. or 4 P.M., arriving at El Verano at 9:28 A.M. and 6:23 P.M.; returning from El Verano at 6:48 A.M. and 3:50 P.M., arriving in San Francisco at 9:20 A.M. and 6:20 P.M. daily. The trip required taking two ferry boats, first to Oakland and then across the Carquinez Straits.

The Sonoma Valley Railroad, now doing business as the San Francisco and North Pacific Railroad, also departed from the Ferry Building in San Francisco, at 7:30 A.M. and 5:10 P.M., arriving in Sonoma at 9:27 A.M. and 7:17 P.M.; and returned to San Francisco at 6:18 A.M. and 3:48 P.M., arriving at the Ferry Building at 8:40 A.M. and 6:15 P.M. daily. Additional excursion trains for campers and vacationers were provided each weekend all summer long.

So good was the business that by the late 1890s local merchant Solomon Schocken and others were making plans to build an electric streetcar system to connect Santa Rosa with Sonoma, and Sonoma with Schellville. Applications were made and newspaper articles written about an electric streetcar, but it all came to naught.

Try as they might, the railways never completely put the steamboats out of business. Even though the attractive steamboat *Sonoma* could not compete with the railroads, it successfully ran up the Petaluma River for many years. Similar vessels, such as those run by Capt. Peter Hauto, provided daily service from Schellville to San Francisco, hauling butter and other agricultural produce.

The railways continued to be important until well into the 20th century, but, like the stagecoach before them, they eventually became only a memory when the automobile and Greyhound bus took their place.

— ROBERT D. PARMELEE

INDEX-TRIBUNE ARCHIVES

Local historian Robert D. Parmelee in the uniform of a Northwestern Pacific Railroad employee, at the Sonoma Depot Museum.

Fish and game abounded in the Sonoma Valley

*F*ish and game were abundant in the Sonoma Valley between 1879 and 1899, but even before the turn of the century, lax state laws, greedy "sportsmen" and community growth began to whittle away at the wildlife population.

The first mention of fish in the first issue of *The Sonoma Index* on April 21, 1879, dealt with carp. Imported from Germany in August 1872 by J. A. Poppe of Sonoma, who raised them commercially, a small number of carp escaped from his ponds into Sonoma Creek and propagated. One old-timer claims this was one of the major contributing factors in "ruining Sonoma Creek as a fishing stream."

The voracious carp were said to eat trout eggs and small trout. Bony and soft, carp were unpopular as game fish, although edible.

"They bite like a trout and make a good fight. One of them weighed nearly eight pounds," said a fisherman in reporting to the *Index-Tribune* in 1879. Carp were also caught with spears and pitchforks, they became so plentiful. That same issue noted that "J. A. Poppe of this place recently shipped 40 carp to Sisson's in Shasta County."

The first mention of salmon appears in a January 1886 *I-T* item noting that "salmon are plentiful in Sonoma Creek and can be seen in large numbers every day." This referred to salmon and steelhead coming up to spawn.

An item in the Jan. 21, 1899, *I-T* noted that recent rains had set "all the mountain streams here a-booming," and that "Sonoma Creek is fairly swarming with salmon and trout on their way to the spawning grounds near the headwaters of Agua Caliente, Hooker, Fowler, Stuart and other small creeks on the east and west sides of the Valley."

An October 1886 item notes that "A. J. Murphy caught 40 fine trout in the Sonoma Creek one day last week inside of three hours." One of those greedy "sportsmen" we referred to is mentioned in an April 30, 1887, item: "Nick Fowler, an employee of G. A. Cornelius, caught 352 trout Thursday, Friday and Saturday in Sonoma Creek."

The biggest trout mentioned was a seven-pounder caught on April 15, 1888, in Sonoma Creek.

The biggest "weight" catch of any fish was reported on March 23, 1889, from Sonoma Creek between Volmer's Hotel and McGill's station (near Schellville): "Thursday morning, John Ludeman of this place speared 300 pounds of carp with a gig." Said the *I-T* editor, "He will please accept the thanks of this office for a nine-pounder."

Catfish were also caught in large numbers in the combination of fresh and salt water at Embarcadero below Schellville. "It is not uncommon for a fisherman to catch several hundred in a single afternoon or morning," said the *Index-Tribune* of May 14, 1898.

Striped bass, from the East Coast, were first introduced to the San Francisco Bay and Delta areas the year *The Sonoma Index* was founded. In 1879 the planting of 132 of these gamefish was reported, followed by another 300 in 1882. They propagated widely, and the sloughs below Schellville and the lower reaches of Sonoma Creek have produced many large stripers for fishermen from the 1920s up to the present day.

The author of this piece remembers catching limits of stripers in the small slough extension of Sonoma Creek right behind the Millerick ranch-house, a stone's throw from where the Schell-Vista fire station now sits. And that was in the 1950s!

Deer abounded in the hills surrounding the Valley between 1879 and 1899, and it was not uncommon for hunters to hike from town and in a few hours bag a buck in back of the Vallejo home or Mountain Cemetery. The deer were even more abundant in the Glen Ellen and Kenwood areas.

One article in the Aug. 11, 1883, *Sonoma Valley Index* noted that "deer are so plentiful that two of our boys are making $4 a day by killing deer and shipping the venison to San Francisco."

Wildfowl also thrived in the Valley of the Moon before the turn of the century. In the Valley and hills flocks of quail made their homes—in such great numbers so as to annoy vineyardists, who demanded an "open" rather than the state-imposed closed season on quail.

A Sept. 12, 1885, editorial in the *Index-*

Tribune noted that "every one of these birds destroys at least 50¢ worth of grapes in certain sections here before it gets into the city nimrod's game bag."

Waterfowl were also plentiful, as the marshlands, tules and sloughs south of town were a natural feeding ground for the birds. Ducks— teal, mallard and sprig—provided good shooting November through January.

Geese of the Canadian honker and snow varieties are also mentioned. The Nov. 26, 1892, issue of the *Index-Tribune* noted: "Wild geese are swarming on the tule lands south of town. They are so thick and destructive on the Senator Jones ranch [now Skaggs Island] that a hunter is employed to keep the voracious birds off the young grain which has commenced to make a fine growth."

The Sonoma Valley Gun Club, perhaps the community's first group of its kind, was organized in November 1892 with the following membership: J. Wadsworth, F. A. Riser, J. A. Perkins, George Cassidy, Ed. Dowdall and F. Grothaus. The club leased land on Harry Fisher's dairy farm.

Predators, scarce today, roamed the hills of the Valley—mountain lions, wildcats and some bear.

An item in the Feb. 5, 1898, *Index-Tribune* reports the killing of the fourth wildcat of the season, plus three foxes, on the Bain ranch a few miles north of town.

It was an era for the hunter and fisherman.

– RML

A few select news notes from the 1880s

Caleb Carriger has 200 orange trees on his place. One tree bore 1,500 oranges, all well developed and of excellent quality. He sold last year 700 oranges from two trees. Jan. 15, 1880, *Sonoma Index*

At a meeting of the school trustees, the following resolution was adopted: Resolved, that this board will not consider any complaints against teachers in the Sonoma public school unless the same be submitted in writing signed by the party making such complaint. The object doubtless is to do away with the numerous and unimportant grievances that form so disagreeable an experience of the common school teacher. This system will identify the complainant, and give opportunity to properly specify the nature of the grievance and enable the trustees to examine into the cause. Jan. 30, 1880, *Sonoma Index*

The total amount of wine shipped from this point between Nov. 22, 1879, and April 1, 1880, is 275,000 gallons. April 10, 1880, *Sonoma Index*

Telephones are all the rage. One has been extended from Pauli's store to connect with the Depot. Others are talking of putting up connecting wires. It is not a bad idea for our businessmen to open communication with their dwellings, and with one another in this manner, as the wires and cost of erection is comparatively trifling. We trust we shall be able to follow suit—well, when our ship comes in. May 29, 1880, *Sonoma Index*

Mr. A. V. LaMotte, superintendent of the Lenni Fish Propagating Co., informs us that the company sometime since shipped 30,000 trout eggs to the Auckland, New Zealand, Acclimatization Society, and has received the report from them that they arrived in better order than any prior lot they had received from other parties. This we consider another feather in Sonoma's cap, and a big, bright one, too. July 1883, *Sonoma Valley Weekly Index*

Last week we made mention of a big potato, weighing three pounds, which was raised on the ranch of Capt. P. N. Stofen. Mr. Martin Muldry has one raised on the same ground which weighs four pounds. Sept. 29, 1883, *Sonoma Weekly Index*

There is now a hard struggle going on in this town between the town cattle and the tramps to decide which shall have possession of the Plaza and the pavilion. At last observation taken, the tramps had the best of it and have gained complete possession of the pavilion, as they greatly outnumber the cattle. Oct. 6, 1883, *Sonoma Weekly Index*

In the past two years, a great deal of attention has been paid by our farmers to tree planting and in a few years this Valley will be equally divided up in vineyards and orchards. A ride through the Valley will show that young orchards are being set out by many of our vine growers who have at least realized that there is more money in a diversity of crops than there is in cultivating one particular kind of product, such as grapes, for instance. Realizing this, Col. George F. Hooper is engaged in planting out 2,000 French prune trees on his farm near this city. Next season, he will also plant 2,000 olive trees in addition to those already growing on the place.
In a few more years, Sonoma Valley will be a heavy producer of all kinds of fruits and pure olive oil, which in time will become as famous as her celebrated wines and brandies. Feb. 11, 1886, *Sonoma Index-Tribune*

Glen Ellen: We visited this picturesque little burg last Monday and found its businessmen in good humor and the place in a thriving condition. We found the [two hotel] landlords at home, and came in for a share of that politeness, affability and entertainment which has made these gentlemen so well known to the traveling public. Jan. 14, 1888, *Sonoma Index-Tribune*

Capt. H. E. Boyes and the hot springs era

Workers drilling on the property of Capt. and Mrs. H. E. Boyes March 18, 1895, made a discovery that would soon lead to the development of one of Sonoma Valley's biggest attractions—natural hot springs.

It was on the same Boyes property, then known as the Agua Rica farm, that the famed Boyes Hot Springs Bathhouse would eventually be built and attract huge crowds year after year here. The Boyes Bathhouse, Fetters Hot Springs Hotel and the Agua Caliente Springs Hotel were to become three of the most popular mineral bath resorts in Northern California in the years that followed.

On that landmark day in 1895 workers struck the flowing well of hot water after drilling

COURTESY, SONOMA VALLEY HISTORICAL SOCIETY

Henry Ernest Boyes, namesake of Boyes Hot Springs.

to a depth of 70 feet. Temperature of the water was 112 degrees, almost hot enough to boil an egg. Accompanying the water was an immense volume of natural gas, which, it was said, was enough to supply the entire city of Sonoma with light.

Several other springs—hot, tepid and cold—surrounded the area. According to aborigine tradition, the hot springs were previously used as healing sources for various Indian tribes of Northern California, who brought their sick with them to bathe in the waters of the health-giving springs.

For two years Captain Boyes had been conducting the search for the hot mineral artesian water and natural gas. After the initial discovery in March 1895, an additional underground stream of hot mineral water was struck, which, according to the *Index-Tribune* account, "burst up to the surface through a seven-inch pipe to a height of several feet above ground amid a vapor of steam that caused the eyes of the astonished well laborers to bulge out like doorknobs." The flow was estimated at 100,000 gallons a day; the temperature, 112 degrees.

Professors and other leading geological and mining authorities flocked to Sonoma Valley to study the newfound springs. The Agua Rica Hot Springs, formed to promote the hot springs' recreational and medicinal values, was soon incorporated. And others proceeded to get into the act, as well.

Dr. Nordin, the new owner of the Agua Caliente Springs Hotel and grounds, employed workers to dig an artesian well with the same hopes in mind. In May 1895 an excellent flow of hot mineral water was found. The stream shot to several feet above the surface of the ground and carried an average temperature of 100 degrees. Dr. Nordin and his crew immediately began making plans to build swimming baths and like facilities. Improvements were also made on the nearby buildings, and interiors were refurbished.

The mineral bath phenomenon continued to bubble with enthusiasm here. In 1896 some 1,600 bathers utilized Captain Boyes' facilities, despite the fact that only three bathrooms were available. Between January and October 1899, over 4,085 bathers had visited there.

– JOHN LYNCH

City enacted tax on dogs, curfew for minors in 1885

*F*rom *The Sonoma Index-Tribune* of Sept. 5, 1885:

In another column will be found ordinances Nos. 21, 22 and 23, as passed by the Board of City Trustees last Wednesday evening, which should be read by everyone in the community.

The first has for its object the levying of a dog tax within the city limits. If the ordinance be enforced to the letter, it will have a tendency to lessen the number of worthless curs that now roam our streets and invade the back yards of dwellings and will also add to the revenue of the city.

Ordinance No. 22 was passed for the purpose of imposing and collecting an annual street poll tax, and is so drawn up that no one can dodge the collector.

The last ordinance, No. 23, is the most important of all.

It declares that it shall be unlawful for minors under 16 years of age to be on the public streets or Plaza at night after 8 o'clock during the months of November, December, January, February, March and April, and 9 o'clock during the remaining months of the year.

This is as it should be. There can be no disputing the fact that the small boy of this town is a perfect nuisance when allowed to remain on the streets at night.

If kept at home of an evening under the watchful eye of his parents, he will be out of mischief and eventually become a useful member of society; but if he be given the run of our streets at night, it is only a question of time when he will develop into a full-fledged hoodlum.

To the end that no such fate shall befall our boys and for the peace and quiet of the community have the Trustees seen fit to pass this order, and we trust the object sought by its promoters will be attained.   – RML

Sonoma's old adobe jail, located on First Street West north of Spain Street, was built by General Vallejo. It was still in use in the 1870s. In 1887 *I-T* editor Harry Granice described the jail as small, poorly ventilated, inadequately equipped and "a disgrace to any civilized community." In 1894 a new jail was constructed, and cells were furnished "with a board bed and a pair of blankets each," Granice reported.

INDEX-TRIBUNE ARCHIVES

First Vintage Festival— a Grecian drama

The Vintage Festival—pageants and kids in costume, music and dancing, good food and, of course, wine. Sonoma's first Vintage Festivals had all these elements but differed from today's Vintage Festivals in many ways.

Our first Vintage Festival took place in October 1896 at the Rhine Farm, two miles east of Sonoma. The festival was an expression of thanksgiving for the vintners' successful fight against phylloxera, a root louse that threatened to destroy California's vineyards.

While current Vintage Festivals are history- and parade-oriented, the first celebration was a mythological drama set in ancient Greece. Authored by Sonoma High School principal Benjamin Weed, the drama was titled *The Vintage Festival*.

Grecian-robed Eva Gundlach presented the prologue. Weed, as the wine god Bacchus, initiated his followers into the joys of wine. "The drama abounds in choruses and drinking songs, the music of which was composed by Mrs. F. T. Duhring," reported the Oct. 31, 1896, edition of *The Sonoma Index-Tribune*.

Local actors included Carl Bundschu, Vernon Goodwin and Miss Claire Hope. "Dancing was indulged in until a late hour in the beautifully decorated wine cellar, which was lit with different-colored incandescent lights," noted the paper.

A natural amphitheater called Pansy Valley, located just north of today's Gundlach-Bundschu Winery on Thornsberry Road, was the setting for early vintage festivals. German vintners Emil Dresel and Jacob Gundlach started the winery in 1858. They brought both German winemaking methods and Rhineland festivals to the Sonoma Valley. Their successors, Charles Bundschu and Julius Dresel, created the Vintage Festivals.

When phylloxera appeared in their vineyards, Julius devised the method which eventually whipped the scourge—grafting phylloxera-stricken cuttings to resistant rootstock.

The second Vintage Festival was held on Oct. 9, 1897, with invitations issued to Sonomans and San Franciscans. City dwellers came by the Tiburon boat to Schellville, then by open carriage to "an arcadia in Sonoma's woodlands."

Local residents came by surrey, spring wagon or saddle horse, and wagon seats were removed to serve as chairs around picnic fires. While families ate and gossiped, fiddlers entertained everyone with songs and dances until kerosene lanterns lit the dusk.

At 9 o'clock the drama, again written by Weed, unfolded with five-year-old Otto Dresel playing "Baby Bacchus." The adult Bacchus, portrayed by San Francisco opera star Robert Bien, solved the problems of a young couple by creating a bountiful grape harvest.

Page one of the Oct. 11, 1897, *San Francisco Call* reported the festival:

"One Eve of Pleasure at the Beautiful Vale of Pansies," "Nymphs in a Love Romance," "Greek Mythology Given Life in a Moonlight Mountain Canyon," "Outdoor Revel at the Rhine Farm."

Benjamin Weed and Eva Gundlach starred as the lovers, while Sonomans dressed in togas and goatskins appeared as nymphs, goatherders, vintagers and messengers. Nymphs included Julie Granice, daughter of H. H. Granice, editor of the *Index-Tribune*. H. Gundlach appeared as a goatherder, while six members of the Bundschu family were vintagers and messengers.

The Oct. 1, 1898, edition of the *Index-Tribune* reported both a "first-class" grape harvest and the presentation of *The Victory* by Weed at the third Vintage Festival. As before, Bacchus comes to the rescue of two lovers, this time by waylaying with Bacchantes a slave sent to kill the suitor. Weed and his wife played the lovers, Robert Bien starred as Bacchus.

The Vintage Festivals were not held again until 1947, reborn through the efforts of local leading citizens, in the forefront of whom was *Index-Tribune* editor and historian Celeste G. Murphy. Benjamin Weed went on to establish the Greek Theatre at the University of California, Berkeley.

The Gundlach-Bundschu Winery received a crippling blow when its San Francisco wine cellars were destroyed in the 1906 earthquake and fire. Prohibition silenced the winery, which did not begin bottling again under the Gundlach-Bundschu label until 1976.

— DONALD NELSON EDWARDS

COURTESY, SONOMA VALLEY HISTORICAL SOCIETY

The Union Hotel and Union Hall (right), where many pioneer festivities took place, was located on West Napa Street between what are today Broadway and First Street West—now the site of the Bank of America.

First electric lights for Sonoma in 1898

Perhaps no other editorial campaign of *The Sonoma Index-Tribune* was as forceful or determined as that for electric light for the city of Sonoma.

Beginning in 1895, the *I-T* ran numerous editorials and news items in its stringent advocacy of "modern electric lights" for the small town.

I-T publisher Harry Granice was especially chagrined by the fact that many other small California towns already had such a sign of community improvement. In an editorial written Dec. 21, 1895, he noted, "It is generally admitted that Sonoma is way behind other towns of her size and importance in the matter of light."

He cited as an example the residence of Julius Fochetti, which was illuminated by gas, and noted, "Stores and dwellings are all illumined with coal oil and tallow candles" with that exception.

The *I-T* proposed that the city trustees "inquire into the practicability of owning and controlling its own lighting system" as it "would no doubt prove a source of revenue to the city and in addition give its people a better, safer and more economic light than that afforded by coal oil and candles."

The city was not interested. Instead, a group of local businessmen formed a private company in its quest for light and named it the Sonoma Electric Light Company.

Although the city finally granted the company permission to start business and the fledgling power plant was begun early in 1898, the businessmen stockholders were left with a burden of financial difficulties.

An *I-T* edition early in that year noted, "The Sonoma Electric Company will be incorporated with a capital stock of $10,000, it was decided. ... Two hundred shares of stock with a par value of $50 each will be offered. Most of it has been subscribed for, with the principal stockholders including F. T. Duhring, C. F. Leiding, Robert

Hall, H. H. Granice, C. Aguillon, Julius Fochetti, S. Ciucci, F. Clewe and S. Schocken."

However, shortly before the incorporation of the company, troubles arose with what the *I-T* called the "pull backs" of Sonoma. The Feb. 12, 1898, editorial commented, "Not satisfied with doing their level best to defeat by misrepresentation the water proposition in their hatred of every public improvement, they are now seeking to discourage several of the promoters of the electric lighting project by telling them that the investment will be a dead loss and that there will be assessments instead of dividends."

Although the articles of incorporation of the company were finally filed with the state in April 1898, two of the original stockholders dropped out and things were not going well for the new company.

After a year's trial run, the company admitted defeat and closed the plant. Soon thereafter, however, a Mr. Astrill took over operation of the company.

From that point, the *I-T*'s pages are curiously bare of any mention of the power plant, but according to PG&E records, Sonoma Electric Light Company was sold to California Gas and Electric Company in 1902. In 1906 the company was assumed by PG&E.   – KATHY SWETT

Basalt rock quarries were a major industry

*I*n the 1880s and 1890s, Sonoma's basalt rock quarries created the town's third-largest industry, after the wineries and dairies. "At one time the industry gave employment to 300 men in this place," reported an August 1897 issue of *The Sonoma Index-Tribune*.

Many of Sonoma's hills, including 658-foot-high Schocken Hill, held granite and basalt deposits left by prehistoric volcanic activity. Jimmy Smith of Cordelia started Sonoma's first quarry about 1880. Two years later, H. C. Manuel opened a quarry northeast of town, employing 40 to 50 men, 16 to 20 horses and getting out an average of 80,000 blocks a month.

The Dec. 11, 1886, issue of the *Index-Tribune* reported:

> H. C. Manuel has finished shipping an order for 150,000 paving blocks for the streets of Stockton, but will be kept busy in supplying an order for an additional 100,000 from another source. He has also secured the contract for supplying blocks to be used in the construction of the sea wall at San Francisco.

INDEX-TRIBUNE ARCHIVES

The original Odd Fellows Hall, built about 1880, was located on Broadway.

INDEX-TRIBUNE ARCHIVES

In the 1880s and '90s, Sonoma's basalt rock quarries were Sonoma's third-largest industry, after the wineries and dairies. In August 1897 the *Index-Tribune* reported that 300 men were employed in the quarries. Many of Sonoma's hills, including 658-foot-high Schocken Hill, shown here, held granite and basalt deposits which became paving blocks for San Francisco, Stockton, Petaluma and San Jose. One of the biggest quarry operators was merchant Solomon Schocken. He purchased 62 acres north of town and west of present-day Mountain Cemetery. Many Italian stonecutters, including Samuele Sebastiani, came to Sonoma as quarry workers. Predecessors of the Clydesdale horses on the farm at Spain and Second Street East hauled stone-laden wagons down Schocken Hill.

Quarries at Sonoma, Agua Caliente and Kenwood furnished paving blocks for San Francisco, Petaluma and San Jose. Several quarries were opened on land owned by Gen. Mariano Vallejo, local grocer Henry Weyl and contractor Agostino Pinelli; but one of the biggest operators was Solomon Schocken, a merchant operating out of the Sonoma Barracks, who purchased 62 acres of land north of town in 1880—in the area now called Schocken Hill.

The basalt block industry of Sonoma received another "boost" this week. S. Schocken of this city, on Thursday last, secured a contract for the delivery to one of the principal cable car systems of San Francisco of 400,000 blocks, which will be used in paving the streets between tracks,

noted the Nov. 25, 1893, edition of the *Index-Tribune.*

The basalt industry suffered a serious setback when San Francisco's street commissioners tried out bitumen, or asphalt, for street paving. But the *Index-Tribune* happily reported, "The basalt block industry, which has been almost at a standstill of late, has commenced to pick up. It had been demonstrated after a trial of several years that bitumen can not altogether supplant block paving."

The Pinelli family had been in the quarry business in Europe, and Agostino Pinelli first mined stone on General Vallejo's property west of Schocken Hill, paying the General $12 per thousand stones as a fee for using his land. Agostino brought to Sonoma many Italian stonecutters, including Samuele Sebastiani—later to become the successful vintner—who drove the horse-drawn wagons loaded with stones down Schocken Hill to the Embarcadero on Sonoma Creek or to the train station in Sonoma's Plaza.

"These [quarries] give employment to a large

number of white men, the year round, at remunerative wages. ... Many of them are married and surrounded by interesting families, own their own dwellings, are members of our churches and secret societies and take an active interest in public affairs," noted an 1886 issue of the paper.

The Jan. 26, 1889, issue of the *Index-Tribune* reported, "The block-making business is giving employment to a large number of men at present. They make from $3 to $5 per day, according to the skill of the men." Blockmakers worked by the piece, with the more skilled workers earning $6 and $7 a day.

A story in the Nov. 25, 1893, edition of the paper demonstrated the hazards of the trade: "About seven months ago, H. Matson, while working at his trade of blockmaker, injured his right hand and for several months was confined to his bed, threatened with blood poisoning. The family, consisting of his wife and two little children, residing in this place, have been reduced to destitution." Readers were urged to assist the Matson family.

Asphalt paving finally destroyed Sonoma's basalt block industry, but today the City Hall in the Plaza and the old Pinelli building [between Lo Spuntino and Zino's on First Street East] stand as two of many reminders of our quarrymen.

– DONALD NELSON EDWARDS

Frustrating fight for an adequate water system

The *Index-Tribune*, representing the interests of the property owners in this town, is in the water fight with both feet.

You can boycott the paper, cuss the editor, threaten to do him up, but you can't pull him down.

The *Index-Tribune* is in favor of a better water system and will favor any proposition that the people will decide upon in mass meeting.

*T*his editorial by feisty *I-T* editor Harry H. Granice was one of many he wrote during the 1880s, 1890s and early 1900s on what was probably the city's biggest local issue—its inadequate water system.

INDEX-TRIBUNE ARCHIVES

The Union Livery Stable in the 1890s. Pictured are Joe Ryan, later Sonoma County sheriff, and Emil Cornelius. A clothing store and microbrewery now occupy the site at Napa and First Street West, adjacent to the *Index-Tribune*.

INDEX-TRIBUNE ARCHIVES

Bonded Liquor Warehouse on West Napa Street, with St. Francis Solano Catholic Church visible at left. John Maxwell Cheney of a pioneer Sonoma Valley family is the man with cart at left. The warehouse was located about where a two-story medical office building now stands.

But despite all his work and arguments, nothing was done about the city's water system—which was built by Gen. Mariano G. Vallejo—while Granice was still alive. He died in 1915, and as late as 1918 the city voters turned down a proposal for the city to bond itself to buy out the local water company. The city finally bought the system in 1933.

It must have been especially frustrating for editor Granice—surely one of the most farseeing men of his time—during the 1880s and 1890s. For during this period, many proposals to improve the city's water system were put forward, but nothing really came of them.

During these decades, in the meantime, the use of electricity and the telephone were making great inroads here.

In October 1887 the *I-T* mentioned that a new Sonoma Valley Water Co., with prominent residents as directors, was going to construct a reservoir on Sonoma Mountain from which a line would run to the city of Sonoma.

Apparently work started on this project but the water never got here, for in 1890 editor Granice was still lamenting the scarcity of water and denouncing "redwood mains likely to burst."

The private system built by Vallejo used the reservoir behind his home, Lachryma Montis, as a supply, and it went to a few customers around the Plaza and in the downtown area.

Granice continued to inveigh about the need for a modern water system, extolling the benefits

for living and fire protection, plus a cut in insurance rates.

He was one of the chief advocates of the Sonoma Fire Department, formed in 1889. But the city didn't give the firemen a proper water supply.

Almost week by week, the *I-T* also reported the success of farmers and businessmen drilling artesian wells.

Merchant Solomon Schocken got an artesian well which was said to be capable of furnishing water for a city of 100,000 inhabitants and water power for a dozen factories. Schocken supplied a number of his tenants with water. Most city residents, of course, were still on wells.

It was even speculated that Sonoma was built on top of an underground river. Yet for all this, as editor Granice was fond of pointing out, Sonoma was the only city in the state without any watering troughs for horses.

In August 1892 he noted that the trees in the Plaza were dying for lack of water. "With the waters from half-a-dozen artesian wells running to waste, this is a most remarkable state of affairs," Granice mused.

In June 1896 St. Francis Solano Church burned down, and the editor remarked, "How helpless our citizens are in case of fire."

Disastrous fires occurred in the 1880s, 1890s and early 1900s, often wiping out several buildings or a whole section of the settled area. On at least one occasion, wine was used to fight one of these conflagrations.

Granice's suggestion for getting a better water system was to bond the city. In August 1896 the city trustees (now the city council) assigned three of their number to investigate how the city could bond itself for a water system.

The trustees also obtained options on several artesian wells, with a view to building up the municipal water system. And in January 1897 a couple of engineers were assigned to report on what would be the best water system for the city.

The engineers came up with two plans: the city could use artesian well water, development of which would cost $25,300, or let a gentleman named L. L. Lewis pipe water to the city from Fowler Creek at a cost of $14,000.

Granice editorialized for a water bond issue on the platform of "Prosperity, Peace and Plenty." A bond election, asking voters to select one of the two systems, was set for June 14, 1897.

For some unknown reason, the date of the election was changed to July 12. And then the state Supreme Court said some of the city's legal wording for the election was wrong. The election was postponed.

In April 1898, three pro-water candidates were elected as city trustees—G. S. Harris, Fred T. Duhring and H. H. Davis.

But later in the month, voters rejected the city's water scheme—90 yes, 56 no. A two-thirds majority was needed.

A corporation of artesian well owners tried without success to get a franchise from the city in May 1898. Another committee was formed to recommend a water system.

Another water bond election in the amount of $15,000 for acquisition and construction of a city water works was set for October 24.

The election lost again, 102 yes, 59 no. Granice wrote, "J. E. Poppe, Chessmore, George Breitenbach and the other anti-water advocates win a doubtful victory."

Granice continued to vent his feelings in his editorials. One was headed, "One hundred and two versus 60."

The city continued to diddle about, with two trustees named to secure options on wells and well sites again. An engineer named Otto Von Geldern outlined a detailed plan whereby Sonoma could get a municipal water system for

$19,170.

Von Geldern headed his report "The Water Problem." That was the same head used in a discussion of the problem, which hadn't changed, in the *I-T* in 1918, 20 years later.

In April 1900 another water bond issue was defeated, although two pro-water candidates were elected as city trustees—G. H. Hotz and Settimo Ciucci.

On July 4 that year, the paper said the city's "ancient" water system was clogged with slime.

In April 1918 a $45,000 water bond issue was defeated, 173 no, 140 yes. Only one thing had changed—the number of no votes was getting bigger.

—JERRY PARKER

Volunteer fire company formed officially in 1888

*I*ndex-Tribune editor Harry H. Granice waged many editorial campaigns until his death in 1915, but one of his most satisfying—eventually—was his constant plea for the establishment of a fire department in the community.

His top priority, along with the fire department formation, was for an adequate, city-owned water works. The two, of course, were intertwined.

Hardly a month went by during the 1880s and 1890s that the *Index-Tribune* didn't report a fire of some kind, many of them wiping out homes and businesses and even large sections of the town. Following each fire, or so it seems in reading through the old newspaper files, would be an editorial advocating (1) a water works and (2) a fire department.

Although Granice never lived to see an enlarged and improved city water system (finally voted by the people in 1933), he was in the forefront when the city's first fire department was born.

Four weeks after the city trustees introduced an ordinance creating a fire department (Oct. 13, 1888), a group of citizens met in the city pavilion in the Plaza and organized the town's first official volunteer fire company.

Editor Granice was a member of a three-man committee named to draft the bylaws, and officers were elected "to serve for three months."

INDEX-TRIBUNE ARCHIVES

Sonoma Volunteer Fire Department, March 26, 1892. Members bought their own red and white uniforms with nominal assistance from the city. Barely visible is the hook-and-ladder fire apparatus. *I-T* editor Harry Granice (circled) campaigned actively for the community to establish a fire department and then became a volunteer.

They were H. Raschen, president; Jas. Albertson, secretary; Granice, treasurer; J. E. Poppe, foreman; C. W. Engelbert, first assistant foreman; and Julius Fochetti, second assistant foreman.

Other charter members of the fire department were Henry Weyl, Jr., John Ludeman, Wm. C. Green, James Martin, R. E. Perkins, George Martin, Englebert, G. A. Goees, A. Schweickhardt, O. Wagner, J. G. Marcy, Swen Church, D. Quartaroli, James Ricci, E. H. Pauli, L. Modini, Geo. Pabst, Albert Sutter and Granville Harris.

At the next meeting of the city trustees, on Jan. 2, 1889, $370 was appropriated to purchase a hook-and-ladder truck, $300 for one hand-powered engine, $80 for hose and hydrants and $50 "for preparing a suitable room for housing the first apparatus."

The new hook-and-ladder truck arrived by train on January 24, and that same evening members of the Sonoma Volunteer Hook and

Ladder Company drew the machine out of the city pavilion and, headed by the 18-piece Sonoma Valley Band, marched around the Plaza.

Said the *Index-Tribune* of Jan. 26, 1890: "The handsome truck and the cheering by the members of the company and spectators would have convinced the most sceptical that the old town was not yet dead by a long shot."

A year later, on Jan. 7, 1891, following the request of fireman H. H. Granice, the city trustees voted an appropriation of $100 toward the purchase of uniforms for the Sonoma Volunteer Fire Company, the uniforms to belong to the fire company rather than individual members.

While the new apparatus helped quell several minor fires and several major conflagrations—and the handsome red uniforms with white lettering were great for morale—lack of an adequate water supply was to hinder the proud Sonoma Volunteer Hook and Ladder Company for many years.   – RML

Twice buried—irate citizens dug up Mr. Wynne

*T*he headline in the Sept. 22, 1883, *Sonoma Weekly Index* read "Twice buried!!" and the story about the death, inquest, burial, digging up (by a self-appointed citizens' committee) and reburial of a Sonoma resident named Owen G. Wynne must have made fascinating reading for *Index* readers back then.

A harsh rebuttal story in the following week's paper, from Justice of the Peace and Acting Coroner F. Breitenbach, made equally fascinating reading.

It all started with Mr. Wynne being found dead at 5 A.M. on the morning of September 15 at the entrance of his workshop and residence situated on the east side of the Plaza. A tailor by trade, born in Ireland, Wynne was age 41, and had lived in Sonoma for nearly four years. The acting coroner summoned a jury, with witnesses, and it was determined by the physician in attendance that the cause of death was chronic alcoholism, the jury rendering its verdict "death from natural causes."

The inquest was held at 10 A.M., and just a few hours later the body was placed under the earth at the cemetery after a funeral procession consisting only of the coroner, undertaker, grave digger and one chief mourner—all riding in the same lumber wagon with the corpse—according to the *Index* reporter.

The hurried and impersonal handling of the case evidently upset a group of local citizens, who gathered to decry the swift proceedings and burial of a fellow resident, calling it "an insult" to the community. What happened next was reported thusly in the *Index* :

An indignation meeting was convened at 9 P.M. the same day with these results: The rude box containing the corpse was unearthed and placed in our public building, the Court House, at 10 P.M., where all the usual formula was carried out in due form on such occasions. At day-dawn the corpse was taken from the rude box, where he (Wynne) had been deposited with boots and filthy garments on, just as lifted from the dust in the street when found

Mountain Cemetery is the resting place of Sonoma's founder, Gen. M. G. Vallejo, and Capt. H. E. Boyes, for whom Boyes Hot Springs is named. Their graveyard markers are pictured above.

INDEX-TRIBUNE ARCHIVES

dead, and by willing and manipulative hands was reduced to a nude state, receiving thorough ablution from head to heels. Then encased in a winding sheet or shroud of linen, he was then placed in one of the most expensive caskets that our town could furnish.

The funeral left our Court House at 3 P.M. last Sunday, where the last funeral rites were rendered by the Rev. Wm. Gafney in a most impressive manner. The body was interred on the hill cemetery, in a plot where Mr. Litzius had already expended $50 to grade, build, fence, etc. which still remains for the benefit of departed neighbor Wynne. We append a list of names who have so liberally tendered their mite to sustain the expense of giving a fellow man a Christian burial. And when you read it you will say that Sonoma is not a bad place to live in—or die in, either.

The list contained the names of 76 donors, some of them among the town's leading citizens, the individual contributions ranging from $5 to 50¢.

In rebuttal, the acting coroner, in a heated letter to the editor of the *Index* appearing in the September 29 issue, claimed that the writer of the previous week's article had misrepresented his actions and libeled him by his "high phrases and falsehoods." Referring to the writer of the "Twice buried" article in the previous week's paper, Breitenbach commented further, "Why this man, who by his peculiar style of writing is as much known as a jackass by his long ears, should have done so mean an act, I cannot imagine, as I have never wronged him by deed, word or thought."

Breitenbach noted in his letter that he had lived in this community for 33 years and asked that those who have known him "and all fairminded men" to compare the statements in his letter to those of his slanderer. Said Breitenbach's caustic letter,

When found dead, Owen Wynne was dressed in his walking suit, with white shirt, brown coat, pants and vest; his clothes were not dirty; he was so

laid into the coffin, which was not a rude box, but a decent casket, such as our undertaker has heretofore sold for $15; the body was taken to his last resting place in the lower graveyard, not on a lumber wagon, but on a spring wagon, hired at the livery stable.

The letter noted that, while the Wynne funeral cortege passed along Sonoma's streets,

There were many people and vehicles standing around, [but] no one fell into line or showed any respect for the passing funeral. ... During the day no suggestions were made to me, or any assistance offered, and when it became manifest to me that the deceased had no friends, who would take charge of the body, and as the same could not remain in a small, closed room, adjoining a family residence until the next day, for sanitary reason, it then became my duty to order the burial. ...

Acting Coroner Breitenbach's letter also reminded readers that the previous week's article in the *Index* failed to state where the indignation meeting was held, nor who the chairman was, nor the names of the committee who dug up the body.

At what saloon, or on what street corner was that meeting held? How much whisky did it take to stimulate the digging committee up to the sticking point? I have been credibly informed by one of the party that they had been all, more or less, drunk, and that a fight and knock-down occurred at the grave over the momentous question as to who should boss the job. A nice crowd that! Indignant citizens indeed! Sir, does your correspondent expect the coroner to wash the body of every drunkard found dead in the road, or of every suicide hanging to a tree? And does he demand that the taxpayers of this county shall furnish a hundred-dollar casket for such occasions?

F. Breitenbach, Acting Coroner

– RML

18 A New Century Ushers in the "Resort Era": 1900–1919

INDEX-TRBIUNE ARCHIVES

In Sonoma Valley's resort era, trains like the above deposited vacationers at Boyes Hot Springs.

An era of vacationers and civic improvements

*F*or many Americans the beginning of the 20th century was a time of unbounded optimism and faith in progress. Although the population in Sonoma had actually decreased with the decline of the basalt blockmaking industry, leaving many unemployed, a new industry was developing, one which would bring people pouring into city and valley. The Sonoma Valley discovered its resort potential and the economic value of tourism.

The railroads first began to promote the Valley to tourists. In 1900 the California Northwestern Railway published numerous requests for Valley residents to open their homes to city visitors. That summer there were more visitors than places to keep them.

By the 1901 summer season, property owners here had begun to respond to the possibilities. Several new hotels were opened, and many existing facilities were expanded.

That year a San Francisco hotel owner named Theodor Richards bought Agua Caliente Hot Springs and straightaway began to make it into a first-class resort. Boyes Hot Springs, for which a stock prospectus had been issued in 1895, finally opened in time for the 1901 season. John Lounibos, an El Verano hotel owner, opened another bathing resort the following year.

In 1902 the *Index-Tribune* published a special edition designed to promote the Valley's charms; and the Southern Pacific Railway began a fervent advertising campaign to attract tourists and settlers from the East.

In 1903 the California Northwestern organized local girls to present wildflowers to railway passengers at each station stop. This popular custom was carried on for many years.

The *Index-Tribune* editorialized, "Sonoma Valley … seems to have a roseate future. … Let those who love solitude and rusticity hie themselves to the hills, for the invasion is inevitable."

More "summer rendezvous" resorts were established too during the 1900s and 1910s. In 1908 George and Emma Fetters opened Fetters Hot Springs. Along with Boyes Springs and Agua Caliente, it became one of the area's leading resorts.

Another resort was opened the following year by Louie and John Parente, who bought and developed 10 acres of land at Verano Springs and opened another resort.

Hundreds of residents took in some visitors each summer. Hotels without hot springs or pools transported their visitors by horse-drawn buses to the major resorts.

Some proprietors catered to certain groups. One of the best-known was Belgium-born Mrs. Mary Nevraumont, who attracted the San Francisco "French colony" to her El Verano Villa.

Both the hotels and the resorts provided entertainment for their customers. During the summer season visitors could attend a constant round of banquets, picnics, vaudeville shows, moving pictures, concerts, dances, teas, garden fêtes and masquerade balls.

These amenities were in addition to luxuriously appointed rooms, tubs for various types of mud and mineral baths, and bathing pools. Guests could also avail themselves of the services of a resident chiropractor, or of facilities for tennis, croquet and archery.

As the Valley became more and more of a resort community, locals, too, enjoyed the social round and began to develop more community events. There was plenty of baseball and horse racing and the beginnings of a rodeo.

In 1909 the Fourth of July celebration had offered little more than a brass band, a parade and speeches in the Plaza for area residents.

Horse-drawn buses carried tourists from railroad depots to Sonoma Valley hotels and resorts, such as this one at Oak Grove.

Three years later the parade was a mile long, and there were 3,000 people in town to join the festivities.

By 1910 the Fourth had been converted into a three-day holiday, with different features each year. In 1916, as the *I-T* observed, "Some 23,000 people came in on the railroads. … Several hundred automobiles [came]. … Resorts did a record business."

The resort business and its family clientele continued to thrive through early liquor controversies and the austerity programs of World War I, which America entered in 1917. The 1918 season was in fact the best ever.

But real changes came with Prohibition in 1919, the year in which both Capt. H. E. Boyes and Theodor Richards died. Not only was Prohibition the Valley's first economic setback in years, but it also changed the character of the resort business.

Many establishments would cater less to the family trade and more to the high-flying patrons of Prohibition days.   – SANDY SANDERS

Jack London in Sonoma Valley

AUTHOR'S NOTE: The following story about Jack London is excerpted from *The People of the Pueblo* by Celeste Murphy, who was personally acquainted with the famous author.

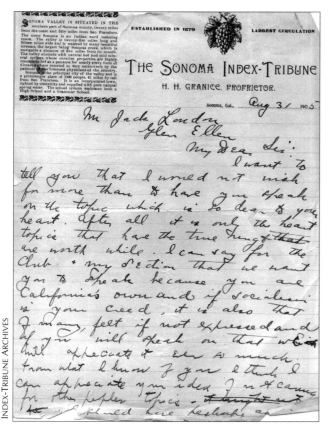

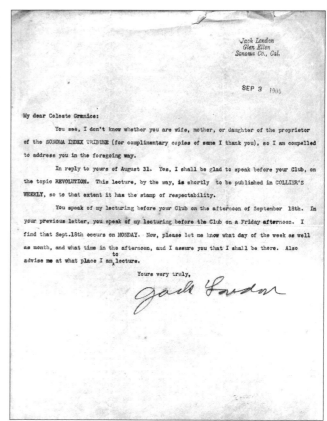

INDEX-TRIBUNE ARCHIVES

Correspondence between the author's aunt, Celeste Granice—then a recent college graduate and later the *Index-Tribune*'s editor—and Jack London in 1905. Miss Granice invited "the famous writer and socialist" to deliver a lecture before the Sonoma Valley Woman's Club, saying " ... we want you to speak because you are California's own and if socialism is your creed, it is also that of many, felt if not expressed, and if you will speak on that we will appreciate it ever so much." London replied that he would be "glad to speak before your Club, on the topic REVOLUTION."

In the fall of 1904 a son of California brought the world's attention to Sonoma and its moons. Jack London came to write his books and build his home where "10,000 Indians once had lived." His romance, *Valley of the Moon,* was just one of his many books, but to Sonoma it is London's greatest work, for through it Sonoma won new and far-flung fame.

Jack London, San Francisco born, and already popular as a writer and lecturer, first came as a visitor to the Glen Ellen home of Ninetta and Roscoe Eames, aunt and uncle of young Charmian Kittredge, who later became Mrs. London, the author's second wife. Mrs. Eames was the editor and owner of the *Overland Monthly,* a prestigious magazine of the era. Enthusiastic over London's work for some time past, she and her husband invited the young author to their picturesque country place, Wake Robin Lodge. London, the fervent apostle of socialism, the keen writer already recognized for

his insight into the laws of life and the ways of men, found in Sonoma Valley peace and inspiration. Glen Ellen, its romantic background and pastoral acres, suggested the great ranch Jack London finally acquired.

One of the author's earliest successes, *The Sea Wolf,* was written while on an outing at Wake Robin Lodge in 1903. After the Russian-Japanese war, where he went as a war correspondent, London returned to California determined to make Sonoma Valley his home. The quiet he once feared would weary him he learned to love, as he rode horseback through the hills with Charmian at his side or sailed the sunny creeks and meandering waterways of Sonoma and Napa counties in his little boat, the Roamer. After London's marriage to Charmian in Chicago, where he was giving a series of lectures, the couple came back to Glen Ellen. From Sonoma Mountain to the floor of the Valley, London bought farms and vineyards, fern-clad canyons, wooded hills, purling streams, redwoods and gay manzanitas—portions of the original holdings of William McPherson Hill, J. Chauvet, Alfred LaMotte, Charles Kennedy, Kohler and Frohling and other pioneers. While adding to his acreage and planning the scientific farm and all the projects of his days of gladness, Jack London wrote constantly.

When literary success appeared greater than anticipated, and editors and publishers clamored for more and more of his work, he built a massive, multi-storied stone house on his ranch. The red rock for the edifice London called the "Wolf House" came from quarries in the Sonoma hills. He built it primarily as a protection to his now priceless library, first editions and autographed copies of books he loved and credited with much of his success, for London was an insatiable reader and reacted to much he read. He built his house, too, as a threshold worthy of staunch friends. Set down among the towering redwoods which had grown up from older giants, the wonder castle, three stories high, commanded a view

of the entire country and the old ranchos down the Valley. One night just before the Londons were to occupy their home, but fortunately before they had moved their library from the stone wine cellars where the books had been housed, a mysterious fire broke out in the still unfinished mansion, sending billows of smoke and flames to the sky. Gaunt chimneys and denuded walls in a grove of blackened redwoods were all that remained of the proud house.

Then came travel to the South Seas, Samoa and strange ports in the ill-fated *Snark,* a boat built to order for London after the San Francisco fire of 1906, and finally abandoned as unseaworthy after the author was forced to make repeated and extensive repairs.

Jack and Charmian came home to California more than ever convinced that life in the heart of the Sonoma hills was life at its best. His 1,400-acre ranch was the pride of the countryside. London, the literary genius, with his touseled hair and friendly mien, was of the people. Sonoma and Glen Ellen loved him well. He had a

Jack London with his daughters Becky (left) and Joan in 1906.

INDEX-TRIBUNE ARCHIVES

INDEX-TRIBUNE ARCHIVES

Jack London often did his writing in the scenic outdoors of his Glen Ellen ranch.

cheery greeting for all—Bill Ping, the white-bearded stage driver with the Southern drawl; Charley Poppe of the country store, with his merry chuckle; Paine, the blacksmith, in whose shop Bob Fitzsimmons, the Australian prize-fighter, made a huge horseshoe for Jack and his admirers around the forge; Pancrazi, who wrote Italian poetry and served good wine; the boys at the Mervyn Hotel and the mineral springs, who were always sure of the drinks as Jack London's bell-decked team drew up at the swinging doors. London loved the cup that cheers, as he acknowledged, but if he ever drank to excess it was unknown to his Sonoma neighbors. His highly colored confession in John Barleycorn made that book a bestseller and was pounced upon as good propaganda by Prohibitionists, then zealously interested in outlawing liquor.

London's death on Nov. 22, 1916, at age 40, was unlooked for by his friends and publishers, although for some time he had had forebodings and failed to heed the warnings of physicians as to organic complications. He died of gastrointestinal uremic poisoning.

When news reached the people of the pueblo that their gifted son had gone from them forever, a great sadness settled over the Valley. There were tears in the eyes of the townspeople that November day when his ashes were interred in the red soil of his Sonoma Valley "Beauty Ranch," whose wild flowers and grasses mantle alike the lowly and the great. Beside the graves of the two little children of whom he wrote in *Burning Daylight,* not far from the old picket fence in the woods, rest the ashes of the author. A boulder, weathered and time-scarred, a stone the builder had rejected when London's big stone house was built, marks his grave. The moon of his Valley shines down upon it.

The ranch continues to be the mecca of hundreds of visitors each year.   — CELESTE MURPHY

AUTHOR'S NOTE: Jack London State Historic Park was created in 1959 when a small portion—about 40 acres—of Beauty Ranch was acquired by the state, partly through a gift from Irving Shepard, London's nephew and an heir to the London estate. The original park included London's grave, the ruins of Wolf House and Charmian's House of Happy Walls. Additional acreage has been added over the years, so that today the park contains more than 800 acres, including many of the ranch buildings and the cottage where London wrote much of his later work.

The new City Hall had four "fronts"

When San Francisco architect A. C. Lutgens designed Sonoma's City Hall, he made all four sides look the same. On each side of the square structure is a set of three arches and, beyond them, a set of entrance doors. Because the merchants on all four sides of the Plaza felt that the building should face in their direction, the architect made all sides of the building the same.

The decision to build a new City Hall was made in 1904. A replacement was needed for the old wooden pavilion in the Plaza. The city asked for bids on the building, but when they were opened in December 1904, the bids were considered too high and were rejected.

Sonoma City Hall and workmen, 1909. Building stones came from quarries in the hills visible in background.

The city trustees decided to ask the voters to approve a bond issue of $10,000 with which to put up City Hall. The city apparently had $5,000 in the kitty to begin with.

The bond issue passed in June 1905—125 yes votes to 17 no votes.

There was great public rejoicing. Bonfires were built in the Plaza, fireworks were shot off. The Sonoma Brass Band gave a concert. Then it was discovered the election was invalid because of some legal technicality.

Another election was held in September 1905. This one passed too, 109 yes, 10 no.

The bonds were sold to a Mrs. Martha Stearns, a wealthy local woman and first president of the Sonoma Valley Woman's Club. Bids were opened in December, and the low bid of contractor John T. MacQuiddy of $15,475 was accepted.

The cornerstone laying took place on Feb. 24, 1906, even though the stone masons were on strike. They were seeking the union wage of $1.50 a day. The event was a gala affair, of the kind old-time Sonomans seem to have loved.

There were speeches by Mayor Julius Poppe and assorted dignitaries. Tribute was paid to special guest Henry Beeson, the last surviving member of the Bear Flag Party of 1846.

The cornerstone was stuffed with city and Masonic records, photographs and newspapers. The laying of it was conducted by the Masons, led by the senior grand warden, Dr. Roden of San Francisco.

As a climax, beloved Luisa Emparan, a daughter of General Vallejo, sang a delightful popular song of that day, "In Dear Old California's Sunny Dells."

There followed a dinner for 200 people.

Work on City Hall had hardly started when the earthquake of April 1906 halted it. It wasn't until June that MacQuiddy's men returned to work. This was due in part to the fact that most banks had closed for an extended period after the earthquake to get their fiscal affairs in order. Then in September 1906, MacQuiddy walked off the job, apparently because of inflation. It was becoming apparent that the building couldn't be completed for less than $25,000 or $30,000, almost double the contract price. In the aftermath of the earthquake and the frenzied rebuilding that was going on, the cost of labor and materials had soared.

The city council readvertised for bids in 1907. The low bidder was James B. Newman, of Napa, at $14,200. Work resumed and all went well until May, when the stone masons and cutters went on strike again. They wanted $6 a day. They had been getting $5.

Newman rejected the demands, and work on City Hall came to a halt.

Index-Tribune editor Harry Granice wrote: "In the meantime Sonoma's white elephant occupies the center of the Plaza, a fitting monument to the slow way they do things in this town."

But the strike was settled in August with a compromise—the workmen returned for a wage of $5.50.

Editor Granice felt better and by January 1908 was moved to write: "Let it be known that Old Sonoma is New Sonoma and that on historic land is growing up a new generation proud of its

historic and romantic background but fraught with the spirit of the times."

The old city pavilion was sold for $100 in the spring of 1908 to a farmer who hauled it away piece by piece to build a barn.

As summer waned, the new City Hall neared completion and sat splendidly in the middle of the barren Plaza. It was decided to dedicate the building on Sept. 9, 1908, Admission Day.

Another grand blowout was held. Bear Flagger Henry Beeson was still alive to be honored. There was a parade with many bands and floats and General Vallejo's old carriage, occupied by two of his grandsons, Carlos and Richard R. (Dal) Emparan.

The speakers included James D. Phelan, an ex-mayor of San Francisco; Sonoma Mayor George Breitenbach and old-time Sonoma merchant F. T. Duhring. There were horse races, musical and literary exercises, and a grand ball.

And once again, the celebration was closed by Luisa Emparan singing "In Dear Old California's Sunny Dells."

COURTESY, SONOMA VALLEY HISTORICAL

The explosion of a coal oil stove, combined with a brisk breeze, faulty fire-fighting equipment and flammable shacks behind buildings on First Street East in Sonoma created an inferno on Sept. 23, 1911. Agostino Pinelli's quick thinking saved his building, when he directed firefighters to pump red wine from his 1,000-gallon tank onto the fire.

Many years later, in the 1940s, the fire department moved from the ground floor of City Hall to a new building on Patten Street, and the space was taken over by an exhibit of model planes that belonged to retired Air Force General "Hap" Arnold. These were sent to the Air Force Academy in 1960 and the ground floor converted into offices for a growing municipality.

The second floor, where city trustees had met, was converted into a combination court and city council chamber in 1953.   — JERRY PARKER

Wine used to quell 1911 disastrous downtown fire

The threat of fire is always an ominous specter to Sonoma Valley residents. Protected as we are by beautiful hills on either side, those same protectors can easily turn into blazing furies once a fire has been ignited.

Although there have been many instances of the Valley fighting intense fires, there has probably never been a more frightening one to the residents of Sonoma proper than the fire of 1911.

"Disastrous fire in business section" read the banner headline of the Sept. 23, 1911, *Sonoma Index-Tribune*.

What had begun as a small kitchen fire in a cobbler's shop on First Street East soon engulfed the entire business block.

A number of factors contributed to the disaster. Although nearly 100 firefighters and a fire engine were on hand five minutes after the start of the blaze (caused by the explosion of a coal oil stove), it quickly became an inferno.

A combination of a faulty "fire-fighting apparatus," inflammable shacks in the rear of the burning buildings and a brisk breeze were responsible for the uncontrollable conflagration.

According to the *I-T*, the "heroic efforts of the firemen were fruitless, no fault of theirs."

From the original cobbler's shop, the fire leaped to the second story of the Poppe flat, occupied at that time by Mrs. Kate Buchan and family and J. E. Poppe and family.

The fire was still burning slowly, and volunteers were able to save all furniture and belongings of the families, including two large pianos.

Up to this point, the buildings in the block

Most of the buildings opposite the Plaza's east side were destroyed in the 1911 fire. Two months later, business leaders were rebuilding.

INDEX-TRIBUNE ARCHIVES

north of where the fire had started were safe, but a sudden change in the wind quickly spread it to the eaves of the Von Geldern building, which adjoined the Poppe block.

The *Index-Tribune* noted, "If at this point, firemen had abandoned the Poppe building, which was obviously doomed, at least two-thirds of the property could have been saved." Instead, the volunteers continued the fight at the building, the fire spreading in an incredibly short time to the Bismarck Hotel, the Barbarin building and Pinelli's two-story structure.

Although most of the furniture and fixtures of these burning buildings had been saved and placed in the Plaza, another wind change sent "a wall of fire clear across the street and into the Plaza, which set fire to the grass and many of the personal effects belonging to Cantoni's bakery and the Bismarck Hotel, which were instantly ablaze and consumed."

Again the wind changed, and the roof of Pinelli's wine cellar on Spain Street and several cords of stove wood blazed. As the fire engine was being used elsewhere, it appeared that nothing could save the structure.

Agostino Pinelli's quick and original turn of thought saved the day. Directing a force of firefighters to his 1,000-gallon tank of wine in the cellar, he helped them connect a large hose and force pump to the same, and "a powerful stream of red wine was directed on the burning wine cellar and wood, and the building was saved."

At one time during the afternoon, the roofs of the Sonoma Mission and the Toscano Hotel caught fire, but they were quickly extinguished. One of the best things the volunteer firemen did was to attach a team of horses to a one-story structure located between the blazing Poppe building and the Sonoma House hotel and drag it to the ground.

The act later was credited with saving the Sonoma House, the Duhring-Ryland property and every house on East Napa Street from Duhring's corner to the Granice, La Gorres and Bates properties.

Although the destruction was indeed costly to the business leaders of the community, by November they had already begun to build again.

One *I-T* story noted, "There is a great activity in the city of Sonoma as clearing of the ruins and rebuilding of structures [takes place]. ... Both the Pinelli and Barbarin buildings will be a great improvement on those destroyed."

– KATHY SWETT

1906 earthquake shook up Sonoma

When the great April 18, 1906, earthquake (of 8.3 magnitude) combined with a devastating fire to wipe out a significant portion of San Francisco, causing thousands of deaths in that city alone, Sonoma, by comparison, escaped with only the worst "shaking up" that anyone living here 90 years ago could remember.

In Santa Rosa, just 25 miles north, more than 100 deaths were reported, most of them from falling bricks and fire which followed. There, five major downtown hotels collapsed totally, and several caught fire and trapped most potential survivors. One of those killed in Santa Rosa was a 21-year-old Sonoman, Chester Trudgen, a drug clerk. The building where he slept collapsed, pinning him beneath the debris. Before help could arrive, the debris caught fire and he was burned to death.

The Sonoma Index-Tribune being a weekly publication, it was four days after the major quake that the paper appeared with local news

stories on the disaster. All of those stories in the April 21 *I-T* were written by associate editor Celeste Granice Murphy, the lone staffer in the absence of her father, editor Harry Granice, who was vacationing in Mexico.

Here is how the lead story appeared:

FEARFUL VISITATION OF EARTHQUAKE
Sonoma Wednesday Experiences Awful Ordeal, and People are Panic-Stricken.

Sonoma's escape from a frightful catastrophe seems almost providential, for Wednesday's earthquake was the most terrific in the history of this place. It was an awful ordeal to have experienced. At 5:11 A.M. the sleeping inhabitants of this Valley were ruthlessly awakened to find the earth in the throes of a mighty earthquake which lasted fully one minute. Buildings creaked and partially collapsed, chimneys toppled and roofs fell in. There were the sounds of falling glass and the cries of the panic-stricken as they rushed pell-mell from their homes to the streets. Little did the people of Sonoma realize at that moment how great a havoc was being wrought away from here. Our damage was confined entirely to the destruction and demolition of buildings. No one was killed or injured.

Adler's new stone building, occupied by G. H. Hotz, caved in on the east side and south end. Clewe's concrete store was badly cracked. The Sonoma Valley Bank building's west wall is bulging. The high school was rendered unsafe for use. The Schocken building is a wreck on the interior. The Poppe store is crumbling on the four corners, and the home of C. Aguillon was so badly demolished that the family had to take refuge in another house immediately.

L. S. Simmons had all his drugs thrown down from the shelves of his store and they are a total loss estimated at $1,000. The Stofen home on Broadway was seriously damaged as were also the Hall residence and that of Mrs. Snyder. Not a chimney in town is standing. At Glen Ellen and El Verano there were also many homes and buildings badly wrecked. This Valley probably sustained damage to the amount of $45,000 or more.

In other stories in the April 21, 1906, *Index-Tribune,* readers learned that no one was injured at the Sonoma State Home at Eldridge, "although the buildings were badly damaged and the patients frightened." At Glen Ellen the new store built by Charles J. Poppe after the recent fire was badly damaged by the earthquake. At the O'Donnell home in Glen Ellen Mrs. O'Donnell fainted and was carried out just as the big stone chimney crashed through the ceiling of the room. Another chimney fell through onto the bed in the guest chamber, but fortunately it was not occupied at the time.

Schools, which had been closed all week, were scheduled to open on Monday. "The high school building will be temporarily abandoned and the recitations will probably be conducted in Dal Poggetto Hall," reported the *Index-Tribune.*

The following week's issue reported that "The Court House in Santa Rosa is practically ruined. The new Masonic Temple there, the fine public library, the big brewery, the shoe factory, two theatres, three of the finest hotels, a score of office buildings and stores all gone. They resemble a monstrous rubbish pile. Five steel vaults are all that remain of the banks."

All Sonoma Valley property owners whose chimneys were damaged were notified that as a precaution against fire, chimneys must be inspected, and that no insurance claims would be paid in case of fire, unless a certificate of inspection could be shown. A local relief committee was organized here by the Sonoma Valley Woman's Club and a local Catholic ladies' group, with a substantial fund collected for the refugees from the earthquake and fire calamity. Tents were erected in the Plaza to shelter the needy.

Celeste Granice Murphy, the *Index-Tribune*'s associate editor, reported on her findings during a lengthy tour of San Francisco, and on the quake and fire aftermath, in the April 18 issue. Her long and detailed story ended with this observation: "Cosmopolitan San Francisco, with its Latin quarter and Chinatown, is no more. Commercial San Francisco, with its massive wharves, its factories, its warehouses, lies prostrate in the gray ashes of that awful fire." – RML

The Sonoma Valley Woman's Club hosted a mission festival in 1912. In front of the ladder are Charmian and Jack London.

Mission San Francisco Solano de Sonoma through the years

The Sonoma Mission circa 1899. A corner saloon, which originally had been in the middle of First Street East, was moved to the front of the mission chapel, all but hiding it.

Joseph Knowland photographed the priests' quarters in 1903 on behalf of the California Historic Landmark League in order to publicize the neglected state of the Mission and raise funds for its restoration.

The 1906 earthquake weakened the edifice substantially.

In this photo (circa 1900) the priests' quarters adjoining the chapel are visible at right.

In 1905 Otto Von Geldern posed in front of the white-picket-fenced Mission. Von Geldern was an early-day engineer of Sonoma.

The collapse of the southwest corner of the Mission occurred on Feb. 12, 1909.

COURTESY, ROBERT D. PARMELEE

By 1910 the pile of rubble left by the Mission's collapse the year before had been removed.

INDEX-TRIBUNE ARCHIVES

The Sonoma Mission Creamery, today an Italian specialty-food emporium, opposite the Mission in 1917.

INDEX-TRIBUNE ARCHIVES

The Mission as it looked in 1930, with the old bell in front. The 1911–13 restoration included removing the cupola and installing a cross. In the 1940s the front was stuccoed.

COURTESY, SONOMA VALLEY HISTORICAL SOCIETY

The Mission in ruins in 1911.

INDEX-TRIBUNE ARCHIVES

In 1918, the Mission occupied an unkempt site, but the building—on which restoration had begun in 1910—looked much better than when it was a hay barn hidden by a saloon.

INDEX-TRIBUNE ARCHIVES

In 1953 the foundation of the original sacristy was uncovered in the Mission's rear courtyard.

INDEX-TRIBUNE ARCHIVES

Today thousands of visitors tour the Mission each year, including throngs of fourth-grade California-history students. Although regular services at the Mission were discontinued in 1881, in 1986 the local ministerial association began conducting ecumenical Christmas and Good Friday services in the remodeled sanctuary.

Saving of the Mission

The old Sonoma Mission did not look like a landmark of California history in 1902. For the preceding 20 years, its owner—local merchant Solomon Schocken—had used the buildings to store hay and casks of wine.

In 1902 Mrs. Laura McBride Powers founded a league to preserve historic buildings throughout the state and convinced William Randolph Hearst of the *San Francisco Examiner* to promote the idea.

Hearst donated $500 to start off a public subscription fund-raising campaign. Community groups like the Sonoma Valley Woman's Club and the Native Sons of the Golden West helped make the fund a success.

In 1903 Hearst bought the Mission San Francis Solano de Sonoma for $5,000 out of the Landmark Fund. The state finally accepted the public's donation of the mission and other historic properties in 1905.

But Carrie Burlingame, a founding member of the Sonoma Valley Woman's Club, recalled that local State Sen. Herbert Slater "presented numerous bills ... for the appropriation of funds" to restore the mission, "only to have them pigeonholed or ... vetoed by governors."

With the state as an absentee owner, the mission was neglected. The *Index-Tribune* reported that the 1906 earthquake had cracked some of the walls. During the winter of 1908–1909, heavy rains caused the east wing and the front wall of the chapel to collapse into ruins.

The collapse spurred local groups, headed by the Woman's Club, to look after the mission themselves. They raised $700, enough to rebuild the front of the chapel with adobe bricks taken from an 1840s Salvador Vallejo building then being torn down, and to put up lumber sheathing to protect other damaged walls.

In the fall of 1909, Sonomans turned out in large numbers to celebrate the dedication of a signpost which marked the location of the original El Camino Real mission bell.

In 1911 Slater introduced another bill for $5,000 to restore the Sonoma Mission, and this time it passed the legislature with the governor's consent.

The *Index-Tribune* informed its readers that the state plan called for "a red-tiled roof to be restored with the original tiles which have been preserved, the repairing of the decayed walls with adobe bricks and the replacing of the belfry with the original bell."

Senator Slater sponsored another bill in 1913, asking for $2,000 more to restore the mission. This bill apparently failed, but his parallel bill for $5,000 to raise a Bear Flag monument succeeded.

In 1914 Gov. Hiram Johnson himself attended a marathon celebration in Sonoma to dedicate the new Bear Flag monument and to rededicate the Mission Saint Francis Solano de Sonoma, the last and northernmost of the Franciscan fathers' chain of 21 California missions. – SANDY SANDERS

Woman's Club civic force since founding in 1901

Sonoma's Plaza—with its wide walks, beautiful trees, ducks and fish pond, fountains, amphitheater, City Hall and old library building—owes much to the Sonoma Valley Woman's Club for its existence.

From its start in 1901, the women's club was really a "ladies' improvement club." The ink on its charter was hardly dry when the ladies approached the city of Sonoma trustees to get them to approve an ambitious plan for city improvements, the major request being the cleaning up and beautification of the Plaza.

The Plaza had existed since Gen. M. G. Vallejo personally laid it out in the late 1830s and, from time to time, had been a center of town activity. But when the ladies got their improvement movement going, the Plaza was in a sad state.

The "ancient" pavilion in the center served as a patchwork jail and headquarters for city government but was in a deplorable state.

All manner of livestock trampled about the grounds, and it apparently looked more like a dusty pasture than a park. The Ladies' Improvement Club (later to be the Woman's Club) began raising money, putting in paths and planting trees. But after two years the project still hadn't gotten that far along.

H. H. Granice, *I-T* editor, said in a May 23, 1903, editorial that after two years of effort, the Plaza looked little better than it originally did. He suggested that the lack of progress partially stemmed from having an "eight-acre Plaza for a one-acre town."

He praised the ladies for their efforts and blasted city trustees for not being more helpful.

Work and improvements progressed slowly, but in 1905 a fountain was built in the Plaza, and in 1906 a cornerstone was laid for the new City Hall. In 1908 grading and filling took place and the old "eyesore" pavilion was torn down.

In 1909 a "Sonoma Day" was sponsored by the Woman's Club, and the town turned out in force to work all one Saturday on the Plaza. Business owners, workers, townsfolk—all grabbed shovels, rakes and wagons, hauled 600

The newly completed Sonoma library, shown here circa 1912, was built with funds from the Andrew Carnegie Foundation, requested by the Sonoma Valley Woman's Club. Constructed on the Plaza's east side, the building is today the home of the Sonoma Valley Visitors Bureau.

INDEX-TRIBUNE ARCHIVES

loads of dirt to the Plaza, and spread and leveled it so that lawn could be planted and paths improved. At lunch, they ate beneath the shade of trees that had been planted several years earlier by the ladies.

Another fountain was built by the Woman's Club in 1909, and the club raised more money in 1910 for Plaza beautification by holding a carnival.

Woman's Club Plaza and library projects continued right on through the era to modern times.

It was the Woman's Club that built the pool and fountain in front of City Hall. The Woman's Club started and staffed the first public library. It was even at the club's urging that the library first got on the tax rolls to gain city support.

The Woman's Club pitched in to preserve the crumbling old Sonoma Mission in the early 1900s. The members also were active in hundreds of other civic projects.

But it is the Plaza that must be forever the crowning achievement of the Woman's Club. The ponds, lawns, trees, gardens and shaded walks may have been changed here and there in modern times, but their birth and inspiration came from those hard-working ladies who first decided to improve Sonoma.

— BILL LYNCH

Sonoma library a Woman's Club project

From its modest beginnings in the Odd Fellows building on Broadway to the modern structure on

West Napa Street, the Sonoma Public Library has been a vital part of Sonoma's history.

No one man played a more important role in the founding of a permanent, financially strong library in Sonoma Valley than Andrew Carnegie. During the 1900s, the well-known philanthropist gave thousands of dollars to small towns across America to aid in the construction of libraries. Sonoma was one of the many recipients.

The story of the Sonoma library begins, however, at the turn of the century, with the founding of the Sonoma Valley Woman's Club in 1901. Two goals of that club were to improve the appearance of the Plaza and to begin a lending library for citizens in the community.

With Mrs. Martha Stearns as president, the first library set up shop in a small room located in the Odd Fellows Hall on Broadway in 1903. There it stayed until April 1906.

At that time, Mrs. Sophia Calderwood offered the use of her small building on First Street East. Rent was $6 per month and club members took turns as librarians.

On Aug. 7, 1909, the city council passed Ordinance No. 101, officially establishing the Sonoma Public Library. The ordinance provided supervision of the library by a board of trustees. That first board included Kate McDonell, Sophia Calderwood, William Rambo, Charles Dal Poggetto and Thomas Brown.

Members of the board were appointed to three-year terms, without pay, and expected to fulfill the following requirements:

- Make library rules.
- Administer all funds given to the library.
- Hire a librarian and prescribe her duties.
- Purchase necessary books.
- Purchase land for the purpose of building a library.
- Exchange books with other libraries.
- Perform all other acts necessary to run an efficient library.

Finally, the board was to see that the library was always free to the residents of the city of Sonoma. The board met once a month to carry out these guidelines and work toward creating an efficient, pleasant library.

The library board appointed Miss Meta Stofen as the first librarian at the rate of $15 per

INDEX-TRIBUNE ARCHIVES

Philanthropist Andrew Carnegie contributed funds for a new library, which opened in 1913.

month, including light janitorial work. The library kept hours from 7 to 8:30 P.M. every evening, with Sundays and holidays excepted, and Wednesday afternoons from 2 to 4 P.M.

In June 1910 the board first learned of the Andrew Carnegie Library grants program, although it did not act upon it until November, when members discussed the proposal at great length.

Carnegie's conditions for lending money for the construction of libraries in small communities were reasonable. He required that city councils pass a resolution guaranteeing the payment of $600 per year for the annual support of the library.

At the May 4, 1911, meeting of the trustees, a letter was read, noting acceptance of the town's application for a library grant provided the City of Sonoma gave $600 per annum for the maintenance of the building.

An architect was hired, Mr. A. C. Lutgens of San Francisco. Soon after the architectural plans were approved by Mr. Carnegie, a contract was let to William Newman, contractor and builder from Napa, at the price of $6,645.

Although that price was some $600 over the money which Mr. Carnegie had given the city, the trustees agreed to raise the additional monies, rather than send the bid back to Carnegie, for fear that the application would be rescinded.

A dance was held early in 1913, and approximately $220 was raised. Most of the work on the new building was completed by April 1913. And, although the exact date of completion and occupation is not known, it is on record that the library board met in the new building, on the east side of the Plaza, for the first time on May 4, 1913.

During the early years of its existence, the library board held several fund-raising benefits to bolster the accounts for maintenance and book purchases for the library.

The library became a landmark in the Valley for visitors and a haven for children and adults over the years. Inevitably, the town outgrew the charming, cozy quarters of the Carnegie library and undertook to build a bigger and more sophisticated structure—the modern Sonoma Valley Regional Library on West Napa Street.

— BECKY GOEHRING

INDEX-TRIBUNE ARCHIVES

The Bear Flag monument in Sonoma Plaza was dedicated June 14, 1914.

The Bear Flag monument

Sonoma's historic Plaza has been the scene of many stirring events, but none more so than the two major occasions associated with the Bear Flag—the original 1846 take-over of the sleepy, unguarded pueblo and its commandante, General Vallejo, and raising of the flag by the Bear Flag Party; and, some 68 years later, the grand ceremonies attending the dedication of the monument commemorating that event.

In 1901, upon the death of Harvey Porterfield, a member of the Bear Flag Party and a Sonoma pioneer of 1838, the *Index-Tribune* recounted how, in 1846, he had helped to raise a flag that was put together on the spot.

"A lone star and a bear were then painted on the body of the flag," explained the *I-T*, "and it was hoisted on a flagstaff that was planted in the ground over the identical spot now occupied by the flagpole owned by the city."

Little was done to formally recognize that event until 1907, when the *I-T* reported that the Sonoma Valley Woman's Club "marked the spot to properly commemorate it [the Bear Flag raising], telling the tale to generations to come."

But in 1910 the *Index-Tribune* headlined that "The Bear Flag pole is no more." The historical flagpole occupying a site on the northeast corner of the Plaza went down and was damaged beyond repair as strong winds swept through the Valley. The *I-T* called the loss of the 64-year-old flagpole "an irreparable loss to old Sonoma,

COURTESY, SONOMA VALLEY HISTORICAL SOCIETY

A Sonoma Valley group on an outing at Mount Tamalpais in August 1904: (top, left to right) Claude Johnson, Emma Hotz, Henry Bates, Gus Hotz; (bottom, left to right) Clara Johnson, Zoe Bates, Frank Burris, Pauline Bates Hayes, Bertha McGimsey and Will Clewe.

whose people were justly proud of it and the early-day associations which it represented."

Henry Beeson, the sole survivor of the Bear Flag Party, reminisced in 1911 that the date was truly June 14 and not the 13th or 15th, as some had said. The original Bear Flag was destroyed during the earthquake and fire in San Francisco in 1906, according to Beeson.

Thereafter the Sonoma Parlor of the Native Sons of the Golden West became the spearhead group in the movement to get a Bear Flag monument, with the valuable support of blind State Sen. Herbert Slater of Santa Rosa. This movement culminated in 1913 as Gov. Hiram Johnson signed a bill to appropriate $5,000 for the erection of such a monument.

When the news reached Sonoma, the *Index-Tribune* reported that it sparked "an impromptu celebration in this city to rejoice over the event in which speech-making, martial music and beating of drums played a leading part amid the wild huzzas of the Native Sons, in which they were joined by almost the entire populace."

Committees were formed, plans perfected and work begun on October 30 of that same year. That day was designated as "Native Sons Day," and some 50 teams, which had been organized with picks and shovels, filled and graded the monument site. Ladies from various organizations in the Valley provided a fine midday luncheon for the workers.

That day and succeeding ones were a success, for on June 13 and 14, "5,000 wildly cheering people watched as Gov. Hiram L. Johnson pulled the cord that released the Bear Flag which draped the monument ... disclosing to view the artistically modeled, perfectly sculptured figure in bronze."

In his address to the enthusiastic crowd, Governor Johnson proclaimed, "The sturdy souls who raised this flag prefigured the destiny of California. ... They had vision of the empire of preeminence which we now possess ... [and] set for us examples in courage and initiative that must ever be our guiding impulse and inspiration."

Special trains from San Francisco, an elaborate parade, horse races, a fireworks display ("the finest and most brilliant display ever seen here") and a grand ball "that lasted until the break of dawn" were major parts of the singular celebration.

The Sonoma Parlor of the Native Sons "deserves every word of commendation, every word of praise," commented the *I-T*, "which made the unveiling of the Bear Flag Monument and the partial restoration of the Mission San Francisco Solano de Sonoma ... the most notable and biggest celebration in the history of Sonoma County."
— MYRON DELONG

World War I spotlighted Sonoma Valley patriotism

*O*n their crystal sets [a type of radio], or perhaps on their new Atwater Kent radio sets—and via daily metropolitan newspapers—Sonoma Valley residents would have learned that the conflict we know as World War I actually broke out on June 28, 1914, in Europe.

But it wasn't until April 7, 1917, that *The Sonoma Index-Tribune* brought the conflict overseas close to home with an editorial titled "On the present crisis." Editor Celeste Murphy urged Sonomans to join with the rest of the nation in supporting President Woodrow Wilson and Congress in halting the autocratic and militaristic German government, and keeping the seas open to all.

The day before, on April 6, 1917, the U. S. had declared war on Germany and the central powers, after Berlin refused to honor the neutrality of American ships. On June 26, the first American troop ship steamed into the Bay of Biscay and landed on the west coast of France at Saint Nazaire. The Yanks had arrived.

A week after the U. S. declaration of war, several Sonoma Valley leaders met at City Hall and voted to organize a Citizens' Defense League. Subsequently, other meetings were scheduled in which a Red Cross Society was established in Sonoma, with a branch at Glen Ellen. More than 200 volunteers became active workers.

Hamil Wagnon, a student at the Chico Normal School and only son of Postmaster and Mrs. John Wagnon of Sonoma, wrote home in April 1917 that he was receiving aviation instruction from Army Corps regulars preparatory to enlisting in the service. He and Dewey

This War Must Be Fought On European Soil

If the peoples of the earth are not to become toiling millions for the Prussian Junkers and the Prussian Krupps, if they are not to be terror-ridden slaves at the mercy of a German Kaiser's will, Prussianism must be driven back within its own borders and kept there.

Not only English freedom, French freedom is at stake. Our own cherished institutions, our free government, all that our fathers fought for, all that free peoples prize, is threatened by an enemy that would impose his own hateful Kultur on every free institution in every liberty-loving land.

That is why the war must be fought on European soil. We are fighting in Europe now that we may not have to fight in America, on the very thresholds of our own homes, later.

We are fighting for the safety and liberty of our children, our homes, our country. No price is too great to pay for Victory.

Americans, you are called upon to back our armies in France, to furnish them the guns and shells and ships and airplanes, the enormous quantities of every sort of supplies that they must have to defeat the Prussian armies and drive them back across the Rhine.

*The War Is Being Fought in Europe—
But It Must Be Won Right Here at Home*

Will You Strike a Blow for American Freedom? Your Support of the Third Liberty Loan Is Your Answer. Invest today in Liberty Bonds—ALL the Bonds You Can

THIS SPACE PAID FOR AND CONTRIBUTED BY
The Following Business Men of El Verano

| Thos. H. Baines | Emmet Mullen | L. P. Kearney | John Basilou |
| L Larbre | Al Dutil | A M Garaventa | Villa Savoy |

War bond support ads like this one appeared in the *Index-Tribune* in 1918.

INDEX-TRIBUNE ARCHIVES

Smith, an 18-year-old Sonoman who quit his job at the Crockett sugar refinery to enter the service, were early war volunteers who received recognition in the *Index-Tribune* under the headline "Sonoma boys are patriots." Irving Shepard, nephew of author Jack London and son of Mrs. Eliza Shepard of Glen Ellen, was another 1917 enlistee in the U. S. Navy, eventually entering the submarine service.

The Liberty Loan bond purchase program—a national fund-raising venture to support the war against Germany—was instituted in the Valley in May 1917. The [original] Sonoma Valley Bank, under Frank M. Burris, was the first local buyer of Liberty Loan bonds, subscribing $5,000, with an additional $6,000 subscribed for clients. The first public sale of bonds followed, the Valley collecting $79,250, exceeding its $75,000 quota. In October a second sale here brought $131,000, beating the $130,564 goal. Two more Liberty Bond sales, the final one in June 1918, were also marked successes. *Index-Tribune* editorials, plus paid advertisements sponsored by local business firms and individuals each week, kept the public aware of the need to support the Liberty Bond campaign.

The World War I period also produced a "spy report" in Sonoma Valley. A foreign-born couple living on Hood Mountain above Kenwood became suspects when local authorities confiscated a wireless radio apparatus from their home. The dismantling of the wireless followed several reports that an unidentified airplane was flying over Sonoma Valley for several nights. No other incriminating evidence was found at the mountaintop house, nor did further investigation indicate that the couple were guilty of anything more than possessing radio equipment, which wartime regulations made illegal.

There were occasional stories in the *I-T* about "slackers" (men who failed to register for the military draft) being apprehended, but far more stories of local boys enlisting and going off to war. Draft numbers were published from week to week with the names of draftees also printed.

Published, too, in the hometown paper were letters from Sonoma boys serving in the war zone. Bert Heugitt of Agua Caliente wrote of his transport ship being torpedoed by a German submarine. Vivid details of serving with the Army Ambulance Corps on the battlefields of Europe were related in letters from Fredrick Duhring

and Donald Campbell, among the first Sonomans to serve overseas.

"On the Fourth of July, 1918, the citizens of Sonoma raised a flag over City Hall in honor of the 117 boys gone to war from this community and surrounding Valley," said a page-one story in the July 6 *Index-Tribune*. The death of a Sonoma soldier, Stephen Nonella, 24, from pneumonia while at the Camp Fremont army hospital, was reported in the Oct. 19, 1918, *I-T*.

"With the news of the signing of the armistice on Nov. 11, 1918, Sonomans were surcharged with the spirit of celebration and rejoicing. ... Flags began to flutter from every flagpole and every automobile. ... The mayor appointed Jesse Prestwood and John Mohr a committee of two to arrange a mammoth celebration. ... The day was a semi-holiday here ... at night there were bonfires in the Plaza and many impromptu parades ... and silent prayers of thanks for peace," the *Index-Tribune* of November 16 reported.

It was following the armistice that Sonomans would learn of the Valley's first battlefield death—that of 18-year-old Frank Bosch, son of Capt. and Mrs. Peter Bosch of Vineburg. A telegram from the government told the parents that he had succumbed to wounds received in battle "somewhere in France," said a front-page story in the Nov. 30, 1918, edition of the *I-T*.

The death, from wounds received in battle, of Pvt. Isadore W. Moskowite, son of Mrs. Anna Moskowite of Schellville, was revealed several weeks later. Also disclosed was the young man's bravery, surviving the experience of lying wounded in a shell hole for five days when all his comrades around him had been killed. After spending some time in the hospital, he went back to active service and three times went "over the top," eventually receiving his fatal wounds.

Sonoma County is officially acknowledged as having lost 19 young men in World War I.

– RML

Glen Ellen offered five hotels, eight saloons

During the early years, Glen Ellen, like her neighbors, was extremely busy during the summer months, and a sleepy little village through

In 1914 the Mervyn Hotel in Glen Ellen was advertised as "the most up-to-date resort in Sonoma Valley."

COURTESY, SONOMA VALLEY HISTORICAL SOCIETY

the winter. Though Glen Ellen was out of the hot springs area and boasted no hot baths, her resorts were always full.

Bay Area businessmen brought their families to the Valley of the Moon. They settled into cottages or tent cabins where they remained until the fall rains. On Friday evenings either of the two railroads that served Glen Ellen disgorged a horde of "commuter" dads and whisked them back Sunday nights.

Camping out was only part of the fun, since there were five hotels—the Glen Ellen, Chauvet, Riverside, Mervyn and Roma Hotels—as well as the Mervyn resort and several others near town to provide dancing and other entertainment.

In 1914 the Hotel Mervyn advertised itself as being the most up-to-date resort in Sonoma Valley and claimed to offer the finest in bathing, boating and fishing.

It seems as though Glen Ellen was a little on the boisterous side during those days, since the citizens felt a strong need for a constable. In 1900 they petitioned the board of supervisors to cut Sonoma Township in two and make Glen Ellen a separate township.

Finally, in April 1901 their request was granted, and the Township of Glen Ellen was established. This included Glen Ellen, Eldridge and Kenwood. J. W. Gibson was appointed justice of the peace, and John R. Allen took over the constable duties.

It is easy to see why a constable was necessary when we discover that there were eight active saloons—Sobbe's, Pancrazzi's, Thierkoff's, The Pioneer, Monahan's, Mervyn Hotel, Hotel Chauvet and another above the slaughterhouse.

There is no doubt that Constable Allen slowed things down some, but probably the trauma brought about by the unbelievable increase of the price of a gallon of wine to 30¢ was even more effective.

However, not all activity was in the saloons. In 1900 Dr. C. C. O'Donnell gave a building lot and $500 toward the building of the Catholic church called St. Mary's. The Congregational church was meeting regularly in the Native Sons Hall on Glen Ellen Avenue [now Arnold Drive].

In the spring of 1903 Jack London brought his family to Wake Robin Lodge for the summer. In 1905 he moved to Glen Ellen and remained until his death in 1916.

Names like Hill, Ranker, Rankin, O'Donnell,

Glen Ellen was a lively resort town in summer and a quiet village in winter.

INDEX-TRIBUNE ARCHIVES

Poppe, Pancrazzi, Gibson, Pagani, Gordenker, Sobbe, Monahan and many others will be found listed among those who have made great contributions to Glen Ellen through the years, but the name of Joshua Chauvet has been associated more than any other with Glen Ellen progress throughout those early years.

In 1853 Joshua Chauvet bought 500 acres and a mill site from General Vallejo. He operated the sawmill there for 18 months before converting it into the foremost flour mill in the county.

By 1880 Chauvet was running a brandy and wine business on the premises. He was making 125,000 gallons of wine. In 1881 he expanded with the construction of a $14,000 winery building. It was three stories high with a storage capacity of over 200,000 gallons.

By 1888 the winery had reached an annual output of 175,000 gallons of wine and 8,000 gallons of brandy. This beautiful stone building beside Sonoma Creek, near Eldridge, was badly damaged in the 1906 earthquake but continued in use for many years.

During the turn-of-the-century years, Glen Ellen was always an active and prosperous village. Though the year-round population never reached the 400 mark, it was a busy township. Joshua Chauvet and his son Henry built the Hotel Chauvet and three other buildings in 1905 and 1906. All of the bricks were made in the local Glen Ellen brickyard.

In 1916 the town had everything that one could find in the big city. Well, nearly everything! For in 1916 Mr. Pancrazzi built a large auditorium on Carquinez Street and showed movies twice a week. In May of that year he showed Jack London's *Burning Daylight* to an audience of 260 and *The Sea Wolf* to 275, plus 100 residents of the state hospital at Eldridge.   – RUSS KINGMAN

COURTESY, MILLERICK FAMILY

The Millerick family home at Schellville (across from Sonoma Creek Winery) circa 1916. Mr. and Mrs. Michael Millerick, grandparents of the late Maj. James Millerick, are pictured with their grandniece Jean Catherine Jensen.

The Don Movie Theatre on East Napa Street was in use as early as 1913 and burned in 1932. Admission was 10¢.

COURTESY, SONOMA VALLEY HISTORICAL SOCIETY

Flu epidemic of 1918

*T*hough influenza was uncommon in Europe and America throughout most of the 1880s, a pandemic and a series of epidemics occurred, culminating in the disastrous killer pandemic of 1918–19.

The worldwide toll from this great plague was 20 to 40 million deaths, and the little town of Sonoma was not spared its share of misery.

The Sonoma Index-Tribune of Oct. 19, 1918, noted, "The germ is still unknown ... although King Alphonso of Spain was one of the victims of the influenza epidemic in 1893 and, again this summer, Spanish authorities repudiate any claim to influenza as a 'Spanish' disease."

The illness was not yet epidemic in this country, but the populace was warned that if it did not take care, such would be the case. A detailed and remarkably accurate description of the symptoms followed, leaving little uncertainty in the minds of readers regarding what to expect if stricken.

Precautions, aimed primarily at preventing contagion, were listed and included isolation, burning of gauzes and napkins, and wearing of masks. (These measures, if followed, are still today recognized as effective, though generally obsolete when vaccine is available.)

General health measures were also explicated (and, again, are still recognized as of value).

Overcrowding, perhaps the single most important factor in generating an epidemic, was also mentioned: "While it is not always possible, especially in times like the present, to avoid such overcrowding, people should consider the health danger and make every effort to reduce the home overcrowding to a minimum. The value of fresh air through open windows cannot be overemphasized. ... Keep out of crowds, period."

The final poetic caveat implored: "Cover up each cough and sneeze. If you don't, you'll spread disease."

By Oct. 26, 1918, a note of panic had crept into the *I-T*'s coverage, as it noted school closings, prohibitions of public meetings and general anxiety.

"Dr. Goban and Hays were kept going night and day, and drug stores—beseeched to furnish specifics for the disease—ran out of supplies."

Among the general populace, two deaths were reported.

By December 28 many cases were still reported, but they were a "light form [resembling] old-fashioned grippe."

Nonetheless, on Jan. 18, 1919, the Board of Health was stimulated by a flare-up to again close schools and ban all public gatherings, including, according to F. T. Duhring, chairman

The author's grandfather, *I-T* editor Harry Granice, was among those who invested in efforts to establish a major brewery here between 1910 and 1916. Granice's championing of the brewery as a home industry came to naught, and the building eventually became the home of the Vella Cheese Factory.

of the local health board, "lodges, churches, theatres, pool rooms, clubs, dances and ... meetings."

A collective sigh of relief must have been breathed when the *I-T* of February 1 finally released some good news—the schools were reopened, the flu ban was lifted, and the Board of Health announced the epidemic was completely under control.   – CLINTON LANE, M. D.

Prohibition a shocker for valley of the vine

Wet or dry?

The Sonoma Index-Tribune, powered by editor Harry Granice's arsenal of piercing editorials, waged the most bitter and certainly the most highly publicized campaign of the era in Sonoma Valley against the evolving forces of Prohibition.

Perhaps never has such extreme contempt been expressed in the annals of the *Index-Tribune* than during those days leading up to the final arrival of "bone dry" Prohibition.

"Obnoxious," "fanatical," "illegal," "selfish," "hypocritical," "foolish" are mere small samples of the battery of jargon slung at those much-scorned "Prohibitionists under the disguise of reform."

There was no question where the majority of Sonoma Valley citizens, and certainly the *Index-Tribune*, stood on that issue.

Such rancor toward the Prohibition-minded forces was understandable. The viticulturists and winemakers of the Valley had a livelihood to protect, as did tavern, resort and roadhouse owners. Certainly, the wine and resort industries made up the backbone of the Sonoma Valley economy at the time. And those businessmen, as well as the everyday guy-down-the-street beer— or wine—drinker weren't about to give up those privileges without a fight.

The first ripples of the Prohibition storm can be traced back to August 1907 when the city trustees passed Ordinance 90, the liquor ordinance, which, among other things, fixed taxes at $60 semi-annually. Also, the ordinance made it a misdemeanor to sell liquor to the intoxicated or to allow women to loiter or remain on the premises where liquor was sold.

INDEX-TRIBUNE ARCHIVES

A number of businessmen protested the ordinance and presented a widely signed petition. They claimed that the so-called anti-liquor ordinance was "directly hostile to our business interests in particular and the future prosperity of Sonoma in general." It was also pointed out that such legislation would be detrimental to the interests of the grape growers and winemakers here "without which there would be little prosperity."

Despite pleas from the businessmen, the ordinance passed 3–2. Trustee H. E. Bates, one of those voting in favor of the ordinance, said that while he did not wish to work a hardship on anyone, he felt nevertheless that the present situation was inviting Prohibition. Hotel and saloon men consequently acquired the services of a Thomas J. Butts of Santa Rosa to help them question the legality of the saloon ordinance.

Although vintners claimed something of a victory when a committee in Washington voted to have wine exempt from a new liquor distribution law (prohibiting liquor from being passed from a free to a Prohibition state), the wine industry here was nevertheless floundering. The financial depression, a growing number of Prohibition states and overproduction were blamed.

But the brunt of the *Index-Tribune*'s editorial hammer was wielded at the so-called reformists. In an editorial titled "The wave of reform and the Sonoma Valley" (Nov. 14, 1908), editor Granice maintained that there was really nothing that needed reforming in Sonoma Valley. "We have no Emeryville track, no Sausalito pool rooms, no San Francisco grafters, nor gambling halls, nor brothels and those other vices which have fastened themselves upon other interior communities."

In March 1911, both houses of the legislature passed the Local Option Bill, giving incorporated towns the option of going "wet" or "dry." An editorial in the March 25, 1911, edition of the *I-T* read, "With beer that is going to make Sonoma the Milwaukee of the West, with wine that has already brought honor and wealth to its makers, with water which is the best chaser ever passed over any bar, it isn't likely that Sonoma will ever go dry."

But it wasn't going to be that easy. Shortly after the passage of the option bill, "wet" forces

COURTESY, SONOMA VALLEY HISTORICAL SOCIETY

The first automobile in Sonoma Valley was a Metz belonging to the Simmons family, represented here by Gladys Simmons (later Dodge) and young Ellis Simmons, circa 1908.

began making claims that the legislature had been duped by the Anti-Saloon League into approving the new law, since the licensing board was not obligated to issue a liquor license even if one was requested.

California grape growers and winemen, meanwhile, began to organize their forces in an all-out campaign against the Anti-Saloon League movement. The California Wine Association, Italian Swiss Colony, grape growers and winemakers throughout the state put up donations to finance the campaign.

Slowly, however, the clouds of Prohibition continued to creep into the picture. In February 1913 the county board of supervisors passed a resolution limiting the number of retail liquor licenses in the Valley. It didn't sit well with the businessmen of Sonoma Valley—or the *Index-Tribune*, as one might guess.

The supervisors were "deceived into passing an unjust, cruel and unfair resolution," a May 3, 1913, editorial read. The local chamber of commerce was also accused of "representing nothing except its own selfish purposes" when representatives appeared on behalf of Sonoma Valley during hearings on the matter.

Supervisor J. H. Weise then motioned to have the resolution rescinded, which prompted a recall campaign against him. The Mother's League in the Valley was the group that was active in trying to recall Supervisor Weise.

Another was one G. J. K. Bigelow, publisher of a competing paper, *The Expositor*.

Bigelow was the subject of several bitter lambastings in the *Index-Tribune* for his Prohibitionist sentiments and campaign for the recall of Weise. A petition for recall was circulated, and the names of those signing the petition appeared in several consecutive editions of the *I-T*.

The recall election was held, and it failed miserably. "Bigelow is rebuked by the voters. He ought to now realize that vilification, abuse and misrepresentation do not win elections—His attempted recall a dead failure," read the headlines in the Sept. 30, 1913, edition of the *I-T*, proclaiming the recall's overwhelming defeat.

But the walls of Prohibition continued to form. Just prior to the recall election, a new county liquor ordinance was passed, specifying where and how and how much liquor was to be dispensed, as well as spelling out other restrictions. One stated that no dance hall or platform could be located within 50 feet of a bar in a bona fide hotel. Later, a prohibitive tax on viticulture products, brought about by the Revenue Emergency Act, was levied.

In April 1914, it was announced that the statewide Prohibition measure would be on the November general election ballot. "This proposition is but another one of those fool laws sought to be put upon our statute books by hypocritical reformers, who need to be reformed themselves," exclaimed Granice in an editorial April 4, 1914.

More strong stands against the Prohibition measure ensued. California, many argued, stood to lose more than any other state, because of its sizeable grape and hop industry. Taxes, it was predicted, would increase dramatically.

With the United States' entry into World War I in 1917, a surplus of food was desperately needed. Congress, in turn, passed a law that shut down every distillery in the U. S., thus preventing the use of grains or other commodities suitable for food in the manufacturing of whiskey or other beverages.

COURTESY, SONOMA VALLEY HISTORICAL SOCIETY

California Telephone and Light had 150 subscribers in 1915, when a photographer captured Nellie Petersen and Josephine Andrieux at the switchboard in the office of the former Castex building on Napa and First Street East.

The Prohibitionists kept at it. Among their claims were that German-Austrian aggression in Europe was to be blamed on beer-drinking.

California voted overwhelmingly against Prohibition, but that didn't stop the "dry" advocates.

President Woodrow Wilson signed the national Prohibition measure in late 1918 to go into effect in July of 1919. An *I-T* editorial charged, "The idea was never promulgated as an honest war measure. The war was just an excuse to further the propaganda of Prohibition cranks."

The "drys" dealt perhaps the decisive blow in January 1919 when the senate voted to ratify the acceptance of the "bone dry" amendment to the national constitution.

Seething headlines in the Jan. 11, 1919, edition of the *Index-Tribune* announced: "Senate votes to destroy our vineyards. Drys win 24 to 15."

Vineyardists and winemen again banded together in an effort to mount some sort of last-ditch legal appeal, but it appeared hopeless. Later, finding themselves right in the middle of the 1919 grape crop (hailed in the *I-T* as "one of the largest and finest in the history of the state"), growers and winemen made pleas to President Wilson.

Determined not to stand by and let their crop go to ruin, vineyardists went ahead and crushed their grapes in the fall of 1919 to save growers from a ruinous and farcical "wartime Prohibition."

Samuele Sebastiani, meanwhile, had pre-pared himself by making improvements in his cannery, purchasing new machinery for preserving string beans and handling tomatoes.

During the interim period between wartime and national Prohibition, wineries such as Sebastiani, Rhine Farm, Joe Sorini, L. Kunde and Pagani & Son were doing a land-office business trying to keep up with the frantic, last-minute demands for their products.

But the snarls that awaited grape growers and winemakers were simply too much. The shock of Prohibition would shake the industry like no drought or pestilence had ever done.

Like dormant vines, the wine industry in Sonoma Valley was about to fall into a deep, winter-like sleep.   – JOHN LYNCH

INDEX-TRIBUNE ARCHIVES

In June 1907 the old Cumberland College building was razed to make room for a new high school. In April 1908 a new $12,000 high school building (above), a block north of today's high school, was dedicated.

19 Sonoma Valley in the "Roaring Twenties": 1920–1929

INDEX-TRIBUNE ARCHIVES

Sonoma Valley Union High School under construction in 1923. It has been 74 years since a new high school was built here.

Present high school opened in 1923

*B*oosted by enthusiastic townspeople and the shameless editorializing of the *Index-Tribune*, Sonoma opened a new high school building in 1923.

As early as May 1921, *The Sonoma Index-Tribune* carried a story which proclaimed: "The board of trustees by unanimous vote decided that a new high school building was most urgent and that an immediate campaign to vote bonds be initiated."

According to that story, the high school's enrollment was larger than that of 119 of the 330 high schools in the state of California, yet its main school building was in worse condition for efficient service than most of them.

Among the pressing needs of the Sonoma Valley district were more classrooms, more adequate laboratories and an all-around new physical plan for the school.

The *I-T* writer noted, "The wretched heating system with its 12 wood stoves, the poor ventilation, the lack of hoods for poisonous fumes in the laboratory, the defective plumbing, the crumbling condition of the walls, without and within; the whole appearance of the plant is such as to provoke the ridicule of visitors."

By June 4, 1921, the board of trustees had decided to call for a bond issue for $115,000 to build a "new magnificent school building." A plan was proposed for a building designed by archi-

INDEX-TRIBUNE ARCHIVES

The 1927 senior class of Sonoma Valley Union High School, from left: (top row) Paul Thompson, William Rambo, Phillip Karst, Edwin Lindley, Barney (James) Bonbright, Tony Souza, Frank Pensar, Len Sperring, Clarence Dowdall, Watson Garoni, Italo Ciampi, Lee Clerici; (middle row) Mr. L. H. Golton, Walter Cliff, William Lund, Miss Bertha Warthorst, Emma Johnson, Ann Johnson, Evelyn Valente, Leah Rouquie, Al Pellandini, John Rauly; (front row) Hazel Weidrick, Evelyn Guerne, Countess Prestwood, Edna Roeder, Eva Schieck, Gladys Fox, Ella Fox, Evelyn Carlson, Ruth Allen, Leah Abbott, Eugenie Tate and Mildred States.

tect W. H. Weeks of San Francisco which would have a capacity for 240 pupils and 10 teachers "in case they are needed." The *I-T* further reported that the proposed building was of solid concrete construction of a mission style of architecture, with courts and a gymnasium. It would also include a hall and stage.

The *I-T*, in a front-page "news story" on June 11, 1921, stated, "The new high school is endorsed everywhere. A campaign for the $115,000 building is gaining great momentum as pertinent facts and figures are digested by the taxpayers. Vote Yes!"

The people of the Valley did, indeed, get the message and, by a vote of 428 for and 192 against, approved the bond issue. "The vote gave the two-thirds as required by law, with 14 votes to spare," the *I-T* proudly stated.

In March 1922 the building contract was awarded to Larsen and Siegrist of San Francisco for the low bid of $108,777, and ground was soon broken.

Finally, on Jan. 19, 1923, the auditorium of

the new high school was thronged with patrons of the school, students and friends when a "splendid dedication ceremony took place."

The *I-T* reported in that issue, "It is planned to add much to the new building as time goes on and finances permit. Landscape gardening, a machine shop, tennis courts, drives and athletic fields are yet to come."

With ample room to expand the facilities when needed, Sonoma Valley residents felt they had made a wise investment. The *I-T* spoke for many in the Valley when it printed, "The dedication of the splendid structure last night marks a new era in Sonoma Valley's educational advancement."

– KATHY SWETT

1923 Mission centennial pageant festival highlight

Sonoma's Mission Centennial will go down in history as the finest achievement of the century just past.

The five-day celebration of the founding of the Mission town was a splendid and fitting climax of 100 years of community development and progress.

*S*o said the opening paragraph of the page-one feature story in the July 7, 1923, issue of *The Sonoma Index-Tribune* recounting the 100th anniversary observance of the founding of the Mission San Francisco Solano de Sonoma, when Padre José Altimira planted the cross here on July 4, 1823, establishing the last and most northerly of the chain of California missions started by Father Junipero Serra.

Judging by the thousands of visitors the Sonoma Mission Centennial brought to Sonoma from June 30 through July 4, and the plaudits won by the community in the metropolitan city press, there seemed little doubt that the event was truly Sonoma's "finest achievement."

The Sonoma Mission Play, produced by Garnet Holme, the noted writer of the acclaimed "Ramona" pageant at Hemet and other outdoor productions, won particular praise from both the press and spectators. Three hundred costumed participants, most of them residents of Sonoma Valley, were cast in roles for the three-episode Mission Play which detailed the founding of the mission, the coming of Gen. Mariano G. Vallejo, the Bear Flag incident and other special moments in Sonoma's storied past.

Members of well-known Sonoma families were in the huge cast: Mrs. Lulu Emparan, Raoul Emparan, Walter Bundschu, Jesse F. Prestwood, Robert J. Poppe, Mr. and Mrs. Ralph Hotz, Adam Adler, Roy Bill, Walter Murphy, Louis H. Green, August Sebastiani, Pierre Rouquie, Carrie Burlingame, Kennon Gilbert, Louis Bosch, Shirley Weise, Edna Cooper and Florence Forni—to name a few. Said Elford Eddy, a reporter for the old *San Francisco Call*, in a feature story about the Mission Play:

Without making comparisons, without qualification, without any explanation of the reason why, it can be stated with authority that Sonoma's celebration was the best thing of its kind any of the

COURTESY, SONOMA VALLEY HISTORICAL SOCIETY

Among participants in the Sonoma Mission Centennial Pageant of 1923 were, from left: (standing) Roburt Stanleigh, Walter Murphy, Carrie Burlingame, Bruce Warren, Raoul Emparan (General Vallejo's grandson), Robert Poppe, Sofia Maldonado; (seated) Minnie Cook, Honoria Tuomey, Luisa Emparan (Raoul's mother), Rose Arrieola and Celia Thomson.

visiting newspapermen had ever seen. And visiting newspapermen always credit themselves with having seen considerable.

That Sonoma, a small city, could stage such a show was a big surprise to these same visiting molders of public opinion. They came intending to consecrate a lot of time to sleep, but after seeing the show, they decided they could do their sleeping after their return home, and tried to remain in circulation 24 hours a day for fear of missing something.

A Spanish ball in the Plaza followed the Mission Play on the evening of Saturday, June 30. Sunday at noon the mission was the setting for a high Mass conducted by San Francisco Archbishop Edward Hanna. A matinee performance of the Mission Play was next. A Wild West rodeo was also on the Sunday afternoon program, followed by Plaza entertainment including a musical revue, classical folk dancing and Spanish fandango in the evening. Monday and Tuesday, July 2 and 3, were also event-filled,

from morning until midnight, highlighted by band concerts and other entertainment. The Mission Play was repeated on July 3 and 4 to sell-out crowds. Seating had been provided for 3,500 spectators, and those seats were filled during every performance.

And who but the sponsors were concerned that the aftermath of the glorious Mission Centennial fête showed some $10,000 in unpaid costs? After appeals for financial aid appeared in the *Index-Tribune*, community residents rallied to pay off the debt, the donors' names published on the front page of their hometown newspaper.

– RML

Sonoma Golf Course dates back to the 1920s

*I*t's a par 72 and has been recognized by such famous golfers as Sam Snead and Byron Nelson as one of the best laid-out golf courses in the United States.

We're talking about the Sonoma golf course, an idea born as the "Valley of the Moon Golf and

INDEX-TRIBUNE ARCHIVES

The handsome clubhouse of the Sonoma Golf and Country Club was destroyed by fire in the early morning hours of Feb. 4, 1952. Some 13 years earlier, Mrs. Alma Spreckels, then owner of the golf course, spent $100,000 transforming the historic old J. K. (Guy) Bigelow mansion into a clubhouse.

Country Club" back in June 1921 in the minds of Boyes Hot Springs resort proprietor Rudy Lichtenberg and golf promoter W. I. Fitzgerald.

They envisioned a golf layout here that would soon rival the famed Del Monte Golf and Country Club which had met with so much favor on the Monterey peninsula.

Lichtenberg, a former prominent Marin county resident, was also a director and organizer of the Golden Gate Ferry Co.

"Mac" McKenzie, then president of the California Golf Association, was brought to Sonoma Valley, and he, with knowledgeable golf professionals, determined that Oak Lawn, the 238-acre ranch of J. K. Bigelow, north and west of El Verano, was the ideal location for a golf course (where the Sonoma Golf Club is today).

On Sept. 24, 1921, Lichtenberg and Fitzgerald, along with a number of prominent Sonoma Valley citizens, signed a five-year lease for $3,000 per year on the Bigelow property as the beginning of the Valley of the Moon Golf and Country Club.

Said the *Index-Tribune* of that date: "The people of Sonoma Valley are awakening to the fact that golf is fast becoming a national sport, and they realize that with the completion of our highways and our new Golden Gate Ferry, they must be prepared to compete with other sections of the state."

To build the golf course, envisioned from the start as 18 holes, the club leaders chose John Clark, famous builder of Crystal Springs, near San Francisco, and other golf courses. The plan was to complete nine holes as quickly as possible, the second nine to follow.

The handsome two-story home of the Bigelows was to be converted into the clubhouse, with dining room, card rooms, lockers, showers and baths.

On June 21, 1924, it was announced that Fred F. Partridge of San Francisco had purchased the Bigelow ranch, including the golf course which had been under lease to the VOM Golf and Country Club. Frank M. Burris, a Sonoma banker who was club president at the time, said that Partridge planned to complete the course to 18 holes and would retain the name Valley of the Moon Golf and Country Club.

Two years later, on Nov. 6, 1926, the *Index-Tribune* reported that San Francisco capitalist A. O. Stewart, representing the Sonoma Properties Co., Inc., had purchased the former Bigelow property, including the golf course and former residence used as a clubhouse by the golf club.

On Friday, July 27, 1928, the new 18-hole golf course, on which $110,000 had been expended, was formally opened, with Eddie Beeler, former golf pro at Lakeside, in charge. The *San Francisco Examiner* on the Saturday preceding the opening carried a page announcement on the new golf course and country club in Sonoma Valley.

When the Depression hit several years later, the golf course, along with the resorts of Sonoma Valley, suffered considerable financial loss. The golf course was saved for the Valley when it was purchased by Alma Spreckels, who owned the Sobre Vista properly nearby.

In later years it was purchased by the late Dr. Cecil A. Saunders, a prominent San Francisco physician. Following his death, ownership passed to his son, William Saunders, a Honolulu attorney, who operated it as one of several "national" golf courses owned by the corporation for a number of years.   – RML

AUTHOR'S NOTE: Bill Saunders and other family stockholders sold the golf course in April 1988 to F. D. B. Enterprises, USA, one of the Fuji Country Company group, a leading golf course managing company in Japan. Sale price was reported in excess of $7.5 million with an additional $8 million subsequently spent on a complete rebuilding of the course and clubhouse.

Popular golf professionals at the Sonoma course since the 1940s included the late Harold Stone and his successor, Jess Reinking; Pat Burtson, presently with the Napa Municipal Golf Course; Ron Blum, now a golf pro in the Pacific Northwest and an NFL referee; and Don Tarvid, the present head pro.

Sheriff Joe Ryan, "terror of bootleggers"

Undoubtedly one of the most colorful lawmen in Sonoma's history was Sheriff Joe Ryan. A 23-year deputy for Sonoma County, who served as sheriff of the county for less than one year, Ryan was known as the "terror of bootleggers."

Ryan came to Sonoma from Elmira, California, as a 10-year-old boy with his parents, who were in the hotel business. His mild-mannered exterior hid a strong and adventurous spirit which would make him one of the best law enforcement officers in the county. One indication of his spiritedness showed itself in the tale of young Ryan and his friend, John P. McDonnel. Ryan and McDonnel were determined to show who had the best mare in Sonoma, and they decided to race through town to prove the point. The race, down Napa Street, was a fast one, and as the boys reached St. Francis Church, Joe's horse fell and landed on top of him.

The accident caused some injury to Ryan, who subsequently had to undergo several operations. This didn't seem to have too much of an adverse effect on Ryan, for he was soon working at the Gravelle stables as a stable boy and as a bus driver for the U. S. Postal Service.

Ryan was appointed deputy sheriff in 1901 by Sheriff Frank Grace, and soon made himself a record as a deputy that was hard for anyone to match. His talent for capturing and arresting criminals was unequaled.

One strange case took place in 1921. Deputy Sheriff Ryan was called to a robbery at the Fischer cottage in Fetters Springs. It was an unusual robbery, as the only things missing were some clothing and a sack of sugar.

Ryan, investigating the scene of the crime, came upon a trail of sugar. Following this, he soon discovered a belt which he identified as the kind worn by the patients of the state hospital at Eldridge.

Ryan then went to the hospital and, upon making inquiries, soon learned that two men were missing, one of them a six-foot-tall Indian. Ryan decided to hunt for them in the nearby hills.

The mystery was solved when a woman from a local store told Ryan that two men answering the description of the patients had been in to buy some food. They were soon captured and returned to the hospital, thanks to the detective work of Deputy Ryan.

In May of the same year, Ryan was called to

Joe Ryan with one of his trotting horses. Before becoming sheriff, Ryan operated a race track behind stables located at the corner of Napa and First Street West.

settle an altercation between two Vallejo "toughs" in George Darling's restaurant in Boyes Hot Springs.

The two, one described as a "navy yard pugilist," had been kicked out of the restaurant and were causing trouble outside. As Ryan was attempting to arrest them, Michael Hayes, the fighter, knocked Ryan down and broke his jaw. Undaunted, Ryan managed to take both men into custody before going to Santa Rosa to see a doctor. Ryan's only comment on the affair was that he "resents the fact that the swelling interferes with his usual good eats!"

In September 1925 John Boyes, sheriff of Sonoma County and former Santa Rosa police chief, was taken ill. It was generally assumed that he would not recover, and steps were taken to decide on his replacement.

Joe Ryan was the favorite candidate of the board of supervisors, and of many of the people of Sonoma County. He had run for the office twice before and was once so narrowly defeated that a recount was called.

In the Sept. 9, 1925, issue of the *Index-Tribune,* a banner headline read "Sheriff Joe Ryan is sworn in." The board of supervisors had chosen Ryan unanimously from a field of eight other candidates.

Ryan, immediately upon hearing the news, had gone to Santa Rosa to be sworn in and to place a $25,000 bond, as required by law.

The new sheriff, wasting no time, celebrated his promotion the same day by rounding up a

COURTESY, SONOMA VALLEY HISTORICAL SOCIETY

Joe Ryan died within a year of being appointed sheriff.

San Francisco ex-convict who had stolen a car and was hiding in the hills in back of the Santa Rosa golf links. Ryan swore he would not be a "swivel-chair executive" and that he would work for "a strong economy in the sheriff's office."

During his first month in office, Ryan established the Women's Christian Temperance Union. Meetings were held at the county jail on Sunday evenings. Ryan felt that the hymns and gospel carried through the evening air to the prisoners just might do them some good, and certainly could do no harm.

Soon after his appointment as sheriff, the 49-year-old Ryan married his longtime sweetheart, Miss Jessie Hiser of Sonoma, a night telephone operator. The couple, not telling anyone of their plans, went to Santa Rosa and were married by Judge Percy S. King. The ceremony was concluded when the judge handcuffed the newlyweds together. As most people thought of Ryan as a confirmed bachelor, his wedding was the cause of much rejoicing.

In October 1925, just over a month after his appointment, Ryan was honored by his deputies with a gift. "In recognition of the esteem in which he is held by his office force and deputies," he was awarded a diamond-studded badge. A wed-

ding gift of a mahogany clock was presented to Ryan and his bride at the same time.

Unfortunately for the citizens of Sonoma Valley, their popular and colorful sheriff was not to bag bootleggers much longer.

Less than a year after his appointment as sheriff, and only seven months after his wedding, Joe Ryan died of a heart attack in the home of his brother, Tom.

His death, in June 1926 at the age of 50, was a shock to the community. Sonoma's "favorite son" sheriff was mourned by all but the criminals of Sonoma County.

He was described in his obituary as "fearless, brave, determined and almost with an uncanny talent for running down and capturing criminals. He became widely known as one of California's best peace officers and was feared by the criminal all along the coast."

Sheriff Joe Ryan, with his diamond-studded badge and colorful history, was certainly one of the most beloved county officials that Sonoma County has ever had.

— SUE MORAN

S. F., Oakland baseball teams trained here

The headline for a front-page story in the Oct. 6, 1923, *Index-Tribune* read, "Prepare for Seals at Boyes Springs." The announcement was not to warn Sonomans that those sleek flippered and whiskered seafaring creatures were migrating inland, but rather that the famous minor league baseball team from San Francisco would be arriving the following spring.

The San Francisco Seals, perennial powerhouse club of the Pacific Coast League, had chosen the resort town of Boyes Hot Springs, with its mineral waters and friendly atmosphere, as an ideal spot to establish their spring training camp once again.

Work started on a grassy-green diamond, and bleachers were erected by local citizens in anticipation of the club's arrival, scheduled for early in 1924. With star players like Pete Compton and Jimmy O'Connell, and trainer Denny Carroll, the arrival of the Seals was one of the most eagerly anticipated happenings in the Valley.

INDEX-TRIBUNE ARCHIVES

The San Francisco Seals' champion Pacific Coast League baseball team of 1923. The team held its spring training sessions in Boyes Springs, taking full advantage of the mineral baths, masseurs and recreational facilities.

The diamond which the Seals used was located where the Fiesta Plaza Shopping Center now stands. When the destructive fire of 1923 roared through the area, the baseball diamond, along with the Boyes Springs Hotel, was destroyed. But community leaders, determined not to lose the recognition and boost to the economy provided by the Seals each spring, laid out a new diamond adjacent to the new Sonoma golf course.

The Seals' team, still committed to training in the area, made its 1924 spring training headquarters in the two-story golf course clubhouse, the former J. K. Bigelow home. With four to six members of the club per room, the players slept on beds resurrected from the ruins of the Boyes Springs Hotel.

Bleachers were erected at the new diamond so that local and visiting baseball enthusiasts could come and enjoy the Seals' daily practices and pre-season games against other Bay Area squads.

While Seals manager George Putnam had high praise for the Valley's hospitality and the accommodations provided, despite the great Boyes Springs fire losses, the ball club and local hosts, Rudy Lichtenberg and Fred Partridge, could not get together on financial arrangements for the 1925 spring training, and the Seals went to Fresno.

The Seals' absence was short-lived and the Fresno experiment called a debacle; the San Francisco team returned here in 1926 with new manager and first baseman Bert Ellison and popular players like Eddie Mulligan, Tim Hendryx, Smead Jolley and Lloyd (Little Poison) Waner. The latter was the brother of former Seals' star Paul (Big Poison) Waner, called up to the Pittsburg Pirates the previous season.

The Seals, with a few defections, continued to be harbingers of spring in Boyes Springs throughout the 1920s, '30s and early '40s. On Feb. 5, 1928, it was announced in the *Index-Tribune* that even the major league New York Giants (many years before they were to move to San Francisco) were considering training in Sonoma Valley's wonderland. Manager John McGraw contemplated the move for some time, because of the mineral springs and the therapeutic benefits of the locale. The move never materialized, however, and the Valley remained the domain of the Seals through the era of manager Frank (Lefty) O'Doul.

When the Seals finally abandoned Boyes Springs, the Oakland Acorns, also of the Pacific Coast League, succeeded them here for several seasons, with legendary and colorful managers like Mel Ott and Casey Stengel at the helm.

Although they no longer practice and train in the Valley, on a lazy spring day it is easy for local fans to lie back and imagine (and some may recall) the sight of the dashing young Pacific Coast League ballplayers, or hear the crack of the ball against a bat and the thud of a long fly landing in the mitt as the final out was made on a Boyes Springs diamond of yesteryear.

– RON CHURCHILL AND RML

Raids on resorts, illegal stills during Prohibition

There were so many little resorts in the Valley in those days—if you were known at all, you could get a drink at any one of them for 25¢.

So spoke a former Sonoma bootleg still owner-operator, who wishes to remain anonymous, when asked what those Prohibition days were like in the Valley of the Moon.

The March 6, 1920, *Sonoma Index-Tribune* featured a front-page account of one of the first "snooping" raids, when Prohibition enforcement officers appeared at the Chauvet Hotel in Glen Ellen. In a closet under the stairway they found some cordials which had been "stored there and forgotten," so the proprietor states, when the country went dry. At the Depot Hotel, also in Glen Ellen, the officers found wine and aqua vita in their search for an illicit still near the area. However, no moonshine was located.

"Exciting incidents mark 'dry' raid," headlined the Aug. 5, 1922, *Index-Tribune*. According to this account, 14 Prohibition enforcement officers, following up investigators' tips, flooded the Glen Ellen district and made a raid on the Ambrose Noe place in the hills back of the Swain ranch.

INDEX-TRIBUNE ARCHIVES

Dedicated in 1923, the Jack London Memorial Library was built by the Glen Ellen Women's Improvement Club at a cost of $15,000. The library had a stage, auditorium, dining room and kitchen. The property was deeded to Dunbar School in 1938 but was eventually torn down when the foundation was discovered to be defective. People in the photo were not identified.

"Ostensibly a goat ranch," the *Index-Tribune* reported, the "goats' milk," which was very popular, proved to be "hooch," and the officers seized three stills, mash and a quantity of "white mule" (un-aged whiskey).

An elaborate account of a raid on the Union Hotel in the April 10, 1920, *I-T* tells how two agents surprised Mr. and Mrs. John Steiner, proprietors, one Friday evening. One officer flashed his "star" upon the table where Mr. Steiner sat playing a game of cards, and informed him that he intended to raid the place.

"Mr. Steiner told him to proceed if that was his intent, and was so little disturbed by the intruder's appearance that he did not even get up from the card table." Another officer, however, was searching the dining room where Mrs. Steiner was, and with a flashlight began ransacking the sideboard and linen chest in search of "booze." In a closet he found "a portion of a bottle of white wine, given to Mrs. Steiner as a present, and she kept it there for her own use when tired from overwork."

When Mrs. Steiner denied having the wine there to sell, the officer is quoted as having said, "Well, if you haven't been selling it, you are a damn fool. Don't think I'm a Prohibitionist; I'm just doing my duty. I like a shot as well as anybody. To tell you the truth, I'm dry right now." He then dashed into the kitchen with the wine. The article concluded that the raid amounted to the "finding of a few bottles of wine and liquor which the proprietor and his wife kept for their own use in what they regard as their home."

A sympathetic tone was always evident in the *I-T*'s accounts, such as the following, of these raids: "The detectives knocked out the bungs of the wine barrels and smashed many bottles, letting the cherished possession of the proprietress, Annie Acquistpace, run out on the ground in the presence of the woman and her little crippled son."

Another article in the Aug. 12, 1922, *I-T* remarked that the raids were a result of reports turned in by a detective named Vail, and "as a result, the resort section of the Valley has turned from a carefree, merry joy zone into a veritable vale of tears. The lid is on."

The Sonoma hills apparently hid a number of stills in those Prohibition days. The late Ted

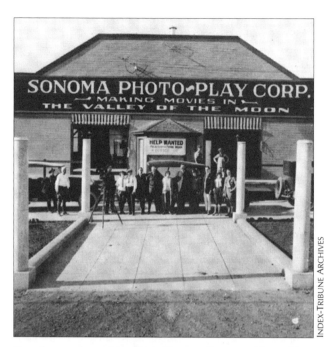

Run by producer Harold J. Binney, Sonoma Photo-Play Corp. was briefly located in Boyes Springs.

Riboni, veteran Valley plumber, recalled building 50 or 60 stills for customers in the Valley. Most of them, he said, were concentrated around Cavedale and Lovall Valley. It was at the biggest one on Lovall Valley Road where two Prohibition officers were killed in a raid, according to Riboni.

"I worked for Marcy and Peterson on Broadway during the day and made special fittings for the stills at night," he said.

One still he built, on what is now the part of The Ranch estates, was discovered when chickens at a ranch below began dying mysteriously. When the owner had his hens autopsied it was found they had died from an overdose of alcohol. It seems the overflow, or mash, had gone into an old well and seeped into the water supply of the chicken ranch below.

The "Prohis" appeared in the Valley right away, traced the seepage to the offending still and put another enterprising whiskey producer out of business.

The Jan. 31, 1925, front page of the *I-T* told of a still seizure by Sheriff John Boyes on a ranch south of town. This was at the home of a local barber, where the sheriff discovered 1,000 gallons of mash, six sacks of sugar, two sacks of prunes and two sacks of barley. The barber was accused of making "jackass brandy" and harbor-

INDEX-TRIBUNE ARCHIVES

The St. Francis fire of 1922. It was started by workmen who were burning off paint. The fire swept through the church, destroying the entire structure.

ing 200 gallons of "hair tonic." He was charged with the manufacture of "moonshine."

Another arrest was made when two stills were discovered in the Cavedale area on the Landis ranch. In an area long known as "the secret pasture," officers discovered two stills and 4,000 gallons of mash. "The illicit liquor plant was a first-class one," the *I-T* reported. "Set up in the isolated spot was a summer kitchen of burlap where the moonshine was cooked up. The stills were of 50-gallon capacity and seven vats of mash were in the process of fermentation."

Tragedy came with Prohibition, too. Local brothers Sal and Albert Carlo, proprietors of the Lark Club House in Agua Caliente, were shot in a bootleggers' war in a San Francisco moonshine plant. And the late George Cavaglia, who was notorious for his still operations, was badly burned when one blew up.

One anonymous still owner, at the same time denying he once operated two giant stills near St. Francis Solano Church, admitted to selling his stuff to local resort owners for $8 per gallon. "I

lived at the El Dorado Hotel. Quartaroli owned it then. It was a real nice place."

Still never admitting to operating those two giant stills, he parted with his secret to successful bootlegged whiskey:

> The best whiskey was put in oak barrels and buried in hot manure piles to age; as it heated up, the tannic acid from the oak barrels would age it in about three weeks. But I never was a bootlegger. A bootlegger is someone caught and convicted. I never was a bootlegger.
>
> – PAT MARTINDALE BONNOITT

St. Francis Church a fire victim for second time

St. Francis Solano Church caught fire and burned to the ground on Thursday, Sept. 28, 1922. This was the second time Sonoma's Catholic church was destroyed by fire. The first time was in June 1896.

The 1922 fire had its origin in a part of the church where workmen from the Muller and Downey company were burning off old paint. A report in the Sept. 30, 1922, edition of the *Index-Tribune* described the fire:

> In some way, one of their blow torches communicated to a hollow column on the front of the church which acted like a flue and started the fire skyward.
>
> The painters, seeing that they were powerless to cope with the blaze and that the ladders by which they had ascended would soon be caught in the flames, made a hurried descent to the ground.
>
> Meanwhile an alarm for the fire department had been rung in, but the engine was at the Sebastiani tract fighting a grass fire which menaced the home of Mrs. Louis Breitenbach. The firemen, however, rushed the apparatus to the church fire, leaving the Breitenbach fire to the Sebastiani protective system.
>
> When they arrived, the church was

a seething mass of flames and it was apparent that all effort should be directed to saving the handsome new parochial residence and other nearby property. A heavy wind sprang up and carried burning embers to adjacent roofs and fields, and for two hours the entire town was menaced.

The firemen fought valiantly, battling back the flames from the priest's house and saving what they could of the sacred statuary and other valuable contents from the interior of the church.

Several times, the old Tivnen property, across the street, took fire as did the Barracchi home two blocks away, the Cheney property, Castagnet barn and other structures. Volunteers, aided by one of the chemical engines from Boyes Hot Springs, repeatedly put out incipient blazes, grass fires, burning trees, blazing fences, etc.

By 3 o'clock, charred embers were all that remained of the stately old

church, built by the late John M. Burke some 25 years before.

The loss at the time was estimated to be $40,000. No loss of life occurred and no one was injured.

Plans began immediately to build a new church, and fund-raising drives took place throughout the remainder of 1922. A big dance to raise funds was held at the St. Francis Hotel in San Francisco in November.

On May 27, 1923, the cornerstone of the new St. Francis Solano Church was laid, and shortly thereafter the church completed its rise from the ashes.   – BILL LYNCH

Boyes Springs wiped out by the fire of 1923

The fire then whipped up again and came down a gap between the foothills and Woodleaf Park and Boyes Springs. The whole settlement was instantly ignited. Flames broke out everywhere. With a cry of horror, people fled from their homes.

COURTESY, SONOMA MISSION INN & SPA

Sonoma Mission Inn at Boyes Hot Springs as it looked in 1927, after it was rebuilt following the 1923 fire. The property was known as the Boyes Springs Hotel until 1928, when directors changed the name "to capitalize on Sonoma's historic and romantic background."

This vivid paragraph was one of the highlights in the *Index-Tribune*'s story of the great fire which scourged Sonoma Valley in September 1923—probably the worst fire ever to occur here.

The fire started in the Glen Ellen area, said the *I-T* of September 23, and blitzed its way to Boyes Springs. Before the winds stopped and the fire could be extinguished, Boyes Springs was wiped out, along with several resort areas around it.

The only conflagration to come close in recent years was the bad fire of September 1964, which swept the west side of the Valley, from Kenwood to the edge of the city of Sonoma. Oddly enough, both fires covered about the same area, but the one in '23 was undoubtedly worse.

The 1923 fire started, according to the *Index-Tribune,* when some men trying to smoke out some bees in Napa County let their fire get away from them on Sunday, September 16.

For the next two days the fire roared and leapfrogged past the firelines, jumped back and forth across Sonoma Creek, and gobbled up homes, hotels, resorts, outbuildings and a vast collection of assorted structures.

Where the Napa bee-chasers were located isn't clear, but the fire entered Sonoma Valley through Nuns Canyon. By midnight the flames had driven out the families in the Trinity Road and Cavedale Road areas.

They fled to Glen Ellen and found the farmers there fighting to save their homes and barns. The winds, pushing the fire like a bellows, spurred the blaze on toward the Spreckels ranch, the Sonoma State Home and Agua Caliente.

In 1923 Sonoma Valley did not have much in the way of firefighting equipment. There were only a few primitive fire trucks here, and putting out brush fires was mainly a job done by men wielding shovels.

Firefighters were conscripted, as the *I-T* said, to combat the fire. The residents of Sonoma came to the aid of their neighbors to try to stop the fire before it spread farther south.

Businessmen in Sonoma and elsewhere closed their stores and hurried to the fire lines with their employees. The schools were closed, and teachers and students fought the fire.

These heroic volunteers checked the course of the conflagration early Monday afternoon. The fire was blocked before it could do much harm at the Spreckels ranch.

The Madrone Vineyards were saved. The State Home at Eldridge was spared. The wind slackened. It seemed the worst had passed.

Not so. Around 2:30 P.M., the fire picked up strength again in the canyons behind the summer resort areas of Agua Caliente Park, Fetters Springs, Sonoma Highlands and Woodleaf Park.

It continued to consume buildings despite the hundreds of firefighters arrayed against it.

During Monday afternoon, Boyes Springs was destroyed.

The *I-T* reported:

> People fled from their homes, some with their belongings packed, some with nothing.
>
> Fed by countless bungalows and cottages in Woodleaf Park and by rows of stores and the Boyes Springs Hotel, the flames leaped high in the air, jumping from one side of the road to the opposite and finally swept across the creek to Sonoma Vista, where it licked up row after row of summer homes.

Help came from all over. The Northwestern Pacific Railroad sent a fire train crew to the Valley, but because the trestles had been burned out, there was not too much it could do. Chief Murphy of the San Francisco Fire Department sent three trucks here.

The fire nevertheless missed a few structures in the Springs area, it was related. The Sonoma Valley Restaurant was saved. Joe Ryan's stable came through. And so did Benedetto's Barber Shop, Stuermer's Garage and the Boyes Springs Bath House. Sam Ganos managed to save his popular restaurant.

Refugees from the fire poured into Sonoma and El Verano, piled into cars and trucks of all descriptions. At 10 P.M. Monday, the fire died down and was finally beaten out.

But Boyes Springs was gone, wrote the anonymous *I-T* reporter. The hotel was a mass of ashes; the little theater, where music and laughter held sway the night previous, was only a memory.

The NWP depot and grass plot were obliterated, the clubhouse was no more, and the Woodleaf store, the busy lumber yard, the new business block, the favorite stores and shops, the good eats places, garages, private homes along the highway and 30 bungalows in the orchard back of the hotel—all were leveled. Rumors of people who had burned to death in the fire turned out to be false.

And one of the most unusual stories was about a little dog left chained to his doghouse as the fire swept through. He dug his way into the ground and the flames passed over him. When the doghouse burned, he gained his freedom and eventually found his family.

The September 29 issue of the *I-T* reported that people were already starting to rebuild at Boyes Springs.

Some businessmen set themselves up in tents. Others erected temporary structures. The state Highway Commission, through Commissioner Harvey Toy, sent word it was now really going to build that road from Schellville to Beltane, in Glen Ellen.

Boyes Springs had a mayor in those days, J. W. Minges. He lost almost everything in the fire, but he and his neighbors never really lost heart.

Minges said: "My plans are not settled, of course, but Boyes Springs will be rebuilt more symmetrically and substantially. Boyes will rise from the ashes again. Fire cannot rob us of our mineral springs, our climate and the whole-souled people who abide here. No siree!"

–JERRY PARKER

The Sonoma Grammar School bus in the 1920s.

INDEX-TRIBUNE ARCHIVES

20 Valley Coped with Depression of the Thirties: 1930–1940

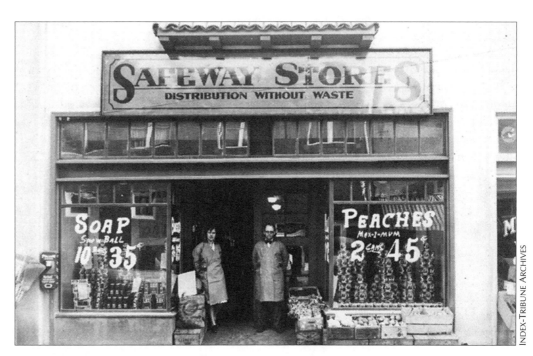

INDEX-TRIBUNE ARCHIVES

The first chain store in Sonoma Valley was a Safeway located on West Napa Street in 1930. R. D. (Ray) Roberts, store manager, and Mrs. Roberts, shown here, advertised canned peaches at two for 45¢. In 1996, when a new 50,000-square-foot Safeway opened, one can of peaches was 79¢.

Despite Depression, progress shone through

*H*ow did Sonoma Valley weather the so-called Depression decade which followed the October 1929 stock market crash?

If one were to judge from the contents of the weekly issues of *The Sonoma Index-Tribune* from 1930 to 1940, locals handled the perilous economic times quite well. In fact, headlines denoting considerable progress shone through the darkness of the Depression years.

Optimism, it appears from news and editorial comment, more than matched negativism.

Those in need found a citizens' emergency relief committee—composed of members of the newly formed Red Cross chapter, Sonoma Kiwanis Club, Woman's Club, Chamber of Commerce and local churches—eager to give assistance. The local VFW post placed food barrels in local stores to collect items donated for the needy.

Food and clothing prices here in 1930 were reasonable. At Sonoma's Safeway store, bananas were priced at 4 pounds for 25¢, picnic hams went for 19¢ a pound and 10 pounds of pure cane sugar cost 48¢. B. Mori's Mission Fruit Market, located between Safeway and the *I-T* on West Napa Street, advertised two fresh loaves of bread for 15¢, two dozen red apples for 33¢ and Burbank potatoes at 8 pounds for 25¢. At the G. H. Hotz department store, ladies' wash dresses were on sale for $1.47, large bath towels for 39¢

each and men's work shirts, 79¢. Eraldi's was offering flannel shirts for $3.95, and worsted and flannel pants went for $3.48 to $6.45. The three barber shops in Sonoma dropped the price of a shave and haircut from $1 to 75¢.

Aid, in the form of jobs for the unemployed, was welcomed here after Franklin D. Roosevelt, elected president in 1932, enacted his National Recovery Act (NRA), followed by his Works Progress Administration (WPA) and Public Works Administration (PWA) programs. Local workers were employed in a variety of community-betterment projects under the WPA, augmented by locally raised funds.

Among these local projects were the Vallejo Home restoration and rebuilding of the chalet at Lachryma Montis; improvement of the eight-acre Sonoma Plaza, including the amphitheater; building of a firehouse at Boyes Hot Springs; and improvements at both the grammar school and high school, which WPA labor made possible, augmented with district funds.

Valley residents further showed their optimism by approving formation of the Valley of the Moon Fire District and taking action to form the Sonoma Valley Chamber of Commerce in January 1930. The census for the city of Sonoma in 1930 indicated a population of 980 people, compared to 957 in 1910, city officials acknowledging the "rather slow growth."

That faster growth was on the horizon for the area was foreseen in announcements in the *Index-Tribune* of a federal bill authorizing $1,250,000 for a "bombing base" in Marin County (later to become Hamilton Field, where more than $10 million was expended in building the important Air Force base); and approval by voters on Nov. 4, 1930, of a $35 million bond issue for construction of the Golden Gate Bridge. A construction start by July 1931 was predicted by chief bridge engineer Joseph B. Strauss. Construction contracts were actually awarded in November 1932, and one year later the local paper reported that a total of 506 men were employed in the bridge construction.

Tourism growth, despite the Depression, was on the increase during the 1930s. The new Sonoma Mission Inn Golf and Country Club course was an attraction for visitors. And local golfers took advantage of a $5 membership fee

The Clewe store on the corner of Broadway and First Street West, circa 1936, formerly the site of the *Sonoma Tribune* and now that of Great Western Bank.

offered to those who wished to play golf any day except Sundays and holidays. More than 3,000 persons swam at the two pools at the Boyes Bathhouse on the July 4th weekend of 1931.

When bad times hit after the stock market crash in 1929, the widely acclaimed golf course here suffered from lack of patronage and went into bank receivership, being operated by a company offshoot of the American Trust Co. (later Wells Fargo Bank) for several years. Subsequent purchasers of the 240-acre handsome links layout failed to make it profitable. In October 1936, with rumors that the golf course might revert to a hayfield or be sold in small parcels as a subdivision, Mrs. Alma B. Spreckels, prominent sugar corporation heiress and owner of the Sobre Vista ranch here, came to the rescue and bought the property.

The Boyes Hot Springs bathhouse, destined to become one of the Valley's major tourist attractions, was purchased in April 1934 by Rudy Lichtenberg, prominent Marin County resident with interests in the hot springs area. Associated with him were his nephews William and Harry Johnson.

The bathhouse at Boyes Springs was where talented musician Art Hickman led his dance band on summer evenings before and after World War I and was credited with inventing a rhythm called "jazz." He and his band were later featured in the Rose Room of the Saint Francis Hotel in San Francisco. Hickman died Jan. 17, 1930, his

INDEX-TRIBUNE ARCHIVES

The 1930 Sonoma High basketball team. Members of the Dragon varsity were, from left: (kneeling) Phillip Bill, Melvin Canobbio, August Sebastiani, "Stinky" Davis, Bill Clewe; (standing) Rinehart Monson, Art Lindberg, Ed Burmester, John Mohr, Jr., Les Sperring, Dale Farrell and coach Dave Pfeiffer.

passing a page-one headline in the *Index-Tribune*.

The 60 patrons of the Schellville post office, established Nov. 14, 1888, learned that by edict of the Postmaster General the 43-year-old post office was permanently closed on Oct. 16, 1931. The area would be served by rural free delivery service out of the Sonoma post office, said the announcement.

Also closed, most of them permanently, during the 1930s, were numerous illicit liquor-making stills in various parts of the Valley. Despite the lessening of Prohibition laws, there were still those amateur booze-makers willing to take chances for their ill-gotten gains. Federal agents swooped down on ranches, homes and businesses to halt the manufacture and sale of illegal and untaxed liquor and wines. These raids were actually a prelude to the national repeal of Prohibition in December 1933, ending a dry regime of 14 years.

The old Don Theatre on East Napa Street was destroyed by fire Nov. 21, 1932, and two weeks later Samuele Sebastiani announced plans to construct a modern 85- x 168-foot theater building on First Street East. A large upstairs hall was included in the plans, as were store buildings adjoining the theater. The $75,000, 400-seat theater opened April 7, 1934, with *Fugitive Lovers*, starring Robert Montgomery and Madge Evans. A dance followed

in the upstairs hall, with an estimated attendance of 1,000 persons.

Lachryma Montis, the home of Gen. M. G. Vallejo, was deeded by his heirs to the State Park Commission on June 5, 1933. Mrs. Luisa Emparan, Vallejo's only living daughter, was chosen curator and custodian of the state landmark, which was dedicated as a state park on July 7.

That same year also saw the purchase of the Sonoma Mission Inn at Boyes Hot Springs by Mrs. Emilie Long, prominent San Francisco hotel owner; and the coming to Sonoma of Dr. Carroll B. Andrews, a Stanford medical school graduate, to enter practice here with Dr. Sophus Boolsen, with offices above the American Trust Co. building, opposite the southwest corner of the Sonoma Plaza. The state's first sales tax went into effect with the signing of a measure by Gov. James Rolph on August 4.

A nudist colony bared itself here in June 1934, with the lease to a health club on a Buena Vista ranch, where eyewitnesses reported naked men, women and children frolicking and sunbathing inside a 10-foot-high wire fence which surrounded the property, the former Waltz ranch.

The old Barracks on Spain Street, erected by General Vallejo for his troops in 1835, were purchased in October 1934 by Walter and Celeste Murphy, copublishers of the *I-T*, from the S. Schocken estate. Plans included restoring the exterior of the two-story adobe along the original lines and making the interior more habitable as a residence for the Murphys, who expressed a wish to make it available to the state at their passing.

Low prices for foods and general items continued in 1935, judging from an *Index-Tribune* advertisement placed by Ray Roberts of the Quality Market: coffee, fresh ground, lb. 15¢; Crystal White soap, 10 bars, 28¢; Campbell's soups, 3 cans, 25¢; catsup, large bottle, 9¢.

Because George "Baby Face" Nelson and wife were reported by a San Francisco policeman and others to have been dining at Parente's resort in El Verano, owner Louis Parente was subpoenaed as a witness at a San Francisco federal hearing, according to a front-page *Sonoma Index-Tribune* story on March 22, 1935. He was one of 33 witnesses subpoenaed by the government in the trial of 18 defendants charged with

The 1936 Sonoma merchants' baseball team at the old ball park, now the site of the Sonoma Marketplace. Team members were (front row) coach Lou Palluci, manager Ray Tynan, Ray Barrachi, Lou Minelli, Lee Clerici; (back row) Nick Lotta, Chris Ganos, John Merlo, Andy Barrachi, Fred Frediger, Jim Weyl, Roz Hotz, Lou Pellandini and Don Smallen.

harboring Nelson, a nationally known criminal who was killed near Chicago after being hunted down by the FBI as a public enemy.

Other 1935 highlights: Despite much publicity and planning, the three-day celebration of the City of Sonoma's 100th birthday in June was canceled by the committee April 19 when only $500 had been subscribed. A parade in town and the annual Sonoma Rodeo at the Millerick ranch was held as planned. The new open-air theater in Sonoma Plaza was dedicated on Memorial Day in honor of city councilman A. R. Grinstead, local attorney, for his personal efforts in improving the Plaza.

Significant happenings in the news of 1936 included the Sonoma Valley Chamber of Commerce's plans to number houses in Sonoma, in preparation for city mail delivery; the dedication of the new Boyes Springs firehouse; Sonoma Valley voters joining the rest of the nation in returning President Franklin Roosevelt to office; the mailing of application forms by Postmaster Walter Murphy and staff to all public employees in the Valley who would come under the provisions of the new U. S. Social Security Act; and a record crowd estimated at 4,300 attending the eighth annual Sonoma Rodeo at the Millerick ranch on Sunday, June 21.

Organization of a Sonoma Valley Historical Society was reported in the Jan. 15, 1937, issue of *The Sonoma Index-Tribune*. Preliminaries were discussed at the home of Miss Edna Cooper,

INDEX-TRIBUNE ARCHIVES

The Rustic Inn in Glen Ellen, circa 1930. The Inn, which burned down in 1974, was formerly known as the Monahan-Shamrock Saloon, among other names, and shared grounds with the Mervyn Hotel and the big picnic area in the late 1800s. The Rustic Inn was a well-known local landmark and a favorite watering hole for many, including Jack London.

with J. P. Serres presiding over an enthusiastic gathering. Dues of 50¢ a year were suggested.

The official opening to traffic of the $35 million Golden Gate Bridge on Thursday, May 27, 1937, was given voluminous coverage in the *I-T*. The opening was followed by a five-day fiesta. The span's economic value to Sonoma Valley, in tourism alone, was constantly cited by observers. In the opening three days, 139,850 autos crossed the bridge.

Contrasting editorials by editor Celeste Murphy appeared side by side in the Dec. 31, 1937, issue of the *Index-Tribune*. One dealt with the "bright outlook" for Sonoma Valley in 1938. The other was a sobering and realistic look at warring factions overseas—with dictator power plays by militaristic German and Italian leaders, civil war in Spain, unrest in China and threats to the British Empire. In it was a plea from the country editor for Sonomans and all Americans to strengthen our system of democracy to resist the insidious "isms" threatening the world.

The new year opened on a discordant note for City of Sonoma residents, who learned that the population of 1,050 was too small to receive free mail delivery service. A communiqué from the Postmaster General's office said Sonoma must wait until its population hit 2,500.

In major realty deals here the old Jones ranch of 10,500 acres, known as the Sonoma Land Co. holdings, was purchased by M. B. Skaggs of the Skaggs chain stores, for $318,000. The 43-acre Van Damme property at Napa and Fifth Street East was sold to Mr. and Mrs. Donald Armstrong of Beverly Hills, who planned to make it their country home. U. S. Navy Commander and Mrs. Charles M. Cooke purchased the 165-acre H. E. Tracy ranch in the hills northeast of town.

The new three-story steel-and-concrete Sebastiani Apartments on Spain Street opened for inspection May 27, 1938. In addition to the 12 modernly equipped units, the Spanish-style building, which cost $50,000, had an Otis elevator to serve occupants, the first in the city's history.

It was in 1938 that Frank Freeman, one of the finest athletes in the history of Sonoma Valley Union High School, caught the eyes of track and field fans, his remarkable achievements in the running broad jump covered both by *The Sonoma Index-Tribune* and the sports sections of the metropolitan daily newspapers. As a junior, Freeman leaped an amazing 23 feet, 3 inches in the May 7, 1938, North Bay League track and field meet at Santa Rosa to establish a new NBL and school broad jump record. He won the North Coast Section meet at Berkeley the following week. During his senior year Freeman won national recognition at the California Interscholastic Federation state meet in Los Angeles. All three of his jumps broke the state broad jump record of 23 feet, 8½ inches, but his best, 23 feet, 10 inches, gave him only second place when Jim Jurkovich of Fresno sailed 24 feet, ½ inch on his final jump.

Freeman, a Glen Ellen grocery clerk, was to achieve greater recognition a year after graduating from Sonoma high school. Competing unattached in the Pacific Association track and field meet May 17, 1940, the 19-year-old leaped 24 feet, 10 inches, the second-best broad jump in the country that year. Heralded as a future U. S. Olympics team member, he subsequently competed for the San Francisco Olympic Club a month later in the National AAU meet in Fresno. A recurring back injury, plus a bad case of nerves, allowed Freeman to place just third in both the junior and senior divisions with a best

More than 200,000 pedestrians crossed the Golden Gate Bridge on its opening day of May 27, 1937. The bridge brought Sonoma Valley new possibilites for growth and heralded the beginning of greater prosperity for the North Bay.

INDEX-TRIBUNE ARCHIVES

jump of 23 feet, 5 inches. Since that meet, Freeman leaped into oblivion, the back injury evidently ending his dream of competing in the Olympics.

"Losses on cherries last season, and the uncertainty of crops this year, have caused local growers to lower the pay of fruit pickers to 25¢ per hour, 5¢ less than last season's," an announcement in the July 8, 1938, issue of the *Index-Tribune* revealed. Staging a sudden raid, Sheriff Harry L. Patteson and Deputy William Cook seized three "jackpot" slot machines in a barroom of Louis Parente's summer resort in El Verano on September 24. No arrests were made. The famous Goldstein vineyard, 535 acres of choice hilltop grape land east of Agua Caliente, was sold the week of October 7 for $32,500 to Louis M. Martini and Silas Sinton, owners of Martini Grape Products, Inc. Tolls came off the

Sears Point toll road November 21, the 11-mile road across the marsh from Sears Point to Vallejo becoming a free unit of the state highway system.

The World's Fair premiere on Treasure Island in San Francisco Bay Feb. 18 and 19, 1939, was attended by many Sonoma Valley residents. High praise was heard for the mural by Kenwood's Al Sondag in the Redwood Empire building depicting the raising of the Bear Flag in Sonoma Plaza. April 21, 1939, was Sonoma County Day at the fair, with hundreds enjoying the Little Fiesta musical group from Sonoma directed by Celeste Murphy and Dan Ruggles.

The year 1940 opened on a sad note, with the deaths of two prominent Valley citizens reported in front-page *I-T* stories. Rachel J. Snyder, daughter of pioneer Sonoman and Fremont Battalion member Franklin Sears, died January

10 on the 640-acre ranch southwest of town where she was born 87 years before. (In May 1944 Vic Leveroni, lessee of the property for 24 years, purchased the home and acreage for what the *Index-Tribune* reported was "about $55,000.") Last rites were held March 23 for Louis H. Golton, Sonoma Valley Union High School principal for 22 years, who died March 21 after suffering a heart attack on a bus while returning from a principals' convention in Long Beach. Mourners overflowed the high school auditorium (later to be named for Mr. Golton) where the services were held.

In May it was reported that Samuele Sebastiani, who was erecting a large basalite building next to the Sonoma Post Office on First Street East for a roller skating rink, also planned to build a modern 12-unit auto court (motel) and grill on recently purchased property on West Napa Street east of the French laundry.

The expansion of the war in Europe came closer to home in July of 1940 when Sonoma Valley postmasters received orders from President Roosevelt to fingerprint all "aliens." In September the military conscription of all U. S. men between 21 and 35 had been signed into law, and preparations were being made to set up draft boards here to handle their cases after registration October 16. August Pinelli was named to represent Sonoma Valley on the county draft board. In November, numbers were assigned to local draftees. Despite the issue of an unprecedented third term, voters returned President Roosevelt to office, FDR defeating Wendell Wilkie in a landslide.   – RML

Wine industry revives as Prohibition ends

> Once again acres can be tilled for wine, ... rich red burgundy and health-giving zinfandel may go on the market along with the golden Johannisberg riesling and fragrant sauternes, ... splendid men and women will now rise up and go to work again to win recaptured glory for vintages yet to be garnered from the vineyards of historic Sonoma Valley.

With these hopeful words, an *Index-Tribune* editorial of July 1933 applauded the demise of Prohibition, a few weeks after California ratified the repeal amendment.

INDEX-TRIBUNE ARCHIVES

During Prohibition Samuele Sebastiani saved his winery by converting it to a cannery. Although Sebastiani Vineyards continued to produce wine for medicinal and sacramental use, it was the cannery that kept the operation alive. Following the repeal of the 18th Amendment, the cannery was rented and Sebastiani returned to the business of making wine again. California was the 16th state to ratify the repeal of Prohibition. In June 1933 the *I-T* reported that "in local precincts the vote was a landslide ... and not a single precinct returned a majority for retention of Prohibition."

At this time most wineries and vineyards of the Valley of the Moon were in varying stages of disarray, with neglected vines, abandoned cellars—businesses either ruined or struggling for survival. And many growers did survive by selling grapes to home winemakers.

Only Sebastiani continued with any sizable wine production during Prohibition, operating under a government permit to make sacramental and medicinal wines.

Destructive as the ban was to Sonoma Valley, the industry had anticipated the repeal of Prohibition as early as October 1932. In that year's grape harvest, growers saw better returns, according to reports: "15 to 22½¢ per pound for red and white wine grapes," said the *I-T*.

The San Francisco market showed vast improvement, and the mood of an entire country reflected the growing resentment toward Prohibition. Change was in the air, and Sonoma Valley vintners and winemakers were eager to begin the process of restoration. Newspaper accounts in the summer of 1933 described the plans of several Sonoma Valley growers and winemakers, as the repeal became official.

• Charles Tribuno, a prominent and wealthy wine dealer of San Francisco, purchased the "A. Sorini property [the present Safeway store site] on the westerly city limits." He planned to rehabilitate an old winery and promote a wide distribution of wines.

• Unidentified buyers purchased the D. Cincera property, including a "fine old winery and comfortable dwelling," at a sale price discreetly described as being between $9,000 and $10,000. This had once been the home of the pioneer wine firm of Berges and Domeniconi, and plans were under way for restoration.

• At Sebastiani Winery, sparkling wines were already being bottled, and orders poured in. Samuele Sebastiani felt certain that the future of the wine industry was assured.

At Pagani Winery in Glen Ellen (formerly Chauvet Winery), owners anticipated their first crush since Prohibition.

Other vintners were not so immediately optimistic. Wildwood Vineyard, run by Arthur (Big Boy) Kunde near Kenwood, had found another market for grapes and given up the actual making of wine. Re-entry into the wine market was uncertain and "famed cabernets were only memories." [In recent years the scenic Kunde winery has won recognition among the Valley's best.]

The Dresel vineyards, a venerable name in wine making, had ceased wine production around 1920 and had no plans for renewal.

And the well-known Rhine Farm (forerunner of today's renewed Gundlach-Bundschu) "suffered from the ravages of the dry laws more than any other vineyard," according to an *I-T* news item. The cellars had been largely dismantled, the vineyards not regularly cultivated.

The Bundschus had moved out of the wine business entirely when Prohibition came, although they kept the vineyards. Many years later, Jim Bundschu told the story of his grandmother, Sadie Bundschu, who actually became a Prohibitionist and tolerated the vineyards only because the yield was sold as table grapes during the dry years. (Not until 1970 did wine making return to the old Rhine Farm.)

In the 1933 crush, local vineyardists were being offered $35 per ton (in contrast to $10–$20 in 1932) and Samuele Sebastiani crushed his largest tonnage to date, adding about 300,000 gallons to his cellars.

Good claret, shipped in the spring for 25¢ per gallon, went up to 45¢ by fall. Eastern capitalists began to show interest in the California wine industry, with offers of investment.

Sonoma winemakers, among others in California, began to visualize the impact of their wines against French products. Most local winemakers aspired to the production of good "vin ordinaire," and it would be several decades before Sonoma Valley varietals received favorable comparison with fine French wines. But a beginning had been made.

The post-Prohibition growers had more immediate, practical concerns. They appealed to the Federal Tariff Commission for a revision on tariffs to protect American wines, citing the cost of production and the need for fair returns to an industry just recovering from setbacks.

And in January 1934, the Independent Growers Union was organized to promote grower interests in marketing, pricing and labeling.

During that same month a *New York Times* writer singled out Sonoma Valley wines for special praise and also described the area as "rich in color and romance." Sonoma was on its way.

Today we may take for granted the miles of lush vineyards, thriving wineries and quality wines, all so accessible, almost at our doorsteps. A measure of credit should go to a persistent group in the 1930s who revived an industry out of the ruins of Prohibition.   — ROSE MURPHY

Millerick ranch rodeo was a Sonoma favorite

Most of today's Sonoma residents may not consider themselves as living in an area that less than 50 years ago still provided a touch of the real "wild, wild West"; but some of our leading citizens not only recall those days, they lived them.

That was a time when cattle still roamed the ranges of Sonoma, tended by working cowboys who, as cowboys have been known to do, periodically indulged themselves in that Western free-for-all called a rodeo—high old times of bucking broncos and cattle-roping, bull-dogging, dust, sweat and a good many broken bones. It is hard to believe that it all ended only about 43 years ago!

COURTESY, MILLERICK FAMILY

Norman Cowan of Glen Ellen, world-champion cowboy, at the Sonoma Rodeo. The first of many annual shows at the Millerick ranch in Schellville took place in 1929.

A few years back, on a quiet Sonoma street, should one have happened to meet winery owner August Sebastiani, or dignified Dr. C. B. Andrews, it might have been very hard to visualize either one of them on the back of a racing mustang, bent over the saddle and the horse's flying mane, lariat in hand.

But actually, both did well in roping contests, and one year August Sebastiani won a trophy. Of course, they were not real cowboys, the working kind who really knew their way around horses and cattle.

The Millerick family was behind it all. They owned the famous Circle M Ranch, known for its racing horses and rodeo livestock.

The founder was Jack Millerick, and the tradition was carried on by his nephew, retired U. S. Air Force Maj. Jim Millerick. With his knowledge of livestock and rodeos, he was able to build it into a real Western attraction, which lured many of the top hands of the rodeo circuit to Sonoma. But there was plenty of local talent involved to give the "big boys" a run for their money.

Ben Meyer always entered the roping contest; Bill Church, the bareback and bull-riding; Jack Bowen and Stanley Gomez, roping and bull-dogging; Bob Thornsberry and Ken Jones were consistent winners in bareback and bull-riding; Dr. Dario Marioni was an occasional bull-dogger; and even Jim Millerick, who bit the dust a lot, contested as a winning bareback rider.

All of this high adventure took place at the annual Sonoma Rodeo, which certainly was the biggest rodeo in the San Francisco Bay Area until the huge Cow Palace events began at the end of World War II. Moreover, the Sonoma Rodeo had the longest consecutive run of any California rodeo, beginning in 1929, continuing right through the war years, and into the 1950s. Not a single year was missed, and everyone in Sonoma was proud of that.

In 1947 there was a two-day rodeo, but unfortunately that one nearly broke its local sponsors. Something on the order of $20,000 had been spent on promotion and organization, but on rodeo days the skies opened with a deluge of rain and the gate receipts totaled only about $8,000. The rain was unseasonable for June, when the rodeos were always held, and the sea of mud that year that saw horses up to their knees,

COURTESY, MILLERICK FAMILY

Vernet Ryan of Sonoma (right) was a Millerick ranch rodeo participant. Note crowded stands in background.

cars up to their axles and cowboys in mud up to their ears will long be remembered.

But in spite of that disaster, the Sonoma Rodeo continued to grow, drawing the big names of the rodeo circuit such as Ben Dobbins, Al Haupt, Ty Stokes and Bob Studnick, known to his friends as "Bronco Bob," the West's bronco-riding champion.

Aside from our own local cowboys and head-liners of the national rodeo circuit, the Sonoma Rodeo also drew stars of the screen—the cellu-loid cowboys who were known and loved by at least two generations of Americans, and probably a good many people elsewhere in the world, and who continue to live on in the late-night movies on television.

The town also turned out to see the likes of Monty Montana and his troop of trick riders; a clever clown called Slim Pickins, who later became a movie and TV star; and Burl Mulkie, who was admitted into the coveted Cowboy Hall of Fame.

Even Will Rogers knew Jack Millerick and dropped by the ranch several times to visit,

because he liked Jack (and everyone he ever met) and because Jack raised one of the best strings of rodeo bucking horses in America—right here in Sonoma.

From the early working cowboy events, the rodeo gradually grew in size and stature. Crowds of up to 8,000 were not unusual, and the town turned out to see the 60 or 70 contestants do their stuff—saddle and bareback bronco riding, calf-roping, team-roping, bull-dogging, and the last event, and highlight of the day, bull riding.

Right up until the last Sonoma Rodeo, these events were really special, a community happen-ing in which all the townspeople were involved, not just the sponsors such as the Chamber of Commerce, AWVS, the Native Sons and the California Highway Patrol.

At least a month ahead of the rodeo, every man in Sonoma grew a beard—they had to, because anyone caught on the Plaza without whiskers was "arrested," subjected to a mock trial and locked in the "hoosegow," a "jail" on the Plaza erected just for such offenders. For a time the entire town turned Western, reliving days that actually were not all that long ago.

In the afternoon of the day before the rodeo, there was a big parade. Everyone who had a horse or could borrow one rode in it. And there were chariots, too, drawn by prancing horses; because up until just before World War II, there were chariot races at the rodeo.

Trick riders would be in the parade as well, and appear the next day at the rodeo. And the Roman riders were something. Roman riding involved a rider standing on the backs of two horses which were ridden at full gallop around the arena. That was exciting!

The evening before the rodeo, there was a huge street dance on the town Plaza. Everyone was there. And you never knew if you might be rubbing elbows with someone like professional boxer Buddy Baer or actor Andy Devine. They were there, too. It was the biggest night of the year.

In the rodeos of the 1930s the admission was $1, and that included an "all-you-can-eat" dinner of beef barbecue, beans and bread. Jim Millerick said he used to feed about 3,000 people. To cook the meat, a crew headed by the Maffei brothers, "Nib" and Oliver, would bury three beeves wrapped in burlap cloth in a special pit at the rodeo grounds, which was near the present Schellville firehouse. They would be buried in hot coals overnight, and the meat would be deemed done by the following day.

Yet another thing that made the rodeo days of Sonoma unique was the "trail drive" of the string of bucking horses, easily 50 strong, right down the highway from Jack Millerick's ranch five miles to the rodeo grounds. The Millerick string carried the Circle M brand and was one of the top rodeo strings in the nation. But the string was sold when Jim Millerick was recalled to active air force duty in the '50s.

Not long after, the Sonoma Rodeo became history. ... Lucky Buck from Petaluma no longer came to spur the broncs, nor the big circuit rodeo stars of yesteryear. ... Whiskers no longer sprouted in June, and the kangaroo court was disbanded.

But those were high old times when the real wild, wild West lived again in Sonoma, if only for a few days each year.   — SAM J. SEBASTIANI

Plaza beautification a Depression-era plus

Despite the fact that the nation was in the throes of the Depression, the early 1930s saw an ambitious plan for the development and improvement of Sonoma's Plaza that was unprecedented.

Guided by a citizens' group calling itself The Plaza Committee and by city councilmen A. R. Grinstead and Cedric Cutter, a number of major projects were completed between 1931 and 1935.

The labor and funding of these various projects were provided by such divergent groups as the Sonoma Valley Woman's Club, Veterans of Foreign Wars, Boy Scouts, Sonoma Volunteer Fire Department and the local Italian community. Even federal assistance, in the form of the Public Works Administration, figured in the transformation of "Sonoma's eight-acre problem" into a beautiful town square.

In March 1931 the city council called for bids for the purchase and installation of a pump and pressure watering system for the Plaza. At the same time, uncultivated areas of the park were cleared of weeds, plowed and replanted with shrubbery.

Also in that month a movement for additional beautification of the Plaza was initiated by a group of Sonoma Valley residents of Italian descent. It was proposed that a large plot lying south of the library, in the eastern portion of the square, be developed into an Italian garden designed and patterned after the best to be found in the Old World.

It was reported that the group of civic-minded Italians who had worked out the idea for the garden felt that, since numerous organizations of the city had taken over plots in the Plaza for maintenance, they, too, might show equal interest by bringing the far-famed Italian Garden idea into the local picture. The cost of the project was estimated at $1,500.

The city council accepted the proposal and plans for the garden in July 1931. Tom Vella, who had worked with San Mateo landscape gardener Peter Canalli on the plans, appeared before the council and submitted the proposal. He stated that funds raised by popular subscription among the Italian population were available, and work

In 1932 Sonomans were just beginning to realize the Plaza's potential as a community park. By 1935 many features of the eight-acre park we know today had been installed.

would start immediately. Plans included a fountain in the center of the garden surrounded by various plantings, walkways and benches.

In February 1932 the city council took steps toward further beautification and improvement of the eight-acre parcel by granting the request of Fire Chief Jep Valente that the firemen's plot be extended to take in a larger area, to be developed by the department.

In March the council approved a comprehensive plan from councilmen Grinstead and Cutter, with plans drawn by landscape artist Edward J. Waterhouse of San Mateo, for nearly $1,200 in expenditures, most for an aquatic garden in a depression on the west side of the park to be surrounded by "beautifully colored rock from a nearby quarry."

Another community group—the Boy Scouts of Troop 9—had a hand in the Plaza development. It was noted in the Feb. 9, 1934, edition of the *Index-Tribune* that the Plaza project which Troop 9 undertook, and for which they gave a benefit dance, was completed that week when the boys planted a lawn and set out shrubs in their section of the Sonoma park north of the library. Forty dollars, plus their work, was put into the beautification of the historic square.

The Sonoma Volunteer Firemen revealed plans in October 1934 for a modern children's playground and landscaping around the proposed site on the north side of the Plaza. The plan called for the purchase of all-steel equipment with every device for recreational pleasure and safety, the expenditure expected to be about $500 to be raised by a benefit dance and popular subscription.

The federal government, through the PWA plan, played a significant role in the Plaza's

INDEX-TRIBUNE ARCHIVES

Index-Tribune editor Celeste Murphy (right) and an unidentified friend admire the original Sonoma Mission bell, circa 1930. The bell, with its belfry, had disappeared in the late 1850s. It was located by Woman's Club members at the old Sutro Museum in San Francisco some 50 years later and returned to Sonoma in 1920.

development when in 1935 plans were revealed for a little theater which many years later was designated, by a bronze plaque, as the Grinstead Memorial Amphitheatre. It was appropriate, in that councilman Grinstead was one of the prime movers on the theater project.

It was noted in February 1935 that

the al fresco theater will be a terraced terrain surrounded by shrubs with a stage and sloping area from which an audience may see all that is enacted. In the past, the City Hall balcony far above the street had to be used, and orators at rallies have had to speak from park benches or trucks.

In conjunction with this PWA project, pools to ornament the Plaza and improve low spots will be completed. ... They are to have walks laid around them and be bordered by stepping

stones. A bordered rose garden is also in prospect.

On Memorial Day 1935, Sonoma dedicated the new open-air theater in the Plaza when exercises for the military dead of this country were held under the auspices of the Bear Flag Post, Veterans of Foreign Wars. Councilman Grinstead, attorney and veteran, was one of the principal speakers at the dedication. – JIM LYNCH

Sonoma finally gets its own water system

*T*he genesis of Sonoma's water system goes back to Gen. Mariano G. Vallejo's time. It was in 1868 that the General put in a modest water system for the city.

The source of supply was Lachryma Montis, the spring behind the Vallejo homestead at the north end of Third Street West. From here, this crystalline product was distributed through redwood pipes to the customers.

The general ran the water company himself. When he died, it was continued by his daughters, Luisa Emparan and Maria Cutter—with the help of Mrs. Emparan's son, Richard Raoul Emparan.

Some time in the early years of this century, the company was sold to the Sonoma Water and Irrigation Company, which also operated a water distribution network in the Boyes Springs area of the Valley.

It was at the beginning of the 1930s that the city trustees, as the city council was called then, agreed that the city water system needed improvement.

In the fall of 1930, it was decided to rehabilitate an old well on the northwest corner of the Plaza both for improvement and for more fire protection.

The well had originally been dug to serve the Donahue railroad, which had its roundhouse, shops and yards in the Plaza in the 1880s.

In March 1931, the city accepted the bids of two local firms for installation of a water system in the Plaza. Mission Hardware, owned then by the late August Pinelli, got the job of installing a pump for the old well with his bid of $395.

M. Lange was awarded the contract for making a concrete-lined pit for the pump with a bid of $169. Pipes were also to be installed in the Plaza.

In August 1931 Sonoma Water and Irrigation announced plans to improve and expand its system by installing 5,000 feet of laterals and other improvements to the tune of $15,000. The company's territory was said to include Sonoma, Sonoma Vista and Agua Caliente. The Sonoma City Council granted it permission to work inside the city and asked that two more fire hydrants be added to the 38 the city had.

However, a movement for the city to have its own water system started when it was learned that Sonoma Water and Irrigation wanted to increase its rates.

With commendable foresight, the council took a straw ballot by mail on this proposition. Over 500 ballots were mailed out in November 1932. Of these, 169 were returned, with 145 votes for public ownership of the water system and 14 opposed.

Almost simultaneously, it was reported in January 1933 that Sonoma Water and Irrigation was having financial difficulties, probably the result of the Depression, which was tightening its grip on the country.

With the results of the straw ballot as a guide, the city council began to plan construction of a water system. This could be done for $33,000, according to a report in *The Sonoma Index-Tribune.*

A bond election for establishing a water system was set for March. Just prior to this time, August Pinelli, who was also a city councilman, said the bonds could be retired in eight years with a profit of $4,000. And insurance rates could be cut 18 percent.

Also prior to the election, the *Index-Tribune* said the water system would make $8,000 annually. This must have been the capper, because the bond passed by a vote of 367 yes votes to 59 no votes.

The bonds were sold to a local resident, Mrs. Beatrice Bulotti, at an interest rate of 4¼ percent.

There must have been some behind-the-scenes action going on, because after the election, the *I-T* reported that a "growing number of patrons" recommended purchase of the Sonoma

Luisa Vallejo Emparan, daughter of M. G. Vallejo, circa 1935, during her tenure as state curator at the Vallejo Home park. In 1933 the State of California purchased the Lachryma Montis homestead and Swiss chalet, and 17 of the 250 surrounding acres. Luisa was the Vallejos' last surviving daughter, the 15th of 16 children.

Water and Irrigation Company's plant here. These "patrons" spoke of the excellence of the spring on the Vallejo property. In April 1933 the council decided to defer action on a new municipal water plant to try to find out how much Sonoma Water and Irrigation might be willing to sell for. After several haggling sessions, the city agreed to buy the company's assets for $24,000.

Perhaps the city's water users felt some sentiment about still being able to drink from General Vallejo's own spring.

As the number of water customers increased, the Vallejo spring became inadequate as a supply. The city dug a half-dozen wells and ran its system with these.

Since 1963 the city's water—and that of the water district in the upper Valley—has come from the Russian River, where it is stored behind the Coyote Dam.

This system was built with county bond issues passed in the 1950s.   — JERRY PARKER

Samuele Sebastiani had faith in Sonoma's future

To most local citizens and visitors here, the name Sebastiani appears to be on, or is in some way associated with, just about every major building establishment in Sonoma.

They're not far from wrong.

Samuele Sebastiani, the man who opened the way for modern wine making in Sonoma Valley, also was a visionary builder of public facilities, commercial buildings and homes around town.

His seemingly endless string of projects began with his founding of the wine operation in 1893. He purchased a building on Fourth Street East in 1903 which he soon converted into a winery. A cannery operation followed at the site.

But the main thrust of the Sebastiani building boom erupted in the 1930s. In late March 1931 Sebastiani embarked on a new house-build-

INDEX-TRIBUNE ARCHIVES

Samuele Sebastiani founded his wine business here in 1893. He later built numerous public facilities, including apartments, a theater, bus depot, hotel and "rollertorium."

ing program on his tract located on Fourth Street East. Two five-room stucco-type homes were the first to be constructed on the tract under contractor L. L. Thomas.

On Nov. 21, 1932, the old Don Theatre burned down. Sebastiani proceeded to take on what turned out to be one of the most significant projects for Sonoma—the construction of the new Sebastiani Theatre on First Street East, across from the Plaza.

In a front-page article appearing in the Dec. 30, 1932, edition of the *Index-Tribune*, Sebastiani explained his intentions in regard to the new theater: "While I am anxious to keep the cost down as much as possible, I propose to allow nothing to stand in the way to give Sonoma a building that will be a credit to the town, and one useful, pleasant and convenient for those who arc to use it."

With the arrival of some 50,000 feet of lumber, work began soon thereafter. Seventy-five pillars, 30 x 30 inches thick, with connecting concrete walls, constituted the main foundation of the building.

In March 1933 the clock tower, 72 feet high, was erected. Len Thomas was also the contractor for the theater project and employed many local mechanics and laborers. There was an average of 30 men on the job at any given time.

John Mohr, then owner and manager of the old Don Theatre, took over management of the new facility as well.

Sebastiani Theatre opened its doors for the first time on April 7, 1934. *Fugitive Lovers,* starring Robert Montgomery and Madge Evans, was the film to be shown. Over 1,000 people attended the opening-day matinees and evening show.

Sebastiani's attention turned toward the northwest corner of the Plaza in early April 1936. There, he announced plans to build a new bus depot.

Just six months later, on October 10, he opened his newly renovated and modern hotel on Spain and First Street West on the northwest corner, once the site of the pioneer Weyl Hall. Formerly the Plaza Hotel, it was renamed, fittingly, the Sebastiani Hotel. Today, it is called the Sonoma Hotel and is owned by John and Dorene Musilli.

Rounding out a rather hectic year of building and planning, work began the first week of

Salvador Vallejo's first home, opposite the Plaza's north side, was demolished in 1936, when its adobe bricks were found to be beyond repair. In 1938 Samuele Sebastiani erected the "most up-to-date" apartments in the Valley on the site.

Sebastiani bus depot and apartments on Spain Street as they looked in 1976. Partly visible, next to the apartments, is the restored 1850 adobe housing Sonoma's oldest dining spot, the Swiss Hotel, long owned by the Marioni family.

COURTESY, FRIENDS OF SEBASTIANI THEATRE

The Sebastiani Theatre under construction in 1933.

December on the construction of a then up-to-date $50,000 apartment complex on the north side of the Plaza, next to the new bus depot. It became known as the Sebastiani Apartments and had the distinction of having Sonoma's first elevator.

Sebastiani had purchased the property from the Poppe estate, and the modern apartments were built on the ground where Salvador Vallejo had an adobe home in 1836.

The apartments opened the last week of May 1938. Living room, bedroom and bath, breakfast room and kitchen were included in each unit.

Directing his energies back toward the winery, Sebastiani began erecting a 75- x 150-foot concrete wine cellar adjoining the main structure. Work began in August 1937.

Included in that expansion project was the addition of several new wine storage tanks of 2,500 gallons and over, a new grape crusher and other machinery.

Rolling his bustling building projects right into the 1940s, Sebastiani applied for, and was granted by the city council, a permit to construct a combined bowling alley and skating rink on his lot next to what was then the post office on First Street East.

The Sebastiani Rollertorium, which it was

eventually named, opened in July of that year. Initially, it was planned to have four bowling lanes along with the skating rink. Evidently, the plans for the bowling alley were abandoned along the way and the rink became the main feature. Sebastiani later built a bowling alley on West Napa Street, along with a restaurant building and Sonoma's first "auto court."

Cottages there were improved, and the restaurant and cafe were operated in conjunction with the auto court, with the bowling alley adjoining. The apartments are occupied rental units today. The former restaurant and the bowling alley have since been converted to other retail and professional uses.   – JOHN LYNCH

AUTHOR'S NOTE: The former Sebastiani Apartments, located next to the old Greyhound bus depot, still exist today under the name Cuneo Apartments, owned by Richard and Mary Ann Cuneo, Samuele's granddaughter. The rollertorium facility later housed a food market, and now is the site of the Mercato retail complex.

Sonoma Valley Chamber of Commerce born

A "get-together" dinner held in March 1930 at the Toscano Hotel, with 32 representatives of the business and professional houses of Sonoma present, was the first step toward the founding of the Sonoma Valley Chamber of Commerce.

At that dinner, organization plans for the chamber were laid, with Joe Baccaglio, assistant manager of the American Trust Co. bank (now Wells Fargo), chosen as the temporary chairman.

According to a speaker that evening, Stanley Jones, president of the Associated Chambers of Commerce of Sonoma County, "Sonoma has been missing many of the good things, as there is no agency to look after the internal or external needs and desires of the municipality."

Interested Sonomans viewed the organization of a chamber of commerce as the wave of the future, the only way that men with "vision" would be able to promote the growing little town.

Jones went on to say that the lack of a chamber had "put Sonoma Valley out of contact with the progressive movement in the area, much to its loss."

Local business leaders were present at that first meeting, including Fred Batto, Herbert Batto, Gary Bartoli, Newton Dal Poggetto, Dave Eraldi, Henry Lourdeaux, O. Maffei, Vic Leveroni, William P. Downey, Joe Andrieux, A. Maffei, Walter Murphy and many others.

The *Index-Tribune* reported in the March 21, 1930, edition, "The men who took the initiative, it is pointed out, are to be commended. They are an enthusiastic bunch who desire that Sonoma Valley shall progress and believe that through organization the community can and will get many of the good things that we are missing today."

On April 10, 100 members on the charter rolls elected 10 directors, who in turn elected Downey as the first president of the chamber. Other officers included Fred Batto as vice president, J. B. Scribner as treasurer, and Wade Wilson as secretary pro-tem.

The directors set the dues at $15 per year.

Among the first projects listed on the chamber's agenda were better bus service, obtaining road maps for motorists and, first and foremost, drawing tourists and new residents to historic Sonoma.

– KATHY SWETT

Sonomans smile when they say "Cheese!"

Wine, history, ideal climate and natural beauty are among those things for which Sonoma Valley is noted.

But we shouldn't overlook one of the community's other significant products—cheese.

Since the turn of the century, when local dairy farmers hauled in their cans of milk via horse and wagon to the old Sonoma Mission Creamery on First Street East, across from the Mission San Francisco Solano de Sonoma on Spain Street, cheese has been manufactured in Sonoma.

Today, two popular cheese manufacturing operations attract scores of visitors from near and far—the Sonoma Cheese Factory on Spain Street, with Pete Viviani and his son, David, as coproprietors; and the Vella Cheese Company on

A young August Pinelli, later a Sonoma "honorary alcalde," in the Sonoma Mission Creamery delivery truck. Since the turn of the century, when local dairy farmers were hauling their milk to the creamery, Sonoma has had a cheese factory.

INDEX-TRIBUNE ARCHIVES

Second Street East, founded by Tom Vella. The latter is a family corporation, with Ignazio A. Vella, Tom's son, the CEO and chairman of the board.

The Vella operation of today is actually a resurrection of a business which opened at the same location back on Nov. 16, 1931. It was on that date that Tom Vella and his then associate, Celso Viviani, opened their new Sonoma Valley Creamery in a converted brewery, originally the home of the Sonoma Ice and Brewing Company.

Made of stone quarried in the Sonoma foothills, the two-story brewery building on Second Street East, north of Spain Street, was owned by a corporation of local businessmen. Steam and lager beer was successfully brewed there before Prohibition laws halted the operation.

Subsequently the Sonoma Ice and Brewing Company became a distributing firm for near beer, carbonated beverages and ice.

When completed in November 1931, the $10,000 project converted the old brewery into a modern creamery for the manufacture of cheese—jack, dry jack, Romano, Romanella and cheddars.

Both Vella and Viviani had worked for Tom's older brother, Joe Vella, the Sonoma pioneer in the cheese-making trade and owner of the Sonoma Mission Creamery—Viviani since 1920, Tom for a lesser number of years.

In 1943 Joe sold his cheese plant to Tom, and Celso. Joe agreed to remain on with the operation, working for them.

In 1945 Viviani and Vella built the present new retail building and plant on Spain Street, at the site once occupied by Fochetti's blacksmith shop and Pete Boccoli's auto repair garage. Celso Viviani and Tom Vella dissolved their partnership, amicably, in May 1948, Vella taking over the firm's Oregon cheese-manufacturing operation.

Pete Viviani joined his father then as a partner, buying him out in 1953 and operating the business alone until 1969, when son David and son-in-law Fred Harland formed a three-way partnership. [Harland left the business in 1990.] Pete and David Viviani have carried on since as the Sonoma Cheese Factory, making Sonoma Jack and cheddar cheeses, and have greatly expanded the Spain Street operation over the years.

Tom Vella, in addition to his Oregon operation, reopened a cheese-making operation on his own on the premises of the old Sonoma Mission Creamery, owned by brother Joe, in the early 1950s, and later rented space at the Sonoma Cheese Factory.

It was in 1969 that the old brewery site was reborn as a cheese-making facility by Tom Vella. In the interim, the old stone structure had been used as a warehouse and mushroom-growing plant. While in the latter capacity, the interior of the former brewery was severely damaged by fire. Tom Vella spent a considerable sum in rebuilding it to provide what is today the popular Vella Cheese Company wholesale and retail facility, filling orders locally and nationwide under the direction of Ignazio Vella.

The products of both Sonoma cheese firms are winners of state and national awards, and Vella cheeses also have the distinction of earning laurels in international competition.   – RML

The Sonoma Barracks through the years

A turn-of-the-century view of Spain Street, looking west, when the Sonoma Barracks (right) had an ornate wooden facade. The historic adobe was built in 1836 by Indian laborers to house the troops of Gen. M. G. Vallejo.

The Barracks building was being refurbished for the Murphys when this photo was taken in 1938.

A newly added balcony was in evidence when the Murphys finally occupied the Barracks.

The east end of the Barracks building was occupied by Solomon Schocken's general merchandise store. The advertising on the store's outer walls provided a backdrop for the crowd attending the dedication of the El Camino Real bell in 1910.

Sonoma Barracks in 1935. The following year, *I-T* co-publishers Walter and Celeste Murphy purchased the Barracks from the Schocken family and began restoring it for use as their residence.

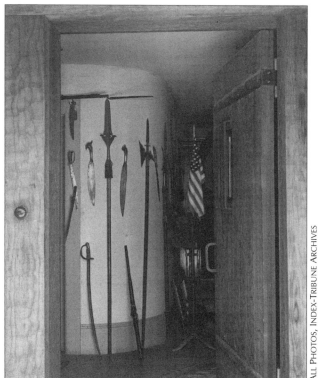

The entrance to the Barracks in 1945, during the period when it was the Murphys' (and briefly the author's) residence. Ninety-nine years earlier, on the heels of the Bear Flag Revolt, the Barracks was the capitol of the California Republic for 26 days.

ALL PHOTOS, INDEX-TRIBUNE ARCHIVES

21 World War II Paramount: 1941–1947

The Sonoma Index-Tribune

SONOMA, "VALLEY OF THE MOON," LAND OF ROMANCE AND HISTORY, SITE OF LAST OLD MISSION, FAMOUS FOR CLIMATE AND MINERAL SPRINGS.

LXIV   TWELVE PAGES   SONOMA, SONOMA CO., CALIF., FRIDAY, DEC. 12, 1941   CITY OFFICIAL PAPER   NO. 20

I NEED YOUR HELP!

"It will cost money to defeat Japan and the Axis allies. Your government calls on YOU to help NOW. Buy Defense bonds or stamps today. Buy them every day, if you can. But buy them on a regular basis.

"Bonds cost as little as $18.75, stamps come as low as 10 cents. Defense bonds and stamps can be bought at all banks and post offices, and stamps can also be purchased at retail stories.

THE SONOMA INDEX-TRIBUNE URGES ALL AMERICANS TO SUPPORT YOUR GOVERNMENT WITH YOUR DOLLARS.

INDEX-TRIBUNE ARCHIVES

During the war years, the *Index-Tribune* urged readers to support the war effort and purchase defense bonds and stamps.

Valley citizens did their patriotic duty

The years 1941–47 were dominated by national events of profound proportions so devastating that survivors are often heard to ask, "Where were you?" when such-and-such happened. Where were you—in Sonoma? The Bay Area? In the military service? Away at school? In an internment camp?!

Wherever you were then, if you had ties to Sonoma Valley, you probably read the *Index-Tribune*. The eight-page weekly, devoted almost exclusively to Valley happenings, provided a unique and valuable service to its World War II–era readers. In these times of wake-up radios and ever-present television, it is difficult to realize that the local paper, more than just reporting, was then the main source of information and instruction that made it possible for citizens to cope with the hassles of wartime living and the transition to a peacetime economy.

The weekly *I-T* was filled with lengthy articles promoting local wartime activities, such as the seven separate war bond rallies, one victory bond campaign, two war chest campaigns, Red Cross war relief drives, solicitations for tennis shoes and hair clippers for soldiers, and sloganized campaigns such as Books for Buddies, Victory Books Campaign, Automobiles for Tanks, Victory Scrap Drive, Tin Can Drive, Food for Victory, War Blood Donors, Clothes for War and War Dog Fund.

INDEX-TRIBUNE ARCHIVES

In 1947 Gen. "Jimmy" Doolittle, one of WWII's U. S. Air Force heroes, was the speaker at a Western States Turkey Show banquet here as a guest of Gen. "Hap" Arnold (at right). Others at table, from left, are V. M. (Bob) Moir, State Chamber of Commerce official, and State Sen. Herbert Slater of Santa Rosa.

Citizen activities in defense of nation and home were given their share of coverage along with discussion concerning the draft board, air-raid blackouts, Home Guard, aircraft identifications, air-raid shelters, Red Cross and Amercan Women's Volunteer Services programs, aircraft warning service, USO, city defense plans and conversion of the Sonoma Mission Inn to Navy use for rest and recreation leave.

Of equal importance were news articles concerning the limitations placed upon citizens by reason of war and how to cope with those restrictions, i. e., gasoline, food and shoe rationing, tire-rationing instructions, first-aid advice, OPA control regulations, 35-mile-an-hour speed limit, tire inspections, rent-control regulations, victory garden directions, notices of restaurant closings due to shortage of food, price lists for turkeys (52¢ a pound) and, most important of all, instructions on how to get and use ration books.

Scattered throughout the pages, as well, were direct news items covering Sonomans missing in action, hero lists, war stories, letters from soldiers, patriotic photographs, patriotic ads, reports on activities of Air Force Gen. "Hap" Arnold as a new personality in Sonoma, rationalizations for internment of citizens of Japanese ancestry and two local war events—the capture of war prisoners at Sears Point and the dropping of a Japanese incendiary balloon near here.

Occasionally, filling what newspaper space was left (an eight-page issue was the weekly norm), there were items on regular happenings such as annual conventions, horse shows, rodeos, turkey exhibits, business news, deaths of prominent citizens (the most notable during those years being General Vallejo's daughter Luisa Emparan and wineman Samuele Sebastiani), marriages, births, and social and school news.

Also making headlines in the *I-T* were ongoing problems with patients fleeing the Sonoma State Home at Eldridge; continual frustrations

INDEX-TRIBUNE ARCHIVES

Gen. "Hap" Arnold with former Army Chief of Staff Gen. George Marshall, author of the Marshall Plan, which rebuilt war-torn Europe.

over delays in making city improvements; the loss of the railroad track up the Valley; and the several-year struggle, under the leadership of Dr. Carroll B. Andrews, with divergent views on his preference to retain the lease for a community hospital at Buena Vista, rather than build a new hospital.

The *Victory for Liberty* minstrel show sponsored by AWVS at the high school, the construction of the cheese factory building on Spain Street, the sale of prominent parcels of real estate such as the golf course and the Sonoma Mission Inn, and the roller skating contest at Sebastiani Rollertorium on the Plaza were major news happenings.

Also reported were deputy sheriff activities such as the gambling raid on Spaghetti Pete's and nuisance complaints about Sun-O-Ma, the local nudist colony—one such complaint even culminating in an altercation between vineyardist-UPI news executive Frank Bartholomew and a nudist over access to the colony through the Buena Vista vineyards.

During these same years, we read of the repair of the Sonoma Mission in 1944 and the arrival and departure of the Oakland Oaks baseball team, which held spring training here.

With the end of World War II, military affairs were dropped from the paper as if they had never happened, and the essential topics immediately became water, street and sewer improvements, the creation of a city planning commission, the funding of the Valley recreation district, the long-delayed opening of the leased hospital at Buena Vista, groundbreaking for Hanna Boys Center, and the building of a new firehouse, police station and jail on Patten Street.

Veterans' problems were not forgotten, however. The paper reported on plans to build a veterans' memorial building and Sonoma's first post-war housing project (intended to be rented for $25 a month exclusively to war veterans and their families) on the Sebastiani property south of St. Francis Solano Church, encompassing some of the homes still standing on Barracchi Way.

The year 1946 saw the most momentous public celebration ever held at Sonoma—the 100th anniversary of the Bear Flag Revolt; and in 1947 the Valley staged its first modern Vintage Festival.

Many of us in Sonoma Valley have personal recollections of those years—searchlights scanning the sky; seagulls that looked like enemy planes; blackouts; school evacuation plans; the sound of the coastal defense guns from San Francisco; playing poker for red ration points; military uniforms everywhere; blue stars (representing sons or daughters serving in the military) hanging in windows, and occasional gold ones; the sound and flash of the big ammunition explosion at Port Chicago; the singing of the national anthem at the end of motion pictures; and, above all, a sense of allegiance and purpose that seems lacking now.   — ROBERT D. PARMELEE

Home guard formed

With the bombing of Pearl Harbor on Dec. 7, 1941, Mayor C. C. Bean, following the example of other towns, called upon citizens of Sonoma to form a home guard to protect the city water supply at the cistern behind the Vallejo home— Lachryma Montis. He assigned two men to guard duty every night, each armed with his own shotgun or rifle. Among the many who volunteered and served were Ralph Hotz, August Pinelli, Dave Pfeiffer, A. R. Grinstead and Dick Watkins.

The city built a cabin at the water works to shelter the guards at night, and the U. S. government provided a formula that would neutralize poisoned water, if detected. Soon the water guard was merged with the aircraft warning service, known as the AWS.

On orders of the U. S. Army, the AWS was terminated on Oct. 1, 1943. At a farewell dinner, George Streiff received the AWS medal and silver star for meritorious service as chief observer; F. W. Dobbel was honored as assistant observer; Mrs. L. Charleston was awarded a 500-hour medal for service as filter center worker, aircraft-recognition instructor and observer; and F. Beinhacker was given a wallet for his extraordinary service as an observer at the age of 80. Of the 30,290 total hours spent observing, the high-point persons were: Roy Pauli, 384; Rube Lange, 350; Mrs. Jep Valente, 326; Mrs. C. F. Wells, 320; and Mrs. T. Morenzoni, 245. Dorothy Bancroft was one of many 200-hour observers who were honored at the dinner.

To protect against a possible air attack beyond the observation points, Sonoma County created ordinance No. 194, providing for a total blackout at the sound of the air-raid warning signal from the City Hall. This meant all automobiles had to pull to the side of the road with lights out and all homes had to be darkened, the ordinance providing for a $300 fine for any violation.

The *Index-Tribune* explained that the warning for an air raid would be a two-minute broken blast by siren and that the all-clear would be a two-minute steady blast. Air raid wardens were appointed by the city and county to check on compliance with the ordinance, assist in preparation of blackout curtains and prepare to give first aid if necessary. The record is not clear, but estimates are that three or four blackouts were experienced.

To thwart the possible impact of an air raid, a defense control room equipped with five telephones was set up in the Sonoma City Hall, pro-

viding direct communication to key defense points such as the fire department, police and sheriff's offices, PG&E, ambulance and hospital. A master map hung on the wall, showing the water and electric lines of the town. It also provided a plan whereby water and electricity could be eliminated from any block, following the plan established in London where one damaged area could be completely isolated without inconveniencing others. A civil defense committee staffed the control room on an almost around-the-clock basis, volunteers being August Pinelli, Howard Moser, Henry Lordeaux and many others.

Protection from damage by incendiary bombs was given a good deal of special attention. Barrels of sand were strategically placed—especially on top of those buildings likely to suffer attack— for use by the fire department and others in smothering an incendiary. Mrs. Warren More and Leilani Burris gave six-hour courses on the subject of gas and incendiary bombs and how

INDEX-TRIBUNE ARCHIVES

Admiral Charles M. Cooke was among the career military men who chose Sonoma Valley for their retirement home. The Cookes purchased the old Tracy Ranch off Lovall Valley Road in 1938. On Dec. 7, 1941, then Captain Cooke was aboard the *U.S.S. Pennsylvania*, flagship of the Pacific Fleet, at Pearl Harbor. When he retired in 1948, Cooke was in command of the U. S. Seventh Fleet.

to deal with them.

Even those of us who lived through those war years don't care to relive them in memory but, on being reminded, can easily recall the sight of the sand buckets and homemade blackout curtains (mostly cardboard fitted tightly to windows), and familiarity with the wail of the fire siren—knowing which meant fire, which didn't. All nostalgic memory-joggers of a worrisome era.
— ROBERT D. PARMELEE

Sonoma's AWVS unit a WW II success story

The Sonoma Index-Tribune in 1941 published an appeal to the women of Sonoma Valley to join the American Women's Volunteer Services (AWVS), a wartime organization. Minimum hours were required, and the only duty was to answer the telephone, "a service which could easily be per-

Sonoma old-timers will remember the "hoosegow" set up in the Plaza when the American Women's Volunteer Services sponsored the Sonoma Rodeo June 21, 1942. Jean Carver, Leilani Burris and Ulla de Britteville are the AWVS members in the photo along with Marine Corps privates John Cooper and David Hawley.

formed by women."

By February 1942, the AWVS was expanding, now providing courses for motor corps drivers and instruction in air-raid protection and identification of various types of bombs.

Requirements were becoming more difficult and expectations of women became more demanding. AWVS courses required knowledge in first aid, map reading and motor mechanics.

Sonoma Valley's membership consisted of enthusiastic, hard-working women, including the following: president and chairman Jerry Casson, Jean Babbel, Myrtle Bowie, "Auntie" Myrtle Casson, Elizabeth Charleston, Mary Clein, Dorothy Ferretti, Emma Finchum, Julia Finchum, Eolene Foster, Ruth Gilbert, Alberta Kiser, Caroline Kline, Faye King, Paula Dreighbaum, Freida Lawrence, Virginia Lowell, Wilma Martinson O'Neil, Lucy Ricci, Faye Stein, Barbara Thomas, Frances Thomson, Margaret Foster Weible and Anna Burris Welch.

In 1942 the AWVS stepped forward to sponsor a popular annual event, the Sonoma Rodeo. According to Jerry Casson,

> It was quite an undertaking. We women didn't know how to take over in the beginning. The men said we would lose our shirts, that it was impossible! It was an extremely bleak time and we saw the rodeo as a source of enjoyment, which people needed, and figured they would come. We stuck our necks out, risking everything, with only $60 in the bank.

The rodeo was a huge success! It made $10,000, netting $2,500 after all expenses were paid. With a portion of the funds, an organ was purchased for musical entertainment. The rest was channeled into various projects.

A recreation program for U. S. Navy personnel returning from the South Pacific was one such project. The Sonoma Mission Inn became a Navy R & R Center, with the AWVS assisting as volunteers. Sonoma also became the retreat for military men based at the nearby Skaggs Island naval communications facility and for recuperating men from Mare Island Naval Hospital.

A picnic was sponsored once a month as a source of relaxation for men and to help

INDEX-TRIBUNE ARCHIVES

amputees from Mare Island Hospital learn to become skilled with new limbs and make other adjustments.

The AWVS and the community all pitched in for the wartime duty of being on call during blackouts and warnings of enemy or unfamiliar aircraft in the area.

The entire town turned out lights. A lookout point was situated over the Sebastiani Apartments. The AWVS had purchased a station wagon which had blackout lights installed for the purpose of being usable during emergency hours.

There were countless other AWVS projects, such as dances, clothing drives and an annual minstrel show. Christmas time was often a sad event for the men so far from home. The women's organization provided morale and cheer during Christmas holidays. Parties were held at Mission Hardware. Farmers contributed fruit, a rare treat then. Decorations, gifts and goodies were bought and donated by townspeople. Local farmers contributed eggs and butter. Families provided cookies and cakes—an unlooked-for treat, with rationing prevalent.

Sonoma Valley women tirelessly served their country, community and those in the military through the American Women's Volunteer Services. During a critical time, the existence of the AWVS boosted the morale of servicemen and provided help, care, provisions and entertainment. More important, a feeling of unity and warmth was offered in a time of uncertainty and upheaval.

– DEBORAH GREBEN

Rationing in Valley during World War II

Cooperating with the war effort from 1942 through 1945 meant limiting the use by folks on the home front of many of life's necessities they had always taken for granted. This was done by the rationing of gasoline and automobile tires, plus sugar and a wide variety of other foodstuffs. That leather was considered at a premium, and important in winning the war, was emphasized by even the rationing of shoes. In charge of the national rationing program which Sonoma Valley residents experienced during those World War II years was the Office of Price Administration,

Specially designed editorial cartoons were sent to newspapers throughout the U. S. by government agencies during World War II. The one above urged readers to conserve fat for use in munitions and medicines.

known fondly, and otherwise, as the OPA. Chairman of the Sonoma Valley War Price and Rationing Board was Max Soley.

Citizens were issued "ration books," each containing lettered stamps good for "points," and designated for use during certain limited periods and in limited numbers.

In a January 1943 issue of *The Sonoma Index-Tribune*, it was reported that the "OPA expects to have 30 billion stamps ready to distribute next month. This exceeds [the quantity from]12 years of continuous production of United States postage stamps."

Local residents volunteered to staff the various rationing boards established here—the first one, in January 1942, a branch of the Sonoma County Tire Rationing Board headed by Judge Thomas Denny, R. R. Emparan and Carrie Burlingame. Sugar rationing registration was put into effect at Valley schools in March of that year, with sign-ups for ration books conducted with the help of teachers, under the leadership of J. F. Prestwood.

Gasoline rationing registration got under way in the Valley in November 1942. Every properly licensed automobile was entitled to an "A" book, good for 240 miles of travel on the basis of 15 miles per gallon. The *Index-Tribune* of Dec. 4, 1942, reported that gas rationing here "is in full swing," with 3,000 A books issued and filed, under a committee headed by J. B. Scribner. There were B, C, D, E and T books, too—ration books good for a three-month period.

Gasoline and tire rationing's importance to the war effort were obvious to the cooperating citizenry, who recognized the ongoing demand for rubber and petroleum products for the many types of vehicles used by our troops. In its Nov. 13, 1942, issue, the *Index-Tribune* reported that

Rationing Days to Remember!

GASOLINE – "A" coupons 14 good for four gallons, valid through March 21; "B" 5 and "C" 5 coupons, good for five gallons, valid indefinitely; "B" 6 and "C" 6 coupons, good for five gallons, valid indefinitely.

TIRES – Periodic passenger tire inspections have been discontinued. Periodic inspection on Truck Tires is required. Tire replacement inspections (on R-1 Application forms) are required when applying for all tires.

MEATS, BUTTER, CHEESE, CANNED MILK, MARGARINE, CANNED FISH, SHORTENING, LARD, SALAD COOKING OILS. – Book Four, red stamps Q5 through S5 valid through March 31; T5 through X5 valid through April 28; Y5 through D2 valid through June 2, (Worth 10 points each. Red tokens used as change.)

SUGAR – Ration Book Four, stamp 34, valid until February 28; stamp 35 became valid February 1, good through June 2.

FRUIT AND VEGETABLES – Book Four, blue stamps X5 through B2 valid through March 31; C2 through G2 valid through April 28; H2, J2, L2, M2 became valid February 1, good through June 2.

SHOES – Airplane stamps No. 1, No. 2 and No. 3, Ration Book Three, valid indefinitely.

BUTTER – Creamery butter rationed at twenty-four red points per pound.

Courtesy of
GOTTENBERG BROS.
GROCER

JACK ALLEN
Broadway   MEATS   Sonoma, Calif.

In support of World War II rationing, local merchants placed ads like the above in *The Sonoma Index-Tribune.* This one appeared Feb. 16, 1945.

following a government request to turn in all tires in excess of five, the Sonoma Railway Express agent, Clarence Philbrook, "has been swamped with rubber and the stage depot looks like a second-hand tire emporium." One man turned in 12. Another showed up with four brand new tires. There were tires in every condition, some the best, and others in the "last ditch."

War Ration Book No. 2 was put out in February 1943, according to the *I-T*, and became a "must" addition to local purses and pocketbooks. This book supplied red stamps covering all meat, canned meat, canned fish, butter, cheese, cooking fats, shortening, salad oil and cooking oil. Officials estimated that approximately 50 percent of the American housewife's weekly food budget would be rationed, with the onset of the new program.

Valley housewives weren't the only ones to feel the rationing pinch. In August 1943 the Sonoma Valley Chamber of Commerce appealed to the OPA for rationing relief on behalf of 14 restaurants and hotels, a number threatened with closure due to insufficient ration points. The *I-T* reported that during recent weekends Sonoma Valley hotels and restaurants had to turn away patrons, with several places deciding to "fold up." The pleas fell on deaf ears and the food division of the OPA refused to intervene.

An attempt by the OPA to place unreasonable price regulations on the sale of California juice grapes through ceilings on wine was finally abandoned, according to an *Index-Tribune* story in December 1943. The federal agency acknowledged, for one of the few times in its existence, that one of its price control programs had miserably failed.

Vintners, including those in Sonoma Valley, had ignored the warning by the OPA not to pay more than $37 a ton for juice grapes. Instead, growers were paid from $75 to $80 a ton by the winemen for grapes that should have brought from $125 to $150 a ton.

Those in the grape-growing and wine-making industries were thus among many others to raise their glasses in a joyous toast when World War II ended in victory for the U. S. and its allies, thanks—in part—to those secret weapons, utilized on the home front, known as ration books.   – RML

Last of Vallejo's children, Luisa Emparan, mourned

A voice is stilled, a smile has faded, a vivacious and esteemed daughter of old Sonoma has passed through the portals of time to Eternity, but memory of her and the love and friendship of family and acquaintances will live as long as life lasts for those who knew Mrs. Emparan—Señora Luisa Vallejo Emparan of Lachryma Montis.

This was the lead paragraph of the story about the death of Mrs. Emparan in the *Index-Tribune* of July 30, 1943.

Mrs. Emparan, who was born at Lachryma Montis, was the last of the 16 children of Gen. Mariano G. Vallejo, the founder of the Sonoma pueblo. She lived to be 87 and, during her long lifetime, was a living connection with Sonoma's earliest history.

Her mother was Señora Francisca Benicia Carrillo Vallejo, after whom the town of Benicia was named. Luisa was a cousin of the screen star Leo Carrillo. Her father, the General, told Luisa and his other children stories of how he came to Sonoma in 1835, when there was almost nothing here except the Mission. Two Vallejo daughters were born here, Maria and Luisa. Vallejo called them his "little Americanos," because they were born after California had become a state.

After being educated at a convent in Benicia and Ursuline Academy in San Jose, Luisa Vallejo married R. R. Emparan in 1881. He was a young diplomat from Mexico serving with the consular service in San Francisco. They lived in San Francisco, San Diego and Mexico City and finally settled permanently in Sonoma. They had three children, Anita, Carlos and Richard Raoul Emparan. Luisa Emparan greatly resembled her father, and the Vallejo likeness was also strong in her children, especially Richard, who died here in 1975.

She was widowed while quite young. Later, after her parents died, she assumed the management of the water system, built by the General, which supplied the city of Sonoma.

She took an active part in the social, cultural and religious life of the community. Music was her major interest and she possessed an enchanting voice. She often moved her audience to tears when she sang such old Spanish songs as "La Golondrina," "La Paloma" and "La Estrellita."

In the old Mission days, she sang the Masses there, and later, when St. Francis Solano Church was built, could be heard in the choir, where her rendition of "Adeste Fideles" or "Noël" brightened the season. She was one of the leaders in the drive to restore the old Mission. Through the years she remained the chatelaine at Lachryma Montis, and, when the Vallejo homestead was sold to the state, she continued to live there as the curator-in-residence.

In the early stages of her final illness, she continued to greet visitors at her bedside. Toward the end she was moved to the Burndale Sanitarium for better care and died there on July 23, 1943.

The funeral was held at Lachryma Montis and was attended by many members of the family and by a vast assemblage of friends.

Among these were Gov. Earl Warren, Leo Carrillo, Joseph R. Knowland, San Francisco Mayor Angelo J. Rossi, Congressman Clarence F. Lea, Sen. Herbert W. Slater, San Francisco District Attorney Matthew Brady, Dr. Fred Butler (superintendent of Sonoma State Hospital), and many pioneer Sonoma Valley and Sonoma County residents, business people, politicans and leaders in the civic and art spheres.

The funeral procession made a circuit of the Plaza—as had been done with her father in 1890—before it moved north to Mountain Cemetery. Here Luisa Emparan was laid to rest near the General. Her son Richard, named the first honorary alcalde of Sonoma by the county board of supervisors, lies not far away.

The story about her death in the *Index-Tribune* closed with some lines from one of her favorite songs:

> Sometimes between long
> shadows on the grass,
> The little truant waves of
> sunlight pass.
> My eyes grow dim with
> tenderness the while
> Thinking I see them,
> thinking I see thee smile.

— Jerry Parker

COURTESY, SYLVIA SEBASTIANI

Three generations of Sebastianis: August Sebastiani holds his son Sam, with patriarch Samuele Sebastiani looking on.

Samuele Sebastiani was 70 when he died in 1944

The man who probably did more than any other to establish the modern wine industry in Sonoma Valley, Samuele Sebastiani, died here in March 1944 at the age of 70.

A penniless immigrant when he arrived in Sonoma at 17, he was also his city's leading benefactor and philanthropist during his lifetime.

His success was due to hard work, determination and intelligence—in line with a true American formula.

The short, stocky Sebastiani came here with the dream of making wine, but first he had to accumulate some money. So he worked in the quarries in the hills behind Sonoma, hewing out cobblestones which were used to pave the streets of San Francisco.

When he had a stake, he began to buy wine-making equipment. Hard-working, tireless,

cheerful, he began to build what became a vast wine-making plant on Fourth Street East near the intersection of Spain Street.

Eventually, he was assisted here by his son, August, who succeeded him in the local wine business. Another son, Lawrence, managed a second winery at Woodbridge, which was later sold. He also had a daughter, the late Sabina Sebastiani McTaggart.

In addition to his winery, Sebastiani built a cannery on Fourth Street East which was a major industry here for many years.

He constructed many commercial buildings around town and numerous homes. And he improved St. Francis Solano Church as well as beginning construction of a school there.

The many commercial buildings he put up are still here, including the Sebastiani Theatre, the former Greyhound bus depot building, the Sebastiani [now Cuneo] apartments and a hall above the theater that was once the major gathering place for public dances and social events. An auto court he built on West Napa Street is today a residential rental complex. The restaurant and bowling alley buildings constructed by Sebastiani at the same site are still used for other business enterprises.

After America entered World War II, Sebastiani built an aircraft observation post atop his three-story apartment house on the Plaza.

Sebastiani worked constantly to enhance the quality of his wines, to increase his production and to expand his outlets—goals that have since been exceeded far beyond his imagination, through the efforts of his son and daughter-in-law, August and Sylvia; their sons, Sam and Don; and their daughter and son-in-law, Mary Ann and Richard Cuneo.

Samuele Sebastiani, in his time, developed markets for his wines in New York and Chicago and other cities in the East and Midwest. Now Sebastiani wines go around the world.

In 1938 Sebastiani made a triumphant visit to his hometown in Farneta, Italy. His wife, Elvira Eraldi Sebastiani, accompanied him. All the villagers turned out to welcome them.

He died on March 26, 1944, at his home in northeast Sonoma. The entire city closed down for two hours during his funeral on March 30. The impressive rites at St. Francis Solano

Church were followed by entombment at Mountain Cemetery.

The funeral was one of the largest ever seen in Sonoma, and there were many lavish floral tributes. This was as it should be, according to the *Index-Tribune's* editor, Celeste Murphy, who wrote, "Every acre of ground he owned was promptly cultivated, and every house he built had its garden. In death as in life he was surrounded by his favorite flowers." — JERRY PARKER

1946 Bear Flag Centennial celebrations

The 100th anniversary, in 1946, of the raising of the Bear Flag in Sonoma Plaza was worthy of not one, but two commemorations—both attended by then Gov. Earl Warren and thousands of enthusiastic spectators.

The governor's first appearance here was on March 10, 1946, when, following a gala parade in which horsemen's organizations from thoughout the state participated, he signed a bill passed by the state legislature allocating $300,000 for placing 9,000 miles of trails in every part of California. Also signed, on the balcony of the Barracks building, was state legislation authored by State Sen. Herbert Slater of Santa Rosa earmarking $7,500 toward the Bear Flag Centennial commemoration June 14, 15 and 16 of that year.

Film star Leo Carrillo, descendant of the same early California family as Gen. Mariano G. Vallejo's wife, Francisca, headed the March 10 parade as grand marshal, later being photographed with Governor Warren in the Plaza for a reenactment of the Bear Flag raising. A luncheon at Rozario's Palms Inn preceded the parade, with Sabina Sebastiani McTaggart in charge of arrangements. Mrs. Warren (sister of Hannah Gordon French of Sonoma), Senator Slater, State Park Commissioner Joseph Knowland, grand officers of the Native Sons of the Golden West and George Cardinet, president of the California State Horsemen's Association, were among other dignitaries introduced at the luncheon.

On June 14, 1946, three days of commemoration of the Bear Flag event 100 years before

INDEX-TRIBUNE ARCHIVES

California Gov. Earl Warren raised the Bear Flag in the Plaza during a special observance March 10, 1946, when he signed legislation allocating funds for the Bear Flag Centennial commemoration. Others in photo include Sonoma mayor John Picetti (facing Warren), actor Leo Carrillo and local resident Marilyn Pinelli Gallagher.

opened here with a colorful pageant—"Romance of the Bear Flag Republic"—produced by Charles E. Pressley, noted dramatist and author of Santa Barbara, on a natural stage lined by trees at the Maxwell Ranch at Verano. Several hundred costumed performers, most of them local citizens, participated in the historic pageant, put on each evening of the three-day fête.

The Bear Flag Centennial Parade was the major event on Saturday, with General of the Air Force H. H. (Hap) Arnold—who had just become a resident of Sonoma Valley—serving as grand marshal, astride a beautiful palomino. Also in the long line of march, in an open limousine, were Governor and Mrs. Warren, who smiled and waved at the responsive crowd witnessing the impressive parade.

The three-day gala June 14, 15 and 16 included barbecues each day on the Plaza, aerial circuses at the airport, street dances and carnivals, band concerts and the Sonoma Rodeo at the Millerick ranch as the Sunday finale.

— RML

Nudist club existence bared at Buena Vista

*I*n July 1944, on a 240-acre ranch above what was then called the Buena Vista Ranch, the Sun-O-Ma Club was flourishing. There were cabins, a swimming pool, a public drinking hall and a general store. People from the East Bay, Southern California and Oregon flocked there. The only thing unusual about this camp was that it was a colony for nudists.

For reasons unknown, federal agents with the Office of Price Administration launched an investigation of the owners, Victor and Emma Staehli, for failure to register the hideout cabins on the ranch and to make reports to the Rent Department.

They discovered more than they bargained for. Although the Staehlis assured the agents they had nothing to hide, the patrons were threatened with loss of gasoline privileges when their car license numbers were taken and turned in to ration boards for checking.

In August of that year a controversy with Frank Bartholomew began. The Bartholomews had purchased the 475-acre ranch below the colony for a country home and farm, with plans to reestablish the old Buena Vista Winery and vineyards made famous by Count Agoston Haraszthy, known as the "Father of California Viticulture." It was necessary for owners and patrons to cross the Bartholomew property to gain access to the Staehli holdings. With 400 to 500 patrons motoring in over the dirt road, the nudist facility became a nuisance and caused damage to fruit crops. Dust settling over the vineyards and orchards rendered the fruit unmarketable.

The nudists were also charged with creating noise and disturbances, destroying cattle guards and carrying away gates which had been erected across the road. The Bartholomews filed suit.

When the case went to court, Superior Court Judge W. D. L. Held issued a temporary restraining order preventing members of the colony from using the road through the Bartholomew property. The judge's order prevailed, even though Mrs. Staehli testified that the road had been in use for 36 years and that no damage had been done to Mr. Bartholomew or his property.

In January 1945 the Sonoma Valley Woman's Club and the Saturday Afternoon Club of Santa Rosa decided to get into the act and passed resolutions asking the Sonoma County Board of Supervisors to forbid nudist colonies in the county.

The resolution stated that the Sonoma Valley Woman's Club did not consider the practice of nudism or the maintenance of nudist colonies in the county to be of any advantage or use to the community. On the contrary, the club-women maintained, they were detrimental and undesirable to the county as a whole.

Consequently, an ordinance was passed by the supervisors which forbade the "mingling of unclothed guests of both sexes." It not only forbade the nudism, but provided penalties for those who "aid and abet the practice or permit their property to be used for such purposes."

Meanwhile, for opposing the practice of nudism, Frank Bartholomew became the victim of an attack in a pamphlet published by Elmer W. Pruett in 1945. A nudist exponent who branded critics of nudism as "obscenists," Pruett defended the practice of nudism and the organization of colonies or camps for the purpose of sunbathing, recreation and real appraisal of the human body.

In April 1945, despite the court order forbidding any but the owners of the nudist colony to use the Bartholomew road, the nudists were continuing to do so. The Sonoma County court order was posted on the gate entrance, but Bartholomew alleged the order was torn down, the chain was cut and Staehli supporters in these actions hinted at gun play if denied access.

Bartholomew had the goods on the "teasers," though, for an official investigator took movies of the goings and comings of the nudist enthusiasts and revealed the pictures in court. That was all that was revealed, however, as the nudists were clothed at the time.

The movies showed Victor Staehli at the disputed gate with a procession of cars going in and later coming out. The cars' license plates were covered with sacking.

A second and more stringent injunction prohibiting Mr. and Mrs. Staehli from trespassing on the ranch was issued by Frank Bartholomew. While the Staehlis were found not guilty of con-

INDEX-TRIBUNE ARCHIVES

It is hard to believe that most of the Sonoma Valley youngsters pictured here are now in their sixties. The Red Cross beginners' swim class was photographed June 20, 1947, at the Boyes Hot Springs big mineral pool. At far left is Red Cross volunteer Mrs. Garrett Welch of Sonoma; at right, Lucien Massa, instructor.

tempt of court, they were found guilty of abusing their personal rights in the matter and therefore lost permission to cross the Bartholomew ranch.

In September 1946 a final decision was reached regarding the road.

A third court decree restricted the defendants from using or burdening said road in any manner or for any purpose beyond the limited, private use thereof by defendants, their family employees and guests in connection with the use of said premises for a single-family dwelling and farm.

In March 1947 the Staehlis declared they would appeal the case to a higher court. That was, apparently, the last of the bare facts publicized in the local paper.

Thus, those Sonoma Valley people who may have been entertained by the nudist colony guests doing their calisthenics in the balmy breezes of the Sonoma hills (and some may still be around to tell about it) had to look elsewhere for their entertainment.   — LINDA GRIEWE

Hollywood stars here for *Sea Wolf* premiere

*I*t was a day the people of Sonoma Valley never forgot.

On March 22, 1941, the cast from the just-released movie *The Sea Wolf*, including Edward G. Robinson and John Garfield, came to Sonoma Valley and were entertained in a gala celebration.

Also with the group from Hollywood was a handsome actor named Ronald Reagan, just starting to get roles in films. Little did anyone know that some years later his real-life role would be to serve as California's governor [and later, President of the United States].

The occasion was the premiere of the movie based on the popular novel by Jack London, at Sebastiani Theatre. The premiere crowned a full day of parties and picnicking at the London Ranch in Glen Ellen and at the beautiful estate of Mr. and Mrs. Elmer Awl (she was the former Alma Spreckels) in Sobre Vista.

The movie stars steamed into San Francisco Bay on the luxurious ocean liner *America* from Los Angeles. During the voyage, the stars had witnessed an onboard premiere showing of *The Sea Wolf.* They were met by Charmian London, widow of the late author, and the author's nephew, Irving Shepard, and his wife, Mildred.

From there, they boarded Greyhound buses and headed for Sonoma Valley and the picturesque London Ranch in Glen Ellen. An account of their arrival here in the March 28, 1941, edition of the *Index-Tribune* read: "When they turned up the hill road to the ranch and saw the vistas and the scenes so well remembered from Jack's book, *The Valley of the Moon,* they were more than ever enthusiastic and so expressed themselves."

A tremendous welcome was given the stars who casually and enthusiastically proceeded to hobnob with journalists and local citizens.

The Sonoma Valley Chamber of Commerce

put on a splendid barbecue, headed by volunteer chefs Oscar Larson and Bill Locarnini, at the London Ranch, and the choicest wines of Sonoma Valley were freely poured.

Members of the Little Fiesta group were in costume and provided musical entertainment. Among the local musicians who played and sang for the stars were Clara Carbonaro, Edward Milkie, Morris Solen, Eolen Foster, June Leveroni, Bette Garrison, William Martinson, Dan Ruggles, Vernon Milligan, Jr., and Carl Dresel.

Following the barbecue, the film stars and other guests drove to the Spreckels estate in Sobre Vista and were lavishly entertained at a reception at the Sea Island house on the grounds. There, according to the *I-T* account, "swimming, warm sunshine and generous hospitality delighted them."

Promptly at 3 P.M. the stars to appear at the *Sea Wolf* premiere left the Awl place and arrived shortly thereafter at the Sebastiani Theatre. A huge crowd was waiting, and the throng of

COURTESY, GREYHOUND LINES, INC.

In 1941 Hollywood celebrities, including the cast of *The Sea Wolf,* came to Sonoma Valley for the movie's premiere: (from left) Kay Eldridge, Charlie Ruggles, Jane Wyman, Ronald Reagan, Alice Talton, Edward G. Robinson and John Garfield.

INDEX-TRIBUNE ARCHIVES

In a Vintage Festival of the 1950s, the roles of Gen. and Mrs. M. G. Vallejo were played by (at right) Julia and R. R. Emparan (General Vallejo's grandson). It was one of the last occasions when a direct descendant of the General was featured in the annual pageant.

Sonomans cheered and applauded loudly as the stars made their way to the stage.

In the party of celebrities were Robinson, Garfield, Reagan, Jane Wyman, Rita Hayworth, Hobart Bosworth, Priscilla and Rosemary Lane, Mary Astor, Charles Ruggles, Ralph Bellamy, Ruth Hussey and Donald Crisp.

Following the personal appearances and introductions of notables, the party returned to Sobre Vista. Later, all left for Oakland, where they boarded specially chartered planes for Hollywood.   — JOHN LYNCH

Vintage Festival revival in fall of '47 a success

The first revival of the Vintage Festivals of 1896–98 was held here in October 1947.

The first revival was dedicated to the 90th anniversary of the California wine industry—the beginning of which is credited to Count Agoston Haraszthy at the Buena Vista winery here in the mid-1850s.

Since then the tradition has remained much the same. The festival represents a time of thanksgiving for the annual wine harvest and encompasses a fond look at Sonoma Valley's rich historic past.

In 1947 the festival was held in October. Since 1948 it has been held the latter part of September.

That first program wasn't a very big show, but it had some of the events which are still standbys today—including the Blessing of the Grapes, a reenactment of the Vallejo-Haraszthy double wedding, tours of the wineries, band concerts, visits to historic homes and dances.

A plaque was also dedicated to Count Haraszthy at Buena Vista. One event of that year which has never been repeated was a roller-skating exhibition. This was held at the old Sonoma Rollertorium on First Street East opposite the Plaza.

Honorary chairman of the first festival was the late 1st District Supervisor James F. Lyttle.

Dr. David Jones was general chairman, Rudy Lichtenberg, vice chairman and Mrs. Marion Greene, treasurer.

Other members of that trail-blazing group included Celeste Murphy, Myrtle Lyttle, Louis M. Martini, Sabina McTaggart, Ethel McDow, Sal Argento, Mr. and Mrs. Oscar Larson, Arthur Kunde, Harriet Jones, Tess Linn, Beth Benedict, Al Rozario, Betty Weise, Mrs. C. Tryon, Gladys Dodge, Polly Black, Mildred Shepard, Eve DeMartini, George Jovich, John Merlo, Jr., Pete Narvaez, Dan Ruggles, Frank Bartholomew, Dick Watkins, Peter Mancuso, Roy Carter, Morris Greenberg, Sally Hollander, Paul Wolter, Lois McVeigh, J. P. Serres, J. F. Prestwood, Mrs. O. I. Palstine, Edna Cooper, James Tate and Ruth McDonald.

The first festival was sponsored by the Sonoma Valley Chamber of Commerce, the Wine Institute, Sonoma County Wine Growers' Association and the State Chamber of Commerce.

In succeeding years, a Valley of the Moon Vintage Festival Association was formed to stage the event. That association continues to function, although there have been times, in the past decade, when the chamber had to step in again to help out.

For many years after its founding, a special feature of the festival was a pageant written by the late Celeste Murphy, Sonoma historian and former editor and co-owner of the *Index-Tribune*.

This pageant traced the history of Sonoma Valley, from the founding of the Sonoma Mission in 1823 and the arrival of General Vallejo to the Bear Flag Revolt in 1846, ending with the brilliant double wedding which united the Vallejo and Haraszthy families in the 1860s.

In recent years, a few of these individual episodes have been included as "happenings" in the festival.

The traditional curtain-raiser for the festival has come to be the picturesque Blessing of the Grapes. This was performed for the first time in 1952 by the late Father Alfred Boeddecker, O.F.M., garbed in the brown robes of the Franciscan order, in front of the Sonoma Mission.

One of the group who created the first festival and helped to carry it on in the early years was Virgil Jorgensen, son of famed California artist Chris Jorgensen, who wrote: "Historical Sonoma is so worthwhile preserving. There is enough of the original left to make it worth the effort, but certainly some inducement should be offered to prospective builders and remodelers to conform to a harmonious general scheme of architecture."

– JERRY PARKER

INDEX-TRIBUNE ARCHIVES

During the fall and winter of 1942, the SP-NWP Railway pulled up the tracks between Sonoma and Lawndale Road in Kenwood. The rails removed were used to build a wartime emergency track from Oakland to the Richmond Shipyards. This photograph, taken in July 1942, shows one of the last freight trains to cross the trestle near the intersection of Highway 12 and Nun's Canyon Road.

Planning commission formed by city in '47

A post-World War II building boom in Sonoma began to make it alarmingly clear to city residents that some formal zoning plan was needed to prevent haphazard growth patterns.

At a Nov. 12, 1947, meeting of the Sonoma City Council, a tentative draft of a General Plan was presented to council members by A. Hahn of Hahn and Campbell Associates, planning engineers of Palo Alto.

After thoroughly studying the city environs of Sonoma, the consultants presented a plan which was based "on the principle that land should be used and developed for the interests of the community as a whole rather than for speculators and the financial interests of a few."

Four types of development were designated by the experts and included: double dwelling or more (apartments), commercial, industrial and residential.

Included in the zoning plan was a provision for "use permits" which would keep the regulations flexible and give the city control over uses which might be objectionable.

Also recommended by the experts was the formation of a city planning commission.

Any proposed building project would be required to go through two public hearings before the commission. The planning commission would then give its recommendation to the city council, which would hold one public hearing before any final action.

The consultants told the council members that they had purposely refrained from contact with any local group so that the material presented would not be biased.

Hahn explained further at that first meeting that the plan was not to be considered something that would never change. He noted that with the further growth of the city, certain modifications would have to be made to the zoning plan.

The city council gave its unanimous consent to the tentative plan and noted that it was worthy of the community's approval.

The city's first planning commission was appointed in January 1948 and included chairman John Picetti, William D. Morgan, Oliver Maffei, Mrs. Tom Vella, Harvey Downey and Edna Cooper.

Members of the city council who also served on that first commission included Mayor August Pinelli, City Attorney A. R. Grinstead and City Clerk Elsie Bean.

— KATHY SWETT

On April 29, 1945, the Sebastiani Rollertorium was the scene of a champion rollerskating contest—a high point in the building's use as a popular entertainment center frequented by servicemen. Today the site is occupied by the Mercato shopping complex.

22 Post-War Growing Pains: 1948–1959

At Nicholas Turkey Breeding Farms near Vineburg, circa 1956, are (left to right) Orell Saffores; Walt Crawford of CNG Breeders, Winton, California; George Nicholas; and Jay Van Omen of Central Hatcheries, Zeeland, Michigan.

Balancing growth with small-town provincialism

The first rumblings of major growth rippled through here in the late 1940s and on through the '50s, jolting Sonoma Valley's seemingly imperturbable state of slumber.

World War II was over. And save for the somewhat perplexing campaign in Korea, where American boys continued to give their lives in battle, the major war theaters were closed. The boys from WW II were home. Families were reunited.

Turning away from the nightmarish memories of worldwide confrontation, holocaust and bloodshed, it was time to set sail for less tumul-

tuous and more productive times.

Utilizing perhaps the only appreciable element inherent in most wars—a strong sense of togetherness—the citizens of a once-sleepy hollow awoke and began directing their energies toward the development of Sonoma Valley.

It was a time of growing pains, a yearning to build and develop. Sonoma Valley in a sense was changing its identity. And, almost simultaneously, outsiders identified and "discovered" the Valley of the Moon and its charm.

The fuse was burning. And ultimately, it led to the big growth boom of the 1960s and '70s.

The Valley blossomed for sure, but in such a way that much, if not all, of the small-town provincialism was retained. Efforts at incorporating one town into another were not always popular.

The formation of all-encompassing Valley-wide districts, such as the Sonoma Valley Sanitation District and the Sonoma Valley Unified School District, were prime examples of escalating growth and the kinds of solutions sought to deal with growth's inherent complexities. But even those efforts were balked at by some.

The pains of provincialism were nearly as great as the pains of growth.

The urge to be productive even entered into the area of natural resources. There were repeated attempts to drill for oil here, all proving futile. It was even thought at one time that a section of the Valley was rich in uranium.

Education seemed to be of particular interest to the growth-minded Valley. Probably, the most ambitious effort of the entire era was the unification of Sonoma Valley schools into one district.

Several new elementary schools were built during the period, all of which are still in operation today. The high school also expanded its facilities. The plea for a junior high school was first heard.

Hanna Boys Center became a reality, yet another example of the desire to develop and promote the welfare of youth.

The somewhat stormy evolution of the new district hospital characterized an intense urge to modernize and have a "proper" facility.

The Valley was extremely eager to acquire a veterans' memorial building of its own.

The desire to pursue the latest phenomenon in the commercial world—supermarkets—resulted in the construction of two of the Valley's major shopping facilities during these years.

Most significantly, they were the futuristic '50s. The passion for modernization set the stage for the growth explosion of the '60s and '70s.

But the massive changes failed to erase the longtime passions of provincialism. In many cases it had a squelching effect on some seemingly important projects.

But, like it or not, it is certainly one of the features that has made Sonoma Valley so unique.

– JOHN LYNCH

Father William O'Connor (center), director of Hanna Boys Center, with golfing notables Byron Nelson and Ken Venturi at Sonoma Golf Course Aug. 12, 1953. Nelson, Venturi and other golf professionals played a match as a fund-raiser for the center.

INDEX-TRIBUNE ARCHIVES

Unification of schools sparked by growth

The formation of the Sonoma Valley Unified School District in 1959 was one of the major achievements in the modern history of this area. Without unification, a quality educational program could not have been developed here.

Prior to unification, the Valley was a patchwork of competing school districts. There were Prestwood and Sassarini elementary schools and the high school in Sonoma. In the upper Valley there were El Verano, Flowery and Dunbar elementary schools. In the southern end of the Valley there were two old pioneer schools, Huichica and Tule Vista.

As their enrollment soared in the 1950s, these schools experienced more and more difficulty in passing the bond issues and tax increase elections they needed to maintain and improve

INDEX-TRIBUNE ARCHIVES

The Sonoma Grammar School was declared seismically unsound in January 1949 after a structural engineer from the State Division of Architecture deemed the building unsafe. August Pinelli, clerk of the school's board of trustees, informed the public that the building would be closed until repairs could be completed. Classes were held in churches and other buildings. The new Prestwood Elementary School opened for classes in the fall of 1950.

their educational programs.

In the spring of 1957, therefore, school district unification was obviously an idea whose time had come.

According to the *Index-Tribune* files, however, the idea of unification of the schools goes back as far as 1951.

In the May 25, 1951, issue it was reported that the augmented County Committee on School Unification had recommended that the Valley unify its seven schools into one district. This came at a meeting at the courthouse in Santa Rosa.

Each of the school districts here had a representative on the county committee. They all voted for unification except the representatives of Tule Vista and Huichica schools. These two old-time schools were phased out when unification finally took place here in 1959.

In May 1957 not one, but two big school bond elections were defeated—one for the high school and one for the Sonoma elementary district.

School officials were polled after these unsuccessful elections by the *Index-Tribune*. The majority expressed the opinion that unification seemed to be the made-to-order solution for their dilemma.

In June 1957, the *Index-Tribune* polled the elected school trustees. They gave the same answer. They all liked the idea of unification—with the exception of the trustees of Dunbar School in Glen Ellen, where the students had always had the option of attending Santa Rosa High or Sonoma Valley High.

This same month, James Nelson, local member of the county Committee on School District Organization, said that group was willing to make a study of school unification here.

He said this after getting the approval of the persons present at a meeting held at El Verano School. There were all of 16 persons in the audience! An augmented county committee began to hold meetings around the Valley in the fall.

At a meeting in December 1957 at Dunbar

School, the problem there was worked out. The Kenwood residents who had students at Dunbar indicated they wanted to maintain their ties with Santa Rosa High School.

The Glen Ellen residents felt they should stick with Sonoma Valley High. The Kenwoodians agreed to build their own elementary school, and eventually did.

Unification got public approval at a positive meeting held in March 1958 at the high school. There were 60 persons at this meeting.

The research done by the county committee was presented. The audience agreed that the unified school district board should have five members, elected on a geographical basis—that is, one representative from each of the school districts.

According to the findings of a "proxy board," school unification would:
- Provide for one governing board responsible for educational planning and operation of all the schools, from kindergarten through high school.
- Provide more flexibility in utilization of school buildings.
- Attract and keep more competent personnel.
- Make it possible to obtain a greater variety of education specialists.
- Facilitate rearrangement of attendance areas.
- Provide for greater independence and freedom from supervision by other agencies.

The tax for the new district would be $1.65 per $100 of assessed property valuation. This figure resulted from combining the 90-cent high school tax with the 75-cent elementary school tax.

The bonding capacity of the district was put at $1,974,937. The bonded indebtedness was $1,227,000, leaving an unused capacity of $747,937.

The bonded indebtedness would be spread over the whole unified school district.

The unification idea had to be put to a vote, of course, and this occurred in October 1958. The

The old El Verano School building on Arnold Drive, now a church, was last used as a school in 1954.

INDEX-TRIBUNE ARCHIVES

measure achieved an overwhelming victory—830 yes votes to 203 no votes.

An election for five trustees was set for Dec. 30, 1958. There were two to be chosen from the Sonoma district and one each from El Verano, Flowery and Dunbar.

There were 10 candidates for the five positions. Those elected and the votes they received were: Dr. Paul Harrison, 605; Towle Bundschu, 542; James Gordon, 870; Frank Buchbauer, 654; Stan Larkin, 604.

The new trustees inherited a district with a budget of $1 million plus, with 3,000 students and 110 teachers.

The trustees took office Feb. 2, 1959. Bundschu was elected president of the board. The trustees began a search for a district superintendent. Their choice was John L. Glaese, then 46, principal of Sonoma Valley High School since 1952. He was chosen from a field of 18 candidates.

Glaese was a graduate of the University of California and had earlier taught at McCloud and Dunsmuir high schools.

During World War II, he had served as an officer in the Air Force.

His starting salary was said to be between $13,000 and $16,000. His salary at the high school had been $10,500.   – JERRY PARKER

Arnold Field built with community support

*I*t was 47 years ago that the Sonoma Valley Athletic Club, which in 1949 was primarily a group of softball enthusiasts, embarked on an ambitious campaign to build a first-class, lighted sports facility adjacent to what would be the

INDEX-TRIBUNE ARCHIVES

Arnold Field under the lights. The facility, built as part of Sonoma Valley's Veterans Memorial project, is utilized for football, baseball and softball. It was formally dedicated in August 1952.

At the Aug. 9, 1952, dedication ceremonies for the Gen. "Hap" Arnold Veterans Memorial Athletic Field, the general's widow, Eleanor (Bea) Arnold, accepted a bouquet from Little League Baseball player Eddie Fassio (No. 9). Maj. Gen. William E. Hall, Commanding General, 4th Air Force, principal speaker at the dedication, is next to Mrs. Arnold. Also visible in photo are Mayor Warren More, the author, Howard Moser, Maj. Gen. W. E. Todd, USAF; two U. S. Navy officers from the Skaggs Island naval radio station, and (in light suit) one of the Arnolds' three sons, Maj. Bruce Arnold.

Sonoma Valley Veterans Memorial building.

Today that complex still remains as Sonoma Valley's premier lighted outdoor sports facility, thanks to the vision and hard work of that original group, some of whom are to this day still involved in the Athletic Club's operations.

We are speaking of Arnold Field, which actually had its inception when SVAC softballers were still using what one observer at the time described as "a $250-a-year horse pasture, poorly lighted, with splintery and ancient bleachers," located off Napa and Second Street West at the present site of the Sonoma Marketplace shopping center.

About that time, the Sonoma County Veterans Committee had acquired a 16-acre site north of Spain Street at the foot of the hillside and had offered the City of Sonoma a 99-year, $1-per-year lease for 12 acres to be used as a veterans' memorial recreation site. The Sonoma Valley Athletic Club eagerly campaigned for acceptance of the proposal.

Spurred on by examples in Sebastopol—where the citizenry raised money to build a new, lighted ball field—and Healdsburg, where "friendship bonds" were sold in the community to finance the installation of some $20,000 in lights at its sports facility, the Athletic Club members began a drive to raise $25,000, once the proposal received the approval of the veterans' groups, chamber of commerce, city council and county board of supervisors.

"A brilliantly lighted athletic field, green turf, comfortable bleachers, softball and baseball diamonds, a football gridiron—a park adaptable to use for a multitude of events—is slowly but surely being molded into a reality by a hard-working group of Sonoma Valley men represent-ing the local athletic club," a front-page article in the Sept. 9, 1949, edition of the *Index-Tribune* reported.

"Within a few short weeks, a 'friendship bond' campaign will begin—a campaign to raise $25,000 for this modern and needed facility," the article read. These bonds would bear no interest and have no specific payment time but, as the Athletic Club pointed out, "are an investment in the community." Sold in $10 denominations, the bonds were to be paid back from receipts from

Gen. "Hap" Arnold and *Index-Tribune* copublisher Walter Murphy in 1947.

various athletic and nonathletic events.

The drive was officially kicked off in early October 1949, under the direction of committee members Howard Moser (chairman), Don McNay (finance chairman), H. A. (Hutch) Whitehead, Dave and Don Eraldi, Louis Fassio, Lloyd Tyler, Art Wilson, Charles Basch, Louis Pellandini and Ralph Downey. *I-T* editor and publisher Robert M. Lynch was publicity chairman. Also a driving force in these early stages was the late Ernie Mangiantini, who served as the Athletic Club's president and later personally took over the maintenance of the ball park. Accountant Tom Pucheu served as bond-drive treasurer.

In February 1950, shortly after the death of one of Sonoma Valley's most prominent citizens, General of the Air Force H. H. (Hap) Arnold, the Athletic Club started an all-out drive for the sale of the bonds. Up to that time, only some $7,000 in bonds had been sold, and the committee decid-ed that canvassing the entire area would be the best way to push the $25,000 drive over the top.

By mid-March of 1950, the stepped-up cam-paign had reached the halfway mark of $12,500. Shortly afterward, it was revealed that what had been referred to as the proposed Sonoma Valley Veterans Memorial Recreation Center would be named in memory of the late General Arnold. This decision came as a result of a joint resolu-tion agreed upon by the county veterans' organi-zation, board of supervisors, Sonoma City Council and the athletic club.

The drive hit the $20,000 mark in July and with that, the first of many volunteer work par-ties began the seemingly endless task of clearing, leveling and otherwise preparing the proposed field site.

From the outset and until the project was completed nearly two years later, several local ranchers and contractors donated their time and equipment to the project. Without this continued cooperation and volunteer spirit it is doubtful that the project could have ever been completed within the original estimated cost—or at all, for that matter.

When the drive reached $21,115, the lights and poles—the most expensive component for the project—were ordered. Finally the Dec. 22, 1950, edition of the *I-T* carried a front-page headline that read, "Xmas present! $25,000 athletic field

INDEX-TRIBUNE ARCHIVES

bond drive goes 'over the top.' "

The actual construction, like the fund raising, took time. Once the leveling and grading had been completed, utility lines had to be dug for the wiring of the massive light towers which were due to be installed in the summer of 1951. Between August 24 and 31, eight silvery 80-foot light poles—each with a total of 160 lights—were installed at the site, thanks again to a large crew of volunteers and the professional expertise of the Raas Welding Co. of Santa Rosa, which had also installed lighting at the new Sebastopol and Healdsburg fields.

Coincidentally, Sonoma Valley's first Little League became a reality that same summer, which eventually spawned the construction of Teeter and Hughes fields, named after John Teeter—founder of Little League in Sonoma—and Charlie Hughes, a longtime sponsor of Sonoma's Little League program.

In the spring of 1952, fencing, grandstands and a backstop were begun. By June the first baseball games were being played on the new field. By July some 12 athletic teams were already utilizing it. Restrooms, dugouts and fencing were completed by mid-July, and dedication ceremonies were set for Aug. 9, 1952.

Prior to the ceremonies an *I-T* editorial dubbed the project "the field that faith built" and invited citizens to join in the dedication "to a man whose handling of young men and airplanes gave our country strength that the enemy will always respect," referring to General Arnold.

It also said that the field would be "dedicated to the boys who gave their lives so that other boys might play freely in a free world … dedicated to the community and its people who dug deep into their pockets, and hearts, so that the faith of a few men with a mission will on August 9 shine down upon the finest community field in Northern California."

The dedication was described as "a gala event with all the pomp and ceremony incident to such occasions plus the beauty of the spot and presence of notables." Following the ceremonies, the Sonoma Little League All-Stars shut out San Rafael 5–0 under the lights.

The start of a new era in local sports—nighttime football games—followed on October 3 when for the first time in history a Sonoma High

School team played a game under the lights at a Sonoma field. The Dragons, under coach C. A. Edsall, hosted Fortuna in a game that brought in over 1,000 spectators, the biggest crowd since the high school began competitive football seven years earlier.

— JIM LYNCH

Water from Coyote Dam first explored in 1959

*W*hile wine has been a key image-builder for Sonoma Valley since the days of the mission padres and early-day vineyardists and winemakers, before and after Col. Agoston Haraszthy, it was man's most necessary liquid—water—that proved an important factor in the Valley's development and growth, particularly since 1959.

That was the year Sonoma Valley residents realized that wells and reservoirs serving city and unincorporated areas might soon be insufficient to cope with the obvious growth of the Valley, and that additional water sources had to be obtained.

The obvious source turned to in 1959 was the Coyote Dam and Reservoir located on the Russian River just outside Redwood Valley in Mendocino County. It had been financed a few years before by the taxpayers of Sonoma and Mendocino Counties—Sonoma paying the overwhelming proportion of the cost.

A vast aqueduct system had been completed from the dam to Santa Rosa. Sonoma Valley residents, along with the rest of the county, had helped pay for the dam and its dependent aqueduct systems. When the question of water need became persistent, city and valley representatives decided to look into the cost of extending an aqueduct system from Santa Rosa to Sonoma.

At the same time, two other potential sources were given consideration—the North Bay Aqueduct, which would require the cooperation and participation of Sonoma, Marin, Napa and Solano Counties; and a local dam and reservoir system or systems.

The biggest question in everyone's mind about Coyote Dam water was what the cost would be to local users—and could there be a firm contract with Valley water users to assure payment of revenue bonds which would have to

INDEX-TRIBUNE ARCHIVES

The Clerici family's spaghetti-eating pet jack rabbit made *Life* magazine in January 1958, when local photographer Richard O'Neil captured the long-eared gourmet on film.

be used to finance aqueduct construction?

In October 1959 it was determined, for the first time, that Russian River water from Coyote Dam could be brought to Sonoma Valley at a cost of approximately $51.74 per acre foot—actually less than consumers were paying at the time. To get the water here, a 13-mile, $2.2-million pipeline from Santa Rosa—already getting the Russian River water—to Sonoma was envisioned. It was estimated that the price per acre foot would decrease and usage of the water increase.

The price was predicated on use by the City of Sonoma and all other existing water compa-

nies in the Valley, and on a supplemental supply being paid for by the Sonoma State Hospital.

The City of Sonoma in 1959 had 1,200 customers, while all the other water companies together had about 2,250 connections.

The state hospital at Eldridge was the Valley's biggest user, with its 3,600 patients and 1,600 employees, and was served from two surface storage reservoirs and some pumping from Sonoma Creek. Water was then processed through the hospital treatment plant.

The feasibility report, prepared by the Sonoma County Flood Control and Water Conservation District, said the Sonoma Aqueduct was designed to meet the needs of all the Valley, including such areas as Schellville and Vineburg, where wells were the principal water source.

– RML

AUTHOR'S NOTE: In May 1960, Valley voters approved the formation of the Valley of the Moon County Water District and elected a five-man governing board.

Water-use contracts for the receipt of Coyote Dam water were signed by the City of Sonoma and VOMCWD on Aug. 7, 1961. Mayor William G. Raymond signed for the city, and Tom Polidori, board chairman, signed for the Valley of the Moon County Water District.

On Sept. 19, 1961, by a 1,254 to 167 vote, VOMCWD voters approved of a $1,250,000 bond issue to be utilized in the purchase of existing private water companies and for the improvement of same.

Meanwhile, the Sonoma Aqueduct was being constructed from the Wohler Intake near Santa Rosa, and Valley citizens looked forward to the receipt of Russian River water.

It was on March 30, 1963, that the first such water arrived here via the new aqueduct, and a significant ceremony in honor of the event was held in Sonoma Plaza.

The following month, April 1963, Sonomans for the first time quenched their thirst, watered their lawns and bathed in water transported from Coyote Dam and reservoir—a source still very much depended upon.

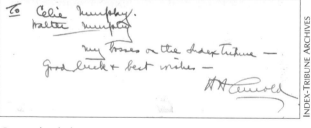

General of the Air Force Henry H. (Hap) Arnold, a columnist for the *I-T* in his retirement, inscribed this photograph of himself "To Celie Murphy, Walter Murphy ... my bosses on the Index-Tribune—Good luck and best wishes—H. H. Arnold."

Gen. "Hap" Arnold, USAF, a famed retiree of Valley

He used to say, "Just call me Farmer Arnold." Farmer Arnold of Sonoma Valley—General of the Air Force, H. H. (Hap) Arnold to the world—was laid to rest on Jan. 19, 1950, with impressive funeral services held at Arlington National Cemetery, Virginia.

The five-star general died of a heart attack January 15 at Rancho Feliz, his country home on the former 40-acre Hall ranch, located off Arnold Drive in the foothills just west of Agua Caliente. The general's beloved wife, Eleanor, was at his side when the end came and was greatly com-

forted by the arrival of their children, Col. Henry H. Arnold, Jr., Capt. William Bruce Arnold, Lt. David Arnold, and daughter Lois and Cmdr. Ernest Snowden. The Arnold sons, like their father, were all West Point graduates.

The evening prior to his death, General and Mrs. Arnold were guests at a birthday party for Walter L. Murphy, retired *Sonoma Index-Tribune* copublisher, held at the Sonoma Mission Inn.

Arnold's body was taken to the Bates & Evans funeral parlor in Sonoma, where an honor guard from Hamilton Field stood at attention all day Monday and Tuesday.

The services at Arlington were impressive. But the tribute Sonoma Valley citizens paid him two days before, in the little funeral chapel on Broadway here, was equally impressive—a warm, grassroots display of affection and thanks. Three hundred people stood in the rain waiting their turn to pass by the casket and pay final respects to their distinguished neighbor, one of the great military leaders in U. S. history.

News and wirephoto services and San Francisco newspapers were present to send word and pictures of the hometown memories to the rest of the world.

It was only a year before his death that Arnold was named General of the Air Force by a special act of Congress. He was personally given this commission by President Harry Truman. He wore the proud decoration of a five-star general.

But the dream of his life was to become a farmer. Even before his new home at Rancho Feliz was completed, he planted his harvest of fruits and vegetables, giving away and selling some of his products, including Crenshaw melons. He also raised white-face cattle.

The Sonoma Index-Tribune was an outlet for many of General Arnold's experiences and sentiments, as he wrote a number of articles for his hometown newspaper. He never asked for or received any compensation from the *I-T*, and jokingly told a Washington, D. C., reporter that he was the poorest-paid scribe in all the world. However, he thought enough of his unpaid job as columnist that on his photograph, presented as a gift to the publishers of the *Index-Tribune*, he wrote, "To Celie and Walter Murphy, my bosses on the *Index-Tribune*."

A lasting friendship developed between the Murphys and General Arnold and family.

The Arnolds participated, and took an interest, in many community affairs, including the first Valley of the Moon Vintage Festival. General Arnold spoke at service clubs here and at many other gatherings prior to the heart attacks which were first noted when he was still in the service.

The war, its hazardous missions and the pressure from the momentous decisions that went along with it made inroads on his health.

While canceling most of his speaking engagements, he felt in improved health after vacations in Alaska and Hawaii and made a personal presentation of his collection of scale-model World War II airplanes to the City of Sonoma for public display at the City Hall. The model planes, presented to General Arnold by various aircraft builders, were in 1958 donated by the city to the Air Force Academy.

His last appearance at a Sonoma community gathering was at the presentation ceremony of the airplane models. He requested that only the Boy Scouts participate with him on the program.

He had great faith in young America and believed that the planes would be an inspiration to youth and an incentive to scientific research and study.

Peace for all and what it would mean for the world and to coming generations was sincerely expressed in General Arnold's very last article written for the *Index-Tribune* in the Christmas edition, Dec. 23, 1949.

Celeste Murphy, the General's editor "boss," made these remarks about Sonoma's "first citizen":

> It was good to have known General Arnold, so kind, so generous, so fine a neighbor with his ready wit and love of good humor. I had heard a lot about "brass hats" and their ways, but "Hap" Arnold had not a semblance of these. He was just a great American, a pioneer of the aviation miracle—the miracle that interested the millions of our young aviators in following an incomparable leader to victory against the tyranny and aggression of two continents.

The Arnolds were always known as fine hosts. At Rancho Feliz they entertained, among others, Adm. Chester Nimitz and Gen. James Doolittle. Moderate in all things, "Hap" occasionally indulged himself in a bourbon old fashioned and never failed to take visiting notables to Jack Walton's bar in the Toscano Hotel or to the Swiss Hotel, operated by the Marioni family, to sample Sonoma specialties.

Born Henry Harley Arnold, the son of a Gladwyne, Pennsylvania, physician, he learned to fly from the Wright Brothers in 1911, four years after his graduation from West Point.

Aviation, military aviation, became his life, and by 1938, he was chief of the Army Air Corps. He was named commanding general of Army Air Forces in 1942 in the War Department reorganization of the general staff.

Under his wise guidance, the United States Army Air Force became a formidable opponent of the Axis powers. He was a particular advocate of the long-range bomber, and one of his last public appearances was to testify in favor of the B-36 at a House Armed Forces subcommittee hearing in San Francisco.   – JOHN LYNCH

Hanna Boys Center opened here in 1949

*T*he Archbishop Hanna Center for Boys, a dream that was born in the minds of three men in 1944, became a magnificent reality on Dec. 2, 1949, when the $1,250,000 facility for neglected boys opened its doors off Arnold Drive here.

The idea for Hanna Center was born in the minds of Rt. Rev. William J. Flanagan, founding director of Catholic Social Service; his assistant and first director of the new center here, Rev. William L. O'Connor; and Rt. Rev. John J. Mitty, Archbishop of San Francisco.

In 1944 Archbishop Mitty approved finances for the opening of a small demonstration center in Menlo Park. The work of Monsignor Flanagan and Father (later Monsignor) O'Connor was so successful that a group of laymen went to work conducting a fund-raising effort to build a larger center. Sonoma Valley was chosen as the site after a widespread search throughout Northern California.

The fund drive, conducted in the 13 counties of the Archdiocese, oversubscribed its goal of $975,000 by nearly $400,000.

On Sept. 19, 1948, over 10,000 people poured into Sonoma Valley to witness groundbreaking ceremonies at which Bishop Fulton Sheen and actress Irene Dunne were key participants.

Fifteen months later, on Dec. 4, 1949, the first 25 youngsters from the Menlo Center moved into their new home, consisting of 12 spacious buildings scattered over 157 acres of rolling hills, formerly part of the historic Morris ranch.

Dedication of the $1,250,000 center took

The Rev. Father W. L. O'Connor, founding director of Hanna Boys Center, greeted the first boys to arrive here in 1949.

COURTESY, HANNA BOYS CENTER

place on May 21, 1950, with an estimated 7,000 persons on hand to see Archbishop Mitty unveil a magnificent statue of Our Lady of Fatima, under whose patronage the center was placed.

Archbishop Mitty and Gov. Earl Warren delivered the key talks of the afternoon. Governor Warren praised the center as an important contribution to the total youth welfare facilities of the state and "a courageous new approach to the problem of juvenile delinquency."

Archbishop Mitty noted that only in a free society could such an undertaking as Hanna Center become a reality, stating, "Hanna Center is a demonstration of what a free people, living in a free society, can do in their own behalf."

The Reverend Father John Roberts, pastor, and Father Raymond Hore, associate pastor of St. Francis Solano Church in Sonoma, assisted the archbishop in the ceremony. St. Leo's Catholic Church had not yet been built.

Succeeding the founding and first director, Monsignor O'Connor, was Rev. James E. Pulskamp, who had been associate director until

INDEX-TRIBUNE ARCHIVES

Joe DiMaggio, the former New York Yankees great, and member of the Baseball Hall of Fame, paid a visit to Hanna Boys Center in the '50s.

1972. O'Connor then remained on staff as Pulskamp's associate.

The late Henri Maysonnave of Sonoma was the first local person to serve on the Hanna Center board of directors, being appointed in April 1948.   – RML

Sonoma Valley Hospital saga full of intrigue

*T*he evolution of the modern Sonoma Valley Hospital at 347 Andrieux Street may be traced back to the 1920s. At that time, there was nothing resembling a hospital in Sonoma Valley, and the handful of doctors who practiced here—there were three in 1923—thought something had to be done about it.

Those pioneer physicians were Drs. Wilford B. Hayes, Allen M. Thomson and Sophus Boolsen.

They had sent a few recovering patients who seemed to need more than home care to a place called the Crane Sanitarium in Boyes Springs, where a motherly nurse, Mrs. George Burns, offered good care.

But the sanitarium burned down in 1923, and Mrs. Burns, known as "Aunty Jo," and her husband retired to a ranch on Burndale Road.

Dr. A. K. McGrath arrived in 1924, and together the four members of the medical fraternity who now had offices here were able to persuade Aunty Jo to put a couple of beds for maternity cases in her Burndale farm home. Eventually a few more beds were added to what became known as Burndale Sanitarium.

Dr. McGrath purchased a nitrous oxide gas anesthetic machine in 1924 for Burndale. This replaced the dangerous chloroform, previously used for surgery.

In 1927 a fifth physician, Dr. Edward J. Finnerty, joined the local medical fraternity.

Burndale was used for over 20 years, but finally Mrs. Burns, then in her 80s, had to give up. Management of the sanitarium was taken over by Dr. McGrath and two other physicians, Drs. Carroll B. Andrews and William J. Newman, but it was obvious that improved hospital facilities were badly needed to serve the growing Valley.

A Sonoma Valley Community Hospital fund was set up, which by May 1945 had grown to $32,618. The citizen's group assisting in raising this money for a new hospital included Edward Graves, August Sebastiani, Joan McGrath, Tom Pucheu, A. R. Grinstead, R. R. Emparan, Paul Wolter and August Pinelli. In 1945 a two-story building (now a winery) in Buena Vista owned by Frank Bartholomew was leased as a new hospital. The building had formerly been a state facility for housing delinquent women.

The first directors of this new hospital were Andrews, Wolter, Grinstead, Pinelli, Sebastiani, Pucheu, Mike Mulas, C. A. Wilson, A. L. Rathbone, Helen Dresel and Sam Shainsky.

During its first two years, the new hospital made a profit of approximately $15,000—this on a room-rate charge to patients of $6, $7 and $8 a day.

Meanwhile, attorney Grinstead and a group were lobbying to get the state legislature to pass a district hospital law, with the idea of creating a hospital district here that would be able to get financial aid through a tax levy.

Grinstead himself wrote the basic district hospital act, which was passed by the legislature in September 1945 and became a model for other hospital districts throughout the state. In January 1946, a successful election was held here to make our hospital a district hospital.

It was allowed to levy a tax of up to 20¢ per $100 of assessed property valuation.

The first hospital district directors appointed by the county district attorney were Wilson, Pinelli, Shainsky, Sebastiani and Mrs. Marion Green. Green was proprietor of the old Woodleaf Store in Boyes Springs.

By 1952 it became obvious that a larger hospital would have to be built. The leased Buena Vista facility had a capacity of only 21 beds, and expansion seemed infeasible. A search for a new hospital site was launched.

A committee which included Bob Gilmore, Dr. Newman and Mrs. Ophelia Larson checked possible sites all around the Valley. Eventually the committee settled on a parcel the district already owned (made available by Sebastiani) on Andrieux Street.

The estimated cost of a new hospital was set at $400,000, and in August 1953, the hospital district board held a bond election for $300,000. The directors already had $164,000 in their building fund.

That 1953 election was defeated, however. The vote was yes 1,849, no 1,107. The measure needed a two-thirds majority to pass. It was pointed out that if only 122 more persons had voted yes instead of no, the measure would have carried.

The defeat of the bond election was mainly due to the work of a committee headed by Dr. Andrews. In its press releases prior to the election, this group claimed that the hospital board had provided neither a detailed budget nor a detailed list of specifications for construction of the hospital.

The Andrews committee also said there was the danger of another, competitive hospital taking over the district hospital's rented quarters at Buena Vista when it moved out.

They suggested that the rented building be retained as a hospital while further planning was done. The committee contended that the planning for a new hospital had been inadequate and that more time was needed to make sure that funds were spent "wisely and economically."

After the narrow defeat at the polls, the disappointed hospital directors set up a fact-finding group to plan for a new election. The group

This converted farmhouse on Burndale Road, Vineburg, served as Sonoma Valley's hospital from 1924 to 1944.

included Homer R. Bosse, Col. John Cotton, W. F. Fitzer, A. L. Ford, Grinstead, Charles Murray, George Nicholas, Tom Polidori and Harry Solen. After several months of study, they recommended that the directors proceed with their plan to build a new hospital at the Sebastiani site on Andrieux Street.

The results of this study convinced the community, with *The Sonoma Index-Tribune* again providing continuous news and editorial support favoring passage of the hospital bond election. A second bond election, held in February 1954, for $262,000 passed by a six-to-one margin. The new hospital was built by A. A. Douglas of Napa. The groundbreaking took place May 20, 1955.

The new hospital opened in January 1957, with a big open house attended by hundreds.

The first administrator was James E. Moore. The board of directors at that time included Gilmore, Shainsky, Mrs. Larson, Colonel Cotton and D. A. Pfeiffer. Pfeiffer served as chairman for many years.

The first major hospital expansion project was construction of the three-story west wing, which was opened in 1972.

To the consternation of the directors and the community, it was discovered in 1977, while a survey was being made for a remodeling project, that the west wing did not have the required reinforcing to make it earthquake-resistant.

How such a terrible thing could have

COURTESY, BARTHOLOMEW PARK WINERY MUSEUM

In 1944, when the community's needs had outgrown the facilities at Burndale, Frank Bartholomew agreed to lease (at a cost of $150–$200 a month) a building on his Buena Vista property for a non-profit community hospital. The two-story building had once been utilized by the state as a residence for "delinquent women."

occurred has really never been satisfactorily explained. The directors filed an $11-million suit against the architects, the firm of Edward Durrell Stone and Associates, and the engineers and others involved. The lawsuit was successful, enabling the hospital to completely rebuild and appropriately strengthen the west wing, while at the same time expanding the east wing and facilities.

– RML

Historic Union Hotel razed for B of A site

On April 2, 1956, work commenced on the demolition of the Union Hotel and adjacent site of the old Union Hall, at the corner of Napa and First Street West, to make space for the modern Bank of America building and parking lot.

The two buildings demolished had a colorful past going back to pioneer times.

The first hotel on the premises was built by a partnership or "union" of three members of the New York Volunteer Army, Col. Jonathan D. Stevenson's Regiment, which served here in 1847. Their names were Dow, Story and Higgins. These three wartime comrades built a two-story adobe building, profited by their venture and sold out in 1851 to P. J. Vasquez, who leased the premises to Tony Oakes, a Portuguese guitarist

and all-around bon vivant.

Tony was so popular that he was elected mayor in 1857. It was said that he frequently played his guitar while sitting on the city council.

The first Union Hotel had a bar at a level below the street, because so much soil on the site had been removed to make adobe bricks. It is said that, during heavy rains, the building would flood and it would take a rowboat to get a drink. Tony sold out in time to miss the destruction of the building in 1866.

John H. Lutgens bought the property and in 1867 built the two-story stone hotel of 30 rooms that stood until 1956. Lutgens leased the building to Frank Oettl, who came West in 1849. A former brothel piano player, Oettl made his own "Havana" cigars out of cabbage leaves, and after the customers had had a few drinks, no one could tell his cigars from the genuine tobacco leaf product.

For the next 20 years new proprietors came and went. In 1891 D. Moore was boss, by 1902 F. Wilde had succeeded him, and in 1905 the hotel was managed by Dr. H. W. Gottenburg, who apparently leased the property from the Leiding estate. Hotel ads of the day specified that you could get full board and room for $1 a day and that every room was equipped with an electric light. Before World War I, the Union Hotel was managed by Frank Koenig.

Just prior to demolition, the hotel dining room was ably managed by Josephine Andrieux. She provided exceptional meals for the Sonoma Kiwanis Club, which met there on Tuesday nights. John Steiner ran the generous bar.

West of the hotel stood the two-story wooden-framed Union Hall, which had been converted to two commercial rentals facing Napa Street. Exactly when the hall was constructed is unknown, but it certainly dated back to the 1880s. The corner rental was leased for a variety of purposes in later years, including a real estate office and a drugstore. By the 1950s it was occupied by the Western Auto store run by Joe Andrieux and Harry Rhodes. Another renter was the Baines and Woodworth radio shop.

Union Hall had formerly been used for a variety of purposes by the community. Church socials were commonly held there, and the hall

INDEX-TRIBUNE ARCHIVES

The Union Hotel at Napa and First Street West was built in 1847 as a two-story adobe and rebuilt in 1867 as a stone structure. Today the site is occupied by the Bank of America.

was large enough for the local high school to play basketball games inside.

Now these two buildings are only memories.

– ROBERT D. PARMELEE

Joan McGrath, Sonoma's first woman mayor

Joan McGrath, a former high school music teacher and then wife of a pioneer Sonoma physician, Dr. A. K. McGrath, became Sonoma's first woman city council member in 1952.

In the spring election that year, Mrs. McGrath easily outdistanced the other five candidates (male) in the election.

City voters had to choose two council members from a field of six candidates. Mrs. McGrath was the top vote-getter, with 403 votes. Sonoma-area soil conservationist Hilton Taylor was second with 195 votes.

In 1952 Mrs. McGrath, a charming, cultivated, dark-haired woman, had been a resident of Sonoma for some 20 years. She came here in

1931 as a music teacher after her graduation from College of the Pacific in Stockton.

She accepted a post at the high school, where she taught until 1937, when she married Dr. McGrath, who had arrived in Sonoma in 1924 fresh out of medical school.

It was undoubtedly her community activities which helped to elect Mrs. McGrath. Although she eventually had six children, she still managed to be a leader in civic affairs.

She was active in the Sonoma Valley Woman's Club, even serving as its president; and she served on boards for the Red Cross, Girl Scouts and Camp Fire Girls. She was a member of citizens' committees which worked for school bond elections.

Mrs. McGrath proved a capable councilwoman, despite a lack of cooperation from her male colleagues at times. In 1956 she ran for reelection and was again the top vote-getter in the field, with 387 votes.

At this point, her colleagues took the hint and elected her mayor. She served until 1960. As mayor, Mrs. McGrath worked for closer coopera-

INDEX-TRIBUNE ARCHIVES

Joan McGrath (center), elected mayor in 1956, is shown with city staffers (from left) Jim Baker, Dorothy Pingree, Hal Crandall and Bruna Urton.

tion between officials of the various cities in the county and was one of the founders of the Mayors' and Councilmen's Association, serving as its first president.

Important projects carried to conclusion during her term as mayor included the remodeling of City Hall, where most of the downstairs space was previously taken up by General "Hap" Arnold's model airplane collection; annexation of the West Napa Street business area; expansion of various municipal services and the appointment of former Police Chief James F. Baker as the city's first administrator.

She also served on the board of directors of the Sonoma Valley Sanitation District, was director of Civil Defense for Sonoma Valley, and was on the executive board of the North Bay division of the League of California Cities. With eight years of inspired community service behind her, Mrs. McGrath thought she could expand the scope of her activities. She ran in the 1960 June Primary Election as a candidate for supervisor from the 1st District.

The incumbent, rancher Carson Mitchell, had held the post since being appointed in 1957. Mitchell did not succeed in getting the required majority of votes, so a run-off was set for November.

In the primary election, Mrs. McGrath got 1,783 votes compared to Mitchell's 2,111. Two other candidates, Louie Minelli and Mel Larson, finished third and fourth.

In the November election, Mitchell squeaked through with a majority of 368 votes. He got 4,951 votes to Mrs. McGrath's 4,583.

Proud of her eight-year record and philosophical about her defeat, Mrs. McGrath went back to teaching, becoming a member of the faculty at El Verano School.

Dr. McGrath died in 1964. In 1966 Mrs. McGrath married Ralph Waterhouse. They moved away from here in 1968, living for three years in Orangevale and later moving to Oakmont, just up the highway from Sonoma.

Mrs. Waterhouse, an accomplished musician, played with the Santa Rosa Symphony from 1931 through the war years. She found her love of music a sustaining interest in her latter years as well.
                                                    – JERRY PARKER

AUTHOR'S NOTE: Sonoma's first woman mayor, who died in November 1995 at the age of 86, was preceded in death by Mr. Waterhouse.

23 Major Growth Years: 1960–1979

The City of Sonoma's first three Honorary Alcaldes: August Pinelli, Henri Maysonnave and Jerry Casson. The honor for community service, bestowed on outstanding citizens annually, was instituted in 1976.

Population, building boom hit Valley

*L*ike that enchanted village in the musical Brigadoon—which only came to life every 100 years—Sonoma Valley slumbered for many years after the first settlement was created here in 1835 by Gen. Mariano G. Vallejo.

But then there was a great, some might even say a rude, awakening along about 1960. For around that time, a new breed of explorer—the modern homeseeker, an even hardier type than Kit Carson—discovered this fabled vale.

California has become the end of the rainbow for this horde of homeseekers, and that rainbow seems to shine in Sonoma Valley with special glory. It is reflected in the area's natural beauty, climate and historic heritage.

For almost a hundred years there was literally no change in the city of Sonoma's population. In 1831 that population was said by local historian Robert Parmelee to be 705. This included Indians, the Sonoma Mission garrison and settlers.

In 1920, according to the veteran present city clerk, Eleanor Berto, the population was approximately 800 in the city. In 1960 the city population was 3,023. The entire Sonoma Valley population was around 20,000. Around 1980 it had grown to more than 40,000.

A building code for Sonoma Valley was enacted in 1960. Construction costs in 1963 in the city more than doubled those of 1962—$2,400,000 compared to $1,068,486. Dr. Charles Allen, Sonoma's mayor in 1963, seemed to hit it on the head when he said in an interview: "The pattern of growth is being established this year."

Building remained at a high level throughout the '60s but really took off with the advent of the '70s.

In 1978 building costs in the city reached what was then an all-time high—$10,136,937. This was almost double the figure for 1977.

The pattern was much the same in the unincorporated area of the Valley, and in both city and Valley the whole spectrum of new building could be seen, with subdivisions, multi-family layouts and commercial projects sprouting everywhere. A certain division in the population emerged, with growth exponents arrayed against those who wanted to slow things down.

City, district and county officials have struggled for decades to keep up with this spectacular growth—building more water lines, sewers and schools.

The Valley of the Moon County Water

District was established in 1960 and began to gear up for the arrival of water from the Russian River, for which bonds were voted in 1955. The water arrived here in 1963.

Before the district was formed, there were several small water companies serving the Valley. The city had its own system. This kind of Balkan-state approach made for rather poor service. The same situation had existed in the schools, but unification in 1959 vastly improved the administration picture.

Reflecting an overall fiscal explosion during recent decades in the Valley, the district school budget went from $449,127 in 1962 (when there were approximately 3,000 students) to $3,125,919 in 1969, when the enrollment was about the same.

The city of Sonoma's budget shows a similar growth, seemingly exceeding any per capita relationship. In 1961, when the city had less than 4,000 residents, the budget was $337,575. In 1969 the city budget was $635,998, almost double, although the population was less than 5,000.

INDEX-TRIBUNE ARCHIVES

Where is everybody? Approaching the Sonoma Plaza from Broadway at high noon on Jan. 1, 1978, neither a car nor a person was in sight.

In 1971 it was $1,307,705—the first million-dollar budget—with the population not much higher than 5,000.

For 1978–79, the city budget was $1,930,817, with the population not quite 6,000.

The period 1960–70 was also considered an era of controversies, one of the biggest being the state proposal for a freeway through the Valley. Back in 1961, state highway engineers conducted local hearings and recommended a route right through the middle of the Valley. A number of people—and their number increased as time went by—wondered if we needed a freeway at all. But almost everyone was agreed that a freeway through the middle of the Valley would destroy it.

Further hearings revealed that most folks thought the freeway—if we had to have one—should be put over by the western foothills.

Opposition to the freeway continued to grow, and by 1967 even Sen. Randolph Collier, considered the father of the California freeway system, said he didn't think a freeway should be built here. He recommended cancellation of the agreement between the county and the state, and the idea died.

The city and county got together in 1963 and asked the Leo Daly Company to prepare a Sonoma-area General Plan for the Valley. Ten years later, the city asked the Gordon Hall Company to revise and update the plan.

That plan seems to have worked well for five years, but a new controversy, over the civic center that was recommended, pitted local factions who took opposite sides. Garth Eliassen, a critic of the city, got an initiative petition to keep the city from building anything at its civic center site on First Street West. The city rejected the ordinance in the petition when City Attorney John Klein said it was illegal. The civic center site became a reality with a court/city council meeting room, plus police department headquarters built there.

The county put together its own General Plan for the rest of the Valley, in line with a state stipulation. Most growth was to be concentrated around the present populous areas, with low density and other requirements supposed to protect the rural areas.

New schools were built, including Altimira

junior high in Boyes Springs, which opened in 1968, and Kenwood elementary, which opened in 1961. Then there was Agua Caliente High School, the so-called continuation school, which opened in 1969.

The state continued to refurbish the landmarks in Sonoma Valley and also opened a new Jack London Park in Glen Ellen in 1960.

The old Toscano Hotel was restored to its 1870s appearance, and the Barracks building underwent a complete restoration, directed by the state parks division, that was completed in 1980.

The new look in housing developments was the mobilehome park. Parks sprouted up all over the Valley, but the city was a little more choosy. It rejected several but wound up with three—De Anza Moon Valley, the pioneer in 1963, and Pueblo Serena and Rancho de Sonoma.

Sonoma's first electric traffic signal was installed at Napa and Fifth Street West in the 1960s.

In 1962 a retirement "city" was planned at Temelec (west of Arnold Drive), the former estate of the late Hearst publisher and Mrs. E. D. Coblentz.

Shopping centers also invaded the city and Valley. Following Valley Mart [now Sonoma Valley Center], established in 1956 by Jim, Tom and Lambro Cordellos, Fiesta took shape in Boyes Springs in 1964. Safeway, Sonoma's first chain store, rebuilt its Fifth Street West supermarket in 1973 when the first became too small.

Plaza West came along in 1977, also on Fifth Street West, and in 1978 the Vineyard Shopping Center opened at the northeast corner of Verano Avenue and Highway 12. The Sonoma Marketplace, largest of them all, was completed in 1979, adding an Albertsons and Longs to the community.

Probably because of the building surge, new banks and savings and loans proliferated in the area during the 1960s and 1970s.

The worst fire in 40 years raged through Sonoma Valley in September 1964, searing 13,000 acres on the eastern ridges from Kenwood to Boyes Springs. There were 30 homes and innumerable outbuildings destroyed.

Residents of Moon Valley and Pueblo Serena mobilehome parks on West Fifth Street ventured into the open the day after the big snow of February 1972, but only with the protection of warm clothing.

A repeat in 1965 caused vast damage in the rangelands south of here, wiping out barns and agricultural buildings and killing cattle. Some beloved old landmarks also burned up in the 1970s, including the Boyes Springs Bath House, Rustic Inn and St. Mary's Church in Glen Ellen, and the Fetters Springs Hotel, the latter operated by Juanita Musson at the time of the fire.

The city's boundaries were pushed out by several annexations.

There were 44 annexations to the city as of 1978, since the first one in 1950. That's when the city annexed the East MacArthur Street property on which Prestwood Elementary School is located. However, 40 of those 44 annexations took place in the period 1960–78. They increased the size of the city (formerly a mile square) by approximately 50 percent.

The drug problem reached even Sonoma Valley in the 1960s, and a furor was caused in 1968 when the high school sent a letter home to certain parents stating their children were "rumored" to be using drugs.

Marijuana busts became frequent. Long hair became a hassle. A new dress code was adopted in 1969 at the high school, and "do your thing"

A new dress code adopted at Sonoma Valley High School in 1969 permitted girls to wear slacks. Most of the girls interviewed by the *I-T* said slacks were "more comfortable and less confining." Pictured here (left to right) are Cathy Marino, Molly Okumura, Donna Giorgi and Robin Smircich. Giorgi wasn't wearing slacks, she said, "because I like myself better in skirts."

INDEX-TRIBUNE ARCHIVES

In January 1968 an honor guard from the Presidio in San Francisco served as pallbearers at the funeral of U. S. Army infantryman John N. Brewer, 20, Sonoma Valley's fourth casualty of the war in Vietnam. Here, the funeral cortege leaves St. Francis Solano Church.

seemed to be the mode.

Heartbreaking stories appeared in the *I-T* in the latter 1960s telling of the death of Valley boys in Vietnam.

The worst aircraft tragedy ever to happen in Sonoma Valley was the crash of an Air Force plane on Mangels Ranch in May 1970, when 13 of the 14 crewmen perished.

In 1972 the hospital opened its $42-million, three-story west wing. The wing had to be rebuilt, because it was discovered that it wasn't reinforced to earthquake standards. Rebuilding it cost $5 million. The hospital district board filed a successful suit against the designers and builders of the wing.

In addition to the biblical plagues of fire and flood, a drought devastated Sonoma Valley for two years in 1976-77. Water conservation and

rationing measures were imposed on all users, and cooperation was splendid.

Another misfortune in the Act of God category was the Dutch elm tree disease, which struck here in 1975. For the next two years, state crews kept busy cutting down all the elms. The cure seemed to be worse than the disease.

In a lighter vein, Sonoma was dubbed by an out-of-town newspaper the "Armpit of the World" after a Ban deodorant commercial was filmed in the Plaza in 1975.

The movie industry also discovered the Valley. *Mr. Billion* was filmed here in 1976. It was a cheerful film but a real turkey.

Lovable Jimmy Stewart dropped into Glen Ellen in 1978 for the filming of some scenes in a "Lassie" television saga.

Maxwell Farm, a 100-acre oasis in the heart of the Valley, was talked about as a civic center site back in the early 1970s. The city of Sonoma took the initiative in the matter but nothing came of the proposal.

In the 1970s the city created the first parks developed here since the Plaza, once General Vallejo's parade ground, was laid out many years

INDEX-TRIBUNE ARCHIVES

The west wing of Sonoma Valley Hospital. It had to be rebuilt because of structural inadequacies.

INDEX-TRIBUNE ARCHIVES

In 1978 actor Jimmy Stewart visited Glen Ellen, where a scene for a motion picture was filmed.

ago. Depot Park, with its museum replica of the old Depot, was completed in 1979. Pinelli Park, in southeast Sonoma, was dedicated the previous year.

Disagreement existed on the site and design of the new regional library on West Napa Street which opened in November 1978, but it is surely a cultural plus.

Crime showed a steady increase in Sonoma Valley between 1960 and 1980, with burglaries and vandalism heading the list.

The Valley was shocked and horrified by the terrorist bombing of the PG&E substation at Leveroni Road in April 1977. This was a new kind of crime, something imported from the fearsome outside world.

Sonoma Valley's people continued searching for the answers. As poet Carl Sandburg wrote about the American people, "In the night, and overhead a shovel of stars for keeps, the people march: 'Where to? What next?'"   – JERRY PARKER

A pickled pair, shotgun blasts and tear gas

AUTHOR'S NOTE: Long before my eldest son, Bill Lynch, became editor and chief executive officer of *The Sonoma Index-Tribune*, he was a news writer, photographer and advertising representative. His talent as a reporter, enhanced by his great sense of humor, was displayed in 1973 when he won national and state recognition for his front-page story in the December 13 issue of the *Index-Tribune* headlined "A pickled pair, shotgun blasts and tear gas." The story, reprinted below, was subsequently picked up by United Press International and sent all over the United States. Bill received two prestigious journalism awards for his story, the San Francisco Press Club award for Best News Story in a Non-daily Newspaper and the California State Fair award for Best Newspaper Story in California in 1973.

Two men, one a baker's assistant and the other a cheesemaker, got pickled Monday night and wound up sandwiched between city police and sheriff's deputies in a four-hour siege of the Sonoma Cheese Factory on Spain Street.

A 34-year-old cheese factory employee, and a 35-year-old employee of a local bakery, who share a small apartment above the cheese factory, apparently had quite a party for themselves Monday night and on into the early morning hours Tuesday.

They were spotted in the store sales room at 3:45 A.M. Tuesday by city patrolman Bob Wieworka. According to Wieworka's report, the two appeared to be having an argument.

Suspecting a possible burglary attempt,

Wieworka called for assistance from the Sheriff's substation in Agua Caliente. Upon the deputy's arrival, both lawmen checked the side and back of the building. At some point in the checkout one of the suspects inside left the sales room, and later the other man also left.

A garbage man making his pickup in the back of the building came out front and reported that he had seen a man with a rifle or gun inside.

A deputy soon spotted one of the men upstairs with a gun in his hand. A few minutes later the man came downstairs toward the front of the building brandishing a double-barreled shotgun. At this point the lawmen backed off to talk over the situation.

A few minutes later, a muffled gunshot was heard from inside. At the time, the officers thought that one of the men had shot the other. They called for more assistance. (As it turned out, the bakery worker had accidentally fired the shotgun and blasted a chest of drawers to bits.)

Cheese factory owner Pete Viviani arrived on the scene as did police chief Gene Cartwright, a second sheriff's unit and six more Sonoma policemen.

Viviani called the store on the telephone and spoke to his employee. He asked him to explain what he was doing and to put down the gun and come out. According to Viviani, the man sounded highly intoxicated. Shortly after that conversation, a second blast was fired out the window from inside the building.

Not knowing who or what the men were shooting at, police chief Cartwright kept hoping to talk them out of the building. Viviani repeatedly called to the pair to come out, but no answers were forthcoming.

Viviani wanted to enter the building to talk the men into coming out, but Cartwright felt that it would be too dangerous.

Tear-gas canisters were fired through the upstairs window. The men inside didn't react. It was speculated that they were "too drunk to be bothered by the gas," or they had finally passed out from overindulgence.

Not wishing to risk getting someone killed, Cartwright tried to play a waiting game and let the tear gas flush the men out.

A Sonoma fire truck was also called to guard against fires that might be caused by the gas canisters when they ignite.

Spain Street, between First East and First West, was blocked off. As the morning wore on, a cold drizzle began falling. A Greyhound bus attempting to turn down the street was stopped at the roadblock at First Street East. While backing up, the bus plowed into a fire hydrant and started a water leak.

Cartwright, Sgt. Bill Rettle and officer Bob Sheets climbed up on the roof in an attempt to gain entrance behind the two suspects.

Leaning down over the front overhang, Cartwright attempted to lob a canister of "CS" gas into the room. It hit a window frame instead, fell to the pavement, ignited and sent deputies and policemen who were downwind scattering out of the gas' path.

As the rain fell harder and the siegers got colder and wetter, it was decided to enter the building and attempt to apprehend the two men.

The gas almost overpowered the lawmen as they entered a side door. Several times they exited, coughing and wheezing, eyes filled with tears.

Cartwright, Rettle, Sgt. Don Bettencourt and sheriff's lieutenant Leroy Kobza moved upstairs with their search and finally located the men hiding in the attic, the shotgun near the bakery worker.

The PG&E substation on Leveroni Road near Broadway was bombed by New World Liberation Front terrorists on April 21, 1977. Thousands in the Valley were left without electricity for many hours.

INDEX-TRIBUNE ARCHIVES

Julius Pagani of Kenwood Winery (center) with successors Marty and Mike Lee, circa 1972. In the old days, customers could take a jug to the winery and have it filled for a dollar.

The men, obviously intoxicated, surrendered without a fuss and were escorted to waiting patrol cars (one of which had a dead battery from using its spotlight through the four-hour affair).

Thus ended the great Sonoma Cheese Factory siege.

Why the baker fired the shotgun is not clear. The pair's account of what happened is confused. They apparently knew they were in trouble when the police arrived, but were either too drunk or too frightened to know what to do.

No one was killed or injured. Twelve lawmen coughed and cried a lot. Several windows were broken. A dresser was blasted to bits. Cheese Factory customers thought there was a bit too much pepper dust in the air that day and the city had a broken fire hydrant.

Cartwright credited Viviani for his help in trying to talk the men out. He complimented his officers and the four sheriff's department officers for their handling of the affair. "Everybody took their time and were careful not to push the suspects into a corner. I'm delighted that we were able to get the men out without firing a shot," the chief concluded.

Both bakery and cheese factory employees may face charges of illegal immigration. The bakery worker will also be charged with illegally discharging a firearm in the city.   – BILL LYNCH

Wineries doubled in the 1960s and '70s

*I*n 1960 five wineries were actively producing wines in Sonoma Valley.

The long-standing cellars of Buena Vista, Sebastiani, Valley of the Moon, Kenwood (formerly Pagani Brothers Winery) and Hanzell were joined by a sudden rush in the early 1970s of new or revitalized wine operations.

In 1969 two families began producing wines in the cozy confines of a garage on Burndale road in Vineburg. Gino Zepponi and Norm deLeuze combined their wine-making talents—and initials—and called their winery ZD.

The following year, a small wine operation on property adjoining Dunbar School in Glen Ellen began to boil with activity again after a long period of silence. Founded at the turn of the century as Lemoine Winery, it was later taken over following the repeal of Prohibition by local vintner Felix Mancuso. His son, Pete, ran the operation from 1950–52. Twenty years later a group of enthusiastic young men cranked things up there again and called it Grand Cru Vineyards.

In 1973 wine producer Frank Bartholomew, who had sold his neighboring Buena Vista Winery in 1968, decided to try making a small amount of wine from the grapes in the vineyards he still owned. The site he chose for a new winery was a two-story building of Spanish-Monterey architecture on his property, which he had purchased at a state auction in 1943. The building was originally constructed by the state as a home for female delinquents. Bartholomew had leased it to the fledgling Sonoma Valley Hospital District, and it had served as the community's hospital from 1945 through 1951. After the new hospital was built in Sonoma, the building was used as a rest home until Bartholomew converted it to Hacienda Wine Cellars.

In 1974 an intense and very meticulous young winemaker named Richard Arrowood was crushing grapes for a new operation in picturesque Kenwood for the very first time. The 250-acre Goff estate was the site, and the handsome two-story French-Mediterranean chateau accommodated tasting, tours, parties and the winery's business offices. A highly sophisticated $3-million winery adjacent to the chateau was completed the following year. Named for the wife of one of the estate owners, the winery was called Chateau St. Jean.

A pair of aspiring winemakers named Jim Bundschu and John Merritt realized their dreams in July 1976 when the century-old doors of Gundlach-Bundschu Winery swung open to the public for the first time in decades.

Located on the Bundschus' Vineburg ranch, historically known as Rhine Farm, the compact winery, which protrudes from the side of a hill, was once a major exporter of wines throughout the world. It all started in 1868. And after a stormy history of major setbacks, including an earthquake, Prohibition, pestilence, fires and spiraling taxes, the 128-year-old, greatly expanded winery was back in business and prospering.

Gundlach-Bundschu's resurrection in 1976 from decades of dormancy brought the total number of existing wineries here to 10.

Certainly, the sudden jump in the popularity of wine consumption was the major factor in triggering the growth of wineries in Sonoma Valley. Younger people began opting for the evening glass of white wine and were gradually turning away from the traditional martini, which, along with other "hard liquor" concoctions, seemed to be the drink of the older generation.

The clean and readily acceptable taste of wine, plus the implementation of more sophisticated technology, sparked the evolution of wine drinking into a popular cultural phenomenon.

Certain grape varietals, the regions in which they were grown, at what stage of development they were picked and how the resulting juice was handled soon became commonplace talk at the dinner table and social gatherings.

Hence, business boomed and visitors filed en masse to the "wine country" to see what all the fuss was about.

Why did the wine business suddenly catch fire in Sonoma Valley? Winemaster Arrowood had a quick and easy answer: "We just have the best growing area to make the finest wines."

Don Sebastiani, youngest member of the highly successful third-generation wine family, has seen Sebastiani Vineyards grow at an astounding pace here in recent years.

INDEX-TRIBUNE ARCHIVES

The "twinning" of Sonoma and the little wine town of Chambolle-Musigny, France, was officially completed Jan. 29, 1960, with a ceremony there. It followed a like ceremony (above) held here the previous September. Participants included (from left) J. D. Zellerbach, ambassador to Italy, and later Sonoma resident and founder of Hanzell Winery; California Lt. Gov. Glen Anderson; high school teacher Waldron Parker (in top hat); Rev. Joel Scott, O. F. M.; Richard Raoul Emparan, grandson of M. G. Vallejo (in background); Sonoma mayor Joan McGrath; and French Consul General Robert Luc.

"Sonoma's just now starting to get a reputation," he explained in 1979. "In wine circles, they're starting to talk about 'Sonoma character' now."

Most vintners agree that the cool, foggy, summer evenings and gentle afternoon breezes here provide for a more desirable growing climate for premium grape varietals.

"Wine is a social thing," Sebastiani remarked. "It's as much a food as it is an alcoholic drink."

It's also very profitable. As Arrowood pointed out, "Consumer interest in wines has increased substantially. And as a result, people have gotten interested in the business."

Sebastiani believes that the reason Sonoma

INDEX-TRIBUNE ARCHIVES

Fishermen down through the years have found Sonoma's sloughs south of Schellville yielding good catches of a fighting and eminently edible fish, the striped bass. CHP officer John O'Brien's catch in the 1960s was as big as his little boy.

Valley experienced a boom in the wine industry somewhat later than the neighboring Napa Valley was due to the latter's easier accessibility from outlying areas. "Napa Valley is a great big valley that follows pretty much the same boundaries as Napa County," he said. "On the other hand, Sonoma Valley is not synonymous with Sonoma County or Sonoma city for that matter. We're not located on a big, main highway. And we're smaller and more cozy than Napa Valley." Business, he added, had been somewhat discouraged from coming here because of those factors.

That is certainly not the case in Sonoma Valley today.   – JOHN LYNCH

High school swim pool was community project

While the *Index-Tribune* took the leadership in instituting and lending all-out support to countless community projects in its first 100 years of existence, one of the most satisfying—despite the fact that it took some 10 years to be completed— was the public fund-raising campaign conducted to raise $50,000 to ensure the construction of the swimming pool at Sonoma Valley High School.

It was back in 1956 that the *Index-Tribune* ran an editorial first suggesting a fund-raising drive for a community swimming pool. Despite only a few encouraging letters to "Pulse of the Public" in reply, the suggestion was repeated both in editorials and the editor's "Musings" column with a certain amount of regularity.

The advantages of such a facility being placed at the high school for student instruction and recreation during school hours, and for community use and Red Cross instruction outside of school hours, were stressed.

A group of local citizens, with high school athletic director Clarence A. Edsall and the *Index-Tribune*'s editor, Robert M. Lynch, assuming the leadership, joined in a preliminary study of the proposal and found it feasible. Students were enthusiastic, and the graduating classes of 1959 and 1960 left gifts totaling $500 toward the pool project.

The swimming pool proposal got a big boost in 1960 when the Sonoma Kiwanis Club, then under the presidency of Dr. Wayne G. Price, adopted it as a club project. The Kiwanians put up money to secure preliminary plans and a cost breakdown and, with the blessing of the school district board of trustees, determined that the project was a worthy one.

The *Index-Tribune* submitted the idea that the pool should become a community-wide project for all of the 80-some active organizations— clubs, lodges, associations, etc.—in the Valley, and soon meetings were held, attended by representatives of many of those 80 organizations and other interested individuals.

Joining with the Kiwanis Club as early supporters of the pool plan were the Sonoma Valley Business and Professional Women's Club, Soroptimists, Rotary Club and the local Red Cross chapter.

An editorial in the *I-T* of July 7, 1960, commented, "What more serviceable monument to community spirit than a swimming pool? For recreation, for teaching—yes, for saving lives."

On August 15 of that year a steering committee of Edsall, Lynch, Price, E. L. Richardson, Bill Candrian and school district superintendent John Glaese was named.

Over the next few years, others took an active part in the fund-raising project. Names we recall—and there were many others—are those of Helen Fernandez, Jim Gordon, C. M. Peterson, Gene Domenichelli, Mrs. James Connolly, Mrs. Charles Allen, Fred Folowell, Ernie Smith, Larry Lancina and Peter Duffy.

As donations came in, the names of the donors and amount given were printed on the front page of the *Index-Tribune*—new donors and old. It was a slow and laborious campaign, and demanded constant news and editorial reminders. By May 1964 there was just $16,324 in the swimming pool fund. Augmenting the individual donations—memorial and otherwise— were benefit events, including dances, concerts, and cake and candy sales. Finally, in July 1966 the $50,000 goal was at hand, and the school district board called for bids on the proposed L-shaped, 175- x 42-foot heated pool with an additional 130-foot width in the diving area. Decking and filtering system and the usual appurtenances were also included.

Gloom hung over the fund-raising committee members' heads on Aug. 9, 1966, when the low

A calf named Chester was donated to the Vintage Festival for a "country auction" in September 1969 by Valley dairyman Bob Leveroni. Shown here with Chester are (from left) Joe Leveroni, Anthony Spina, Elizabeth Leveroni, Stacy Pina and Patricia Leveroni.

bid came in at $84,800 by Christensen & Foster of Santa Rosa. But with the reduction of the kiddies' wading pool and a few other items, a subsequent bid of $79,000 was approved, the school district board agreeing to authorize the sum needed above the $50,000 in community donations.

Work was started on the high school pool August 28 of that year. The swimming pool was completed on Jan. 15, 1967, some 10 years after that first editorial in the *I-T* suggested a community pool built with community-donated funds. On Saturday, June 17, 1967, a warm, sunny afternoon, the pool was formally dedicated, with famed sportscaster Ernie Smith the master of ceremonies. There were swimming and diving exhibitions, and aquacade and a ribbon-cutting ceremony.   – RML

Thirty homes destroyed by wildfire of 1964

There were times that not even the Pacific Ocean could have stopped it.

That's what Ralph Matteoli of the state division of forestry had to say about the intensity of the

INDEX-TRIBUNE ARCHIVES

A youngster checks out the ruins of a home destroyed by the wildfire of September 1964.

memorable, raging and destructive fire which burned over 10,000 acres, destroying homes and other structures in its path in the Valley of the Moon between Saturday, Sept. 19, and Wednesday, Sept. 23, 1964.

The wind-maddened blaze, which started in the Nelligan Road area on the Torrieri ranch near Kenwood, probably from a downed power line, was thought to have been contained on Saturday night. But on Sunday hellish winds clocked at 70 miles per hour brought the dying embers to life again, and soon the eastern hills on Sugarloaf Ridge were a burning, smoky inferno which defied the ever-growing number of men, pieces of equipment and few air tankers that could be utilized.

The winds drove the fire south and east, and by noon Monday it had crossed Nuns Canyon behind the Shirley Weise ranch and headed for Trinity Road, reaching there in early afternoon.

The firefighters' goal was to attempt to keep the blaze to a minimum width and to "pinch it off" before it reached the Hot Springs residential area.

At midnight the wall of flame had pushed beyond Trinity Road, destroying acreage on the Bouverie and Teller properties near Glen Ellen, but residences there were saved.

By 7 A.M. Tuesday the fire crossed Cavedale Road and continued to spread over the ridge to Moon Mountain Road and then into the lower hills of the Agua Caliente–Fetters Springs–Boyes Hot Springs area, where homes from which occupants fled at the last minute were consumed by the seemingly unstoppable tidal wave of fire.

As the fire converged on the Agua Caliente area, forestry chief Matteoli, in charge of the firelines, diverted practically all pumpers from the north to make a stand at Boyes Springs, with the Valley of the Moon Fire District crews at the forefront.

The Sonoma Fire Department, one of many mutual aid units assisting, was ordered to get most of its equipment to Mission Highlands to protect those hilltop residences in the event the fire could not be halted at Boyes Springs.

Sometime after 3 P.M. on Tuesday, aerial tankers braved the still high winds and dangerous canyon downdrafts to bomb the head of the fire at Caliente Creek canyon with fire retardants.

Some residences, including that of the J. B. Severances and Bob and Philomene Severance on Siesta Way, became innocent targets of the bombers from above—some of their payload splattering with force on roofs, walls, fences and autos.

But the bombers quelched the blaze, pinching it off. The fire's spread was stopped, virtually on the outskirts of Sonoma, and the bulldozers and hand troops held it.

By noon Wednesday, September 23, the fire had been diverted completely away from the Sonoma–Springs area and was burning out above Cavedale, under control.

Over 600 men fought in the fire, perhaps the most destructive of all time here. There were 75 pieces of rolling equipment used, including that of the State Forestry, the fire departments representing Sonoma Valley, and the many outside communities which responded with trucks and personnel. Four air tankers and 12 bulldozers were also used.

Twenty-seven homes were destroyed by fire, and several others badly damaged. Twenty-five of the homes lost in the holocaust were in the Boyes Springs area. One was on Cavedale Road and another on Trinity Road. Many smaller outbuildings, sheds, pumphouses and the like were destroyed.

The Torrieri brothers, on whose ranch the fire started, lost four structures, the loss estimated at $120,000. Loss of homes and structures alone totaled well over $500,000, according to estimates.

Among the lucky ones who saved their homes was *Index-Tribune* news editor Jerry Parker, who with members of his family braved the flames licking within a few hundred feet of their Cavedale Road residence and, with some outside help, managed to prevent the fire's hungry tentacles from engulfing the hillside residence.   – RML

Editor's note: The author, *Index-Tribune* publisher Robert M. Lynch, won the San Francisco Press Club's first-place award for Best News Story in a Non-Daily Newspaper in 1964, in recognition of the outstanding stories and photographs he produced during two days and nights covering the Valley of the Moon fire.

The milk-producing industry has long been an important part of Sonoma Valley's economy, with the Stornetta, Leveroni, Mulas and Mertens dairies the leading producers. Above, Alex Stornetta is shown with some of his Guernsey herd in the 1970s.

INDEX-TRIBUNE ARCHIVES

INDEX-TRIBUNE ARCHIVES

A Nov. 1, 1979, gathering of Sonoma city officials: (left to right) Richard Rowland, public works director; Nancy Parmelee, mayor; Eleanor Berto, city clerk; Ed Steinbeck, city planner; Brock T. Arner, city manager; and Al Mazza, fire chief.

Carrie Burlingame, a free spirit 'til her death at 100

Sonoma Valley's Carrie Burlingame, who died in December 1975 at the age of 100, was a free spirit all her long life. She was one of the Valley's unforgettable characters.

The daughter of Horatio Appleton, she was born on his ranch, located where the Fiesta shopping center now stands in Boyes Springs. Mrs. Burlingame combined outdoor activities with intellectual and cultural pursuits throughout her life. Nature, history, art and civic projects were her major interests.

She saw the transformation of Sonoma from a sleepy little pueblo into a modern city.

She was friends with many of the legendary figures of the Valley's past, including Jack London, General Vallejo and the Haraszthy family.

She poured her special knowledge into many articles about the history of Sonoma Valley, many of them printed in *Saga of Sonoma*, published in 1954 by the historical society, of which she was a charter member.

A member of the Sierra Club and the Audubon Society, Mrs. Burlingame made many camping trips through the Sierra over the years.

She was a pioneer motorist and drove across the country when there were hardly any roads.

She was a knowledgeable, self-taught botanist and ornithologist. She wrote poetry and illustrated it with her own charming sketches of flowers and scenes in nature.

As a member of the Woman's Club, she devoted her considerable energies to such projects as the founding of a library here (which occurred in 1913), improvement of the Plaza and the restoration of the Sonoma Mission.

She spent her last years in a rest home where her friends frequently visited her. They found a white-haired little lady of indomitable spirit, whose mind remained forever alert but whose spirit chafed against the infirmities of old age, the loss of sight and hearing.

That spirit was released Dec. 1, 1975.

Sonoma's General Plan was adopted in 1974

The city of Sonoma's General Plan is a slim, 40-page booklet with a gold cover setting out guidelines for the area's future growth.

It was adopted in September 1974, after many public meetings (of the town-hall type) and study sessions. These began in the fall of 1973 and were held all over Sonoma—at the Veterans Memorial, at the high school, at City Hall.

Unfortunately, the sessions never attracted an audience of more than 75 or 100 persons. But countless hours of work and wrangling went into the creation of the plan.

The General Plan was put together by the Hall and Goodhue Design Group of San Francisco. It superseded a plan created in 1963–64 by the Leo Daly Co.

Gordon Hall conducted most of the meetings on the plan.

A common format for most of the meetings was a group of panel discussions led by members of the city council and the city planning commission. Audience comments were included in the discussion.

As various proposals evolved, they were discussed, and the results of these discussions served as the starting point for future sessions.

Gradually the outlines of a plan emerged.

INDEX-TRIBUNE ARCHIVES

Sonoma's beautiful Plaza, captured early one summer morning by local photographer Richard O'Neil, was declared a national historic landmark in 1961.

In the statement of community goals in the plan, a perceptive analysis of the area and its people and what they wanted was furnished. It said:

> Over the years Sonoma has become a unique, historic town with a wealth of natural and man-made beauty. There is a great sense of place in Sonoma.
>
> People have thoughtfully preserved some older buildings while introducing a refreshing mixture of new styles.
>
> There is natural, ongoing concern, therefore, about typical suburban subdivisions of single-family houses on small lots which reduce Sonoma's semi-rural character and there is concern about widespread development of multi-family housing of poor appearance which seems out of place in single-family neighborhoods.
>
> Similarly, there is concern about large commercial centers of a type not compatible with Sonoma's small-town character and there is concern about unsightly industries within the city limits.
>
> There is also concern about preserving natural creeks, the lush backdrop of wooded hills and the long-range vitality of agricultural activities.

The General Plan attempted to combine idealism with practical considerations. As residential and commercial developments proliferated throughout the city, however, the emerging outline of the new city has not, on occasion, seemed to be what anyone expected.

The General Plan had a number of key proposals. The one that created the most controversy was the proposal for a town center, "guiding new commercial and civic uses to vacant land near the Plaza."

This included a shopping center proposal for Napa and Second Street West. Throughout the General Plan discussions, there was a split between the city council and the city planning commission on this issue. The council favored putting a shopping center at the end of West Napa Street. The city planners stuck with the

INDEX-TRIBUNE ARCHIVES

Judge Ray Grinstead in 1966.

General Plan's Second Street West shopping center.

When it came time to adopt the plan in September 1974, the council reluctantly went along with the downtown town center.

As of 1979 the shopping center was under construction at the site, on property owned by the Sangiacomo and Sebastiani families.

The General Plan recommended a civic center site on Spain Street near the Plaza. Land in that neighborhood was unavailable, so the city council did the next best thing, it would seem, and bought 12 acres on First Street West opposite the Veterans Memorial Building.

The present City Hall would be retained indefinitely, it was said.

The residential development section of the General Plan said the most intensive forms of

residential growth should be guided toward the areas west of the town center near Sonoma Creek.

Perhaps the major recommendation in the "circulation" (traffic) section of the plan concerned Highway 12.

Highway 12, it stated, should be rerouted from Broadway to Arnold Drive south of Petaluma Avenue. Route 121 is designated as the chief east-west route for traffic going from Napa to Petaluma and Highway 101.

The environmental resources section of the General Plan urged protection of agricultural land and Sonoma Creek. This would be done by discouraging isolated subdivisions. It also recommended that no public roads be developed along the foothills in an east-west direction north of the town center, to protect the unique backdrop of hills.

Development of neighborhood parks and pedestrian- and bike-paths was also urged.

Revisions are allowed in the General Plan. Such requests are considered by the city planning commission and city council. There have been six revisions in the plan since it was adopted. Four other applications have been rejected.

"Sonoma can yet look forward to retaining much of its rural character and historic charm," the original General Plan states. As city residents watch the growth going on around them, they certainly hope so.   – JERRY PARKER

Judge Ray Grinstead cared about community

*F*ew people have done more for the Sonoma Valley community than the late Judge A. R. (Ray) Grinstead.

Grinstead died in 1966. He was thrown by a horse in May and remained in a coma until his death in July.

The entire Valley mourned the longtime lawyer who, during a lifetime of public service, was a justice of the peace, city councilman, city attorney and Sonoma Court judge.

Grinstead was thought of as the father of Sonoma's Plaza. For it was back in the 1920s, when he became a member of the city council, that he suggested something be done to improve the barren site of the Plaza—as initially urged by a committee of the Sonoma Valley Woman's Club.

A member of the Sonoma Kiwanis Club, Grinstead got his own club to support the project. Money was raised for a landscape architect, and a plan for the Plaza adopted.

That plan included the features of the Plaza so beloved today, such as the rose garden, duck pond and outdoor amphitheater.

Other clubs and service organizations were persuaded to help with the Plaza project. Old-timers such as August Pinelli worked with Grinstead. The Plaza bloomed and became the lovely oasis it is today—surely the city's greatest asset.

Grinstead also created the State of California's district hospital law. This occurred because of the need to build a modern, tax-supported hospital in Sonoma Valley to replace the old Burndale Sanitarium.

Legislation to permit formation of a tax-supported entity for California communities seeking a funding source for hospitals was needed. So Grinstead prepared a draft of a hospital district law.

The legislature eventually passed such a law, and Sonoma Valley got its district hospital in the year immediately after World War II.

The first district hospital was located in a former state-owned building leased from Frank Bartholomew on his Buena Vista Rancho, which later became the Hacienda Winery.

The son of a high school principal, Grinstead was born in Glenn County and, after graduation from the University of California, was also a teacher for a time. He obtained his law degree in 1913. Grinstead served in World War I as a second lieutenant in the army.

He came to Sonoma in 1923 and married Emily Poppe, a member of a pioneer family here. He set up his law practice in the Poppe building on First Street East.

The Grinsteads had three children, Hugh, Robert and Jean.

One of the most beloved members of the Sonoma Kiwanis Club, Grinstead was its song-leader, wrote many musical skits for the club, and acted as a warm and witty toastmaster at many of the club's affairs.

The club honored the memory of Grinstead

with a plaque placed at the open-air performance center at the Plaza amphitheater after his death.

A man of kindly disposition as well as a unique sense of duty, Judge Grinstead had a host of friends in the community—some of them even among those who came before him while he was on the bench.

He could often be seen in conversation with one of these friends at various points about the city, frequently in front of his own charming office building.

                                                           – RML

Orchardist Herb Batto is shown in August 1967 with some of the pears from his orchards. The bins of fruit were shipped to the Vineburg weighing station before being transported to canneries. The pear crop would be light that year, but of good quality, Batto told the *I-T*, and the prune crop would be harvested next. Thirty years later Sonoma Valley pear, prune and apple orchards have disappeared, replaced by vineyards (and subdivisions).

When "write-ins" toppled incumbents

*T*wo incumbent city councilmen, both longtime residents of Sonoma and men noted for their civic contributions, were ousted by two write-in candidates in the municipal election of 1972, one of the most interesting elections in the city's long history.

Mayor John Lobsinger and councilman Chet Sharek were toppled by Tom Pitts and Dan Ruggles. Pitts was a newcomer to Sonoma, but Ruggles, an old-timer, had a background to match that of the incumbents.

The election revolved around one big issue— Villa Vallejo, a 120-unit housing development that had been proposed for property on West Spain Street, right next to the Vallejo home property and the Congregational church.

The election was a classic confrontation between exponents of growth and those favoring open space and retention of what they termed the city's historic heritage.

The two write-in candidates were pledged to maintaining that historic heritage. Voters had a clear-cut choice because there were no other candidates besides the challengers and the incumbents.

Pitts got 693 votes; Ruggles, 633; Sharek, 543; and Lobsinger, 514.

This victory was attributed in part to what *I-T* editor Robert M. Lynch termed "block" voting in an analysis he wrote prior to the election. Noting that Pitts had strong support in the mobilehome park where he lived, Lynch said this might prove significant in the election.

This was indeed the case. The incumbents decisively outpolled their challengers in precincts on the east side of the city. But on the west side, where the mobilehome parks are located, the incumbents were swamped and the write-ins gained an overall majority.

A week after the election, the developer withdrew the plans for Villa Vallejo.

The controversy had emerged in February

Sears Point International Raceway held its first event Dec. 1, 1968. Major auto and motorcycle races, attracting thousands of spectators, are held here annually.

INDEX-TRIBUNE ARCHIVES

when the *I-T* reported that the city planning commission voted 4–2 for Villa Vallejo. In so doing, the commission turned down a plea from the state that it be allowed to buy the 12 acres and make it part of the Vallejo home layout. The state had made its presentation at a meeting of the city planners in January. Voting for Villa Vallejo were planners Lee Tunkis, John Benzon, Paul Harrison and Paul Hoffhous. Voting against it were Ross Strickland and Ronald Preston.

The Congregational church filed an appeal against the planners' decision. The council rejected this appeal, 3–1, at an overflow hearing held February 28.

Voting for Villa Vallejo were Mayor Lobsinger, Sharek and councilman John Switzer. Voting to delay the project for consideration of the state's offer was councilman Henry J. Riboni. Councilwoman Nancy Parmelee abstained because her husband was attorney for Mrs. Annie Montini, owner of the property where Villa Vallejo was proposed to be built.

The February 28 hearing went on for three hours, and 25 persons spoke—some for, some against the housing project. The opponents of Villa Vallejo were individual speakers and others who represented the Congregational church, Sonoma Valley Environmental Council, Sonoma League for Historic Preservation and the state Department of Parks and Recreation.

The opponents of Villa Vallejo presented many arguments, but their major points revolved around open space and maintaining the character and heritage of Sonoma. They spoke of the "rape of progress" and said the Valley was going to be "engulfed in housing developments."

The proponents criticized the intervention of the state, spoke of the $11,000 in taxes the housing project would return annually to the city, and said the state had too much tax-free property in Sonoma anyway and that property rights had to be taken into consideration.

The two sides were sort of summed up by Paul Jess, representing the project opponents, and councilman Switzer.

Jess said the council should consider the interest of the other 30,000 people in the Valley rather than approve a controversial development for 120 families. Councilman Switzer said

that when it came to open space, "You can take a hike."

The write-ins announced their candidacies at the end of March. Both said they wanted to preserve the historic heritage of Sonoma but neither mentioned Villa Vallejo.

Prior to the April 11 election, the Villa Vallejo opponents were very busy. They enlisted the help of many volunteers and went door to door to hand out literature and explain their side of the issue.

On election day, they even stood the required distance from the polls handing out pencils to voters. There were no pencils (for writing in a name) in the voting booths, where ballots were marked with a little metal stylus.

In withdrawing the plans for Villa Vallejo after the election, the realtor involved wrote to the city that he was taking action because the state was apparently serious about buying the property.

The state did request $375,000 with which to buy the 12 acres, plus an additional 18 acres to the west and north of the Vallejo home. This was allocated in the 1972–73 budget.

The state said it was going to plant vineyards on its new property. To date, the financially hurting state department of parks and recreation has been unable to fulfill its promise.

Chess tournaments were popular events in the Sonoma Plaza during the 1960s. Local resident and renowned sculptor Marian Brackenridge, pictured at right, was among participants.

INDEX-TRIBUNE ARCHIVES

In May 1967 a swarm of bees made the pages of the *I-T* when they cooperated with painters, who were replacing the brand name "Signal" with "Enco" at Lee Clerici's service station on Broadway. The bees blotted out most of the old name before taking off. The low price of gasoline then is probably of greater interest today than the bees.

Gasoline crisis of 1973–74

*I*n the great gasoline crisis of 1973–74 our troubles did not begin with the Arabs. Most United States oil came from domestic sources, and only 10 percent came from the Middle East.

The oil embargo was sparked by what was known as the October War. But the shortage in Sonoma was being felt as early as May 1973.

In May suppliers set quotas on local dealers, and one had been forced to close. Others limited their hours or closed certain days.

Explanations for the shortage varied. Some said it was because foreign governments had expropriated U. S. refineries abroad. Others talked about how conservationists had blocked construction of the Alaska pipeline and limited offshore drilling. Still others claimed that the oil

companies were trying to get out of undesirable contracts with distributors and dealers.

By the beginning of October, gasoline cost from 38.9¢ to 45.9¢ per gallon in Sonoma. Station operators were fighting the Cost of Living Council, which controlled their price increases while suppliers' prices rose. Local dealers did not join a dealers' boycott, but they, too, felt the pinch.

The oil embargo was the catastrophe, the final blow. Valley citizens hoarded gas in their garages, sometimes illegally close to water heaters. They stored extra drums in car trunks, creating "Molotov cocktails." And they bought locking gas caps. But few wanted rationing.

Station operators here noted that price increases went to the oil companies, not to dealers. They observed that there seemed to be plenty of crude oil, but not enough refineries to process it.

Sometimes the crunch of cars was so bad that no one could get into or out of a service station. Dealers' hours were irregular and sometimes a secret to all but preferred customers. Most operators limited the number of gallons per customer. They closed on weekends but tried to be open for commuters.

Some said the environmentalists had miscalculated priorities. Others thought the crisis was the result of oil companies' or politicians' maneuverings.

At the beginning of March the Sonoma Valley Chamber of Commerce organized the odd-even rationing system, with 70 percent of the local dealers participating. Those whose cars had even-numbered license plates could get gas on even numbered days. Those with odd numbers, or with personalized license plates, got gas on odd-numbered days. The 31st of any month was to be a free day, if stations were open. Further, motorists could get gas only if they needed at least half a tank.

Saturday and Sunday closings continued, as did limits on the amount of gas purchased. But the lines were shorter after the chamber's plan was initiated.

A Federal Energy Office official from San Francisco insisted to Sonomans that the crisis was real, that old oil wells were drying up as soon as new ones were drilled and that consumption was increasing too fast.

"Sometime soon," he warned, "we must stop relying on fossil fuels."

Sonoman Allen Pangborn agreed with him: "Pretty soon ethyl alcohol made from grapes or potatoes will be cheaper. That's what they did during World War II."

The oil embargo ended in March. By May, the long lines were gone, but the prices ranged from 48.9¢ to 63¢ per gallon in Sonoma.

Having learned what a rare and precious commodity gasoline was, customers were prepared to face more price increases in the future. No more was heard about alternative fuels.

That spring the major oil companies quoted large quarterly profits.

No one, back then, would have foreseen that gasoline prices would someday reach those of today, especially for self-serve.   – SANDY SANDERS

Fire razed Boyes Springs bathhouse April 17, 1969

*I*t was the end of an era when the Boyes Hot Springs bathhouse was destroyed by a fire early on the morning of April 17, 1969.

Established as a resort in the 1880s by Capt. H. E. Boyes and rebuilt after the disastrous Valley fire of 1923, the bathhouse received its death blow in the 1969 fire. Proprietor Luis Vela kept the gutted place open with portable buildings for a couple of more seasons and said he had plans to build a Holiday Inn motel at the site, but nothing came of this.

The 24,000-square-foot vacation mecca was razed by one of the most spectacular fires ever seen in Sonoma Valley. Flames and burning gases rose 100–150 feet in the air during the height of the blaze and were visible as far away as Kenwood.

Lost in the fire were the indoor tennis court (formerly a dance hall and roller skating rink), the two cafes, bar, lounge, front lobby, offices, plus various deck and shade areas.

The locker room facilities, exercise room and resting tables were in a section of the building that was saved. They were never restored and, after several years in a dilapidated condition, were obliterated in another fire.

Mel Schwarz, the chief of the Valley of the Moon Fire Department, directed the efforts of the firefighters. There were 45 men at the blaze and 13 trucks. A number of these firemen and trucks were from other Valley departments responding under the mutual aid plan.

The loss was estimated at $75,000–$80,000, but replacement was estimated at $1,000,000.

Schwarz said there was no evidence of arson in the blaze, which was reported about 12:30 A.M. by an unknown informant who walked into the Boyes Springs firehouse of the VMFD.

The catastrophic blaze threatened to spread to several nearby buildings—whose walls were blistered from the heat—but firemen saved them by hosing them frequently. The firefighters used an estimated 100,000 gallons of water on the fire. No one was injured, although at one stage of the fire three firefighters had to dive off a roof that started to disintegrate beneath them.

The bathhouse was then owned by Vela and his father-in-law, Dr. Russell Wright, team physi-

INDEX-TRIBUNE ARCHIVES

INDEX-TRIBUNE ARCHIVES

The Boyes Hot Springs bathhouse and resort (at left) was destroyed by a swift-moving fire in 1969.

cian for the Detroit Tigers baseball team. Vela was the active manager of the resort. He was involved in many civic projects and at one time was president of the chamber of commerce.

He left the community and went to Florida with his family a few years after the fire.

The bathhouse was the inspiration of an Englishman who made a unique contribution to the Valley's history, Capt. H. E. Boyes. He uncovered an old mineral spring first dug by Dr. Thaddeus Leavenworth. The latter reputedly said he learned of the healing properties of the

mineral waters from the Indians.

The bathhouse attracted huge crowds of vacationers and pleasure seekers during the 1880s and 1890s and remained almost as popular after it was rebuilt in the 1920s.

The resort was the spring training ground for the old San Francisco Seals and Oakland Oaks of the Pacific Coast League.

Colorful managers such as Lefty O'Doul and Casey Stengel could often be seen on the diamond opposite the bathhouse.

After their workouts the athletes relaxed in

Fire destroyed the old Fetters Hot Springs resort hotel on March 23, 1975. The blaze reportedly started in the kitchen on the ground floor of the hotel which housed Juanita Musson's restaurant. A waitress occupying an upstairs room died in the early-morning fire.

the hot mineral pool and later took a plunge in the big, Olympic-size swimming pool. One spring, when constant rains prevented use of Lichtenberg Field, Stengel conducted baseball practices for the Oaks inside the big empty swimming pool inside the Boyes bathhouse.　　 – RML

VOM Water District formed

In the May 26, 1960, edition of the *Index-Tribune* it was reported that the voters of the upper Sonoma Valley area had given overwhelming approval to the formation of a county water district for their area.

Prior to that time, water for most of the upper Valley was furnished by two privately owned water companies, the Sonoma Water & Irrigation Company and the Mountain Avenue Water Company. There was also a water company in Glen Ellen.

A citizen's committee was formed in June 1959 to study the feasibility of establishing a municipal water district to service the Hot Springs–El Verano area. Sonoma County Planning Commission member Thomas Polidori, a resident of El Verano, headed the study committee, with the support of county supervisor Carson Mitchell.

There had been a good deal of concern expressed by Valley residents about the water supply source in Sonoma Valley, with the fear there was the danger of a shortage due to the increasing population.

The formation of the water district, it was thought, could expedite the delivery of the Coyote Dam water to the Valley via the Sonoma Aqueduct, as well as provide an agency which could investigate other water sources in the Valley.

The committee felt that consolidation of the two private water companies into one public body would conceivably produce a more efficient service and lead to reduced or, at the very least, equalized rates.

The consulting firm of Stone and Youngberg of San Francisco, which specialized in municipal financing, was hired by the Valley of the Moon Fire District to determine the financial feasibility of forming a municipal water district in the area.

The firm reported that the formation of a county water district which would buy out the two privately owned water companies was possible. They noted that the district, which would have approximately the same boundaries as the VOM Fire District, would have an assessed value of $5,000,000 and annual revenues of between $50,000 and $60,000. It would also have taxing powers.

The acquisition of the privately owned water companies, Stone and Youngberg reported, would most likely be financed by a bond issue. By a vote of 406 to 246, the voters of the upper Sonoma Valley area approved the formation of the Valley of the Moon County Water District.

They also elected the first board of directors for the district: Polidori, Arnold Griewe, A. L. Ford, Martin Carlson and Mel Larson.

At their first meeting, which was covered in the July 7, 1960, edition of the *Index-Tribune,* the board received its official charter from the Secretary of State's office in Sacramento. Guided by Richard Ramsey of the Sonoma County Counsel's office, they also elected Polidori to serve as the first chairman of the board.

From that moment on, the water use and service in the upper Sonoma Valley has been managed by the Valley of the Moon County Water District.　　 – BECKY GOEHRING

Thirteen air force men lost in crash

Early on the foggy morning of Monday, May 5, 1970, a T-29, two-engine, propeller-driven air force transport plane took off from Hamilton Air Force Base. A few moments later it lost radar and radio contact with the base. Sometime soon after this it crashed on the Mangels Ranch near Sears Point in Sonoma Valley. Thirteen airmen perished in the crash, Sonoma County's worst air disaster.

The first man to reach the scene was John Davieau, foreman of the Mangels Ranch. The scene that met his eyes looked like a battlefield. Burning wreckage and bodies littered the eucalyptus-dotted slope. In the center of this carnage, the plane's tail remained upright, seemingly a memorial for the dead.

One man survived the crash, Capt. George A. Burk, 29. He was discovered about 35 yards from the wreckage by Davieau. He was badly burned on the face and body and was in a state of shock.

"My God, please help me," he moaned. Davieau, who tried to shut those who were dead from his mind, said, "It was the guy hollering for help who really shook me up."

Davieau had been out on one of his inspection trips about the ranch, checking cattle, when he noticed smoke and went to the scene of the crash in an isolated area of the huge ranch.

This was about 8:45 A.M. Rescuers quickly converged on the scene, including Schell-Vista and Sonoma firemen, Sheriff's deputies, California Highway Patrolmen, Norrbom's ambulance, a team from Hamilton AFB with several ambulances, and the coast guard, which sent three helicopters.

Captain Burk was airlifted out and later in the day was flown to Brooke Army Medical Center at Fort Sam Houston, Texas, a burn treatment center. He miraculously recovered.

The air force cordoned off the area and gathered the dead. The bodies were marked by little black flags with white crosses. Eleven were quickly located, but the last two were not found until late Monday afternoon.

They were taken to a morgue at Travis Air Force Base.

The T-29 was on a routine training flight to Spokane, Wash. Among the dead was an airman who was "hitching" a ride to his home in that city.

Air force investigators scoured the scene for days, aided by experts from as far away as the Wright-Patterson Air Force Base in Ohio.

– JERRY PARKER

Dr. C. B. Andrews founded VOM Boys Club

Dr. Carroll B. Andrews retired in 1973 after 40 years of service to his community as a doctor and community benefactor.

The Nebraska-born physician graduated from Stanford Medical School and came to Sonoma in 1933. In addition to his tireless service to his patients (doctors used to make house calls, remember?), Andrews also worked to establish a district hospital.

Such a hospital was set up here in 1945 in an old two-story building (now a winery) owned by Frank Bartholomew. It was a great improvement over the old Burndale Sanitarium, the makeshift hospital used earlier. The present hospital on Andrieux Street was opened in 1957.

Dr. Andrews had a keen interest in community affairs. It was in keeping with his generosity, then, when he bought the old Sonoma Grammar School in 1952 (abandoned in 1949 when its structural integrity was found faulty) and turned it into the Community Center.

This building is used for many cultural, musical and artistic purposes today. Some years after he bought it, Dr. Andrews made an outright gift of it to the community.

It also housed for a number of years the Boys Club, of which he was the principal founder. The club was formed in the early '60s and made its headquarters at the Community Center until it moved into the former Hospital Linen Service building on First Street West. Now known as the Valley of the Moon Boys & Girls Club, it has grown into an organization serving hundreds of Valley youngsters, both boys and girls. Here they enjoy sports and games of all kinds.

Over the years, Dr. Andrews trained many

INDEX-TRIBUNE ARCHIVES

The Valley of the Moon Boys Club, the brainchild of Dr. Carroll B. Andrews, was formed in the early '60s. Today the club's membership of 1,700—and its name—also includes girls.

new doctors in his office. Most of them stayed in the community. He passed away here on July 11, 1990.

Sonoma Mission's 150th birthday observed

The 150th anniversary of the founding of the Sonoma Mission—the last and most northerly of the 21-mission chain which begins at San Diego—was observed by Sonoma Valley in 1973.

A series of events were planned from May through September to mark the Mission Sesquicentennial. And the *Index-Tribune* published a 48-page illustrated booklet giving a history of the Mission.

The sesquicentennial was planned by a non-profit corporation called the Mission Sesquicentennial Commission, formed in February 1971.

The members were chairman Robert D. Parmelee, Mary Bundschu, Robert H. Cannard, Camille Cochran, Robert M. Lynch, Henri Maysonnave, Dick Menefee, James F. Millerick, Morie Morrison and Henry J. Riboni.

The first sesquicentennial event was a house and garden tour on May 27.

Events held during June included a Plaza art show, ox roast, garden party and arts and crafts festival, Bear Flag Day ceremonies, antique show, Petaluma-to-Sonoma walkathon and horse show.

Events which took place in July included a big rodeo and pioneer day, tours of historic monuments, a square dance festival, Fourth of July celebrations here and in Kenwood, a stamp exhibit, a turkey barbecue, and a DAR plaque rededication for Capt. William Smith, the only Revolutionary War veteran buried in California.

The big day, of course, was July 4th. It started with a rededication and blessing of the Mission by Bishop Mark J. Hurley of the Santa Rosa Diocese. There was a big parade at 11 followed by a chicken barbecue in the Plaza.

At 2:30 P.M., patriotic ceremonies were held on the north side of the Plaza. Maysonnave was chairman and Congressman Don Clausen was the speaker.

The Sonoma Valley Chorale entertained, and

during the afternoon there were also special dance programs and folk dancing.

The day concluded with a spectacular fireworks display at Arnold Field. A barbecue in September and the Vintage Festival that month were the last events of the Mission Sesquicentennial.   – RML

Almost overlooked: 1978–79 stories

AUTHOR'S NOTE: During research for this book, it became evident that some significant events during an exceptionally "happening-filled" 1978 and 1979 had been omitted from the *Index-Tribune*'s centennial issue, probably due to early-deadline and space considerations. The 114-page special issue had to be printed well in advance of its July 1979 publication date because of press capacity limitations at that time. Among these "overlooked significant happenings" that are part of the Sonoma Valley story are the following from the *I-T* pages:

First industrial park

Jan. 5, 1978—The $1,200,000 Sonoma Industrial Park, the first project of its kind in this area, is now under construction on Eighth Street East.

Ads on the Barracks east wall

Jan. 26, 1978—Workmen employed by the state Department of Parks and Recreation started tearing down the east wall of the historic Barracks building—the wall on which the colorful old advertisements for Monotti's grocery store, Levi Strauss jeans and Folger's coffee are remembered by many Sonomans.

Sonoma's two major-leaguers

April 13, 1978—John Henry Johnson, the 21-year-old former Sonoma Valley High School baseball star, did the unexpected Monday night at the Oakland Coliseum when he threw a two-hit shutout for the Oakland Athletics in his first appearance ever as a major-league pitcher, beating the Seattle Mariners, 1–0. It was the home opener of the season for the A's.

Johnson, son of Theron and Clarice Johnson of Boyes Hot Springs, is the second Sonoma High graduate to make it to the major leagues. The first was Dan Briggs, son of Mr. and Mrs. Lee Briggs of Sonoma, who was drafted by the California Angels' organization in 1970 and was called up to the parent club on June 16, 1976, from the Angels' triple-A Salt Lake City farm team as a first base-man-outfielder.

Briggs and Johnson, both plagued by injuries during their respective careers, are no longer in baseball but still hold the distinction of being the only two Sonoma Valley boys to have played in the majors.

County funds for Depot Museum

March 30, 1978—James Vanderbilt, leader of the Sonoma Valley Historical Society's project to raise funds for the rebuilding of the Sonoma Depot for use as a museum, received word that the Sonoma County Board of Supervisors has allocated $10,000 toward the project. The original depot burned down in January 1976. The county grant, plus insurance money and city funding received, will assist the historical society's public fund-raising drive to cover the estimated $114,000 cost of recreating the original depot for use as a museum of Sonoma Valley history.

Mrs. "Hap" Arnold dies here at 91

June 29, 1978—Eleanor P. (Bea) Arnold, widow of World War II's General of the Air Force, Henry H. (Hap) Arnold, died Monday at Sonoma Valley Hospital at the age of 91.

First Sonoma policewoman

July 27, 1978—Sonoma has its first policewoman, Beverly A. Sevier, 24, of Benicia; and she beat out 70 candidates (mostly men) for the job.

Marketplace ground breaking

Oct. 12, 1978—A ground-breaking ceremony was held yesterday for Sonoma's newest shopping center, the Sonoma Marketplace, to be located at Napa and Second Street West.

Hello to new library

Nov. 2, 1978—They moved the books out of the old Sonoma city library yesterday, and it marked the end of an era. The quaint, yellow-brick building in the Plaza, built in 1913 with the assistance of an Andrew Carnegie grant, is being replaced by the big, new regional library at 755 West Napa Street.

INDEX-TRIBUNE ARCHIVES

Jim Lynch of the *I-T* staff interviewed John Henry Johnson during an A's game at the Oakland Coliseum.

State buys additional 700 acres of Jack London Ranch

Jan. 4, 1979—The California Public Works Board has allocated $1,069,200 for the purchase of an additional 700 acres of the original Jack London ranch in Glen Ellen, which will be added to Jack London State Historic Park, it was disclosed this week. At the time of the famed author's death in November 1916, his ranch encompassed some 1,400 acres.

The park, opened to the public Sept. 1, 1960, was created in 1959 when a small portion—about 40 acres—of Beauty Ranch was acquired by the state, partly through a gift from Irving Shepard, London's nephew and an heir to his estate. The original park included London's grave, the ruins of Wolf House and Charmian's House of Happy Walls. Additional acreage has been added over the years, so that today the park contains more than 800 acres, including many of the ranch buildings and the cottage where London wrote much of his later work.

Approximately 190 acres of the London Ranch is still held by Jack London's heirs. Milo Shepard, a grandnephew, heir and most recent executor of the author's estate, initially created a 40-acre vineyard on the retained acreage.

He has expanded it into 130 acres which today produce merlot, cabernet sauvignon, cabernet franc, zinfandel, pinot noir and sirah wine grapes. Kenwood Vineyards leases the acreage, which is still under Shepard's supervision.

Now semi-retired, Shepard is still deeply involved in the technical handling of Jack London's literary works, and working with colleges and universities in assisting students and other researchers of the famed author's writings.

Hospital board's first woman president

March 22, 1979—The newly elected president of the Sonoma Valley Hospital board, Marie Cherms, is the first woman named to the previously male-dominated

Interior of the Sonoma Valley Regional Library on West Napa Street.

position. Holder of a master's degree in home economics from the University of Rhode Island, she was a school teacher before the birth of a first child, Lois, now 21. She and her husband, Frank, coordinator of research for Nicholas Turkey Breeding Farms, also have a son, Mark, 19. Marie has taken an active role in the community since moving to Sonoma a number of years ago.

Exchange Bank's grand opening

March 29, 1979—Grand opening ceremonies were held March 24, for the new Sonoma branch of the Exchange Bank at 435 West Napa Street. The 5,000-square-foot, $358,119 structure features Spanish-style architecture, with balconies both inside and outside the building. Founded in 1890 by Manville Doyle, this is number 14 of the bank's branches, all in Sonoma County. Richard Jonas is branch manager.

Pizza parlor success story

May 31, 1979—Mary's Pizza Shack, the most successful pizza parlor in the history of Sonoma Valley, celebrates its 20th anniversary today, with the public invited to come in and enjoy a piece of anniversary cake at the new business site at 18636 Sonoma Highway. Founder Mary Fazio first opened her business in 1959 in a tiny cottage on Highway 12 in Boyes Springs.

Depot Museum dedicated

June 21, 1979—The Depot Museum, an exact replica of the 100-year-old Sonoma railroad depot which burned down in 1976, was dedicated today under the auspices of the Sonoma Valley Historical Society, with some 200

Horses and riders at Jack London State Park.

people in attendance. James Vanderbilt, the museum's director, was master of ceremonies for the program. The historical society raised over $50,000, the city contributed its $50,000 insurance money and Sonoma County gave approximately $50,000 for the rebuilding of the historic depot. The museum is open Wednesday through Sunday, from 1 to 4:30 P.M.

First store to open in Sonoma Marketplace

June 28, 1979—Albertsons supermarket became the first business to open in the Sonoma Marketplace shopping center at Napa and Second Street West yesterday. A ribbon-cutting ceremony, participated in by city, chamber of commerce and Albertsons officials, highlighted the 9 A.M. opening of the 28,000-square-foot supermarket which employs 60 people.

Sebastiani Vineyards' expansion plan rejected

July 12, 1979—Sebastiani Vineyards' revised five-year expansion plan for its long-established winery on Fourth Street East was rejected on a 3–2 vote by the Sonoma City Council Tuesday night. Major reasons for the plan's defeat centered on its "out-of-scale" plan for the site so close to residential areas, and increase in traffic volume.

Index-Tribune centennial edition published

July 19, 1979—Printing of more than 12,000 copies of the 114-page 100th anniversary special edition of *The Sonoma Index-Tribune* was completed this week, with subscribers receiving the history- and photo-filled centennial edition with today's regular weekly issue. Tours of the newspaper plant will be offered at an open house for the public on Saturday.

INDEX-TRIBUNE ARCHIVES

The front cover of *The Sonoma Index-Tribune*'s 100th anniversary edition, published July 19, 1979. Cover design and art work were by noted Sonoma Valley artist Jack Bradbury, an *I-T* staffer.

$11.5-million Schellville plant expansion

Aug. 2, 1979—Construction of new facilities now in progress at the Sonoma Valley sewage disposal plant on Eighth Street East in Schellville will enable it to handle a peak winter load of 16½ million gallons per day as compared to the present capacity of approximately 11 million gallons. The additions to the sewage plant and the new pipeline are being built at a cost of approximately $11.5 million. The federal government is paying 75 percent of the total cost, the state 12½ percent and the county 12½ percent.

Voters OK new police station

Sept. 20, 1979—City of Sonoma voters at Tuesday's special election approved, by a narrow margin, Measure 2, a plan to build a new police station on First Street West, opposite the veterans memorial building. There were 747 yes votes, and 691 noes. Measure 1, an initiative ordinance submitted by city critic Garth Eliassen calling for an election before the city could act on developing a civic center site opposite the veterans' building, also won—by just 41 votes. Measure 1 was termed illegal by city attorney John Klein, but Superior Court Judge Bryan Jamar ordered the city to hold the election following an appeal brought by Eliassen. Jamar did not give any opinion about the legality of the ordinance.

Sonoma League for Historic Preservation's 10th birthday

Oct. 18, 1979—The Sonoma League for Historic Preservation is celebrating the 10th anniversary of its founding this

INDEX-TRIBUNE ARCHIVES

Hand-inserting the nine sections of the *I-T*'s centennial issue proved a formidable task in 1979. Even editor and publisher Bob Lynch (above) joined in. Today an automated inserting machine handles such chores.

INDEX-TRIBUNE ARCHIVES

James Vanderbilt (center), director of the Sonoma Valley Historical Society's Depot Museum, and mayor Nancy Parmelee at the museum's dedication June 21, 1979.

month. Margaret Eliassen was founder of the League in 1969 and has been given credit for many of its early accomplishments. A few of its projects to date have included assisting the city in creating appropriate lighting for the Plaza; sponsoring a local historic landmarks photography contest; restoring the Toscano Hotel on Spain Street; moving the historic old Vasquez House, donated by Mr. and Mrs. Robert M. Lynch, from its location behind the *Index-Tribune* to its El Paseo location and remodeling it for use as League headquarters; compiling "The Sonoma Valley Historical Resource Survey," which was completed in 1978; and hosting events like "Cutting Day," offering a free exchange of plants and nursery information.

Vietnamese "boat family" welcomed

Oct. 25, 1979—The Vietnamese "boat family" adopted by the Sonoma Valley community finally arrived here Sunday, bringing to fruition the months-long efforts of a steering committee, headed by Sandy Piotter, and its many volunteers.

The family of eight, headed by En Ngo, 42, and his wife, Hue, 34, consists of their five children: Van, 12; Phu, 10; Tuyet, 9; Hao, 7; and Trung, 5; and Mrs. Ngo's sister, Ken, 17. Mr. Ngo was a rice merchant in Vietnam. The family fled their country at the time of the Communist takeover. Mr. Ngo booked passage for them on a small, refugee-filled craft, later rescued from the turbulent South China Sea. In the months preceding the Ngos' arrival, the Friends of the Boat People had been busy collecting financial support and donations of food, clothing and other necessities, locating a house and finding a translator to help overcome the language difficulties.

Sonoma Post Office is 130 years old

Nov. 1, 1979—The Sonoma Post Office turns 130 years old next month, along with post offices in San Francisco and Monterey. They share the distinction of being the oldest California post offices established after the American occupation. Alcalde Lilburn Boggs was named Sonoma's first postmaster on Nov. 8, 1849.

Historian-author Richard Paul Papp in his book *Bear Flag Country,* published in 1996, reveals that a post office and mail routes for Sonoma were established about June 27, 1849, and the Sonoma Post Office was actually operating at least six months prior to the creation of Sonoma County itself, and more than a year before California became a state.

Voters approve
Warm Springs Dam (again)

Nov. 8, 1979—Sonoma Valley voters joined with those of the county Tuesday in support of continuing construction of the Warm Springs Dam, as 79,524 of the county's 247,231 registered voters (54.2 percent) went to the polls. County Measure A, which asked the board of supervisors to withdraw from its agreement with the U. S. Army Corps of Engineers to participate in the $240-million flood control, water supply and recreation dam project, received a resounding defeat—56,537 voting no (72.71 percent) and 21,213 (27.28 percent) voting against continuance of the dam project. The great support for the dam indicated by the vote was even more significant, considering that voters in 1974 endorsed the project by the slim majority of 51.2 percent. Despite the fact that $40 million has already been expended on the dam project, a well-organized opposition, led by environmentalists, staged a very visible and vocal campaign. They said the dam was not needed, would cause population growth, raise taxes and destroy trout streams, vineyards and orchards. From the overwhelming approval given Warm Springs Dam at Tuesday's election, it is obvious that the vast majority of voters believed otherwise.

Buena Vista Vineyards, winery
sold to major European firm

Nov. 8, 1979—Buena Vista Winery and vineyards, founded here by Count Agoston Haraszthy in 1857 and recognized as California's oldest winery, has been sold to A. Racke, a corporation that is a major European producer, exporter and importer of wine and liquor, it was learned this week. Young's Market Company, a large Los Angeles-based wine, liquor and food distributor, has owned the winery since purchasing it from Frank H.

Known as the Vasquez House for its early-day occupants, the 140-year-old building in the El Paseo complex off First Street East serves as headquarters for the Sonoma League for Historic Preservation.

Bartholomew in 1968. Dr. Georg Moller-Racke, chairman of the German corporation, stated that the company's objective is to maintain and enlarge upon Buena Vista's position as a producer of premium wines.

Sonoma's second
set of traffic signals

Nov. 15, 1979—Starting Monday, motorists will be required to take note of the red, yellow and green vagaries of the newly installed traffic signals at the intersection of Napa and Second

INDEX-TRIBUNE ARCHIVES

The "Spirit of '76" was captured in many Sonoma Fourth of July parades, in past years, by the local trio of Jeff Ball, school district superintendent John Glaese and Roberta Slater.

Street West. Sonoma's second-ever signalization project was paid for by the developers of the new Sonoma Marketplace shopping center located at the downtown intersection. Another traffic signal at Four Corners (Broadway and Leveroni Road) is scheduled for completion before Christmas, it was learned yesterday.

Part Three

SONOMA VALLEY NEWSMAKERS
1980–1996

As We Come to the End of Our Story

Introduction
to
Part Three

Sonoma Valley Newsmakers, 1980–1996

Part Three, covering the period 1980 through 1996, found the author often asking himself, "Is this history?" while researching the *Index-Tribune* files. Somehow, what occurred in Sonoma Valley in the past 16 years seemed hard to classify as "historic," because the so recent happenings were part of my own week-to-week life. But that is probably how *I-T* editor Harry Granice, my grandfather, would also have felt had he decided to write a book during his tenure from 1884 to 1915.

So, for this "modern-day history" recap in *The Sonoma Valley Story,* I relied, for the most part, on the front-page stories appearing in our newspaper. As the reader can appreciate, selecting the "most important" stories from close to 1,500 front pages—averaging five to six stories on each front page—from the period 1980 through 1996 alone, was a real challenge for me. Had I attempted to excerpt something from every single front-page story, this book could have had the bulky appearance of an *Encyclopedia Brittanica,* its weight capable of cracking your coffee table or bookcase.

Upon reflection, this concluding part of *The Sonoma Valley Story,* like the two sections preceding it, may have a dominant theme as you read about the past in this most special Valley of all the earth. That theme is growth. When and if a sequel to this book is ever written (and I hope it will be), perhaps its emphasis will be on how the Valley dealt with that growth.

24 New Beginnings and Sad Endings: 1980–1985

August Sebastiani, who joined his father, Samuele Sebastiani, in the wine business in 1934, nurtured the family's Sonoma winery to national prominence before his death in 1980 at age 66.

INDEX-TRIBUNE ARCHIVES

1980

*T*he year 1980 began on a sad note. *The Sonoma Index-Tribune*'s lead front-page story on February 21 told of the death of August Sebastiani, "as familiar to Sonomans in his striped overalls as the old Mission and Blue Wing landmarks a few blocks from his winery." The 66-year-old patriarch of the local wine family died on February 16 at his hillside home following a lingering illness and series of operations for cancer.

The funeral Mass at St. Francis Solano Church on February 21 was attended by an overflow throng of mourners estimated at more than 800. Burial was in Mountain Cemetery, close by

the winery which he had nurtured to national prominence since joining his father, Samuele Sebastiani, in the wine business in 1934.

Other significant 1980 happenings included the groundbreaking, on April 7, for the new 6,000-square-foot, $588,440 Sonoma police station on First Street West, across from Arnold Field; approval, in May, by the Sonoma County Board of Supervisors to expend $261,000 for 35 acres of Maxwell Farm for a regional park; reopening (on June 13) of the Sonoma Mission Inn after a multimillion-dollar refurbishing by developer Edward Safdie; the announcement by city officials that by September some 59 utility poles, plus thousands of yards of cable for electric service and telephones, would be eliminated by the current undergrounding project, the third such project in Sonoma; adoption by the city council, on August 11, of an ordinance limiting growth to 100 new housing units per year.

1981

*B*y the end of February 1981, the new Sonoma police station at 175 First Street West was open for business, the move from the old Patten Street station adjoining the firehouse virtually complete.

At Sonoma Valley Hospital, groundbreaking ceremonies signifying the start of the $5,700,000 construction project—which was to include a new one-story east wing and parking facilities, and make the west wing seismically sound—were held March 1. The long-awaited project was the culmination of a successful multi-million-dollar lawsuit against those responsible for architectural engineering errors discovered in 1977 in the relatively new west wing which state inspection officials declared seismically unsafe. Building of the east wing was completed before contractors tackled the rebuilding and seismic corrections to the west wing. Patients formerly housed in the west wing were accommodated in both the new wing and original central section of the hospital while the west wing was being strengthened and brought up to state seismic standards.

1982

*T*he year 1982 started off positively for *The Sonoma Index-Tribune*, which became California's most honored weekly in its circulation category, winning eight awards in various classifications, including the coveted first-place plaque for General Excellence, in the annual California Newspaper Publishers Association Better Newspaper Contest.

The oldest winery building in California, the press house of Buena Vista Winery's Haraszthy Cellars, Sonoma, built in 1862, was opened after a complete restoration. Special May 15 ceremonies were presided over by officials of the A. Racke firm, the winery's owners.

The official dedication of the new Sonoma branch of the Bank of America, formerly site of the historic Union Hotel and Union Hall, at Napa and First Street West, took place on May 22.

Judges at the first annual San Francisco Fair and Exposition Sourdough French Bread Competition in June voted Gratien Guerra and his Sonoma French Bakery makers of the finest French bread in and around the nine counties of the Bay Area.

1983

*S*onomans who thought Mother Nature unusually generous with her rain quota during the winter of 1982 and spring of '83 had their suspicions verified on Saturday, April 23. On that date 1.38 inches of rain was measured by state Department of Parks & Recreation personnel on the weather gauge located at the Vallejo Home state monument, pushing the season's total to an all-time city seasonal record of 54.17 inches. Normal average rainfall through April is 27.32 inches. Amazingly enough, Sonoma city's record rainfall to that date was considered a pittance compared to measurements recorded by gauges in other parts of Sonoma Valley. What must be an all-time, all-Valley record of 112.45 inches of rain for the season was measured through April 25, 1983, by Nelson Custer in Plant Operations at the Sonoma State Hospital, Eldridge.

Introduced as the newly selected principal of Altimira Middle School at the May 24 meeting of the Sonoma Valley Unified School District board of trustees was Marilyn Kelly, 42, who would soon leave her post as principal of the Brittan Acres School in the San Carlos Unified School District. She succeeded Bruce Griewe, who had become principal at Agua Caliente Continuation High School. Prior to being named principal at the Brittan Acres School, Ms. Kelly was principal for seven years at Central Middle School in the San Carlos district.

On July 16 the city of Sonoma formally dedicated its spacious, two-story, newly remodeled firehouse at 32 Patten Street, with mayor Henry Riboni as master of ceremonies. Features of the half-million-dollar fire station project included a glass solarium fronting the entrance, designed to help heat the facility during the winter. At the dedication Fire Chief Al Mazza expressed thanks to city officials, the paid and volunteer firefighters, and everyone involved in the development of

INDEX-TRIBUNE ARCHIVES

A painting by a New Zealand artist, showing a fly fisherman and leaping rainbow trout, is held (above) by Audrey Barnard of the Sonoma Valley Chamber of Commerce and the author, in 1984. The watercolor commemorated the 100th anniversary of the 1883 founding of New Zealand's famed trout fishing industry which was started with fingerlings shipped from the old LaMotte Fish Hatchery on Sonoma Creek near Glen Ellen 114 years ago. The original painting was presented by the U. S. Ambassador to New Zealand to California Gov. George Deukmejian, who had a duplicate sent to the chamber of commerce here. It is now in the collection of the Sonoma Valley Historical Society's Depot Park Museum.

the new station. In his remarks, Mayor Riboni included a brief history of the Sonoma Volunteer Fire Department, which was founded in 1888.

Ralph Hahn, 40, vice principal for three years of Santa Fe High School in Southern California's Whittier School District, was chosen July 26 as Sonoma Valley High School's new principal by the board of trustees, after a lengthy search. He succeeded Harold W. Gray, who retired after 14 years.

David W. Eraldi, World War II navy veteran, local clothing merchant, founder of the Sonoma Valley Athletic Club and the "father of Arnold Field," died August 24 at the age of 62.

The redevelopment plan for the Sonoma Community Redevelopment Agency was formally adopted Monday, November 28, by the city council. The policy statement included a two-point resolution that the agency directors shall have no power of eminent domain and shall not condemn private property for public purposes. Funded through county tax revenues, city redevelopment projects here have included the public parking lot

behind the Barracks and Toscano Hotel north of Spain Street, remodeling of City Hall [and, most recently, the remodeling of the old Carnegie library building in the Plaza].

1984

Sonoma Valley's significant happenings in 1984 included two headline sports items in the February 15 issue of the *Index-Tribune*. The high school wrestling team, coached by Roger Winslow, won its first Sonoma County League Championship since 1969. Freshman Tony Edwards upset an El Molino opponent in the heavyweight division of the SCL tournament on Saturday, February 11, to clinch the undisputed title for the Dragon grapplers. It was his first and only win of the season. During his three subsequent years in high school Edwards was to become the SCL's top heavyweight wrestler.

The other sports headline of February 15 proclaimed the hiring of Mick O'Meara as head varsi-

INDEX-TRIBUNE ARCHIVES

Ralph (Babe) Pinelli, former major league infielder who became a celebrated umpire, was a popular resident of Sonoma Valley from 1956 until his death here in 1984. In photo with him is the Rev. Father John Roberts, a beloved pastor of St. Francis Solano Catholic Church here from 1946 until 1968.

ty football coach at Sonoma High. An assistant grid coach the past three years here, O'Meara succeeded Stan Augustine, who resigned that post in January. A graduate of Santa Clara University, O'Meara served as offensive coordinator for the King City High School football team for four years, prior to coming to Sonoma.

In politics, Janet Nicholas of Sonoma posted a stunning upset over incumbent Bob Adams in the June election for 1st District Supervisor, winning 51.4 percent of the vote to Adams' 30.5 percent.

The city council on September 17 voted to grant a use permit for the 75-room downtown Sonoma Valley Inn, after four hours of testimony. The council upheld 4–1 the planning commission's decision to grant the use permit, after voting 3–2 to certify the final environmental impact report. Extending the length of the council meeting were discussions calling for design changes, concern over PCB (polychlorinated biphenyls, possibly carcinogenic compounds) monitoring at the site, then the location of PG&E's corporation yard; and a request by councilman Kenneth McTaggart that the city conduct an in-depth study of tourism's role here before making a decision on the hotel proposal.

Deaths of two prominent Sonoma Valley residents—retired major league umpire Ralph (Babe) Pinelli, 89, and George Nicholas, 68, turkey mag-nate, were recorded in the Oct. 24 and Nov. 28, 1984, issues, respectively, of the *Index-Tribune*. Pinelli, who wrote a book titled *Mr. Ump*, retired from baseball and settled here after umpiring in the 1956 World Series, where he was behind the plate when Don Larsen of the New York Yankees on October 8 pitched the only no-hit, no-run game in World Series history, a 2–0 victory over the Brooklyn Dodgers. Pinelli was a genial, well-liked personage in the Valley, where he willingly spoke at countless dinner events and was an active booster for youth baseball.

Nicholas, whose company was recognized internationally as tops in the turkey production field, was the epitome of a Horatio Alger success story. A 1934 graduate of Petaluma High School, where he won fame in the Future Farmers of America as California's first Star Farmer, he studied poultry breeding at UC Davis from 1934 to 1937, moving to Sonoma Valley in 1939 with his bride, the former Eleen (Johnnie) Johnson of Petaluma. Here he started the Nicholas Turkey Breeding Farms on Napa Road. In those days the big, dark-feathered "broad-breasted bronze" turkey variety was in vogue, with Valley growers like Art Walters and Harvey Griffin in the forefront. Using the emphasis on genetics taught by Dr. V. S. Asmundsen at UC Davis, George Nicholas in a few years had captured the Western states turkey-breeding market, and later became the world's first major breeder to switch entirely to white-feathered turkeys. When he and the other shareholders sold the company for close to $10 million in 1978, Nicholas Turkey Breeding Farms, with headquarters still in Sonoma, provided over 60 percent of the breeding behind the world's turkeys, its eggs producing an estimated 140 million turkeys throughout the world. [Although now owned by a British conglomerate, world headquarters for Nicholas Turkey Breeding Farms remain in Sonoma, where George Nicholas hatched his first turkey eggs nearly 60 years ago.]

On November 27, 1984, the Sonoma County Board of Supervisors unanimously approved the Boyes Hot Springs 30-year redevelopment project. The 325-acre Boyes project area was slated for street infrastructure improvements, adding curbs and gutters and improving drainage flows; and providing offstreet parking, plus more road improvements along, and including, Highway 12.

COURTESY, SONOMA MISSION INN & SPA

The Sonoma Mission Inn at Boyes Hot Springs, built in 1926, has become one of Northern California's top-rated resort hotels and spas following multi-million-dollar facelifts and state-of-the-art expansions in recent years. The first major modernization, which included all new guest rooms, spa, tennis courts and a second pool, was completed in 1980 by then owner Edward Safdie, an East Coast developer. Rahn Properties, a Florida-based owner and operator of hotels, purchased the inn from Safdie in 1984, adding 70 rooms and convention facilities.

The project, which is paid for by tax increments, was anticipated to cost $26.3 million, with nearly $5 million destined for housing improvements.

Sonoma Valley and County were connected to the 911 emergency telephone system in December.

In a major end-of-year property transaction, Rahn Properties, a Fort Lauderdale, Florida-based hotel owner, operator and developer, filed a use permit application with the county to add 70 guest rooms to the Sonoma Mission Inn—in anticipation of a future purchase of the luxury resort then owned by New York and California real estate investor Ed Safdie. Safdie bought the aging

queen of North Bay resort hotels, built here in 1926, for a reported $2.5 million and undertook a multi-million-dollar refurbishing of the existing 96 rooms, building and grounds. Following the renovation in 1980, Safdie boasted the Inn would be "the finest luxury inn in California, netting $5 million by 1985 and creating an additional $25 million a year in the local economy." [The sale by Safdie to Rahn Properties for $16.5 million was confirmed March 31 by the resort's new general manager, Peter Henry. The new owners, who took over April 15, immediately embarked on a 70-room expansion project.]

The Vintage House senior center saga

INDEX-TRIBUNE ARCHIVES

Jerry Casson (second from left), founder of Vintage House, participated in groundbreaking ceremonies for the senior center on May 21, 1988. Hundreds of visitors, most of them contributors to the $1-million project's building fund, took part in the open house when doors opened on Feb. 19, 1989, following a gala dinner and dance the evening before in the center's Stone Hall. Others in photo, from left: Mayor Larry Murphy; J. R. (Bob) Stone, fund drive leader; Vintage House board president Wanda Stamos; and 1st District Supervisor Janet Nicholas.

That Sonoma Valley is blessed with perhaps the most caring and generous residents of any like-sized community has been proven time and again by the volunteer and monetary support given worthwhile causes and projects, small and large. No better example is the remarkable saga of Vintage House—The Jerry Casson Multipurpose Center for Seniors, which opened its doors here in February 1989.

Miss Casson, a retired social worker, for years a Valley leader in assisting those in need, founded—with devoted associates—the nonprofit center for older adults in 1977 with assistance from a one-time federal grant and community contributions. Rental space for the seniors' center was graciously provided by the Sonoma Congregational Church on Spain Street. Looking to the future, Casson and crew subsequently established a building fund, the earnings from donations and various fund-raising events—spaghetti and hot dog feeds, dances and rummage sales, etc.—reaching close to $50,000 in 1985.

Impetus was added the next year when Vintage House received a $127,099 state Senior Center Bond Act contract. The city's contribution of a building site was followed by approval from the Sonoma County Board of Supervisors of $61,000 in Community Block Grant funds and the formation of an all-out building fund campaign committee headed by J. R. (Bob) Stone. Some 20 community leaders volunteered their services as solicitors for the building fund drive, joining in the effort with the original Vintage House building fund campaign board members, with early-morning strategy sessions held weekly. Citizens, businesses, churches and other organizations responded to solicitations made by volunteers.

The architect's depiction and site plan for the proposed new Vintage House were submitted to the city in March 1987 by architect Victor Conforti. The 200-foot-long building, to be built on city-owned land bordered by First Street East, Second Street East and the bike path, would replace the rented church quarters on Spain Street.

While founder Jerry Casson was recovering from a stroke, in June 1987, the Vintage House board voted unanimously to name the new building for her. The public, in an obvious tribute to her good works, responded with overwhelming support of the building project during the remainder of 1987 and throughout 1988—so much so that as of Dec. 31, 1988, the Vintage House Building Fund board was able to announce that an unbelievable $1,028,432 had been subscribed.

In terms of receipts and community support, it was believed to be the most successful fund-raising project in the history of Sonoma Valley. Actually, the amazing sum raised proved in the end to be needed. Forced to increase its stated building cost goal on several occasions—due to the imposition of certain fees by governmental and special district entities, plus other unforeseen costs—the committee of volunteer fund-raisers in the fall of 1988 finally set its goal for $965,000.

It was on Saturday night, Feb. 18, 1989, that a benefit event called "The Gala" celebrating the opening of Vintage House was held. There were 250 people who contributed up to $100 a plate to attend the sold-out dinner, dance and ceremonies. The next day, Sunday, hundreds of people thronged the special open house, applauding the beautiful building which was officially dedicated.

1985

*T*he entrance of 1985 coincided with the exit of dedicated and dynamic Helen Fernandez from her post as executive director of the Sonoma Valley Chamber of Commerce after 12 years. The effervescent community servant who came here in 1958 with her husband, Barney, was honored at a sell-out testimonial dinner February 14 at the Sonoma National Golf Club.

First Place, General Excellence—the highest statewide award presented annually by the California Newspaper Publishers Association— was again won by *The Sonoma Index-Tribune*. The honor was bestowed February 16 at CNPA's 97th annual convention held at the Fairmont Hotel, San Francisco. It marked the third time in four years that the First Place, General Excellence recognition was given the *Index-Tribune*, which had also achieved the same distinction in 1981 and 1983.

Frank H. Bartholomew, known as Bart to his friends, a former president of United Press International, who intertwined bylines with grapevines in a colorful and exciting 70-year career, died March 26 at his Buena Vista Vineyards ranch here at the age of 86 after a long bout with cancer. It was only a year prior to his death that Bartholomew's book, *Bart: His Memoirs*, was published, telling of his fascinating life as a journalist. He walked and talked with notables of the world, dodged Japanese bullets and bombs as a World War II correspondent, covered the Japanese surrender aboard the *U. S. S. Missouri* in Tokyo Bay, and managed to squeeze in two more wars as an eyewitness correspondent— along with helping to make Sonoma Valley wine history by restoring to life the Buena Vista vines and wines which originated here in the 1850s under the guidance of Hungarian nobleman Col. Agoston Haraszthy.

After more than two years in the planning process, Roger Hillbrook's controversial Four Corners motel-convention center proposal was narrowly defeated May 13 by a 3–2 vote of the Sonoma City Council. Although Hillbrook had scaled down his original use permit request for a 160-unit motel to 80 units, and the project had city planning commission approval, a council

Betty Stevens, veteran docent and keeper of the archives at the Sonoma Valley Historical Society's Depot Museum, met up with movie star Martin Sheen one day in 1984. The depot site was used by the actor in filming a scene for one of his motion pictures.

majority voted disapproval. A unanimous vote was subsequently made to pre-zone the property to single-family residential.

Sponsored by the 60-year-old Sonoma Kiwanis Club, the founding of a second group, Kiwanis Club of the Sonoma Plaza, took place June 19, with Samuel A. Soter named president. The new club, which set Wednesdays at noon for its meetings, held its official charter ceremony in August.

The City of Sonoma's 150th birthday celebration held June 21–24, 1985, was dubbed a huge success. The antiqued-silver commemorative coins, made as a keepsake (and fund-raiser) for the event, met with the favor of all, and sales (at $5 each) were brisk. Activities began with a gala street dance on Friday evening, with official opening ceremonies on Saturday, following a morning walking tour of historical landmarks. Other weekend features included performances by the

Sonoma City Opera, the Odyssey Stage Company and the Sonoma Vintage Theatre troupes. A special performance of the Sonoma Valley Chorale and its *Pictures of the Past* musical and yesteryear fashion show took place on the Buena Vista Winery grounds. In the Plaza the annual Sonoma Kiwanis Club Turkey Barbecue became the "Town Picnic," with Western music, a Navy band and strolling barbershop quartet adding to the varied activities. Closing ceremonies, presided over by mayor Jeanne Markson on Monday night, were attended by an estimated 200 townspeople who shared a giant birthday cake, community singing and reflections from city officials on Sonoma's changing scene over the past 150 years.

Fire danger and community safety were the concerns at the August 12 city council meeting when that body banned the sale and use of all fireworks, even the so-called "safe and sane" variety, within the city limits. Those who disapproved

INDEX-TRIBUNE ARCHIVES

Sonoma's annual Fourth of July fireworks display, put on by the Sonoma Fire Department, compares favorably with those held in larger communities in the Bay Area. Public donations help the firemen light up the sky on the Fourth. The spectacle is even more appreciated, especially by youngsters, ever since the city banned the sale and use of all fireworks in August 1985.

of the ban—mostly youngsters—would henceforth have to get their pyrotechnics kicks at the Sonoma Fire Department's grand Fourth of July fireworks display held at the northern edge of town annually.

His swearing-in as president of the California Newspaper Advertising Executives Association, North, was one of two significant honors conferred in 1985 on Bill Lynch, assistant publisher and advertising director of *The Sonoma Index-Tribune*, the weekend of September 14–15 at the CNAEA's annual sales conference in Palm Springs. At the same time, Lynch accepted, for the second year in a row and the fourth time in five years, the Advertising Excellence cup, the state's top CNAEA advertising award. Competing against the state's largest weekly newspapers (circulation over 10,000), the *I-T* ran away with the overall excellence award by taking first-place honors in six of the 11 judging classifications, second place in one, and third place in three others.

Bruno Banducci, a member of the original San Francisco 49ers professional football team and three-time All-American lineman at Stanford University, died September 15 from an apparent heart attack at Sonoma Valley Hospital. A math teacher since 1975 at Sonoma Valley High School, where he had also served as an assistant football coach, Banducci had been under treatment for lung cancer discovered in July.

After 106 years as a weekly, *The Sonoma Index-Tribune* would be published twice a week (Tuesdays and Fridays) starting Tuesday, Nov. 5, 1985, "to better serve our readers and advertisers," editor and publisher Robert M. Lynch announced September 19.

The brainchild of Sonoma schoolteacher Vicki Whiting, the "I-T's Kids" page made its debut in the Oct. 30, 1985, issue of the local paper and became a regular Tuesday feature. It is geared for children between the ages of two and 10.

A use-permit application to build a major shopping center on a 9.44-acre parcel of Maxwell Farms was filed November 22 with the City of Sonoma by Ken Niles, local resident who was the Sonoma Marketplace shopping center developer. Niles had an option to purchase the acreage, and requested city annexation and pre-zoning approval.

25 Major Changes, Losses and Accomplishments: 1986–1990

COURTESY, SEBASTIANI VINEYARDS

Sylvia Sebastiani, matriarch of Sonoma's prominent wine family and owner of Sebastiani Vineyards, is a lifelong resident of the Valley.

1986

The prominence of the Sebastiani family in the California wine industry was emphasized following the Jan. 3, 1986, announcement that Sam J. Sebastiani, 45, had been asked to step down as president of Sebastiani Vineyards. For weeks afterward, newspapers and wine publications throughout the U. S. told of Sam's ousting by the winery's board of directors, consisting of his mother, Sylvia, 69, board chairperson, and her two other children, Don Sebastiani, 32, and Mary Ann Cuneo, 38.

Mrs. Sebastiani announced that she was "promoting" herself out of the board chairman-ship, while remaining owner of the firm, and named her son, Don, then serving in Sacramento as a state assemblyman representing the 8th District, chairman of the board and chief executive officer. Richard Cuneo, 45, senior vice president and secretary-treasurer of the winery, was named president and chief operating officer on an interim basis, until a search team composed of family members selected a permanent president.

In the Sonoma Valley, where the Sebastianis have been looked upon as Sonoma's "first family" since winery founder Samuele Sebastiani became the town's leading benefactor starting in the 1930s, local residents acquainted with the principals expressed sadness and concern over the breakup. The community reacted as if it were a

COURTESY, SEBASTIANI VINEYARDS

Don Sebastiani

part of the family, and shared its discomfort when wine writers and the news media throughout the country publicized the family split.

While all of the underlying reasons leading to the surprise change in management still remain known only to family members, the ambition of the personable 45-year-old Sam and his goal of producing and marketing prize-winning premium wines—in addition to the less expensive and so-called "jug" wines popularized by Sebastiani Vineyards in the past—reportedly brought tremendous expenses which Sam said were necessary to "turn it [the winery] around." The expenditures, described as "excessive" by board members, were cited as a chief factor in Sam's dismissal, along with a lack of communication with them.

That Sam's goals in improving the quality of Sebastiani wines were being realized could not be denied. In a gold-embossed press kit prepared by Sam, Sebastiani's unprecedented 95 top wine competition awards won at various national, state and local judgings, during 1985 alone, were listed.

On March 10, 1986, A. Martin Adams, 42, president and chief executive officer of McCormick Distilling Company in Weston, Missouri, was named the new president of Sebastiani Vineyards—marking the first time in the 81-year

history of the winery that a non-family member had functioned as its chief operating officer. [Adams served as head of the firm for two years, with positive results. He subsequently accepted advisory roles with the Kendall-Jackson and Kunde wineries before establishing his own importing firm. Adams and his family still reside in Sonoma.]

It was also in March 1986 that the ousted Sam Sebastiani announced plans to establish his own winery. In April he said he had chosen the name Villa Aquila, or Home of the Eagle, for his new wine venture, working with his wife, Vicki, whom he named office manager. Sam had adopted the eagle as a personal symbol and illustrated it on his labels during his six-year term as president/chief operating officer of Sebastiani Vineyards.

Deciding that Villa Aquila was "not pronounceable" (and learning that an Aquila winery already existed in Bolinas), Sebastiani in June changed the name to Sam J. Sebastiani Winery, with the permission of his mother, Sylvia Sebastiani. At first, Sam and Vicki made the office of Sam J. Sebastiani Winery at their Eagle Rock Ranch home in Sonoma, Sam using facilities in both Napa and Sonoma counties to bottle and produce his wines. But he let it be known that his plan was to eventually build his own winery here.

[The March 15, 1989, cover of *The Wine Spectator* trade magazine pictured brothers Sam and Don Sebastiani in an amicable pose. An accompanying story by writer James Laube indicated that family differences had been worked out. A month later Sam and Vicki were breaking ground for their new Viansa Winery on a knoll in

COURTESY, SEBASTIANI VINEYARDS   COURTESY, SEBASTIANI VINEYARDS

Mary Ann Cuneo   Dick Cuneo

the Schellville district, south of town. Viansa is a contraction of their names, Vicki and Sam. Viansa Winery, modeled on an Italian wine village, has a courtyard with landscaping that features olive and fig trees, manzanita trees and Italian wildflowers. Its wines and culinary specialties, along with the setting overlooking an expansive wildfowl refuge, make it a popular attraction for visitors.]

In January 1986, the removal of power poles, overhead cable and wires in the downtown sectors of the city of Sonoma continued with another major joint undergrounding project involving the city, PG&E, Pacific Bell and Storer Cable TV. The $600,000 project, known in city parlance as "Underground Utility District No. 4," covered West Napa Street, from First Street West to the intersection of Fifth Street West. This one was preceded by like projects in the early 1970s for the area around the Plaza, and four years later the section involving Broadway and a portion of West Napa Street

The winter's heaviest storm, the worst since 1982, dumped six inches of rain on Sonoma Valley on February 14, driving a number of Glen Ellen residents from their flood-ravaged homes along Sonoma and Calabazas Creeks, virtually submerging Schellville and wreaking devastation on homes, businesses and farmland throughout the Valley. Indirectly, but tragically, the storm was also related to the death of two Kenwood youths who drowned after their inflatable boat capsized the following Monday afternoon in the raging flood currents of Sonoma Creek near Kenwood. Schellville ranchers reported not only the destruction of 4,000 acres planted in prime oat hay, but also the drowning of some livestock.

Culminating a 20-month process which began with city staff–led town meetings and ended with a series of council and planning commission joint hearings, the Sonoma City Council in February put its stamp of approval on the final 1985 General Plan Update. The previous city General Plan had been drafted in 1974.

The Sonoma Valley Hospital Auxiliary, its members known fondly as the Pink Ladies and also (since the recent acceptance of male volunteers) the Golden Boys, celebrated its 30th year in existence with a dinner dance at the Sonoma Mission Inn on March 8, 1986. Since its founding

Vicki and Sam Sebastiani

INDEX-TRIBUNE ARCHIVES

in 1956, auxiliary members have raised many thousands of dollars and donated thousands of volunteer hours to the hospital. [A large part of the donated funds came from receipts of the group's As Is Shop, offering quality used items since it opened in 1957. Located on West Spain Street, it is estimated that the little shop raised more than $3 million, used to buy high-tech medical equipment and provide educational grants for hospital staff personnel.]

The purchase prices of homes and acreage in the Sonoma Valley, which for years were "steals" compared to the average costs in other parts of the Bay Area, inched into six figures and beyond to mark the spring season of 1986. Local realtors interviewed said the price for the type of property most in demand—a three-bedroom home with a large lot—had been listing for between $135,000 and $250,000. And, as one realtor put it, "The supply is limited."

Jordan (John) Basileu, Sr., 93, pioneer El Verano businessman and longtime hunting and fishing columnist for the *Index-Tribune,* died on March 19 at a local convalescent hospital. A native of Greece, he had lived here since 1910.

The completely redesigned and rebuilt west wing of Sonoma Valley Hospital was unveiled to applauding crowds of visitors on Saturday and Sunday, April 19 and 20. This was the wing in which a major construction defect was discovered in 1976. The hospital district board sued the architect and builder, receiving some $3 million in an out-of-court settlement, giving the district a substantial "cushion" for the complete reinforcement, general remodeling, new east wing and $13-million general expansion project which followed.

Oak Hill Farm, 1,000 acres of rich farmland and scenic mountainside east of Glen Ellen, off Highway 12, is being protected for all time, for the appreciation of everyone, thanks to the generosity of its owners, Ann and Otto Teller. In addition to over 300 acres of wildlife sanctuary previously given to the Sonoma Land Trust, a local, non-profit organization, 677 acres were also gifted to the trust by the Tellers, making it the largest conservation easement in the county.

Simmons' Pharmacy, a Sonoma business landmark, closed its doors at 29 East Napa Street on May 6, 1986, never to fill another prescription nor serve a chocolate malt over its white marble fountain again. The late L. S. (Dad) Simmons opened

INDEX-TRIBUNE ARCHIVES

Englishman David Pleydell Bouverie, on a visit to the U. S. in 1933, fell in love with Sonoma Valley, later purchasing 500 scenic acres near Glen Ellen. Before his death at age 83 in December 1994, the retired architect and philanthropist had placed most of those 500 acres into the Bouverie Audubon Preserve for the public to enjoy in perpetuity.

the Valley's first pharmacy here in 1903.

Sale of Sonoma Skypark, the 22-year-old Eighth Street East aviation facility, was announced May 19 by its owner, Jean Tate. Buyers were a group of Fremont aviators—Ron Price, John Carmichael and Alan Ward.

Down to 27 members, the Glen Ellen Women's Club, chartered in 1904, voted to revoke its charter the first week of June 1986, and disbanded. Once the focal point of many Glen Ellen women, the club was first called the Glen Ellen Improvement Club and took its latest name in 1939. The organization was devoted to community and self-improvement, and assistance to charitable causes. Gladys Holman, club president, said, "When I found the 1904 charter, I shed tears. But I've reconciled myself. Many of the members are old and tired. It's sad, but the time has come."

Following an inter-club debate and mock election, Sonoma Valley Rotary Club members in June indicated they would favor permitting women as members of the present all-male international service organization. The local vote was 14 in favor, with 13 opposed. The trial vote was the result of a recent ruling by the California State Court of Appeals, which determined that, under the laws of this state, Rotary is prohibited from excluding females from membership, the outgrowth of a case involving the Rotary Club of Duarte. [Altimira School principal Marilyn Kelly and Sonoma attorney Barbara FitzMaurice made history here on Wednesday, Nov. 25, 1987. They became the first women ever to be inducted into the 41-year-old Rotary Club of Sonoma Valley, an all-male bastion since it was chartered here in 1946.]

Gloria Ferrer winery, Sonoma Valley's first champagne-making facility, held a grand opening for the public July 3–6, with tours and tastings. The winery, owned by the Ferrer family of Spain, is located west of Highway 121 in the Schellville foothills.

David Pleydell Bouverie, Glen Ellen rancher, architect and property owner since coming here in 1946, was applauded by a large gathering on July 26 at the dedication of Gilman Hall, a spacious assembly hall and auditorium on his property. The facilities were built in connection with the 300-acre-plus Bouverie Audubon Preserve, set aside for preservation in 1978 by Bouverie. As architect of the new $230,000 building, originally a hay

The Sonoma City Council's approval, by a 3–2 vote, of developer Ken Niles' Maxwell Village shopping center project triggered enough opposition, and signed petitions, to create a spirited referendum election—the first in Sonoma's history—on Jan. 13, 1987. Proponents, like those in left photo, outnumbered and outspent opponents, like woman in right photo.

barn built in the 1950s, Bouverie designed it to serve as a center for nature education and recreation. He also gave more than 20 acres of land fronting his property on Highway 12 for a wild-flower preserve.

Developer Ken Niles' controversial Maxwell Village shopping center project was approved in a 3–2 vote of the Sonoma City Council after a six-hour-long session that began Monday evening,

M. F. K. Fisher, world-renowned food writer, spent the last 23 years of her life on the Bouverie ranch, near Glen Ellen, in a cottage built to her specifications by David P. Bouverie.

August 11, and ended at 1:45 A.M. the next day. [The decision triggered a strong reaction from those opposed to the 9.44-acre project adjacent to Maxwell Farms Regional Park, leading to a successful petition campaign to put the issue (Measure A) before city voters in Sonoma's first-ever referendum election, held Jan. 13, 1987. After a sometimes bitter, name-calling campaign, in which Niles and his backers spent $65,000 and the opponents $13,000, voters approved the shopping center. In a turnout of 55.6 percent of registered city voters, 1,509 voted yes, 1,200 no. Cost to the city (taxpayers) for the special election was $8,000.]

M. F. K. (short for Mary Francis Kennedy) Fisher, internationally famous food writer, was saluted by the Sonoma County Wine Growers Association on Aug. 9, 1986, for her contributions to the world of food and wine. The ceremony for the 78-year-old writer-gastronomer followed a champagne reception and preceded a lavish din-ner at the Sonoma Mission Inn on the eve of the sixth annual Sonoma County Wine Auction. A resident of Glen Ellen since 1969, Fisher is the author of such well-known works as *How to Cook a Wolf, Consider the Oyster, A Cordiall Water, Among Friends* and *Sister Age*. [In ill health for several years, Fisher passed away June 22, 1992, at her Glen Ellen home at age 83. The friendly and personable writer who made many friends in Sonoma Valley "went out with courage, grace, strength and a lot of love," said her daughter Kennedy Wright, who was with her mother at the end.]

INDEX-TRIBUNE ARCHIVES

Adele Harrison, among those who founded FISH (Friends in Sonoma Helping) in 1976, is still active as the coordinator of the volunteer organization which assists needy families in the Valley.

Dr. William Levinson, who once served as an assistant to state Superintendent of Public Instruction Bill Honig, was named the new superintendent of the Sonoma Valley Unified School District on October 2. The 44-year-old Levinson, former head of Reed Union School District in Tiburon, succeeded Dr. Bob Geurts, who joined the Sonoma County Schools office. There were 100 candidates for the post.

FISH (Friends in Sonoma Helping) celebrated its 10th year of providing assistance to the people in the Valley, through its corps of nearly 100 volunteers, in October 1986. Churches, civic groups and businesses contribute clothing, money, food and baby items; supermarkets and bakeries pass on their surplus; and donations of clothes, time and money are received from the public. During 1986 alone, FISH spent $17,171 on food and $2,275 on special client services, delivered groceries 1,287 times from Schellville to Kenwood, aided two dozen mothers in helping them locate layettes, and sponsored the cheese giveaway program of which 600 Valley families took advantage. Adele Harrison is the longtime coordinator for FISH.

The Sonoma Valley High School football team completed its perfect (5 wins, no defeats) season by coasting to a 35–0 victory over Analy here November 14 and winning the Sonoma County League championship. In North Coast Section post-season play, the Dragons defeated Fortuna, 28–14, before being ousted in the playoffs by San Marin.

1987

Announcement of the sale of the historic 35-acre Armstrong estate, with its graceful two-story Italianate residence, at the corner of Napa Street and Fifth Street East, Sonoma, to Kenwood builder-developer Steve Ledson, was made as 1987 made its Sonoma Valley debut. Known as Orange Lawn, the house was thought to have been built by Daniel Young, head of the Presbyterian Church's Cumberland College here, in the early 1880s. The property changed hands several times, with Charles Van Damme, widely known San Francisco Bay ferry boat captain, acquiring it in 1910. Mr. and Mrs. Donald Armstrong, former Beverly Hills residents, bought Orange Lawn from the Van Damme heirs in 1938, moving here with their children, Anne and Donald, Jr. Armstrong kept a flock of sheep on the acreage. After her parents' death in the 1950s, Anne Armstrong Procter fell heir to the scenic property. It was Mrs. Procter, a retired nurse and flyer who ferried military aircraft as a WAC during World War II, who sold the property to Ledson. He announced plans for what he called an "elite estate development" for the site.

Sonoma City Council members, at a meeting the last week of January 1987, echoed previous suggestions that the county board of supervisors implement growth control measures in the unincorporated part of Sonoma Valley. They recommended that the county scale down its buildout as the city had done with its 100 units per year restriction, and not continually expand roads to accommodate an increasing number of cars.

Fund raising for the restoration of Jack London's ranch cottage got off to a grand start after the California State Parks Foundation received $300,000 in February from a donor who wished to remain anonymous. Putting a foundation under the small cottage where London lived from 1911 until he died in 1916, shoring up the barns and installing protective fencing around some of the buildings were among long-range plans for the park. The entire project, which will restore the buildings to the period in which London was carrying out innovative ranching methods, was estimated to cost $1.2 million, according to park ranger Greg Hayes.

In preparation for a six-month, seismic rehabilitation and renovation of the historic City Hall in Sonoma Plaza, city officials on March 16 joined in lugging desks, chairs and related office equipment to temporary headquarters being set up in the firehouse and a rented house on Patten Street. [Sonoma's City Hall, originally completed in 1908, was rededicated the evening of Jan. 22, 1988, at a public open house, after being closed for nine months to undergo a major restoration. A $100,000 State Historic Preservation Grant helped pay for the reconstruction and earthquake proofing, which cost the city close to $900,000.]

The new traffic signal at Broadway and MacArthur Street began functioning on Wednesday, April 15. The signal, costing $110,000, is the first constructed and financed solely by the City of Sonoma.

Ceremonies were held Saturday, May 23, at Mission San Francisco Solano de Sonoma to mark the re-installation of the last symbolic bell on the Mission trail, together with a plaque dedicating the site. Members of the Sonoma State Historic Parks Association, along with state officials and local dignitaries, participated. The inscription on the plaque, created by Anthony Stellon, nationally known Sonoma sculptor, reads: "The End of the Mission Trail, 1523–1823 – The Mission Trail marked 300 years of Spanish-Mexican settlement. It traveled as far south as Guatemala and traversed Mexico to advance through 11 of our present-day United States. In 1823 Mission San Francisco Solano was founded, marking the last and northernmost outpost on the historic Mission Trail."

The 100th anniversary of Sonoma Parlor No. 111, Native Sons of the Golden West, was celebrated on the evening of July 18 with a gala dinner and dance at the Sonoma Valley Veterans Memorial Building. The NSGW parlor was chartered here on July 20, 1887.

The kindergartners who entered Sonoma Valley schools in September 1987 are—pause and think about it—the class of 2000. How many of

Centerpiece of the 35-acre Armstrong estate development at Napa and Fifth Street East is the graceful two-story residence built in the early 1880s known as Orange Lawn. Once owned by the Van Damme family of San Francisco Bay ferryboat fame, and more recently by Mr. and Mrs. Donald Armstrong and daughter, Anne, the estate was sold in 1987 to builder-developer Steve Ledson. Many large homes, matching the grace of Orange Lawn, residence of the Ledsons, have been constructed on the historic acreage.

INDEX-TRIBUNE ARCHIVES

A plaque containing the names of the 10 local men who gave their lives in the War in Vietnam was unveiled during Veterans Day ceremonies Nov. 11, 1987, at the Sonoma Valley Veterans Memorial Building.

these brand-new students will persist through 13 years of schooling and receive high school diplomas in the summer of the first year of the next millennium? If present state trends hold, 30 to 40 percent will drop out and will not join the ranks of high school graduates in the year 2000.

James R. Lynch, a fourth-generation member of the family which has published Sonoma Valley's newspaper since 1884, was elected president of the Sonoma County Fair for 1987–88 by a vote of its board of directors on October 20. Presently business manager and chief financial officer of *The Sonoma Index-Tribune*, Lynch succeeded Paul Valente of Two Rock in the top fair post. Valente is a former Sonoma resident and graduated from high school here. Lynch was appointed to the fair board in January 1981 upon the recommendation of outgoing 1st District Supervisor Brian Kahn.

Wednesday, Oct. 28, 1987, marked the closing of the local municipal court in Sonoma as a county cost-cutting action. Pleas from local lawyers and city officials to keep the court open went unheeded. The court facility, adjoining the police station on First Street West, was built with both city and county funds. It is used evenings for meetings of the city council and city commissions.

Veterans Day ceremonies on November 11 at the Sonoma Valley Veterans Memorial Building paid a special tribute to this community's Vietnam War dead. A plaque containing the names of local men who gave their lives in the Vietnam conflict

was unveiled and dedicated to their memories. Donated by Mr. and Mrs. A. G. Phillips of Glen Ellen, the marker lists the names of Richard Andrew Renning, Sigurd Martin Messer, Lawrence Lee Petersen, Robert Allen Fenton, John Newton Brewer, Dean Harry Burns, Theodore Glen Feland, David Allen Kardell, Reginald Victor Maisey, Jr., and Denis O'Connor.

An open house celebration on Sunday, November 23, marked the opening of Sonoma Valley's spacious new, 1800-square-foot Pets Lifeline animal shelter at 19686 Eighth Street East. Visitors, most of them donors to the Pets Lifeline building fund, expressed their approval of the building with its glistening masonry walls and spacious runs for dogs and puppies, and the three rooms for cats—the latter already dubbed the "Kitty Hilton."

INDEX-TRIBUNE ARCHIVES

Inside the "Kitty Hilton," a three-room section for cats awaiting adoption at the Pets Lifeline animal shelter, which opened Nov. 23, 1987, on Eighth Street East.

1988

A replica of the stately pillared residence of Count Agoston Haraszthy was gradually being completed in 1988 on the historic rolling vineyard lands of Buena Vista Rancho in Sonoma Valley's eastern foothills. It is a monument authorized by Antonia Bartholomew, owner of the 400-acre parcel, to recognize Haraszthy, called by many the father of California's wine industry, and to memorialize her late husband, Frank H. Bartholomew. The latter, with his devoted wife, purchased the virtually dormant Buena Vista vineyards and winery in 1943, and through research, industriousness and skill brought about a rebirth of the historic vineyards, wines and Haraszthy legend. Mrs. Bartholomew also revealed on Jan. 8, 1988, that the old Buena Vista Vineyards acreage owned by them was being put into a land trust "in order that this beautiful and historic property will be preserved, and not ruined by the promiscuous building that has already destroyed so much of our Valley's special beauty and historic heritage." It was to be called Bartholomew Memorial Park.

[Mrs. Bartholomew lived to see the completion of the Haraszthy Villa replica before her death in Sonoma on Sept. 29, 1990, at the age of 90. Her dream, and that of her husband, the opening of the 75-acre public park, with the villa, vineyards and picnic area amidst a sylvan setting, was realized on Aug. 22, 1992. Among those welcoming visitors that day were William W. Godward, the Bartholomews' longtime friend, confidant and attorney, the project leader; and park manager Jan Haraszthy, grandson of Count Agoston Haraszthy. Two years later the Bartholomew Park Winery, with its historic museum, was added and has become a popular feature for visitors.]

The week of Jan. 11, 1988, marked the end of an era in Sonoma. Generations who had become accustomed to opening their door and finding a quart of milk, a pint of cream and a dozen eggs on their doorstep first thing in the morning would henceforth be buying their dairy products at the store. Matthew Graves, the Clover-Stornetta milkman since 1964, and the Valley's last home delivery milkman, said goodbye to his milk truck and route, which the dairy firm said would not be replaced.

Two of Sonoma Valley's oldest dairy families still contribute greatly to the milk supply available from store shelves in Northern California. Through several generations, the Leveroni and Mulas dairies have continued as major milk producers. Members of these families are shown in the photos above, taken in 1989. At left, the Leveronis: (left to right) Joe Leveroni holding daughter, Erin; Pat Leveroni Stornetta with sons, Rob and Matthew; the late Bob and Louise Leveroni (she is holding grandson Timothy Stornetta); and Bea Leveroni. Right photo: Mitch Mulas, wearing cowboy hat, works the family dairy with his sons and daughters, from left, Mike Mulas, Carolyn Mulas, Vickie Medeiros and Ray Mulas. Not pictured are Nilda Mulas, Mitch's wife, and Mario Mulas, Mitch's brother. Other prominent dairy family names in the Valley are Mertens, Montini, Ferreira and Johnson—not to forget a respected "retired" name, Alex Stornetta.

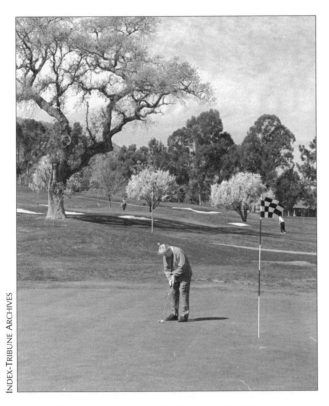

INDEX-TRIBUNE ARCHIVES

The 18th green at the par 72 Sonoma Golf Club course. The original course dates back to the late 1920s. It was purchased in 1988 for some $7.5 million by F. B. D. Enterprises USA, Inc. A sum, said to exceed the purchase price, was later expended in redesigning and upgrading the course and reconstructing the clubhouse, both recognized as the North Bay's finest.

Sebastiani Vineyards exercised its option to buy the former Woodbridge Vineyards Association winery near Lodi, it was announced here on April 5. [The Sonoma winery opened its bulk wine operation in Woodbridge in May 1991 after renovation of the buildings and installation of new equipment. Sebastiani's decision to move its Country Wine operation to the Lodi site was announced in August 1987, following several years of haggling with the City of Sonoma over expansion of the winery at its present location on Fourth Street East. Don Sebastiani, board chairman for the family-owned company, said at the time that its premium wine facility would remain in Sonoma.]

Sale of the Sonoma National Golf Course by the family of the late Dr. Cecil A. Saunders of Sonoma was officially announced April 14, 1988, with the selling price reported to be in excess of $7.5 million. Purchaser was F. B. D. Enterprises USA, Inc., a California corporation and wholly

owned subsidiary of F. B. D. Ltd., a Hong Kong corporation. F. B. D. is one of the Fuji Country Company group, a leading golf course managing company in Japan.

The dedication of the new 90-acre Maxwell Farms Regional Park at Highway 12 and Verano Avenue took place on Saturday, May 21, 1988. Joseph Rodota, director of the Sonoma County Regional Parks Department, was master of ceremonies for the dedication program, jointly sponsored by *The Sonoma Index-Tribune* and the county. A bronze plaque was unveiled, including the statement that "this park is a living legacy of George H. Maxwell's hope that this place be given to the purpose of conserving our natural resources and developing our best potentials." Activities for young people at the event included a "mud mania" competition, kite contest and wagon rides.

City of Sonoma voters who went to the polls June 7 decided by a margin of 1,410 to 1,091 that they didn't like the idea of paying the historically unpaid city council members $300 a month each. Although it was only an "advisory" vote, and a majority of council members could, by state law, still vote to give themselves a monthly salary, all five said they would stand by the public's opinion on the matter.

[On Wednesday, Aug. 2, 1989, the city council voted 4–1 to pay themselves $250 a month in addition to their monthly $255 vision, dental, medical and life insurance premiums which are paid for them by the city. Only one member of the council, Phyllis Carter, adamantly opposed pay for serving, saying she would donate her salary to charity. It was estimated that the salaries would cost the city $15,000 annually. As it turned out, not a single check for councilmembers' salaries was ever written. The city council which succeeded the 1989 pro-salary body on Dec. 19, 1990, introduced an ordinance, adopted Jan. 8, 1991, rescinding the past council's action.]

Four visitors from Kaniv, Sonoma's sister city in the Soviet Union, were given a warm and emotional welcome Friday, July 8, as scores of citizens joined local officials in greeting Nicolai Zharko, mayor of Kaniv; Aleksei Bely, director of a farm complex; Zinaida Tarakhan, museum director; and Alexander Maslov, translator. Months of preparation by the Sonoma Sister Cities contingent, led by Mary Cort, culminated as the four

Ukrainians were embraced in the Plaza by new and old friends. Cort and 20 other local residents had been guests of honor in Kaniv in September 1987. Kaeti Bailie was the first Valley resident to visit Kaniv, in 1985, to assess its potential as a sister city.

Kenwood, the scenic upper-Valley community where the Southern Pacific Railroad built a stone depot in 1887, observed its 100th anniversary on Saturday, September 10. Hosting the historic occasion was the Kenwood Community Club, with a potluck lunch at the venerable Kenwood Depot on Warm Springs Road a highlight of the day.

A change in the management structure of *The Sonoma Index-Tribune*—which took effect in January 1989—was announced in the Dec. 16, 1988, issue of the local newspaper by Robert M. Lynch, editor and publisher. William E. (Bill) Lynch, 45, director of advertising and assistant publisher, assumed the role of editor and chief executive officer. Bill's brother, James R. (Jim) Lynch, 40, the paper's longtime business manager, was named chief financial officer and assistant CEO. Their father, then in his 42nd year at the *I-T*, would continue as publisher.

1989

*J*anet Nicholas became the first Sonoma Valley woman to chair the county board of supervisors on Tuesday, Jan. 10, 1989. Also the first woman elected as a supervisor from the 1st District, Nicholas became the third board chairwoman in the county's history. The first was the late Helen Putnam of Petaluma. Helen Rudee of Santa Rosa was the second. Nicholas, 43, who was starting her second supervisorial term, succeeded Jim Harberson of Petaluma as board chairman.

The 100-year-old residence known as the Marcy house, slated for demolition last October, was transported up Broadway and around the Plaza to its new site on First Street West in the pre-dawn darkness of Wednesday, March 1, 1989. The pioneer house was donated to the Sonoma Sister Cities Association for its headquarters, with the city agreeing to a 25-year lease of land near the police station in exchange for ownership of the house and $1 a year in rent.

Nicolai Zharko (center), mayor of Kaniv, Sonoma's sister city in Ukraine, proved to be an appreciative and personable guest in July 1988 when he and three other Ukrainian officials visited here and enjoyed a picnic in the Plaza.

Spontaneous combustion, involving oil-soaked rags used by a volunteer clean-up crew, caused a swift-moving fire which destroyed the historic 87-year old St. Andrew Presbyterian Church building at 16290 Arnold Drive on Palm Sunday, March 19. The rags had been placed in a container outside the church the day before, after 17 parishioners, members of a work party, had put a last-minute shine on the rich fir and mahogany interior of the former carriage house and stables, built in 1902 for sugar magnate Adolph Spreckels' country estate. It wasn't until 6:30 P.M. Sunday that the blaze broke out, and by the time firefighters arrived on the scene, the building was a raging inferno. Miraculously, the large handmade, walnut-on-oak Celtic cross on the outside of the church remained intact, only singed around the edges, while the rest of the structure was consumed by the flames. Pastor Richard Gantenbein and congregation pledged to rebuild on the site. [The pledge was fulfilled. On April 12, 1992, a gleaming white, $2.1-million new church was dedicated on the same site.]

The Valley experienced its most brutal murder spree in modern history on the morning of April 14, 1989, when Ramon Salcido, a winery worker and resident of Boyes Hot Springs, killed seven people—his wife, 24; two of their daughters, ages 4 and 1; his mother-in-law, 47; his wife's sisters, ages 12 and 8; and a fellow worker, 35, an assistant winemaker where Salcido was employed. Wounded, but escaping death, were a 2-year-old daughter of Salcido's and a 33-year-old supervisor at the winery where he worked.

The deranged killer was arrested five days later near his hometown in western Mexico where he had fled. In an interview on a Mexican television station Salcido confessed to the killings. [On Nov. 16, 1990, some 19 months after the bloody episode shocked Sonoma Valley residents, a San Mateo County Superior Court jury sentenced Salcido to death. His trial cost Sonoma County taxpayers in excess of $500,000. As of January 1997, he was still on San Quentin's death row.]

The old El Dorado Hotel, opposite the north-west side of the Sonoma Plaza, was sold for $2 million cash on May 3rd to Fred and Chili Kohlenberg of San Francisco. Their partner in the hotel venture is Claude Rouas, who was given full control of the project, from remodeling to management. Rouas, at the time, owned and managed the highly rated Auberge du Soleil restaurant in

Rutherford, the popular Piatti Italian restaurant in Yountville and the elegant L'Etoile restaurant in San Francisco. A Piatti restaurant, with a large outdoor dining patio, was among features planned for the El Dorado, which had been vacant since January 1988 when it was closed by creditors and forced into bankruptcy. [The completely renovated and remodeled Plaza landmark, with modern guest quarters and Ristorante Piatti, opened to the public in 1990.]

More than 200 people jammed Andrews Hall in the Sonoma Community Center for a May Day town meeting in which concerns over the fast pace of development in the Valley were expressed. The meeting was sponsored by SOLVE (Save Our Local Valley Environment). The standing-room-only audience was urged to "speak out" during the two-hours-long session, and the response was forthcoming, with residents expressing their thoughts about growth, traffic congestion and proposed developments—mostly in opposition.

Reviving a family tradition, with roots dating

Sonoma was host to the start of the Coors International Bicycle Classic on Aug. 11, 1986, with some of the world's top cyclists, including Tour de France champ Greg Lemond of the U. S. (inset) participating. Hundreds of local citizens were on hand, in and around the Plaza, to witness the start of the Sonoma-to-Sacramento leg of the race, eventually won by Bruno Cornilett of France's Peugeot team. Lemond, of the U. S. Red Zinger team, tied for second.

back to 1904, Bob and Fred Kunde and family announced on June 28 that they planned to build a winery in Kenwood, on the site of their Kinnybrook Ranch. [The new winery, a full-production facility with crushing, fermentation and aging cellars and bottling line on the premises, released its first vintage Sept. 1, 1991. The 31,000 square feet of wine caves dug into the hill behind the winery, and the tasting room, opened to the public in 1992.]

J. Bruno Benziger, 64, cofounder and patriarch of Glen Ellen Winery, passed away peacefully in his sleep the morning of July 10 at his Glen Ellen residence. The irrepressible and innovative Benziger spent 25 years with the family-owned import-export business of Park, Benziger & Co., Inc. in White Plains, New York, before moving his family from there to Glen Ellen in 1981 and founding the Glen Ellen Winery. With his five sons and two daughters involved, Benziger's reasonably priced Glen Ellen Proprietor's Reserve wines became one of America's most popular wine labels in less than a decade.

Richard J. O'Neil, 74, dean of Sonoma Valley photographers, who operated a studio in downtown Sonoma from 1945 until his retirement in 1987, died on Sunday, July 9, 1989, at the local hospital. He won national recognition when his photo of a local spaghetti-eating jack rabbit occupied a full-page spread in *Life* magazine in 1958, and after *Family Circle* magazine published one of his photos. But it was his photographing of high school and elementary school graduating classes that won him local recognition, appreciation and the friendship of countless students over the years. He also took many photographs which appeared in *The Sonoma Index-Tribune*, to whom he rendered many valuable services.

More than 200 members celebrated the 20th anniversary of the Sonoma League for Historic Preservation at a luncheon held at the old Vallejo home on Aug. 18, 1989. Formed Dec. 3, 1969, the league was the brainchild of Margaret Eliassen, whose dynamic leadership guided the organization through its early years and who was active until her death in 1976. Through the years, the League has saved several historic structures and made sure that others were preserved, put the Sonoma Plaza on the National Register by compiling Sonoma's first historic survey, established a

Kenwood resident Tommy Smothers raised his hands in triumph after defeating his opponent during the trials of the World's Champion Pillowfighting Championships, an annual feature of the Kenwood Fourth of July celebration.

resource library of important information about the town's past, restored the Toscano Hotel kitchen, sponsored walking history tours and, through its unique, annual Historic Preservation Awards program, has generated an appreciation for local history and a desire for preservation.

The Bay Area's most destructive earthquake since 1906 on the evening of Tuesday, Oct. 17, 1989, snapped gas and water lines, sparked fires and crumpled buildings and freeways, killing at least 250 people—between its epicenter near Santa Cruz north to the Golden Gate—before subsiding into the slow, rolling motion that brought relatively light damage to Sonoma Valley. A Valley

INDEX-TRIBUNE ARCHIVES

Jack "The Masher" Derrickson of Sonoma, shown here with his wife, Pearl, achieved well-earned recognition for donating $50,000 to Guide Dogs for the Blind by collecting and recycling aluminum cans and old newspapers over a period of a dozen years. Highlighting awards and recognition received was a personal letter of commendation from President George Bush in August 1989.

of the Moon Water District main beneath Riverside Drive was damaged by the temblor, as was a VOMWD 25,000-gallon water storage tank in Agua Caliente.

By comparison, San Francisco's Marina district was hard hit by the quake. Residences were destroyed or badly damaged and fire devoured an entire block, causing concern to some Sonomans with relatives or friends living there. In the East Bay, lives were lost and motorists injured when freeways collapsed. A number of Sonomans told of the horror of being in the shaking stands at Candlestick Park where the third game of the World Series was just about to start with 62,000 Giants and A's fans looking on. The quake that caused the rescheduling of Game 3 also knocked out power on the east side of Sonoma for about three hours, after two electric lines fell from their pole supports, according to PG&E. But, in comparison to the Bay Area, Sonoma Valley lucked out.

Jack "The Masher" Derrickson, who in 1989 reached his goal of donating $50,000 to Guide Dogs for the Blind by recycling aluminum cans and stacks of old newspapers in Sonoma Valley for more than a decade, announced March 6, 1990, that he was reluctantly calling it quits. "It was

doctor's orders," said his devoted wife, Pearl, whose health, like Jack's, had deteriorated. Derrickson, 76, said his own eyesight problem since youth—he is considered legally blind—was an impetus to assist the Guide Dogs program, even though he had never used a guide dog himself.

It took the persistent "Masher" 12 years and four months to recycle the 150,448 pounds of cans and 817,665 pounds of newspaper required to achieve his goal. Highlighting the widespread recognition and awards he received over the years was a personal letter of praise from President George Bush on Aug. 18, 1989, commending him for the kind of people-to-people generosity "and special touch which is beyond the power of the government to give."

1990

*E*leen (Johnnie) Nicholas, 74, the widow of George Nicholas, and matriarch of Sonoma Valley's prominent turkey breeding family, was bludgeoned to death in her Bennett Valley home April 6 by a mentally ill 24-year-old who had known her his entire life and who had been employed by her at the 950-acre Bennett Valley ranch. The young man reportedly "made admissions" to Sonoma County Sheriff's detectives and, after a court examination, was committed to a state mental hospital.

Wanting to keep busy and earn a few dollars at the same time, Mary Fazio opened a pizza parlor in a tiny roadside cottage in Boyes Hot Springs back in 1959. The business, known as Mary's Pizza Shack, prospered beyond her wildest dreams, and, before long, family members became involved. In 1990 a new and spacious restaurant was built on the west side of Highway 12, down the road from the original location, where the menu was expanded but pizza remained its basic ingredient. By 1990 there were seven family-owned Mary's Pizza Shacks throughout Sonoma County. In June of that year the family signed its first franchise agreement for a Mary's pizza restaurant in Napa. A second franchise followed in Novato.

[As the year 1997 opened, there were two franchises in Northern California communities, in addition to 11 family-owned Mary's restaurants in

Sonoma Valley's Mary Fazio, central figure in the success story of the Mary's Pizza Shack expanding restaurant chain, is pictured in the tiny kitchen of her original Boyes Springs pizza parlor 38 years ago.

Sonoma County—all of them spawned in a tiny, roadside stand in Boyes Springs 38 years ago. The Valley got its second Mary's with the opening of a branch in the Mercato shopping complex in downtown Sonoma in February 1994. The other family-owned restaurants are located in Rohnert Park, Petaluma, Windsor, Sebastopol, Santa Rosa (2), Fairfield and Dixon.]

A bit of old Sonoma was lost the night of Sept. 19, 1990, when fire destroyed the 99-year-old Duhring building opposite the southeast corner of the Plaza. The structure housed the venerable Mission Hardware store and its adjacent tenant, Brundage's coffee and tea shop. Onlookers, some with tears in their eyes, watched as firefighters worked in vain to prevent total loss of the business landmark.

Examination of the fire scene by state and local officials determined, following a month-long investigation, that the blaze had been set intentionally by a person, or persons, unknown, in an accessible space behind the structure. Among things saved were the building's graceful old cupola and flagpole spire, and many of the structure's original bricks from 1891. These were later used in the new building, which was built to conform

with the old architecture. A determined citizens' fund-raising campaign encouraged the Duhring family, owners of the property, to use the salvaged mementos in recreating the exterior facade when they rebuilt on the pioneer site.

[It was a year and a half after the fire, May 29, 1992, that hundreds of townspeople turned out to applaud the newly constructed building, whose distinctive arched windows, brick walls, awning and corner cupola were faithfully rebuilt to match the originals. Mission Hardware was one of five tenants of the new Duhring building.]

At the annual National Newspaper Association convention in Kansas City, Missouri, Sept. 21–24, 1990, *The Sonoma Index-Tribune* was presented with eight awards in the NNA Better Newspaper Contest. This eclipsed 1989's seven awards won by the *I-T* in the national com-

Lifted from the ashes of the disastrous fire which destroyed the 99-year-old Duhring building in downtown Sonoma on the night of Sept. 19, 1990, was the building's graceful spired cupola, a landmark opposite the Plaza's southeast corner. Like the phoenix, it was reborn, and today adorns its rebuilt perch.

petition which is open to the National Newspaper Association's 6,000 member newspapers. Publisher Bob Lynch and his wife, Jean, attended the four-day convention and trade show, and proudly accepted the awards on behalf of the entire newspaper staff.

At a November 1 meeting, the Sonoma Valley Ministerial Association decided to remove the nativity scene from the Plaza, where it had been displayed on the lawn in front of City Hall for 35 years. The decision by the ministerial group to place the crèche in front of the Congregational church on West Spain Street was made in order to conform with Supreme Court rulings, and to respond to residents who protested to city officials that the prominent placement of the crèche in the Plaza implied endorsement of Christianity, and offended people of other religious beliefs.

Celebrating Golden Gate Transit's new Route 90 bus service which began operation Nov. 4, 1990, from Sonoma Valley to San Rafael and San Francisco, POST (People of Sonoma for Transit) sponsored a continental breakfast gathering at Vintage House on November 13, with officials of the Golden Gate Bridge, Highway and Transportation District, the City and County of Sonoma, and Metropolitan Transportation Commission in attendance. Later in the morning everyone gathered in front of the Sonoma City Hall for a public ceremony, highlighted by a ribbon-cutting beside one of the new Route 90 coaches. Speakers at the ceremony, while acknowledging that it was the cooperation between city, county and bridge district that made the dream of Sonoma-to-San Francisco public transit come true, special credit was given to the role played by POST, under the dedicated and forceful leadership of Sonoma resident Jim Karabochos, a bus driver for Golden Gate Transit, who got the idea to establish People of Sonoma for Transit back in 1978.

Familiar Sonoma scenes: At left, one of the magnificent Clydesdale horses on the Castagnasso property, on East Spain Street east of the Mission, accepts attention from passersby. Right photo shows the wide variety of participants in the annual Hit the Road Jack Walk/Run, an annual benefit for local charities which attracts hundreds of entrants.

26 Still Fresh in Our Memories: 1991–1996

INDEX-TRIBUNE ARCHIVES

A ribbon-cutting ceremony on Sept. 3, 1991, was the first in a series of community events observing the 100th anniversary of Sonoma Valley High School which first offered classes in the abandoned Cumberland College building, a block north of the present high school, in the fall of 1891. The present high school building opened in 1923. Wielding the scissors (center of above photo) was retired Judge Malcolm Champlin, 80, of Oakland, whose father, the Rev. Charles C. Champlin, was a member of the high school's first graduating class in 1894.

1991

The man whom many called "Mr. Sonoma" died Wednesday night, Feb. 20, 1991, at Sonoma Valley Hospital. August L. Pinelli, 88, lifelong Sonoma resident, Mission Hardware store proprietor and an active leader in the community's development for more than half a century, had been in ill health for several years and had been hospitalized on several occasions.

He was born Aug. 1, 1902, in a home on the south end of First Street East, and used to joke, "I never got out of the block"—referring to the fact that he was still in business at Mission Hardware at Napa and First Street East until the historic Duhring building was destroyed by fire in September 1990.

Despite his health problems and age, Pinelli worked as coproprietor of the store with his partner, Preston Cornelius, right up to the time of the fire. Pinelli was easily the merchant with the longest continuous service record in Sonoma—which is not surprising when you consider that he went to work in the F. T. Duhring hardware store at the age of 14. Nor in all probability will his service to the City of Sonoma—as a city councilman, mayor, fire and water department leader, school board member and chairman of countless local campaigns and projects—soon be surpassed.

On the opening day of school, Sept. 3, 1991, a ribbon-cutting ceremony began what school officials and community leaders hoped would be a series of commemorative events marking the

100th anniversary of Sonoma Valley High School, which opened in the fall of 1891 with 35 students. Prior to the ribbon-cutting on the high school's front steps, a continental breakfast was held with past and present administrators, teachers, school board members, students and community members dedicated to the cause of education, in attendance.

Robert V. (Bob) Leveroni, 73, whose love of the land and pride in accomplishment made him one of the most respected agriculturists in Sonoma County, died of a heart attack on September 24 while in the midst of preparations for the polenta and venison feed he hosted annually for a large group of friends. The prominent dairyman-vineyardist was born here Aug. 26, 1918, to the late Victor and Elmira Leveroni, and began working with his father on their 650-acre ranch as a boy of 14.

Santa Rosa resident Mike Cale, 47, was appointed October 10 by Gov. Pete Wilson to fill the 1st District Sonoma County supervisor's seat vacated by Sonoma's Janet Nicholas, who accepted an appointment to the state parole board in June 1991.

The governor selected Cale, a professional environmental planner and former police officer, over 15 other applicants, all residing in the

INDEX-TRIBUNE ARCHIVES

Charles E. (Chuck) Williams (left), founder of the vast Williams-Sonoma cookware chain, greeted Dan Ruggles, an old friend, during a return to his roots Feb. 13, 1992.

Sonoma Valley.

A Sonoma Valley growth policy, limiting new housing in the unincorporated areas to 90 units per year, was approved by Sonoma County supervisors on December 10. Crafted over a period of months by a cross-section of local leaders, the plan appeared acceptable to all, builders and developers included.

During the short public hearing no one spoke against it. The new policy was said to offer a solution to the rapid rate of recent growth in the Valley where building skyrocketed to 231 units a year—a number that greatly exceeded estimates set down in the county's General Plan. The Sonoma Valley Growth Management Ordinance, adopted as a 45-day urgency ordinance that took effect Jan. 1, 1992, went back to the county planning commission for fine-tuning and more public hearings before it would become part of county zoning law, subject to change when the General Plan is updated.

1992

*S*am J. Sebastiani got approval Feb. 13, 1992, to restore about 90 acres of unused wetlands northeast of his Viansa Winery in Schellville for migrating ducks and geese. The county Board of Zoning Adjustments gave Sebastiani its okay after adding a condition that adjacent landowner and winemaker Fred Cline be included in the final designing of the duck pond to make sure his interests are considered. Sebastiani has joined with Ducks Unlimited to provide the sanctuary. DU, a non-profit corporation, is funding the $50,000 project through a donor program, with Sebastiani providing the land and management of the area.

Charles E. (Chuck) Williams, who parlayed a love of cooking and exquisite taste in functional kitchenware into the multi-million-dollar national and international Williams-Sonoma retail stores and catalog cookware giant, returned to his roots here February 13. Williams captivated a near-capacity crowd as the first celebrity guest participant in a "Conversations on Food and Wine" series at Andrews Hall in the Sonoma Community Center.

Williams first came to Sonoma in 1947 as a young home builder. In 1953, following a trip to

France, he purchased a small hardware store on Broadway from Ralph Morse. Selling off all the hardware, he renamed the store Williams-Sonoma and stocked it with cookware, much of which he had become fascinated with during his visit in France. A local "foodies" group encouraged him to open a store in San Francisco, which he did in 1958—the start of his novel cookware outlet which in 1992 exceeded $300 million in annual sales. Following his presentation at Andrews Hall, Williams renewed acquaintances with many long-time Sonomans.

The old Civil War-era cannon that a General Wagner supposedly donated for display in Glen Ellen at the turn of the century will remain there—despite being sold to a Civil War buff in New Jersey. A hue and cry was raised in the little village in February, when it was learned that owners of the London Lodge, on whose property the cannon has been displayed since 1905, had sold the 1862 relic for $6,000.

The motel owners, who sold the cannon as part of a plan to spruce up the Lodge's parking lot, said since it rested on their property, they felt they were within their rights to sell it. But when townspeople rallied 'round the aging howitzer, circulating a petition to save it, an anonymous donor offered $6,000 to cover the cost. The *Index-Tribune* kept the issue before the public, and finally the New Jersey buyer was talked into releasing his hold on the cannon. The Sonoma County Board of Supervisors got legal possession of it because of its historic value, and the board subsequently deeded it to the Glen Ellen Fire District, its present custodian.

Becky London, daughter of famed novelist Jack London and a resident of Glen Ellen since 1983, died at a Sacramento nursing home on March 26. She was 89 and had often held court at the Jack London Bookstore, owned by Russ and Winnie Kingman, where she regaled visitors from around the world with her stories of "Daddy."

The Naval Security Group Activity at Skaggs Island celebrated its 50th birthday May 1–2, 1992, with special ceremonies and entertainment. Located off Highway 37 on 4,390 acres with a circumference of 15 miles, the naval reservation was commissioned in 1942 after the start of World War II. Here, radio messages from Hawaii, Japan and countless ships at sea have been beamed down

INDEX-TRIBUNE ARCHIVES

The community of Glen Ellen, like one of its old-timers, Hazen Cowan (above), embraced the old Civil War-era cannon in their midst since 1905. The owner of the property on which the cannon was displayed sold it to a collector for $6,000; but such a stir was created in February 1993 that the buyer got his $6,000 back and Glen Ellen retained its cannon.

from the stratosphere and relayed by land to other U. S. Navy stations up and down the West Coast for the past half-century.

Officers and enlisted personnel have, over the years, been involved in Sonoma Valley activities. Through an "adopt-a-school" program, naval personnel tutored Prestwood Elementary School students and helped out in the school's computer lab. They have also played a major role each year in putting on the Ox Roast in Sonoma Plaza, a benefit for the Sonoma Community Center.

[Along with many other military installations throughout the country, the Skaggs Island naval unit here was eventually put on the government's "shut down" list. The announcement came in July 1992 that its closing was slated for September 1993. Official closing ceremonies actually took place on June 18 of that year, and the once thriving Navy community that housed 83 families, with many more commuting from neighboring towns, was to become a ghost town, after 51 years.

Its future use has yet to be announced by the federal government, although many suggestions

COURTESY, D. AMBROSE

The Skaggs Island U. S. Naval Group Activity, commissioned here in 1942, was an important radio relay station during World War II and for some years afterward. Out in the marshland "boonies" off Highway 37, the naval base, until its closing June 18, 1993, carried a Sonoma address, with a small branch of the Sonoma Post Office serving the 83 families on the once bustling military base, now a virtual ghost town.

have come from local sources. The property, located off Highway 37 at the southernmost end of the Valley, is actually only an "island" because it's surrounded by sloughs and levees. It includes dozens of single-family homes and duplexes; a three-story, 77-unit apartment-style barracks; a four-lane bowling alley, small theater, post office, 40-seat cafeteria; and a community center which features a bar, kitchen and ballroom. There are also a swimming pool, racquetball and tennis courts; an indoor basketball court and gym; a par-course, boat-launching ramps and softball field; and its own wells, water treatment and sewage treatment plants. Much of the unbuilt-upon, Navy-owned land is leased to farmers who grow barley hay.]

A $63.5-million bond issue that would have paid for a new high school and controversial site on Carriger Road was soundly defeated by Sonoma Valley Unified School District voters at the June 2, 1992, election. Measure A on the ballot, which would also have converted the 1923-built high school on Broadway into the district's second middle school and improved the five elementary schools, was clobbered when 62.2 percent of the voters opposed the measure. To pass, the bond issue needed approval from two-thirds

of the voters.

Sonoma Index-Tribune editor Bill Lynch was among bond issue supporters shaken by the defeat of the measure. Like his predecessors, staunch supporters of schools and education, Lynch had clearly expressed his support through his many pre-election editorials.

A 1992 study, conducted by a Napa-based wine industry accounting firm, indicated that phylloxera, a root louse which infects and eventually kills vineyards, is once again becoming the scourge of Napa and Sonoma Valleys. Experts predict the insect, which a century ago wreaked havoc in Sonoma Valley, will cause most of the Valley's 6,000 acres of vineyards to be replanted by the end of the century. The financial impact on Valley vintners is tremendous, local growers say. To replace an existing vineyard can cost $15,000 to $20,000 an acre, said Angelo Sangiacomo, one of the owners of V. Sangiacomo and Sons. In addition, it takes a minimum of three years before the new vineyard begins to produce. Sangiacomo said there is a bright side to being forced to replant. "It gives growers the chance to correct any mistakes made in the past. Overall, we feel the replanting is going to improve wine," he said.

Riding a wave that saw Democrats swept into office throughout the state and nation, former Sonoma city councilwoman Valerie Brown won the Nov. 3, 1992, election for the 7th District State Assembly seat, soundly defeating her Republican opponent and former 1st District Supervisor Janet Nicholas of Sonoma. Brown received 94,026 votes to 54,996 for Nicholas. Brown, whose only political experience had been a two-year stint on the city council, took the assembly post formerly held by Republican Bev Hansen, who did not run for re-election.

1993

Citing racism, Altimira Middle School officials decided in April 1993 to change the school's long-time mascot, the Apache, to a more politically correct wolf. Native Americans are on record as being opposed to the use of the designation "Indians," or any related connotation, as school mascots or for sports teams.

The new million-dollar Glen Ellen Village

Market, which includes a branch of the Sonoma Valley Bank, opened quietly for business on April 29. The site, at the corner of Arnold Drive and London Ranch Road, was for many years occupied by the historic Rustic Inn. The new store is owned by Dale Downing and Don Shone, who also own the Sonoma Market in Sonoma.

Sonoma Valley Bank on May 6, 1993, became the community's only independently owned and operated bank. A spokesman for the local financial institution announced it had sold enough stock to local residents and raised cash enough to buy out the majority stock held by Napa Valley Bank Corporation.

Celebrating its 20th season, the Sonoma Valley Chorale, under founding director Jim Griewe, once again played to sellout audiences May 8 and 9 at the Veterans Memorial building. The Chorale, numbering 140 members, ages 14 to over 80, won applause for its show titled *One More Time*, featuring a variety of old and new favorites including songs from the musicals *Cats, Les Miserables, Jesus Christ Superstar, Oliver* and *Phantom of the Opera*.

Approval of a 450-seat, four-screen movie theater, to be built in the old Fiesta Market building at 18615 Sonoma Highway, was given by the Sonoma County Board of Supervisors on June 29, 1993, after a 90-minute public hearing.

The September 28 announcement by the Glen Ellen Winery of the sale of its Glen Ellen and M. G. Vallejo brands to Heublein, Inc. stunned the Sonoma Valley. Ironically, according to Michael Benziger, 41, one of the family owners, it was the financial inability to expand to meet the demand for the two brands that brought about the sale to Heublein. "If we did nothing, we would have lost our competitive edge and begun to disintegrate," he said. The deal with Heublein, which owns such alcohol giants as Smirnoff vodka and Christian Brothers brandy, was said by some wine industry experts to top $100 million. The Benzigers retained their rapidly growing Benziger and Imagery Series brands, as well as the Jack London Road winery and ranch in Glen Ellen and about 85 acres of surrounding vineyards.

The new Friedman Bros. family-owned home improvement center at 1360 Broadway, Sonoma, opened on December 14. The 25,000-square-foot center is a branch of the Friedman family's sprawling flagship store in Santa Rosa which opened in 1971. The firm was founded in Petaluma in 1946. The Sonoma store occupies six acres, formerly the site of Farrell's Lumber and

COURTESY, SONOMA VALLEY CHORALE

The widely acclaimed Sonoma Valley Chorale under founding director Jim Griewe observed its 20th season May 8 and 9, 1993, with a repertoire of numbers wrapped up in a show titled *One More Time*, at the veterans' memorial building. In the fall of 1995 Chorale members flew to Europe where they sang for receptive audiences in Sonoma's sister cities of Chambolle-Musigny, France, and Greve, Italy—plus encore-demanding music lovers in Paris and Milan. At full strength, the Chorale is composed of 140 members.

Hardware and more recently Yaeger & Kirk.

Altimira Middle School's principal since 1982, Marilyn Kelly, 52, was selected to become the new superintendent of the Sonoma Valley Unified School District in December 1993. She replaced Biefke Vos Saulino, who resigned effective December 31, after just 15 months on the job.

Drawing on generous community support, the Sonoma Valley Hospital Foundation raised $51,000 in 1993 to purchase state-of-the-art eye surgery equipment used for cataract surgery. The Ocusystem II device is used in conjunction with the Zeiss microscope and camera acquired through funds raised by the hospital foundation in 1992. Through a variety of fund-raising events and donations, the nonprofit foundation, since its founding in 1982, has funded the purchase of many thousands of dollars worth of equipment and other items for Sonoma Valley Hospital. Carolyn Stone has been president of the foundation since its inception.

1994

Sonoma Valley Unified School District trustees learned at the end of January that local taxpayers were willing to pay only between $30 and $40 per year to improve the overcrowded and badly-in-need-of-repair schools. The message came in the form of results from a telephone survey that was conducted by a polling firm earlier in the month. The news was discouraging to school officials and volunteers who hope to raise from $21 to $47 million for school building improvements, in the wake of the crushing defeat of the $63.5 million bond issue in June 1992.

Although it fell six points and one game short of attaining the ultimate dream of battling for the California State Championship, the Sonoma Valley High School boys' basketball team completed its greatest season in the school's history on Friday, March 11, 1994, losing to San Lorenzo High School, 53–47, in the California

INDEX-TRIBUNE ARCHIVES

Sonoma Valley High School experienced its greatest basketball success in varsity history when the 1993–94 Dragon team (24–7) won the North Coast Section Division III ICF championship. The team, coached by Phil Rosemurgy (front, far right in photo), went on to come within one game of playing for the state Division III title. Team members shown above are, left to right: (front row) Matt Gabriel, Trevor Unverferth, Mark Perry, Bobby Alexander, Ross Guptill, Shane Bresnyan, John Florance, Ryan Morefield; (back row) assistant coach Andy Sallee, Darrell Butler, Linc Isetta, Brenton Sanders, Noah Larson, Kevin Unverferth, Miguel Rosas.

Prominent Valley businessman Gary Nelson (left photo) was fund drive chairman for the successful Field of Dreams sports field campaign. The campaign had the support of more than 1,000 local contributors of money, labor, equipment and materials. Right photo, a takeoff on the motion picture *Field of Dreams*, shows Oakland A's pitcher Dave Stewart in a cornfield with members of local youth teams. The implied slogan, of course, was "Build it and they will come!"

Interscholastic Federation Northern California Division III playoffs semi-final on the UC Davis court. In compiling a 27–4 record, the Dragons, coached by Phil Rosemurgy, were co-champions of the Sonoma County League—their third title in four years—and had captured the North Coast Section Division III championship March 5 by upsetting the same San Lorenzo team 71–46.

The Sonoma Valley Field of Dreams "came true" Sunday, April 17, 1994. Grand opening ceremonies for the seven-acre sports field park, built through the contributions of money, labor, equipment and materials supplied by more than 1,000 Valley supporters, were highlighted by dedication of a monument, containing the names of those supporters. The successful community project was completed in response to a shortage of playing fields for Valley youth. Serving with fellow volunteers on the project, shovel in hand, was *I-T* editor Bill Lynch, who praised the Field of Dreams team at the dedication. "We built this field without tax money, during a recession, in less than a year and a half. We did it as a declaration of our commitment to the youth of Sonoma Valley," Lynch stated. "The names of this field's creators will become part of the realized dream and demonstrate, for those future generations, the good that unselfish service can bring."

The Field of Dreams adjoins the Sonoma Police Department property off First Street West at the base of the northern foothills. It features two Little League baseball fields, a softball field and a full-sized baseball field, plus a general practice and play area. In the fall the fields can accommodate two large soccer fields plus a small field for younger players.

Measure B on the June 7, 1994, ballot, the $27.5-million bond issue to improve local schools, won 70.1 percent approval from Sonoma Valley voters, with 6,562 voting yes and 2,799 (29.9 percent) opposed. A two-thirds vote was needed for passage, something the $63-million school bond election in 1992 failed to achieve by a wide margin. That bond issue, much more ambitious than the June 7 measure, would have included a brand-new high school and conversion of the present Broadway campus into a second middle school. In the successful election, voters authorized funds to be spent for renovations, repairs and improvements to schools in the district.

Don Sebastiani, who took over as president of Sebastiani Vineyards more than eight years ago, revealed on June 17, 1994, that the Sonoma wine firm became the fifth largest winery in the country after selling six million cases so far this fiscal year. The 90-year-old winery, second largest family-run winery in the world, reported an overall growth of about 17 percent over 1993.

Brock Arner, Sonoma's city manager for nearly 15 years, resigned that job effective July 31 to accept the city manager position in Sausalito. Arner, 46, will receive a salary and benefits package totaling $111,000 annually, and a new home that Sausalito would build for the city manager to rent. The new job is a step up from his current salary of $79,116.

The Sonoma City Council on July 5, 1994, voted to close down its hoosegow—for good—as of August 1. Faced with costly staffing problems and fearing liability claims if an inmate dies or is injured in the temporary holding cell that passes for a jail, the city took the action despite the complaints of some law enforcement officials, such as the CHP, who used the holding cell regularly. The local police didn't have enough staff to monitor cell occupants as required by law. Prisoners arrested here must now be transported to Santa Rosa for booking.

The Sonoma Charter School, one of the first 100 of its kind allowed in the state, opened its doors September 6, to approximately 230 kindergarten through eighth-grade students for the first day of alternative public education in the Valley. Charter schools are schools organized by teachers, parents and community members. They are unique because, even as public schools, they are free from most state education regulations, allowing for increased flexibility in their policies and procedures. The schools are given money from the state for students' daily attendance. However, no money is provided by the state for charter school

INDEX-TRIBUNE ARCHIVES

The above photo, taken March 28, 1995, shows Sonoma's Bank of America branch shortly after the failed robbery attempt of an armored car ended in the shooting deaths of a Loomis security company guard and his bank-robber assailant, a 64-year-old ex-con. The latter's accomplice, a woman, was later captured after abandoning a Loomis bag containing $200,000, which was recovered.

start-up costs. Thanks to an effective community volunteer effort, with support from *The Sonoma Index-Tribune*, $140,000 in donations was raised, and the Sonoma Valley Unified School District authorized the use of the old Flowery School facilities at Agua Caliente. Countless hours of work were put into upgrading of the site by volunteers.

1995

What is believed to have been the first death-related bank robbery in Sonoma's history occurred at the Bank of America at 35 West Napa Street on the afternoon of Tuesday, March 28, 1995. Two people died in a blaze of gunfire after armed robbers tried to get away with more than $200,000 in cash being delivered to the downtown bank. When the violent bloodshed ended just after 2 P.M., two lay dead in front of the bank—the 34-year-old Loomis security company guard who was transporting the money into the bank, and his suspected assailant and would-be bank robber, a 64-year-old ex-con with a history of holding up banks and armored trucks.

A female suspect, who was in a gray car with the ex-con in front of the bank and who attempted to walk off with the Loomis bag containing the $200,000, was later caught several blocks from the scene and identified as a 35-year-old resident of Glen Ellen, mother of three sons. She had been forced to abandon the bag of money in the breeze-way of a restaurant across the street from the bank in her attempt to flee the area. Somehow the woman escaped the fusillade of bullets fired by the Loomis driver that killed her accomplice. The armored car driver reportedly fired 18 rounds at the duo in the gray car after his partner was gunned down. Miraculously, the bullets also failed to hit any of several innocent bystanders in the area. The Glen Ellen woman, a brunette, is believed to have donned a blonde wig, large sunglasses and extra outer clothing for the robbery attempt. Those trappings were found abandoned in a nearby lot shortly after her capture. [She was tried by a jury and convicted of first-degree murder with special circumstances in Sonoma County Superior Court in May 1996. The following month she was sentenced to life in prison without parole. As of this writing she is at Valley State Prison for Women in Chowchilla and has filed a notice of intent to appeal the jury's ruling.]

Hired in March as Sonoma's city manager, Pamela Gibson, 50, began her first day on the job Monday, May 1, meeting a crowd of active local citizens who came to welcome her during a reception at the General's Daughter restaurant. The former assistant city manager in San Juan Capistrano, Orange County, Gibson replaces Brock Arner, who served as Sonoma's city manager for 15 years before leaving last July to assume the same role for the city of Sausalito. Gibson, a one-time newspaper reporter and author of several books on Orange County and San Juan Capistrano history, brings 18 years of experience in municipal government with her. She is the first woman to fill Sonoma's highest appointed position and the second woman city manager in the county.

A wet spring was made wetter by mid-May rains which put the damper on outdoor pursuits for Sonoma Valley individuals and athletic teams. The National Weather Service said the spring rains are merely an extension of the systems that hit California all winter, dumping 49.59 inches in the city of Sonoma alone.

The mystery and conjecture over what caused the 1913 fire that destroyed author Jack London's four-story stone Wolf House was solved at the London ranch above Glen Ellen on the weekend of May 19–20, 1995—at least to the satisfaction of a "dream team" of 10 arson investigators from around the country. Led by retired San Jose State professor Dr. Bob Anderson, the arson investigative team determined that the cause of the fire was accidental, with oily rags the probable culprit. Many, including Jack and Charmian London, suspected that the fire was caused by arson shortly before the imposing stone edifice was completed. The arson experts believe the fire began in the dining room, which unlike the multitude of other fireplaces (there was one in every room) had a wood mantel and paneling. They suspect that oily rags, perhaps soaked with linseed oil used to polish the wood, were left near the hearth by workers. The fire started in the middle of the night, Aug. 23, 1913. By the time the Londons arrived on the scene, the magnificent structure was ablaze throughout. The home London said would last for 1,000 years was gone in a matter of minutes.

Two Sonoma Valley volunteer groups, seeking

Part of the 1995 team of top U. S. arson investigators are pictured above inspecting the ruins of Jack London's four-story stone Wolf House, destroyed by fire the night of Aug. 23, 1913, shortly before its completion.

to build two different facilities for youth, got a financial boost, courtesy of the Sonoma County Board of Supervisors, on May 23, 1995. Representatives of the Valley of the Moon Boys & Girls Club and the Sonoma Skate Society learned that the supervisors had approved an allotment of $353,297.87 to the VOMBGC building project and $72,666.66 to assist the Skate Society in its plans to build a skate park. Both have plans to build facilities at Maxwell Farms Regional Park. The money comes from a refund the county received because of a new way of handling state property tax transfers. Other funding requests were granted to a variety of youth organizations and school districts in Sonoma County. If sufficient additional funds can be raised through public subscription, as urged in *I-T* coverage and editorials, the

INDEX-TRIBUNE ARCHIVES

Fran Meininger, director of the Sonoma Valley Boys &
Girls Club, and architect Michael Ross look over plans
for the proposed new $3-million youth facility to be
constructed on a site in Maxwell Farms Regional Park.

Boys & Girls Club would move from its crowded
present home on First Street West into a new,
$3-million facility in the park. The skatepark,
which skateboarders and in-line skaters have long
been clamoring for, is estimated to cost $100,000.
Public fund-raisers are also planned by the Skate
Society.

A granite or marble memorial to the many
Native Americans buried next to Mission San
Francisco Solano in Sonoma was, in June 1995,
proposed for placement at the Mission. Edward
Castillo, Native American studies coordinator at
Sonoma State University, made the recommendation, based on his discovery in mission archives of
the names of 896 Native Americans who were
buried in two graveyards—one next to the
Mission, partway under First Street West, and the
other a bit farther east under a field on the
Castagnasso property where several Clydesdale
horses graze. From the missionaries' records,
Castillo concluded that an unusually large number of Native Americans who worked and wor-
shipped at the Mission died there between the
time it was founded and when it was secularized—from 1823 to 1834.

The purchase, for $2.2 million, of the 24-acre
property adjoining Sonoma Valley High School on
the south was announced Aug. 15, 1995, by jubi-

lant Sonoma Valley Unified School District officials. Remembered by old-timers as the
Matsuyama family ranch, during the months of
negotiations it was referred to as the Dolcini-
Wallman property, names of subsequent owners,
before it was sold to a large development company
in 1990. The company, which had planned to build
86 houses on the acreage, declared bankruptcy
after failing to make scheduled payments to the
Dolcini-Wallman family heirs. Funds for the purchase of the property were made available
through the passage of the $27.5-million school
bond issue in June 1994. The extra land will allow
the high school to grow without having to move,
school district superintendent Marilyn Kelly said.
The high school expects 400 additional students
by the year 2000.

After three years of study, 25 public hearings
and hundreds of hours of hard work, the city's
1995 General Plan was unanimously adopted by
the Sonoma City Council on August 30. It marked
the fourth General Plan in the city's history, previous plans having been approved in 1964, 1974
and 1985. Likened to a city's constitution, state
law requires that every city and county have a
General Plan. It must address seven state-man-
dated topics called "elements"—land use, housing,
circulation, open space, conservation, public safety and noise. While its critics feel the adopted plan
allows too much leeway for increased development
and growth, Sonoma officials point to a significant
change in the plan, which shrinks the city's sphere
of influence by nearly 72 percent. The sphere des-
ignates land limits surrounding Sonoma into
which the city can expand during the next 10
years. The shift is intended to curb urban sprawl
as much as possible.

St. Francis Solano School celebrated its 50th
birthday on the weekend of Sept. 16–17, 1995.
Sister Mary Daniel, who was principal when the
school opened a half-century ago, was among
those present for the celebration, welcomed by
principal Francine Maffei.

Long known for its fine wines, Sonoma Valley
may soon be looked to for fine beer. The Benziger
family, who sold its very successful Glen Ellen
wine label to Heublein, Inc. in 1993, had said that
it would concentrate on its upscale Benziger wines
at the winery in Glen Ellen. While they'll continue to make premium wines, they have announced

Former Secretary of State Henry Kissinger and former Secretary of the Treasury Lloyd Bentsen are pictured above with Mr. and Mrs. Gary Nelson of Sonoma on Oct. 27, 1995, at the Sonoma Valley Veterans Memorial Building. Kissinger and Bentsen were among several distinguished speakers heading a Nelson Associates business conference here.

the purchase of 20 acres of land in front of the Arrowood Winery off Highway 12 near Glen Ellen, on which they plan to establish a microbrewery in 1996.

Important personages whose faces most Sonomans see only in newspapers, magazines and on television screens were brought to the Valley on Oct. 27, 1995, by Gary Nelson, head of the Gary D. Nelson Associates personnel placement firm based in Sonoma. Speakers thrilling the 450 business-men and -women from around the state attending the Nelson Business Conference at the Sonoma Valley Veterans Memorial Building included Dr. Henry Kissinger, former Secretary of State; Lloyd Bentsen, former U. S. Senator and Secretary of the Treasury; and nationally known sports attor-ney Leigh Steinberg. The day-long program, titled "Future Promise or Future Shock," focused on four major issues facing business—diversity, econom-ics, politics and technology. The speakers, for the most part, were optimistic about the U. S. and its future, with new technology playing a role in the opportunities offered.

John Lasseter, 38, an Academy Award-win-ning director of animated films who has lived in Sonoma since 1992, brought to the Valley in 1995 a gala preview showing of *Toy Story*. The first ani-mated feature film ever made entirely by artists using computer technology, it was directed and co-written by Lasseter, with Disney the producer. The *Index-Tribune* reported that the sneak pre-

view at the Sebastiani Theatre, on November 11, would be a benefit for local public schools. Lasseter and his wife, Nancy Tague, have two of their three young children in local schools. In addition to applauding Lasseter and the clever film's two key characters—Buzz Lightyear, a space-action character with an ego, and Woody, a pull-string, talking cowboy—the sell-out crowd attending the preview enjoyed a silent auction, cocktail party and dinner. Lasseter was voted a Special Achievement Award by the Academy of Motion Picture Arts and Sciences for pioneering the animated computer technology used in *Toy Story* and created at his Pixar Animation Studios in Point Richmond.

[Lasseter was one of two luminaries from the Valley of the Moon in the spotlight at the annual Academy Awards presentations on March 25, when he accepted his award for *Toy Story*. Mare Winningham, 36—a Sonoma Valley resident since 1993 with her husband, Bill, and their four sons and daughter—had been nominated for an Oscar

John Lasseter, the Academy Award-winning director of *Toy Story* and Sonoma resident since 1992, is pictured above with his three sons (from left), Sam, 3; Paul, 5; and Ben, 6. Lasseter arranged for a sneak preview of *Toy Story* here Nov. 11, 1995, as a benefit for local schools.

INDEX-TRIBUNE ARCHIVES

Mare Winningham, a Sonoma Valley resident since 1993, was nominated for a 1995 Academy Award for her role as a singer in the movie *Georgia*. Although not chosen, she said the nomination and attending the Academy Awards extravaganza was a great honor. She has since shared her talents with local audiences in two benefit performances for the Sebastiani Theatre here.

for best supporting actress for her portrayal of a singer in the movie *Georgia*. Although she wasn't chosen, Winningham said the experience "was funny, amusing, heady and a great honor for being in a film I will always love."]

The Sonoma Valley Visitors Bureau received its 100,000th visitor of the year in December 1995. This is the first time the bureau, which operates visitor information centers on the Plaza and on Highway 121 south of town, has broken the 100,000-visitor mark for a 12-month period. During the 10 years in which statistics have been kept, the number of walk-ins increased from 13,683 in 1985 to 101,613.

A zealous advocate of the state's Ralph M. Brown Act and the public's right to know, *I-T* editor Bill Lynch was named a winner of the prestigious James Madison Freedom of Information Award for 1995. The award is conferred annually by the Northern California chapter of the Society of Professional Journalists.

1996

*I*nvitations to 525 descendants of the original Bear Flag Party were sent out Jan. 13, 1996, asking them to join Sonoma in celebrating the 150th anniversary of the first Bear Flag raising on June 14, the day the flag was raised in the Sonoma Plaza in 1846.

A 29-year-old Sonoma baker, Craig Ponsford, baked his way into the hearts and palates of an international judging team, astounding competitors from eight other countries by winning the Olympics of the baking world, the 1996 Coupe de Monde de la Boulangerie (World Cup of Baking) held in Paris, France, in February. Ponsford, representing the family-owned and -operated Artisan Bakers, made four breads that are popular in America—*ciabatta*, an Italian bread; beer bread; cornbread; and rye bread—and the required baguette. Ponsford competed against bakers from France, Switzerland, Japan, Denmark, Austria, Belgium, Poland and Luxembourg.

Sonoma got its first official city flag in April, following a city-sponsored contest which attracted 200 entries. The winning flag design, by free-lance

INDEX-TRIBUNE ARCHIVES

Craig Ponsford astounded competitiors from eight other countries by winning the 1996 Coupe de Monde de la Boulangerie (World Cup of Baking) held in Paris, France.

writer Joseph Staub of Sonoma, was one of five finalists presented to the city council, who made the selection. The new city flag contains a bear, star and City Hall, and utilizes the colors red, green, blue and white. The flag was made in time for display at the June 14 Bear Flag Sesquicentennial observance in Sonoma Plaza.

A Sonoma Valley mother of three who had been stalked, harassed and abused by her husband for more than a year was fatally shot in the head by him on the morning of April 16, 1996, shortly after she arrived at a residence on East MacArthur Street, Sonoma, where she worked as a housekeeper. Police said Avelino Macias, 37, shot his wife, Maria Teresa Macias, 36, at point-blank range before firing at least two shots into the doorway where his mother-in-law was standing. She was struck in the legs. He then sat down next to his mortally wounded wife and fired one shot into his temple, killing himself. In April 1995 Theresa Macias had filed a restraining order against her husband, declaring him physically and emotionally abusive. In October she moved out of the apartment she shared with her husband, and subsequently become an outspoken advocate for Hispanic women in abusive relationships.

[Following the tragedy, criticism was heaped on both the sheriff's and district attorney's office for failure to respond appropriately when previously alerted, despite the fact that the victim had signed restraining orders against her husband. A county task force on domestic violence was formed and steps taken to overhaul the policies and practices of the sheriff's and district attorney's office in dealing with domestic violence.]

Sonoma Valley rolled out the red carpet for noted PBS television journalist and author Bill Moyers and his wife and producer, Judith, the weekend of April 19–20. Before the weekend was over, it was obvious that the Moyerses and local audiences had blended into a mutual admiration society. "It was really one of the rare moments that I've had in the course of my work. I felt among friends," Moyers told a group of reporters. "There was such a feeling of community," he said.

The Moyerses' visit was first prize in a national contest won by Sonoma's independent bookstore Readers' Books for its Sonoma Valley Poetry Festival in August 1995. The contest was tied to

INDEX-TRIBUNE ARCHIVES

Mayor Dick Dorf holds Sonoma's first official city flag, designed by local resident Joseph Staub, one of five finalists in a 1996 contest judged by the city council. The flag was completed in time to display at the June 14 Bear Flag Sesquicentennial observance.

the television poetry series hosted by Bill Moyers and its companion book, *The Language of Life: A Festival of Poets*. The Valley poetry extravaganza back in 1995 was a two-week event that culminated in an evening block party and poetry reading. East Napa Street was closed between First and Second Streets East as local residents read their own and others' poetry from soapboxes up and down the street.

A Friday night reception, at which children and adults read their poems for the Moyerses, a book-signing session the following morning and a Saturday evening appearance before a sell-out crowd of 2,000 in the high school gym were highlights of the weekend.

Gasoline prices reached what could be an all-time high for Sonoma Valley motorists on April 18. While prices varied from station to station, the average local price for a gallon of regular unleaded gas (self-service), $1.30 at the end of March, hit $1.52 that day. Valley service station owners said the prices had jumped as often as twice a week.

INDEX-TRIBUNE ARCHIVES

New attractions, like the four-screen Sonoma Cinemas in the Fiesta Center, which opened in June 1994, have been among a number of business additions and improvements in Boyes Hot Springs and environs in recent years. First phase of a $20-million pilot project funded with county redevelopment agency funds in 1996 will include a gateway arching over Highway 12 at the southern entrance to the Springs area, along with streets and landscaping improvements.

The stations pass the added costs on to consumers, in order to make a profit. Factors blamed for the hike in gasoline included new state regulations, the high price of crude, two refinery fires and a cold winter using up fuel supplies.

Boyes Hot Springs and its environs experienced an improved appearance, and its business people and residents in 1996 continued to be enthusiastic about plans and funding approved for a pilot project to give the Springs a viable community identity. Architect Dan Nichols, one of the designers of the project guidelines, said he sees the Springs area being "rejuvenated as a destination" rather than a corridor through which to travel, and having "an identity distinct from Sonoma's." Utilizing funds approved by the county's redevelopment agency, former 1st District Supervisor Janet Nicholas sparked initial action in upgrading the Springs area and having long-standing structural eyesores razed and general neighborhood improvements instituted in the fall of 1986. Her successor, Mike Cale, has carried on, and worked with community and business groups, the Verano Springs Association and the Valley Improvement Project of the chamber of commerce to spark ideas for the Springs and help obtain redevelopment money to assist in paying for them.

The first phase of the $20-million pilot project is to include a gateway arching over Highway 12 at the southern entrance to the Springs. Other improvements such as sidewalks, lampposts and landscaping are scheduled to follow.

Dan Ruggles, "Mr. Music" to his longtime Sonoma Valley admirers, was honored on the occasion of his 85th birthday on Sunday, March 21. Andrews Hall at the Sonoma Community Center, which Ruggles promoted greatly through the years, was the setting for the musical birthday bash and dedication of the center's Daniel T. Ruggles Music Library. While singing, playing the organ and piano, and organizing the musical arts were his first loves, Ruggles has been a community leader in many capacities during his 65 years in Sonoma. He served as a city council member for four terms, president of the Community Center for 10 years, ongoing leader in the General Vallejo Memorial Association and Honorary Alcalde of Sonoma for 1980. And even at 85, that sweet baritone voice brought spontaneous applause from the throng in attendance, as Dan teamed up with several female vocalists in love-song duets during the birthday salute. Cedora Scheiblich and Ruggles, who sang together under the tutelage of the heralded voice teacher Madame Beatrice Bowman here a half-century ago, performed one of those duets. After their nostalgic rendition of "I Love You Truly," Scheiblich quipped, "Fifty years ago, if Dan and I didn't sing that song at a wedding, it wasn't considered legal."

A major safety concern of Flowery School parents and staff was eased on May 3, when ceremonies were held to mark the installation and operation of the long-awaited traffic signal on Highway 12 at the crosswalk leading to the schoolgrounds. Initial requests had been made to state authorities for signalization of the school crossing many years before.

A record attendance of 102,000 racing fans packed into Sears Point Raceway for the Save Mart Supermarket 300/NASCAR Winston Cup auto races the weekend of May 4–5. Reputedly the single biggest one-day sporting event in Northern California due to its Sunday attendance, it helped to fill Valley hotels and restaurants with out-of-town visitors. Millions of fans across the country viewed the races via ESPN television.

The controversial opera *The Dreamers,*

financed by a $100,000 grant from the General Vallejo Memorial Association and presented by the Sonoma City Opera group, premiered at the Sebastiani Theatre in Sonoma on Saturday evening, July 27. Complimented by many in the sellout audience, including Sonoma's "Mr. Music," Dan Ruggles—to whom the opera was dedicated— it had been criticized by Association members led by Bob Cannard, whose foundation grant funded the opera. Detractors claimed it was racist and portrayed General Vallejo in a bad light. William W. Godward, president of the San Francisco Opera Association, was among prominent Bay Area music and art personages attending the premiere.

A devastating blaze that began July 31 as a small wildland fire on Cavedale Road quickly blew out of control, devouring more than 2,000 acres of wildland, 100 acres of vineyards and crops, two homes and adjoining buildings, before it was contained two days later. While the fire raged, 75 homes in its path were evacuated. Cause of the fire, which resulted in property damage of $3 million, was a power line hitting a tree.

The City of Sonoma in August officially adopted Patzcuaro, Mexico, as its sister city—adding to its other siblings which include Chambolle Musigny, France; Greve, Italy; and Kaniv, Ukraine.

With the overcrowding of Valley public schools becoming a major problem, the Sonoma Valley Unified School District board on September 10 voted, 3–2, to apply for $100,000 in state funding to plan exactly how a multi-track, year-round school program would work here. The vote took place after a standing-room-only session of students, parents and teachers who expressed a wide range of opinions on the year-round school proposal.

Also on the education front, Sonoma Valley school trustees voted 3–1 in September to ban the use of calculators through third grade, in the teaching of mathematics, with limited use thereafter. The ban, opposed by most teachers here, was said to be the first of its kind adopted by any California public school district.

Mobilehome park residents, along with the City of Sonoma, were greatly relieved in October when a Sonoma County Superior Court judge upheld the city's mobilehome rent control ordinance. The owner of one of the mobilehome parks had filed suit to overturn the ordinance, adopted in 1992 when the same owner sought to raise base rent levels from $151 to $191 per space.

Had the court's decision favored the park owner, it could have financially devastated the

Continued on page 300

INDEX-TRIBUNE ARCHIVES

This 1996 photo taken at Altimira Middle School gives some indication of the overcrowding problems being faced throughout the Sonoma Valley Unified School District. To alleviate the year-round school schedules being considered, another school bond issue to fund additional classrooms was under study as 1997 began.

The Bear Flag Sesquicentennial

INDEX-TRIBUNE ARCHIVES

Several hundred Sonoma schoolchildren waved miniature Bear Flags in front of the huge state emblem draped in front of the City Hall prior to the gala Bear Flag Sesquicentennial observance which kicked off here June 14, 1996. The picture was sent by the Sonoma Sesquicentennial Committee to newspapers throughout the state to publicize the event, which drew large crowds. Gov. Pete Wilson was the principal speaker at colorful opening ceremonies.

After two years of planning, Sonoma's Bear Flag Sesquicentennial observance in 1996 took place with a series of colorful events, highlighted by an activity-filled Friday, June 14. That was the date on which 33 American rebel-patriots, in 1846, raised the crudely made Bear Flag in Sonoma's Plaza, establishing their short-lived California Republic in protest of Mexican rule.

It was perhaps déjà vu that 150 years later, a group of an estimated 100 protesters, most of them transported here from the Bay Area, protested the protesting Bear Flaggers' actions in a noisy display designed to disrupt—for the first time ever—the community observance of the historic happening.

Law enforcement officers stood by at the Plaza in front of City Hall, where throngs had gathered for the opening noon ceremonies, as the nonlocal protest group attempted to drown out, with whistles, drums and catcalls, keynote speaker California Governor Pete Wilson. The noisy demonstration was also carried on during presentations by a Native American, Hispanic vocalist and the consul general of Mexico, who were invited program participants.

By contrast, the next day, Saturday, a local group called the Bear Flag Resistance Committee, staged a peaceful march—in opposition to the community observance—along Highway 12, followed by a cultural presentation and rally in the Sonoma Plaza amphitheater. The all-day use of the amphitheater by the Valley protest group was

arranged for by the Bear Flag Sesquicentennial committee in response to their request for recognition. There, speakers gave views on a variety of subjects—exploitation of farmworkers, the need for better response to domestic violence and the need to address Hispanic and Native American concerns. Native American, Hispanic and Chicano musicians, poets and dancers also participated in the Saturday program.

An estimated 2,000 people lined Broadway and the entrance to the Plaza applauding 500 participants—most of them in costume—in the half-mile-long opening procession Friday, which culminated in front of City Hall.

A lone Native American, tribal elder of the Kashia-Pomo/Miwok

Sonoma's Honorary Alcaldesa and Alcalde for 1996, Carolyn and Bob Stone (left), served as official greeters at the many activities associated with the historic event. At right, local citizens, dressed in clothing of the period, participated in a tableaux depicting the raising of the Bear Flag on Sonoma Plaza on June 14, 1846. Several hundred descendants of the original Bear Flag party members were guests of the Sonoma Valley Historical Society at a memorable luncheon reunion held at Depot Park.

tribe, led the parade up Broadway, with young Russian sailors, bagpipe-playing English, bayonet-carrying Spaniards and colorfully dressed Mexicans. All represented the many different nations that played a part in early California—and Sonoma's —history. They were followed by a raggedly dressed contingent wearing coonskin caps, the Hometown Band and, finally, a large group of men from the Native Sons of the Golden West bearing a gigantic Bear Flag.

Several hundred descendants of Bear Flag party members, from throughout the U. S., also marched in the procession.

Governor Wilson told the crowd that the roots of California "from the high Sierras and low deserts, to the majestic coastline and the magnificent Sonoma Valley of the Moon, were planted here, in this very Plaza, 150 years ago today."

On succeeding days and weekends, reenactments of the Bear Flag raising were witnessed by large gatherings, as were the exhibits at the Depot Museum, programs and displays at the Sonoma Barracks, a Bear Flag Music Festival in the Plaza, with tie-ins to the annual Kiwanis Turkey Barbecue, Fourth of July celebration and Red, White and Blue Ball.

The reenactment of the end of the California Republic's 15-day reign on July 9 in Sonoma Plaza culminated the Bear Flag Sesquicentennial observance, with some 200 onlookers standing quietly by for their living lesson in history. Local historian and author Robert D. Parmelee was master of ceremonies.

A time capsule, containing mementos of the Sesquicentennial commemoration, community statistics of the present era and related items, was buried in a September ceremony near the Bear Flag pole, to be dug up and reminisced over at the 200th Bear Flag raising commemoration in the year 2046.

city and forced 49 park residents to pay thousands of dollars in back rent. An appeal of the judge's decision was expected.

After 34 years at Sonoma Valley High School—as a student, teacher and administrator—vice principal Bob Kruljac, 53, departed his familiar campus home on November 1 to become principal of St. Helena High School in Napa County.

Following a lengthy and spirited November 14 public meeting, filled with sharp divisions of opinion from the audience, the Sonoma City Council by a 4–0 vote (one abstention) approved granting of a use permit for The Lodge at Sonoma, to be built at Four Corners. The controversial 154-room hotel, convention, center, restaurant and commercial center will be located on the west side of the intersection of Broadway and Leveroni Road. The city council vote overturned the recommendation of the city planning commission, which

in October had voted to deny the building permit. Ironically, back in May 1985 the city council, by a 3–2 vote, denied a use permit for a much smaller (80-unit) motel-convention center on the same site.

At a mid-November public hearing at the FAHA Hall, Verano, close to 30 Valley residents spoke out in opposition to a state plan to lease 735 "surplus" acres on Sonoma Development Center land for vineyard or orchard planting to help shrink the state budget deficit. Environmentalists, open-space advocates, riding and hiking enthusiasts in the audience of some 100 people favored public use of the acreage. The state has identified the SDC open land and thousands of more acres of state-owned land across California as "underutilized," ordering 10 percent of it to be sold or leased for profit each year. A state spokesman said vineyards would probably be the most profitable long-term use of the land.

INDEX-TRIBUNE ARCHIVES

Typically Sonoma: This scene at the corner of Spain and First Street East—where the driver of a Mack truck waited patiently at the corner to allow a mother duck to escort her family (staying strictly within the white lines of the crosswalk) to the pond in the nearby city Plaza. While neither sleet nor snow might stay the mail carrier on his appointed rounds, the female mallard and her brood slowed him up a bit.

27 The Author's Musings

The author with Jim Millerick on a research trip to Wingo, a historic settlement in the Schellville sloughs.

After writing my weekly "Publisher's Musings" column for 44 years in *The Sonoma Index-Tribune*, I put a stop to it on Sept. 15, 1995. I wanted to utilize my time for the research and writing needed for putting together this book. Now, after a year and a half, *The Sonoma Valley Story: Pages through the Ages*, has been completed.

Producing *The Sonoma Valley Story* was a great experience. I discovered that limited literary talent can be made up for with enthusiasm and a deep interest in your subject—plus the assistance of those on the *Index-Tribune* staff who shared my interest and were always there when needed, giving of their time and expertise.

Some personal sacrifices were necessary. My hay fever, dormant for years, was reactivated.

Turning the yellowed pages of dusty, long-stored newspapers—the brittle, aged newsprint tearing and flaking off at my touch—proved an irritant to my senses and sinuses.

The tired old blues behind my trifocals will never be the same, after squinting over reels of faded microfilm copies of *The Sonoma Index*, *The Sonoma Valley Weekly Index*, *Sonoma Tribune* and *The Sonoma Index-Tribune* of the 1880s and beyond.

My patient and understanding wife of 55 years was deprived of several long-planned vacation junkets. Also, our cherished time at The Cabin in Plumas County comingling with the wild animals and birds—and our wild, but nice, human neighbors down by the lake—also played second fiddle to The Book.

My golf game suffered immeasurably. Friends, mostly betting types looking for a pigeon, called to invite me and my wallet out to the links. They grew tired of hearing my excuse: "Sorry, but I have to work on The Book."

Fortunately, these same friends didn't spot me on the two rare occasions that I visited the Sonoma Golf Club course while the book was in the preparation stages. They never would have believed that I was driving a golf cart in search of an oak tree to photograph. Or that I had a putter in my hands on the 18th green only to provide our photographer with the picture we needed for Chapter 25.

During these golf course field trips, the conscientious author didn't even take time to play a few holes. I may never break 100 again, just because my priorities were not in order. Instead of having a golf club in my hands, trying to emulate Tiger Woods, I had a tiger by the tail—The Book.

Of lasting memory will be a research trip taken to Wingo, with my escort none other than "The Major," Jim Millerick, whose rodeo and ranching family is synonymous with the history of Schellville and environs.

As we bumped along in his pickup truck, my special tour director hardly stopped for a breath as he told stories: about the miles of flatlands and their past and present owners; about the once wide waterways, now narrow and clogged, and the boats that sailed them; and the still-standing old railroad bridge that had to be raised and lowered in its working days. The verbal history was interspersed with the Major's colorful adjectives and phrases.

A stop at the historic old Wingo bridgemas-ter's headquarters, for many years an occupied private residence, was a particular treat. After traversing a structurally suspect plank bridge, we entered the old building with the original station sign "WINGO" still hanging out front. A chat with the elderly resident of that treasure amidst the tules was frosting on the cake.

Just a week after our Wingo tour, the special implanted device that kept Jim Millerick's long-ailing heart beating gave out. The man who rode bucking broncos in his youth; flew search and rescue planes in Alaska during World War II, a B-29 bomber in the Korean War and later the big B-52s; and who piloted the author to Wingo in his bouncing truck died at his duck club while fixing breakfast for friends.

Other side trips can be looked upon with pleasure—to the Vallejo Naval and Historical Museum; enjoying the hospitality of Sonoma historian and author Robert Parmelee, whose files provided numerous photos which otherwise would not have been available.

I visited our own Sonoma Depot Museum so often that I felt almost like one of its accommodating docents. I came away from each visit with a deeper appreciation for this best-kept secret in our midst and of the people who staff it for the Sonoma Valley Historical Society.

Putting together this book has been an experience from which I greatly benefited. I learned more about our so special Valley in a year and a half of research than I did during a half-century of residing in this chosen spot of all the earth.

Finally, you can't believe how many times friends have asked, "How's the book coming?" Nor can you believe how good it feels to finally reply, "It's done!"

Appendix

— The Sonoma Index-Tribune Chronology —

1852 Alexander Cox founds the *Sonoma Bulletin*

1879 Benjamin Frank founds *The Sonoma Index*

1881 Celeste Granice born to Harry H. and Kate Granice in Santa Clara, Calif.

1884 *The Sonoma Tribune* purchased by Harry H. Granice and renamed *The Sonoma Index-Tribune*

1901 Celeste Granice graduates from UC Berkeley

1902 Harry Granice founds the *San Rafael Independent*; Celeste Granice becomes the *Independent*'s editor

1904 Celeste Granice joins her father at the *Index-Tribune* as associate editor

1905 Celeste Granice marries Walter Murphy

1915 Death of Harry Granice; Celeste and Walter Murphy purchase *I-T* from Granice estate

1920 Bob Lynch born to Ernest and Ramona Granice Lynch

1937 Celeste Murphy publishes *The People of the Pueblo*; Celeste and Walter purchase the Sonoma Barracks and begin refurbishing it for their residence

1941 Bob Lynch marries Jean Allen

1946 Bob Lynch completes Navy service, joins *Index-Tribune* staff

1949 Celeste and Walter Murphy retire from the *I-T*; Bob Lynch named editor and publisher; Robert and Jean Lynch begin purchase of the *Index-Tribune* from the Murphys

1953 *I-T* wins first awards in statewide competition

1962 Death of Celeste Murphy, Walter Murphy

1965 *I-T* goes from "hot" type to "cold" (offset printing)

1969 Bill Lynch joins staff of *I-T*

1972 Jim Lynch joins staff of *I-T*

1975 John Lynch joins staff of *I-T*

1979 *I-T* publishes 100th-year anniversary edition

1980 Bob Lynch installed as president of California Newspaper Publishers Association and president of California Press Association

1981 Bob Lynch reelected president of California Press Association; desktop computers installed at *I-T*

1985 *I-T* goes from once- to twice-weekly publication

1989 Bill Lynch named editor and CEO; Jim Lynch named CFO Assistant CEO; Bob Lynch named Newspaper Executive of the Year by California Press Association

1992 *I-T* starts *Community Voice* (serving Rohnert Park and Cotati); Sonoma Valley Publishing division established

1996 *I-T* establishes web site on the Internet; Bob Lynch observes 50th anniversary with *I-T*

1997 *Index-Tribune* publishes *The Sonoma Valley Story*

— City of Sonoma Honorary Alcaldes & Alcaldesas —
(Recognition of Outstanding Community Service)

1976 August Pinelli

1977 Henri Maysonnave

1978 Jerry Casson

1979 Robert M. Lynch

1980 Daniel Ruggles

1981 Paul and Adele Harrison

1982 Gail Fehrensen

1983 Chester Sharek

1984 Evelyn Berger

1985 Alan and Sandra Piotter

1986 Nell Lane

1987 James Metzger

1988 Helen Shainsky

1989 Jerold Tuller

1990 Ernest and Loyce Power

1991 Jo Baker

1992 Ligia Booker

1993 James Vanderbilt

1994 Nancy Parmelee

1995 George Watson

1996 Bob and Carolyn Stone

1997 L. C. (Pete) Peterson

— City of Sonoma "Treasures" —
(Recognition of Outstanding Achievement in the Arts)

1983 Marian Brackenridge, Ted Christensen

1984 M. F. K. Fisher, James Vanderbilt

1985 Anthony Stellon

1986 Daniel Ruggles

1987 Irma Wallem

1988 C. Carl Jennings

1989 Helene Minelli

1990 Otto Hitzberger

1991 Linus Maurer

1992 Norton Buffalo

1993 James Griewe

1994 Stanley Mouse, Fred Parker

1995 Jo Anne Connor Metzger

1996 Toni Kuhry-Haeuser

— City of Sonoma Mayors, 1850–1997 —

John Cameron	1850–1851	John Picetti	April 21, 1942–April 17, 1946
Israel Brockman	Aug. 6, 1851–April 10, 1852	August L. Pinelli	April 17, 1946–April 20, 1948
Jesse Davisson	June 5, 1852–Feb. 20, 1854	David W. King	April 20, 1948–April 18, 1950
S. B. Bright	May 6, 1854–May 6, 1854	Warren D. More	April 18, 1950–April 20, 1954
T. K. Chambers	May 12, 1854–May 20, 1854	Hilton D. Taylor	April 20, 1954–April 17, 1956
S. B. Bright	May 27, 1854–May 19, 1855	Joan McGrath Waterhouse	April 17, 1956–April 19, 1960
D. Cook	May 19, 1855–May 12, 1856	William G. Raymond	April 19, 1960–April 17, 1962
John Andrews	May 20, 1856–May 20, 1856	Sal J. Gomez	April 17, 1962–April 21, 1964
Peter Campbell	May 24, 1856–June 7, 1856	Charles L. Allen	April 21, 1964–April 19, 1965
A. C. McDonald	June 14, 1856–Aug. 16, 1858	Talbert W. Bean	April 19, 1965–Oct. 12, 1970
D. Cook	Aug. 20, 1858–June 8, 1861	John W. Lobsinger	Oct. 12, 1970–April 18, 1972
William Ellis*	June 8, 1861–	Henry J. Riboni	April 18, 1972–March 10, 1975
J. R. Snyder*	April 25, 1868–	Nancy Parmelee	March 10, 1975–March 9, 1976
Otto Schetter	June 11, 1878–July 15, 1882	Henry J. Riboni	March 9, 1976–March 12, 1979
E. Wegener	Sept. 3, 1883–April 21, 1884	Nancy Parmelee	March 12, 1979–April 15, 1980
A. F. Haraszthy	April 21, 1884–April 16, 1888	Henry J. Riboni	April 15, 1980–April 27, 1981
Charles McHarvey	April 16, 1888–April 21, 1890	Jerold W. Tuller	April 27, 1981–June 15, 1982
R. A. Poppe	April 21, 1890–April 18, 1892	Kenneth S. McTaggart	June 15, 1982–June 13, 1983
H. Weyl	April 18, 1892–May 2, 1894	Henry J. Riboni	June 13, 1983–Nov. 27, 1984
J. H. Seipp	May 2, 1894–Dec. 4, 1895	Jeanne M. Markson	Nov. 27, 1984–Nov. 12, 1985
R. A. Poppe	Dec. 4, 1895–May 6, 1896	Jerold Tuller	Nov. 12, 1985–Dec. 1, 1986
J. H. Seipp	May 6, 1896–May 4, 1898	Nancy Parmelee	Dec. 1, 1986–Dec. 2, 1987
F. T. Duhring	May 4, 1898–April 21, 1902	Larry Murphy	Dec. 2, 1987–Dec. 8, 1988
Julius E. Poppe	April 21, 1902–April 16, 1906	Henry J. Riboni	Dec. 8, 1988–Dec. 6, 1989
G. H. Hotz	April 16, 1906–April 20, 1908	Kenneth S. McTaggart	Dec. 6, 1989–Dec. 4, 1990
George Breitenbach	April 20, 1908–April 18, 1910	Valerie Kent Brown	Dec. 4, 1990–Dec. 4, 1991
Michael E. Cummings	April 18, 1910–April 20, 1914	Larry Murphy	Dec. 4, 1991–Dec. 2, 1992
Carl Von Hacht	April 20, 1914–Feb. 6, 1918	Phyllis Carter	Dec. 2, 1992–Dec. 1, 1993
Charles (Carlo) Dal Poggetto	Feb. 6, 1918–June 17, 1921	Anthony Cermak	Dec. 1, 1993–Dec. 7, 1994
Fred Bulotti	July 26, 1921–April 18, 1932	Phyllis Carter	Dec. 7, 1994–Dec. 6, 1995
Jep Valente	April 18, 1932–April 15, 1940	Richard C. Dorf	Dec. 6, 1995–Dec. 4, 1996
Charles Clifton Bean	April 15, 1940–April 21, 1942	Albert C. Mazza	Dec. 4, 1996–

*Acting in lieu of mayor ❖ Courtesy, Eleanor Berto, City Clerk of Sonoma 1959–

— Sonoma County 1st District Supervisors, 1852–1997 —

1852–53	O. Shattuck, Sr.	1869 73	J. H. Griggs	1921–33	Frederick Lowell
1853–54	H. G. Heald	1874–79	W. K. Rogers	1934–35	W. C. Woodward
1854–55	Robert Smith	Aug. 1879–Jan. 1880	John Tivnen	1935–45	Howard Knight
1855–56	D. McDonald	July 1880–Jan. 1881	David Stewart	1945–57	James F. Lyttle
1856–57	James Prewitt	Jan. 1881–July 1884	E. E. Morse		
1857–58	Wm. Hagans (possibly Hagan)	Oct. 1884–Jan. 1889	John O'Hare (possibly O'Hara)	1957–65	S. Carson Mitchell
1858–Jan. 1859	Alex Copeland			1965–75	Ignazio Vella
1859	E. Swift	1889–93	M. K. Cady	1975–81	Brian Kahn
Jan. 1859–1860	W. M. Wilson	1893–97	J. Joost	1981–85	Bob Adams
1861–64	N. Fike	1897–1901	T. C. Putnam		
1864–67	A. B. Aull	1901–1913	Blair Hart	1985–91	Janet Nicholas
1867–69	E. W. Frick	1913–21	J. Weise	1991–	Mike Cale

Courtesy, Sonoma County Registrar of Voters. Note: The number of supervisors and the boundaries of the districts have changed since the formation of the county, and district numbers are not clear until about 1921. The years shown indicate a range of years in which elections may have been held, not necessarily the years between which the supervisors served.

— Glossary of Local Place-Names —

Agua Caliente: Brush up on your Spanish if you don't know that the name of this little community around Highway 12 means "Hot Water" —a reference to the hot springs that once drew tourists from near and far.

Altimira Middle School: The school on Arnold Drive was named for Padre José Altimira, the zealous Spanish priest who founded the Sonoma Mission in 1823. There's been talk lately of changing the name due to the padre's harsh treatment of Indians, but no official moves in that direction have been made. (Jack London Middle School has been suggested as an alternative, but in the past, some people frowned on naming things after the turn-of-the-century author because of his Socialist leanings.)

Arnold Drive: The road that stretches all along the west side of the Sonoma Valley was named for World War II hero Gen. H. H. (Hap) Arnold, commander of the U. S. Army Air Corps, who moved to the area during the war and later retired there.

Boyes Hot Springs: The town was named for Capt. Henry E. Boyes, a former English naval officer who founded a resort in the area in the late 19th century.

Dunbar Elementary School: The school in Glen Ellen was named for Dunbar Road, which in turn was named for Mary and Alexander Dunbar, who bought the surrounding land in 1867.

Eldridge: The site of the Sonoma Developmental Center on Arnold Drive was named for Capt. Oliver Eldridge, who helped choose the location back in 1890.

El Verano: This town was once one of a string of resort communities, and its name in Spanish means "the summer place."

Fetters Hot Springs: This former resort town, like its neighbor Boyes Hot Springs, was named for its founder, who in this case was entrepreneur George Fetters.

Flowery Elementary School: No one seems to know for sure how this school got its unusual name, says school secretary Pat Taylor, who has researched the question. She's been told, however, that perhaps it's because so many wildflowers grew near the school's former site (which is now occupied by the district's Sonoma Charter School). An alternative theory postulates that in the early part of the century, when there were only about 15 students, many of the kids were girls with "flowery" names such as Rose and Daisy.

Glen Ellen: The "Glen" part of the name of this village refers not to a man but to the vale in which the town is nestled; the "Ellen" is in honor of Ellen Stuart, one of the early settlers.

Hanna Boys Center: The late Archbishop Edward Hanna of San Francisco gave his name to this home for troubled boys, founded by the Catholic Church. Hanna died in 1944, the same year the idea for the center was born.

Kenwood: This town at the northern end of the Sonoma Valley was probably named by some of its founders after their former home, the town of Kenwood, Ill. Some historians say, however, it may have been named by settlers of English descent after Kenwood House in London, England, a famous landmark built in 1616.

Prestwood Elementary School: This school's namesake, Jesse Franklin Prestwood, was one of the first four graduates of Sonoma Valley High School back in 1896. He served as principal of the old Sonoma Grammar School (now the Sonoma Community Center) for 42 years starting in 1908.

Sassarini Elementary School: Originally this school was going to be named simply "Sonoma Elementary School." But in 1958, shortly after the school opened, it was renamed in honor of Calvin Sassarini, respected former principal of Prestwood School, who died in an auto accident.

Sears Point: No, the racetrack and the nearby promontory that juts out into San Pablo Bay weren't named for the department store. Instead, they were named after Franklin Sears, whose ranch once occupied the site. Sears was a cousin of trapper-turned-miner Granville Swift, another well-known Valley resident in the mid-1800s who took part in the celebrated "Bear Flag Revolt" and later built the Temelec mansion.

Skaggs Island: The naval reservation south of Sonoma (recently abandoned by the navy) was named during the Depression after financial giant M. B. Skaggs, founder of the Safeway and PayLess stores. It seems that the farmers who formerly owned the property fell on hard times during the '30s, and in return for financial backing from Skaggs they gratefully named the island after him.

Schellville: This little community south of Sonoma was named by the Northern Pacific Railroad sometime before 1888 for Theodore Schell, who owned 160 of the surrounding acres in the 1850s.

From a story titled "What's in a local name?" by the late Dennis Wheeler, former Sonoma Index-Tribune *staff writer.*

— Sonoma Valley Wine Producers —

Adler Fels	Glen Ellen Winery	Nelson Estate
Arrowood Vineyards and Winery	Gloria Ferrer Champagne Caves	One World Winery
B. R. Cohn Winery	Gundlach-Bundschu Winery	Ravenswood Winery
Bartholomew Park Winery	Hanzell Vineyards	Robert Hunter Winery
Benziger Family Winery	Haywood Winery	Roche Winery (Sonoma Coast appellation)
Buena Vista Carneros Winery	Homewood Winery	Schug Carneros Estate Winery
Carmenet Vineyard	Kaz Vineyard and Winery	Sebastiani Vineyards
Castle Vineyards	Kenwood Vineyards	Smothers/Remick Ridge
Chandelle	Kistler Vineyards	Sonoma Creek Winery
Chateau St. Jean	Kunde Estate Winery	St. Francis Winery
Cline Cellars	Landmark Vineyards	Stone Creek Wines
Coturri Winery	MacRostie Winery	Tantalus Wineries
Cutler Cellar	Matanzas Creek	Valley of the Moon Winery
Deerfield Ranch Winery	Mayo Family Winery	Viansa Winery
Fallenleaf Vineyards	Moondance Cellars	Wellington Vineyards

Note: Many wineries produce wines under a label different from the name listed above. List current as of March 1997, compiled with help from the Sonoma Valley Vintners and Growers Alliance and the Sonoma Valley Visitors Bureau.

Bibliography

Emparan, Madie Brown, *The Vallejos of California.* San Francisco: The Gleeson Library Associates, University of San Francisco, 1968.

Fredericksen, Paul, "The Authentic Haraszthy Story," a historical research project by the Wine Institute for the Wine Advisory Board, reprinted from *Wines and Vines,* 1947.

Galloway, R. Dean, "Rowena Granice." *Pacific Historian.* 24 (1): 105–124. Spring 1980.

Granice, Harry H., "Hunted Down; or, Five Days in the Fog: A Thrilling Narrative of the Escape of Young Granice." San Francisco: Women's Publishing Co., 1875. Reprinted by R. Dean Galloway. Turlock, California, 1975.

Haraszthy, Agoston, *Grape Culture, Wines, & Winemaking.* New York: Harper & Brothers Publishers, 1862.

Historical Atlas of Sonoma County. Oakland: Thomas H. Thompson & Co., 1877.

Houghton, Eliza P. Donner, *The Expedition of the Donner Party and Its Tragic Fate.* Chicago: A.C. McClurg & Co., 1911.

Hunter, Alexander, *Vallejo: A California Legend.* Sonoma: State Historic Park Association, 1992.

McKittrick, Myrtle M., *Vallejo: Son of California.* Portland, Ore.: Binfords & Mort, 1944.

Menefee, C. A., *Sketchbook of Napa, Sonoma, Lake, & Mendocino.* 1873.

Murphy, Celeste G., *The People of the Pueblo.* Sonoma: Sonoma Index-Tribune, 1937.

Papp, Richard Paul, *Bear Flag Country: Legacy of the Revolt.* Published under the auspices of the Redwood Empire Collectors Club, Petaluma, Calif. Forestville, Calif.: Seraphim Rose Press, 1996.

Parmelee, Robert D., *Pioneer Sonoma.* Sonoma: Sonoma Index-Tribune, 1972.

"Pioneer Register," appended to vols. 2–5 of Herbert Howe Bancroft, *History of California.*

Rawls, James J. and Walton Bean, *California: An Interpretive History.* Sixth edition. New York: McGraw-Hill, 1993.

Rawls, James J., *Indians of California: The Changing Image.* Norman and London: University of Oklahoma Press, 1984.

Rosenus, Alan, *General M. G. Vallejo and the Advent of the Americans.* Albuquerque: University of New Mexico Press, 1995.

Sievers, Wald and Robert D. Parmelee, "Railroads of the Valley of the Moon." From *The Western Railroader,* Vol. 22, No. 3, Issue No. 231, January 1959.

Smilie, Robert S., *The Sonoma Mission: San Francisco Solano de Sonoma.* Fresno: Valley Publishers, 1975.

Sonoma Valley Historical Society, *Saga of Sonoma: In the Valley of the Moon.* Second edition. Sonoma: Sonoma Index-Tribune, 1968.

Teiser, Ruth and Catherine Harroun, *Winemaking in California.* New York: Mc-Graw-Hill, 1983.

Acknowledgments

Special thanks to James B. Alexander ❖ D. Ambrose ❖ Robert Arnold ❖ The Bancroft Library ❖ Meg Scantlebury and Bartholomew Park Winery Museum ❖ Chris Berggren/ Custom Image Photographic Services ❖ Suzanne Brangham ❖ Mary Bundschu ❖ California Department of Parks and Recreation ❖ California Historical Society ❖ California State Library, Sacramento ❖ Shirley Christine ❖ Joan Cochran ❖ C. M. (Charlie) Cooke ❖ The Denver Public Library, Western History Collection ❖ Betty Stevens, Diane Moll Smith and the Sonoma Valley Historical Society's Depot Park Museum ❖ Ron Duer ❖ Ida Rae Egli ❖ Capt. Howard Ehret, USN (Ret.) ❖ Fairfield (Calif.) *Daily Republic* and Foy S. McNaughton ❖ Frank H. Bartholomew Foundation ❖ Friends of Sebastiani Theatre ❖ R. Dean Galloway ❖ Greyhound Lines, Inc. ❖ Gundlach-Bundschu Winery ❖ Hanna Boys Center ❖ Jan and Mianna Haraszthy ❖ Jean Lynch ❖ Mary's Pizza Shack ❖ Brian McGinty ❖ Monica McKey ❖ McNaughton & Gunn ❖ Kathleen Duarte Menghetti ❖ The Millerick family ❖ Helene Minelli ❖ Mark Newberry ❖ Bob Nicholas ❖ Nicholas Turkey Breeding Farms ❖ Robert D. Parmelee ❖ Sandra Piotter ❖ Presentation Archives, San Francisco ❖ William Ramsay and Janet Ramsay Lombardo ❖ James J. Rawls ❖ *The Sacramento Bee* ❖ Sylvia Sebastiani ❖ Jason Breaw and Sebastiani Vineyards ❖ Milo Shepard ❖ Society of California Pioneers ❖ Sonoma City Clerk Eleanor Berto ❖ Sonoma County Registrar of Voters ❖ Sonoma County Wine Library ❖ Sonoma Developmental Center ❖ Sonoma League for Historic Preservation ❖ Sonoma Mission Inn & Spa ❖ Sonoma Valley Chorale ❖ Sonoma Valley Regional Library ❖ Sonoma Valley Vintners and Growers Alliance ❖ Sonoma Valley Visitors Bureau ❖ Sonora (Calif.) *Union Democrat* and Harvey C. McGee ❖ Sunset Magazine ❖ University of California, Davis ❖ Vacaville Heritage Council ❖ Vacaville (Calif.) *Reporter* and Richard Rico ❖ Vallejo Naval and Historical Museum ❖ and the staff of *The Sonoma Index-Tribune*, especially Jill Boeve, Gina Bostian, Jack Bradbury, Chandra Grant, Carol Harvey, Bill Lynch, Jim Lynch, Bud McCulligh, Robbi Pengelly, Yvonne Pomeroy, Brandon Warner and Jeanette Wetenkamp

Index

Page numbers in **boldface** type indicate references to illustrations; there may be additional references in text on these pages. Personal names in CAPITAL LETTERS are those of contributing writers.